The *British Novel* *since the Thirties*

AN INTRODUCTION

RANDALL STEVENSON

B. T. Batsford Ltd · *London*

For William and Rosamund Christie

Printed in Great Britain by
Billings, Worcester

Published by B. T. Batsford Ltd
4 Fitzhardinge Street, London W1H 0AH

British Library Cataloguing in Publication Data

Stevenson, Randall
   The British novel since the thirties: an introduction.
   1. English fiction—20th century—History and criticism
   I. Title
   823'.009   PR881

ISBN 0 7134 4663 3
ISBN 0 7134 4664 1 Pbk

Contents

Preface

> Despite the funeral sermons that have been constantly pronounced over
> its death, the novel has probably never been more various, more
> interesting, more inventive, or more international in its sources and its
> scopes than today.

Malcolm Bradbury adds to his general assessment of contemporary
fiction a particular qualification:

> ...if there is evidence of great creative vitality and invention in the novel
> now, then where in it does the contemporary British novel stand?
> Certainly it does not seem to stand very high in terms of critical attention.

Bradbury goes on to suggest that critics have concentrated on 'the
period of Modernism', and that 'the period since its decline or
disappearance has been a vague one' partly as a result.[1] The present
study is directed towards dispelling this vagueness by showing how
the novel has developed in Britain in the past half-century or so. The
nineteen-eighties are as distant from *Ulysses* (1922) as *Ulysses* itself
was from the novels of mid-Victorian times: as the twentieth century
advances towards its end, there seems more and more need for a
general assessment of what has happened in fiction since Joyce wrote.
As Bradbury and other critics sometimes suggest, the period is a
more worthwhile one than is often supposed: it can also be seen to
possess a certain coherence, particular patterns of evolution arising
from the situation of the novel established in 'the period of
Modernism' in the first three decades of the century.

This situation is outlined in Chapter One. Other chapters divide
the developments which have followed into three main periods,
while a last chapter considers separately the progress of
'experimental' fiction since the nineteen-thirties. General historical
divisions of this sort provide a framework for analysis perhaps more
appropriate for fiction than for either poetry or drama: as E.M.
Forster suggests, 'prose, because it is a medium for daily life as well as
for literature, is particularly sensitive to what is going on'.[2] Several
other commentators have also remarked that a characteristic of
twentieth-century writing is the insistence with which it has been
shaped by what has gone on in the violent and changeful history of
the times.

As Malcolm Bradbury's comments suggest, fiction in the twentieth century has also become increasingly international in outlook. Any study of the novel needs to take account of the international aspect of fiction in English, and of the implications of contacts with other languages and cultures. Some of these are considered throughout, and are further assessed in conclusion. Even general restriction to the British context, however, leaves problems of scope and choice: there are obviously limits to the number of authors who can be discussed in a single volume, and to the extent of attention to each. A completely comprehensive survey of the period can only be undertaken in a directory: several of these are already available, and are listed in the Bibliography. In the present volume, major authors' careers are considered in detail: others, however, are approached through concentration on one or a few representative examples of their work. This is particularly the method in Chapter Four: there is little point in attempting a complete account of writers whose reputations are likely to alter substantially as their careers advance beyond their present state. Throughout, the central concern is in any case not only with surveying the work of individual novelists, but with indicating general patterns to which their fiction contributes; developments in the vision of the novel in the later twentieth century as a whole. Any readers disappointed by omission of a cherished novel, or even novelist, should find in this way some scheme into which they may fit their favourite item for themselves. Such a possibility is after all in accord with the tactics of some recent fiction, one of whose practitioners remarks

> ...the contemporary author proclaims his absolute need of...co-operation, an active, conscious, *creative* co-operation. What he [the reader] is being asked to do is no longer to accept a ready-made, completed world...but on the contrary to participate in an act of creation, in the invention of the work.[3]

No critical writing about fiction can fail to be influenced by the evolution of theories of narrative in the past twenty years: some of those outlined in Gérard Genette's *Narrative Discourse* (1980) have been especially useful to the present study. Since, however, it is intended for non-specialist readers—for any interested novel-readers, in fact—as well as for students of literature, conventional terminology is mostly retained throughout. Ease of access has also been a priority in the choice of editions from which quotations are taken. Wherever possible, references are to currently-available paperback editions of the novels. Publishing details of these are given in footnotes which, as they rarely contain other information, need not distract readers from the text.

More than half a century of fiction provides an enjoyable but challenging range of material, and I am very grateful for help I have received in writing about it. The idea for the study originated in various ways with William Christie and Cairns Craig, and with Tony Seward, who has been a patient and very encouraging editor throughout the project. I'm also indebted to Cairns Craig, Peter Keating, Oddvar Holmesland, Jon Curt and many others, including several generations of students in Edinburgh University's Department of English Literature, for their advice or ideas. The comments of John Cartmell, Brian McHale, Roger Savage and Colin Nicholson have improved individual chapters: I am especially grateful to Ron Butlin and Gavin Wallace, who helped me with the whole study.

Sandra Kemp's meticulous concentration on the typescript, along with her wide and wonderful reading of contemporary fiction, greatly improved and made a pleasure several stages of writing and revision. For further help with the work involved, and very much else besides, my major debt is to Sarah Carpenter, one of much more than only gratitude.

1

The Novel, 1900-1930

'I find your novel unreal just as you find mine to be so... All that *your* school of novelists has to say about the novel seems to us nonsense', remarked Hugh Walpole in his open *Letter to a Modern Novelist* published in 1932.

Walpole's own novels are now often forgotten, but they were popular during the twenties and thirties, and the comments in his *Letter* are a useful introduction to the situation of the novel around 1930, and to some of the questions which confronted its authors. One perplexity for the novelist in the nineteen thirties, as Walpole's remarks indicate, was the existence of a divergence in opinion about the proper nature of fiction. This was very differently envisaged by authors whose views could be seen as dividing them into the sort of opposing 'schools' Walpole mentions. His particular use of the word 'modern' in his *Letter* helps to suggest the nature and origin of such divisions in contemporary opinion. Walpole's own career as a novelist stretches back to 1910, and continues long after 1932, and yet it is emphatically the puzzling young writer to whom his open letter is ostensibly addressed whom Walpole considers modern, and not himself. Clearly, 'modern' in his view refers to a style of writing practised only by some novelists in the modern period, and certainly not by all his contemporaries. His *Letter* describes the appearance of such a specifically modern style, which seemed to Walpole 'nonsense' because, among other shortcomings, it disdained the traditional strengths of fiction—character; storytelling which leads the reader from page to page; and what Walpole calls 'that *arrangement* of the older novelists, the placing of things in order... the crisis at its proper time, the ending neatly rounded off'.[1]

Walpole's recognition of a 'modern' school of writing which discards or re-shapes earlier conventions has been strongly confirmed by later critics. Stephen Spender, for example, whose own poetry began to appear around 1930, later remarked 'I see the "moderns"... as deliberately setting out to invent a new literature as a result of their feeling that our age is in many respects unprecedented, and outside all the conventions of past literature and art'.[2] Walpole's *Letter* names Marcel Proust, James Joyce, and

D.H. Lawrence as part of the 'modern' school: later critics have often added the names of Virginia Woolf, Ford Madox Ford, and Dorothy Richardson; and sometimes also included Henry James and Joseph Conrad. Though such 'moderns'—modernists as they are now usually called—did not really see themselves as a school, all can be considered as sharing in the attempt (also visible in the poetry of the period) to 'invent a new literature' different in style and technique from the work of their predecessors. This urge sharply distinguishes them from contemporaries, Walpole among them, who, whether or not they regarded their age as unprecedented, did not feel the need to alter 'the conventions of past literature and art' in recreating it in their novels. Since it is the modernists who are generally considered as among the greatest and potentially most influential of twentieth-century authors, overshadowing the work of the past fifty years, their fiction demands careful consideration as a preliminary to any account of the progress of the novel since 1930.

How then did the modernists seek to alter the conventions of novel writing? What new styles and techniques had their work made available by 1930? Walpole's *Letter* is not the only expression of hostility between moderns and contemporaries: the modernists themselves produced several such statements, often usefully illustrative of their own stylistic preferences. Indeed, Walpole's *Letter to a Modern Novelist* might almost have been a reply to one such statement, Virginia Woolf's essay 'Modern Fiction' (1919) which, along with a later essay, 'Mr. Bennett and Mrs. Brown' (1924), firmly delineates her own priorities as a writer. These are strongly contrasted to those of her immediate predecessors, whom she identifies as 'the most prominent and successful novelists in the year 1910...Mr. Wells, Mr. Bennett, and Mr. Galsworthy'. Woolf's quarrel with these Edwardian novelists centres upon their realist method, which she thought to entail faithfulness to the perceived, objective world, at the expense of interest in the perceiver—the human subject with all his or her complex thought-processes and emotions. In 'Modern Fiction' she complains that 'the enormous labour of proving the solidity, the likeness to life, of the story is not merely labour thrown away but labour misplaced'. She adds in 'Mr. Bennett and Mrs. Brown' that Bennett, Galsworthy, and Wells 'have laid an enormous stress upon the fabric of things...they have looked very powerfully, searchingly, and sympathetically...but...never at life, never at human nature'.

Her belief that such novelists concentrate too exclusively on 'the fabric of things' led Woolf to accuse them in 'Modern Fiction' of being 'materialists', and she extends this criticism in 'Mr. Bennett and Mrs. Brown' by showing in detail the incapacity of the technique, specifically of Arnold Bennett, to represent effectively a hypothetical character, Mrs. Brown. Through over-exclusive attention to observable, objective aspects—the facts about Mrs. Brown's appearance, dress, background, material circumstances, and so on—the soul or inner nature of her character is ignored, and she fails to come to life.[3] Significantly, Woolf's low opinion of the Edwardians was later supported, in very similar terms, by D.H. Lawrence's criticisms of John Galsworthy's novel sequence *The Forsyte Saga* (1906-28). Lawrence also protested that Galsworthy's methods were incommensurate to the task of creating vital characters: he finds in the case of the Forsytes that 'not one of them seems to be a really vivid human being'. This failing Lawrence attributes to 'the collapse from the psychology of the free human individual into the psychology of the social being'. Such beings suffered, in Lawrence's view, from being 'too much aware of objective reality', and being too close to the 'materialist' spirit of their time.[4]

Such criticism probably reveals as much about the convictions of Woolf and Lawrence as it does about Bennett or Galsworthy. Bennett does not ignore the psychology of his characters, whom he occasionally presents with some of the subtlety, and even through some of the methods, which Woolf was later to employ herself. Galsworthy is quite explicitly critical of his Forsyte characters, whom he uses to exemplify and satirise the materialist tendencies he disliked in his age. Nevertheless, he does admit that, as Lawrence suggests, it is not the individual psychology of characters which interests him, so much as their existence as types, through whom he can satirise a whole society. And for all the occasional inwardness of his characterisation, Bennett does at times import into his fiction a distracting volume of fact and documentation, as Woolf suggests. In *Anna of the Five Towns* (1902), for example, he interrupts a dramatic scene between the heroine and her future husband with a two-page description of the room in which their conversation takes place.

H.G. Wells seems a still clearer example of a novelist committed to objective documentation at the possible expense of development of 'the psychology of the free human individual'. He suggests in *Kipps* (1905) that 'the business of the novelist is not ethical principle, but facts', and later remarked 'I had rather be called a journalist than an artist'.[5] This apparent distaste for art in the novel was the centre of a dispute with Henry James: supplementing the quarrels of Woolf and Lawrence with the Edwardians, this further reveals the stylistic preferences which inform the work of the modernists and separate it from the fiction of their contemporaries. Wells was irritated by some of the criticisms James made in his 1914 review of contemporary novelists—'The Younger Generation', as he called them in the title of his essay. James protested about the style of Bennett in *The Old Wives' Tale* (1908) in terms similar to those used by Woolf and Lawrence:

> ...the canvas is covered, ever so closely and vividly covered, by the
> exhibition of innumerable small facts and aspects...a monument exactly

not to an idea, a pursued and captured meaning, or, in short to anything whatever but just simply of the quarried and gathered material it happens to contain.[6]

James was similarly critical of other contemporary novelists, Wells and Walpole among them. Like Bennett, these writers seemed to him to place in their novels a 'slice of life' simply transcribed from reality without being 'wrought and shaped' by a technique highlighting or giving significant form to their material. As an alternative to this 'slice of life', James praised Joseph Conrad's method of telling his story not directly but through the interpolation between author and subject matter of a narrator through whose consciousness the events of the novel are perceived, and in whose words and narrative arrangement its story unfolds.

Conrad's narrator Marlow—'a reciter, a definite responsible intervening first person singular' as James calls him—appears in such novels as *Lord Jim* (1900), *Heart of Darkness* (1902) and *Chance* (1913). In *Lord Jim*, for example, the reader learns the story of Jim supposedly through overhearing Marlow's presentation of it to a group of friends in the course of an immense after-dinner monologue. The presence of Marlow allows Conrad to avoid the direct, extended denotation of objective reality for which James, Woolf and Lawrence blamed the Edwardians. He concentrates instead partly upon the means by which reality is perceived; upon its reflection in the individual mind; and upon the effect this has upon a narrator whose responses to his world, his re-telling of his experience, form the substance of the novel. Conrad's work thus comes to concern the 'intervening first person singular' as well as the story which the narrator mediates for the reader: part of the interest of *Lord Jim*, for example, is in Marlow himself, as well as in Jim, the ostensible subject of the novel. The interpolation of a narrator also offers a focus for the novel's attention, a centre around which its characters and episodes can be structured. This allows its material, as James wished, to be 'wrought and shaped' into a satisfactory artistic form—a significant ordering of life rather than the raw, shapeless 'slice' which, rather unfairly, he considered the work of Bennett and Wells to be.

The aesthetic preferences which disposed him to admire Conrad's style also shape James's own fiction. In discussing his own work James speaks of an 'instinctive disposition...which consists in placing advantageously, placing right in the middle of the light, the most polished of possible mirrors of the subject'. He illustrates the operation of this 'disposition' with

> ...such unmistakeable examples as...that of Lambert Strether in *The Ambassadors*...I should note the extent to which these persons are, so far as their other passions permit, intense *perceivers*, all, of their respective predicaments.[7]

James does not employ Conrad's device of a narrator, telling the story of *The Ambassadors* (1903) in his own voice, yet he effects a rather similar restriction of point of view on the events narrated by confining himself exclusively to the perspective of a single character, Strether. His thoughts, reflections and perceptions provide, as James claims, a 'polished mirror' for the complicated developments in the Parisian society through which he moves. Because Strether is such an 'intense perceiver' he offers a precise, flexible perspective from which to examine his predicament. James's concentration on him and his thoughts also allows an unusually intimate, detailed examination of the way a character's experiences modify his consciousness and outlook. Wells, in fact, replied to James's criticisms by suggesting that the latter's interest in individual consciousness, throughout his work, was far too finely detailed; absurdly fussy in its sensitivity; and consequently bewilderingly over-elaborate in language and organisation.[8]

In subject matter, Conrad and James differ radically. The former spent some of his early years as a merchant seaman, and is one of the first of many novelists in the twentieth century who have examined the encounter of British life and values with distant foreign places and peoples, sometimes under colonial rule. Many of Conrad's characters are involved in lonely struggles with alien circumstances or hostile elements, far from the support of a familiar society—a considerable contrast to James's complex anatomies of social manners and relationships. Nevertheless, their decisions to concentrate upon an individual character as a perceiving centre through whom the world of the novel is focused for the reader bear some comparison. Their employment of 'an intervening first person singular' can also be seen as an early instance of what developed into one of the dominant features of modernist fiction: its desertion of the perspective of the omniscient narrator—objectively reporting on the world of the fiction in the manner of Bennett, Galsworthy, Wells, and their Victorian predecessors—in favour of a more subjective point of view. It is this focus on the 'psychology of the free human individual', rather than the 'psychology of the social being', or 'objective reality', which Lawrence favours in criticising Galsworthy. It is also a development which Virginia Woolf advocates in distinguishing 'Modern Fiction' from the work of her immediate predecessors. Instead of their 'enormous labour of proving the solidity, the likeness to life, of the story' Woolf goes on to suggest that the novelist should 'look within' and

> Examine... an ordinary mind on an ordinary day. The mind receives a myriad impressions, trivial, fantastic, evanescent, or engraved with the sharpness of steel. From all sides they come, an incessant shower of innumerable atoms; and as they fall, as they shape themselves into the life of Monday or Tuesday, the accent falls differently from of old... Life is

not a series of gig-lamps symmetrically arranged; life is a luminous halo, a semi-transparent envelope surrounding us from the beginning of consciousness to the end. Is it not the task of the novelist to convey this varying, this unknown and uncircumscribed spirit...? We are not pleading merely for courage and sincerity; we are suggesting that the proper stuff of fiction is a little other than custom would have us believe it.[9]

Woolf's distinction of 'the proper stuff of fiction' from the custom of her predecessors is one of the most significant expressions of the priorities which separate the modernists from their contemporaries. Novelists have always 'looked within' and 'examined the mind'. Woolf and the modernists, however, sought a new intensity and exclusiveness of concentration within the envelope of individual consciousness. This involved a break with the conventions of earlier fiction, and the development of new techniques able to record the atoms of impressions as they fall. Such technical developments can be seen to begin with Conrad and James, and to reach a final stage in the novels of Joyce and Woolf in the twenties. In the years between, significant innovations also appeared in the work of Dorothy Richardson, Ford Madox Ford, and D.H. Lawrence.

Rather like Virginia Woolf, Dorothy Richardson sought an alternative to 'current masculine realism' and attempted to create a 'feminine prose...moving from point to point without formal obstructions'. In her novel-sequence *Pilgrimage* (1915-38), she uses brief, half-formulated phrases, linked by ellipses, to imitate the random succession of thoughts, memories and 'myriad impressions' in the mind of her heroine. This is often considered to be the earliest example, in the English novel at least, of the method of transcribing characters' thoughts 'without formal obstructions' which came to be known as 'stream of consciousness'. (The phrase originates in the writings of Henry James's brother William.) Richardson's invention, however, has not secured her reputation. A contemporary reviewer unkindly remarked 'the bleak truth is that Miss Richardson perfected a way of saying things without having anything to say...an excellent manner execrably applied'.[10] A fairer criticism might be that Richardson's use of this 'excellent manner'—which the reviewer saw as belonging to 'modern fiction...the subjective novel'—is restricted in *Pilgrimage* by its application to a less than wholly modern subject matter. Following throughout its thirteen volumes the experience of a semi-autobiographical heroine, *Pilgrimage* really belongs with a group of chronicle novels written in the early years of the twentieth century. These include Compton Mackenzie's *Sinister Street* (1913-14); Somerset Maugham's *Of Human Bondage* (1915); and Arnold Bennett's *Clayhanger* series (1910-18). These novels all trace at great length the development of a single individual, usually one whose experiences closely resemble those of his author. Rather than 'modern...subjective novels' they are late examples of the *bildungsroman*, the novel of personal development, such as Dickens's *David Copperfield* (1850), popular in the Victorian period.

Like *Pilgrimage*, Ford Madox Ford's *Parade's End* (1924-28), which concerns the experience of Christopher Tietjens before, during and after the First World War, initially appeared as separate volumes and is of considerable length when assembled. Like Richardson, Ford employs his stream of consciousness only intermittently, though sometimes for quite extended periods. His transcription of the contents of his characters' minds is stylistically very similar to Richardson's, presenting thought in short reflective phrases, interspersed with ellipses. Unlike Richardson, however, Ford presents extensively consciousnesses other than that of his central character, though Christopher Tietjens remains the principal figure. The inclusion of other characters' reflections contributes to a range of ironically disparate versions of events; of variable recollections of experience. This dramatises very successfully some of the tensions in a war-time society uncertain of its own stability or of how meaning can be derived from the bewildering phenomena abroad in the world at the time. Though posterity has rather overlooked both Richardson and Ford, it has done so with a good deal less justice in the latter case.

Ford's reputation may have suffered partly because, even by the time his *Parade's End* tetralogy began to appear in the nineteen twenties, his work was likely to have been overshadowed by the more spectacular achievements of Joyce, and also perhaps of D.H. Lawrence. Lawrence was chilled by the sterility of modern industrial civilisation and its threat to the freedom and spontaneity of the individual. In his greatest novels, *The Rainbow* (1915) and *Women in Love* (1921) he increasingly turns away from the diminished possibilities of the wider world to examine the potential of fulfilment through personal relationships. Envisaging sex as an integral part of such relationships, Lawrence presented his characters' sexuality with an explicitness largely new to the novel; one which led him, like Joyce, into trouble with censorship. It has perhaps also encouraged subsequent readers to see him as primarily concerned with the expansion into new areas of the novel's subject matter, rather than with the sort of innovation in fictional technique which distinguishes the work of the modernists. Lawrence's plots and narrative structure can seem conventional: *Sons and Lovers* (1913), for example, his first successful novel, partly belongs with the semi-autobiographical chronicles mentioned above. But the intensity of Lawrence's interest in 'the psychology of the free human individual', and in the effect upon his characters of the ebb and flow, wonder and disillusion of powerful emotions released in their relationships, also led him to develop new fictional styles for presenting subjectivity.

This is partly a simple matter of the increased extent to which

Lawrence directs his readers' attention upon individual consciousness. Actual experiences in his novels—sometimes even single lines of conversation—are often followed by several paragraphs or even pages devoted to minute examination of his characters' reflections and emotions. The intimacy with which Lawrence seeks to present this inner experience often leads him to a distinctive intermingling of characters' inner voices with his own more objective authorial tone. This may be seen, for example, in the following passage from *The Rainbow*, which traces the thoughts of Lawrence's heroine Ursula as she walks out one spring morning:

> Again she felt Jesus in the countryside. Ah, he would lift up the lambs in his arms! Ah, and she was the lamb. Again, in the morning, going down the lane, she heard the ewe call, and the lambs came running...stooping, nuzzling, groping to the udder...Oh and the bliss, the bliss! She could scarcely tear herself away to go to school.[11]

It is clear that the voice which says 'ah' and 'Oh...the bliss, the bliss!' is not wholly Lawrence's own, but really a partial transcription of Ursula's, though this is not conventionally marked for the reader by such phrases as 'she said' or 'she thought'. This technique of presenting a character's thoughts or words partly mediated through the voice of the author—usually called Free Indirect Discourse—is a very common fictional technique, certainly not one invented by Lawrence. But the frequency of Lawrence's use of it, often sustained for pages at a time, is a distinctive extension of the novelist's means of 'looking within' and examining the mind. Though Lawrence never employs the more direct entry into the mental experience of his characters offered by stream of consciousness, his sustained presentation of their thoughts and inner world clearly associates him with 'the modern...subjective novel' as it was developed by other modernist writers.

The greatest of these is James Joyce, who consummates in *Ulysses* (1922) all the trends of earlier years to interpolate between reader and fictional world a 'first person singular', whose subjective experience forms the substance of the novel. Much of the Dublin world of *Ulysses* is seen only insofar as it is reflected in the mind of Leopold Bloom as he wanders around the city. Joyce's stream-of-consciousness technique presents the inner life of Bloom—the myriad associations, reflections, and movements of his mind in response to external stimuli—so successfully that be becomes more intimately and wholly available to the reader than any character from earlier fiction. As one critic later remarked, in *Ulysses* 'Joyce rewrote for the modern novel generally the definition of a man'.[12] Joyce's stream of consciousness, however, is used most purely and uninterruptedly not in presenting Bloom himself, but in following in the last section of the novel the thoughts of his wife Molly as she lies in bed with him, her mind hovering on the verge of sleep. Joyce does not follow Ford and Richardson in interpolating ellipses to mark transitions from thought to thought. Instead, he omits punctuation entirely from the last 40 pages of *Ulysses*, enhancing the sense of Molly's ideas, emotions and memories as a mingling flood, a seamless, stream-like continuity.

Such disdain for punctuation in Joyce's development of stream of consciousness is only one of an array of innovative techniques and unconventional devices which made *Ulysses* seem thoroughly unfamiliar, even unintelligible, to early readers and reviewers. Some were further deterred by the frank detail in which Joyce follows Molly's thoughts about sex, or Bloom's visit to the toilet. Many early critics found *Ulysses* deliberately shocking, and fairly few guessed that it would come to occupy a pre-eminent position among twentieth-century novels. Despite some reticence of her own about what she saw as occasional indecency, Virginia Woolf was one of Joyce's earliest admirers, praising *Ulysses* in her 'Modern Fiction' essay (before she had even seen a complete copy of the novel) for its attempt 'at all costs to reveal the flickerings of that innermost flame which flashes its messages through the brain'.[13]

Just as Henry James's priorities predisposed him to admire Conrad, Woolf was naturally in favour of work which satisfied her feeling that 'the proper stuff of fiction' is created by entering the mind and following its movements. By the time Woolf came to write her best novels in the twenties, *Mrs Dalloway* (1925) and *To the Lighthouse* (1927), she had developed her own technique for recording the 'atoms' of impression, not quite identical to Joyce's stream of consciousness. Whereas Joyce often presents the thoughts of his characters 'without formal obstructions' or any intrusion of his own voice, Woolf constantly interpolates phrases such as 'she said', or 'she thought to herself'. This provides a reminder that thoughts are being reported, mediated by an authorial consciousness, though one which is occasionally intermingled with the inner voices of characters rather in the manner of Lawrence's use of Free Indirect Discourse. The distinction between Woolf's interior monologue and Joyce's stream of consciousness is a fairly slight one, however, and has often been overlooked. It is clear enough, in any case, that each technique participates in the initiative of the 'modern...subjective novel' to find methods which present the inner workings of the mind, rather than the 'objective reality' whose documentation so disfigured for the modernists the work of Edwardian realists such as Bennett, Galsworthy, and Wells.

As discussed thus far, concentration upon individual consciousness involved the modernists in the creation of new styles and uses of language, sentence by sentence and page by page in their fiction. Concentration upon subjectivity also involved changes in the overall structure of the novel. As E.M. Forster suggests in his study *Aspects of the Novel* (1927), writers conventionally present a story which is 'a narrative of events arranged in their time sequence—dinner coming after breakfast, Tuesday after Monday, decay after death, and so on'. Wells's title, *The History of Mr. Polly* (1910), or Bennett's description of *Anna of the Five Towns* as 'a history/homely and rude', are reminders of the Edwardians' allegiance to this sort of historical, chronological order, as the structuring basis for their fiction.[14] Walpole, however, observed accurately that this conventional '*arrangement* of the older novelists, the placing of things in order' was discarded by the modernist novel, partly in consequence of its reliance on individual consciousness. Though experience can be organised into historical order for narrative purposes, it does not always exist in the mind in that way. Memory can precipitate various disordered, distant events into present consciousness, mixing past and present. Thus in following the thoughts and memories of individual characters, the modernists could amend or ignore conventional chronological order.

This begins to be evident in the work of Conrad, who describes *Lord Jim*, for example, as 'a free and wandering tale'.[15] It is made so partly by his use of the narrator Marlow, who presents events not always in the historical succession in which they must be supposed to have occurred, but in the order in which he happens to recollect them, or in which they have become mutually associated in his mind. Even when not employing a narrator, Conrad continues to eschew serial chronology in his fiction. In *Nostromo* (1904), for example, he dramatises the chaotic history of a politically-unstable South American republic through an appropriately non-historic, non-chronological narrative. Ford Madox Ford, who collaborated with Conrad in writing several novels, later explained as follows this sort of decision to amend conventional chronology:

> it became very early evident to us that what was the matter with the Novel, and the British novel in particular, was that it went straight forward, whereas in your gradual making acquaintanceship with your fellows you never do go straight forward...To get...a man in fiction you could not begin at his beginning and work his life chronologically to the end. You must first get him in with a strong impression, and then work backwards and forwards over his past.[16]

This working 'backwards and forwards over the past' was a tactic Ford employed himself: in *The Good Soldier* (1915), for example, his protagonist Edward Ashburnham reflects on the various episodes in the history of his wife's infidelities, apparently arranging them in the order of their recurrence in his memory, rather than strictly chronologically. The first part of *The Good Soldier*, originally entitled *The Saddest Story Ever Told*, appeared in 1914 in Wyndham Lewis's short-lived periodical *Blast*, which called for a renovation of styles of painting and included new, formally innovative poetry by Ezra

Pound and T.S. Eliot. The inclusion of Ford's work in such a journal is a reminder of the way developments in techniques and structures for the novel participated in a much wider modernism; a general reassessment of artistic priorities and styles taking place in Britain at the time. Ford continued to 'work backwards and forwards over the past' in *Parade's End*, in which, as in *The Good Soldier*, events are often presented through characters' retrospective reflections upon them.

The novels of Woolf and Joyce, more fully committed than those of Ford or Conrad to entering characters' consciousness, also show a freer alteration of the conventional chronology of the novel. An immediately striking feature of *Ulysses*, or of *Mrs Dalloway*, is that each apparently concentrates on the events of a single day. In fact, this extreme concentration does not greatly curtail the reader's acquaintance with the whole spread of characters' lives: rather, it alters the manner in which such acquaintance is made. Bloom's thoughts during his day in Dublin—or Mrs Dalloway's during hers in London—are frequently interrupted by an association with present events of memories of the past: from this intermingling of past consciousness with present awareness, an extensive history of the previous life of each character can be assembled. This sort of emphasis on memory, and its use to reintegrate past experience with present impressions, are also important elements in the fiction of Marcel Proust. His *Remembrance of Things Past* (*A la Recherche du Temps Perdu*, 1913-27) is concentrated, like the work of Woolf and Joyce, within the experience of individual consciousness. It exhibits a whole repertoire of associations by the narrator of past events with present ones; and of attempts to regain lost fragments of experience by means of an intermingling of memory and present consciousness, shaped and fixed in art. Proust's twelve-volume novel began to appear in English translation in 1922 and may have been an influence in the background of Woolf and other novelists around that time. *A la Recherche du Temps Perdu* is at any rate a reminder that the energy for innovation in the British novel, and the sort of energy expressed in Lewis's *Blast*, should be seen as part of a general urge towards transformation of styles very widespread in European art as a whole in the early years of the twentieth century.[17]

This widespread appearance of the urge to 'invent a new literature', as Stephen Spender called it, suggests that it may indeed be best considered in terms of Spender's belief that the age was 'in many respects unprecedented, and outside all the conventions of past literature and art'. Certain events and developments in the early part of the twentieth century are often proposed as sources of the feeling that an insistently modern world had come into being, requiring a rejuvenated, modernistic literature for its assimilation. One of the most obviously influential of such events is the First World War. J.B. Priestley, himself a popular novelist in the twenties, later remarked

> No intelligent and sensitive European — and writers can hardly succeed
> without intelligence and sensitivity — could escape the terrible impact of
> these four years...the war was there, all around them .[18]

Ford's *Parade's End*, one of the few successful novels to attempt description of the war itself, and of life in the trenches, is also the best account of its effect on society on the home front. Ford dramatises at length the erosion and collapse of a securely, perhaps complacently, self-confident pre-war society. Its values, habits, faith, and even morals are radically challenged and permanently altered by economic or ideological changes brought about by the events of 1914 to 1918. The war is described in *Parade's End* as a 'crack across the table of History', and seems to have been similarly apprehended as an irreparable fracture of the continuity of history and experience by many other novelists. Virginia Woolf, for example, talks of the war as being 'like a chasm in a smooth road', and D.H. Lawrence suggests that one of its consequences was that 'there is now no smooth road into the future'.[19] Some such feeling of disjuncture perhaps underlies the differences between *The Rainbow* and *Women in Love*, which Lawrence had originally intended as parts of one long novel, *The Sisters*. *The Rainbow* (1915) is an account, almost in the sort of chronicle form discussed earlier, of development through the cycles of three generations of family life, ending in a qualified optimism despite the encroaching threats of modern industrialisation. Published after the war, *Women in Love* (1921) is much less optimistic, ending with at best an equivocal realisation of Lawrence's faith in personal relations as an alternative to the despair of the wider world.

The effects of the war are also occasionally apparent in Woolf's fiction. *Mrs Dalloway* is partly concerned with the mental breakdown of one of its shell-shocked victims. *To the Lighthouse* incorporates the sense of the 'crack' in history, the disjuncture of present from past, as a feature of its structure. The novel's first and third sections are written almost entirely as interior monologues of members of the Ramsay family, presenting their thoughts and aspirations sympathetically. These sections are separated, however, by a second part which with cruel independence of human thought or aspiration objectively documents the destructive effects of time, mortality, and the war upon the family. Such bleak disjuncture of the parts of *To the Lighthouse* helps to indicate the sense of separation from the Edwardian era some novelists felt after the war. Such feelings may account for the vehemence of the rejection, by Woolf and others, of the work of 'the most prominent and successful novelists in the year 1910'. Their work must have seemed to belong to an Edwardian age now irrevocably shattered and lost.

Nevertheless, it is significant that in criticising those novelists, Woolf picked on December 1910 as the approximate date on which 'human character changed',[20] and on or about which, in her view, fictional styles should have changed correspondingly. Likewise, it is worth noticing that Wyndham Lewis's *Blast*, and Henry James's discussion of 'The Younger Generation' belong to 1914, immediately before the First World War rather than during or after it. It would be misleading to consider the war as the sole source of the changes in the mood of the age. As Priestley goes on to remark, 'the First World War settled nothing. What it really did was to speed things up, to heighten temperatures already rising before 1914, to widen and deepen splits in the Western mind'.[21] Much of the ideology which might have contributed to such 'splits in the Western mind' was available before the war. In developing analysis of the mind's operations, conscious or unconscious, Freud's work, for example, might be seen as an influence upon novelists of the time. It can at least be usefully compared to their increased concentration on the subjective self, and on the operation and perception of individual consciousness. Like Freud's, Einstein's theories began to appear long before the war. As early as 1905, he radically questioned assumptions about the character and interrelation of space and time. His inference that all values and measurements should be seen as dependent upon the point of view of the observer may have encouraged reliance on an 'intervening first person singular', an 'intense perceiver' as the subjective centre of the novel. Einstein's suggestion that time was not an independent universal order, but depended for its measurement and understanding upon the perspective of the individual, likewise bears comparison with the increasingly internalised chronologies of Joyce and Woolf. Their tendency to mix memory, anticipation, and present thought into a fluid stream of consciousness is also analogous with the thinking of a distant relation of Marcel Proust — the popular French philosopher Henri Bergson, who advocated the understanding of time and consciousness as a continuous, homogeneous flux, falsely ordered and subdivided by clock or calendar.

These and other contemporary developments in philosophy, along with the disruptive and disillusioning effects of the First World War, combined to form a general challenge to the stability and certainty with which the world had hitherto been understood. The new philosophies questioned the validity of such fundamental co-ordinates for experience as those of space and time. The old orders and social relations were altered by the war, which also challenged the belief in progress which had partly replaced declining religious faith in the nineteenth century, later attracting such social prophets as H.G. Wells. Such general uncertainty increased the need, in the growing absence of alternatives, for artists and writers to create order and meaning for their world, but also made their task unusually difficult. As the critic David Daiches remarks, 'the great surge of experimentation in fiction...was in large measure caused by the novelists' search for devices that would enable them to solve the problem of the breakdown of a public sense of significance'.[22] This apparently increased disorder of a world which, as Henry James insisted, still had to be 'wrought and shaped' into art, perhaps also made novelists unusually self-conscious about the nature of their task, and about the devices that could be discovered to assist it. At any rate, art and the processes by which it is created begin to figure prominently as subjects of early twentieth-century fiction.

This development of artistic self-consciousness is central to Joyce's first published novel, *A Portrait of the Artist as a Young Man* (1916), a largely autobiographical account of the development of a single individual, Stephen Dedalus, from childhood towards maturity. Unlike other contemporary autobiographical chronicles, however, Joyce's *Portrait*, as its title suggests, is concerned not just with Stephen's general progress towards adulthood, but specifically with his development of an interest in the nature of art and of the wish to become a writer. This wish to become a fully-fledged artist, and his rejection of the religion which had dominated his early years, resemble—or 'portray'—Joyce's own early experience. Lengthy sections of the novel devoted to Stephen's discussion of artistic priorities are also partly Joyce's own examination of issues which had preoccupied him during his development as a novelist. *A Portrait of the Artist as a Young Man* was first published as a serial in the *Egoist*: its immediate successor in that magazine was Wyndham Lewis's *Tarr* (1918), which similarly presents artistic issues of interest to its author through the discussions of a semi-autobiographical artist-hero. This concern within the novel for the processes of artistic creation further reappears in Woolf's *To the Lighthouse*, incorporated in the figure of a painter, Lily Briscoe. Her struggles to order her experience into a satisfactory, coherent visual form are analogous, and co-terminous, with Woolf's ordering and structuring of the novel itself.

A similarly self-conscious concern with art and its methods appears in Joyce's *Ulysses*. Joyce eschews the stylistic homogeneity of conventional novels, presenting Bloom's experience in an array of contrasting styles. These range from newspaper headlines, catechism, and parody of other literary forms, to the stream of consciousness which Joyce developed largely for himself. At one level, such extended experimentation with language and style makes *Ulysses* the clearest illustration of a concern shared by all modernist writers. A distinctive feature of their fiction (further discussed in Chapter Five) is its readiness to establish or experiment with new linguistic forms: the language of modernist novels often shows as a result a complexity and particularity previously more often associated with poetry.

Joyce's stylistic diversity in *Ulysses* is also part of the novel's wider investigation of writing and fictional form. The whole novel is in a way a gigantic parody, a reworking of Homer's *Odyssey* with Bloom as a sort of modern Ulysses. This general parody is greatly diversified by the literary or other mimicry in the individual styles of each section of the novel. As a result, it is virtually impossible to read *Ulysses* for its story alone. Instead, the reader is repeatedly forced to take account of the varying ways that the story is told, and through such constant questioning of the way fiction represents reality, obliged to scrutinise the whole diverse enterprise of relating the world in words, and words to the world. This sort of self-conscious examination within the novel of the language, problems and practice of writing fiction has continued to interest authors in the latter part of the twentieth century, especially the later generation of experimental novelists considered in Chapter Five. Modernism and its questioning of convention also continues to be more generally influential. Joyce and other innovative writers of his time challenge readers to reconsider the nature of fiction, and to reconstruct for themselves fictional worlds complexly envisaged through the consciousnesses of characters, often expressed in diverse linguistic styles and unusual chronological structures. Such challenges have in some ways permanently altered the relationship between writer, novel, and reader. The latter is required by modernist writing to participate more actively in the imaginative creation of the fictional world envisaged, and becomes, in the view of one recent critic, 'no longer a consumer, but the producer of the text'.[23]

Though such strikingly original works as *Ulysses* have naturally continued to affect later writers and readers in various ways, there are also factors which have inhibited the influence of the modernists. Many writers in the twenties, Woolf among them, saw their age as a transitional one whose literary experiments would be developed and perfected by subsequent generations of novelists. The success with which such 'experiments' were completed, however, may paradoxically have limited their effect. Ezra Pound remarked when *Ulysses* was first published, '*Ulysses* is, presumably, as unrepeatable as *Tristram Shandy*...you cannot duplicate it'.[24] Along with other modernist works, Joyce's novel may have been considered so technically sophisticated or unique as to discourage attempts at imitation. Lack of contemporary popular success may also have restricted the immediate influence of the modernists. Sometimes altering familiar approaches to character, and often omitting the '*arrangement* of the older novelists', the unconventionality of the new fiction initially made it difficult to read and understand, as Walpole complains in his *Letter*. Modernist fiction certainly did not immediately interest a wide public, despite the excitement it aroused in literary circles. Although Virginia Woolf, for example, has come to be regarded as one of the most significant of modern English authors, she sold relatively few copies of her novels at the time of their first publication. In his letters to Wells, Henry James likewise laments the absence of a wide readership, from which his stylistic complexity generally debarred him. The attentions of the censor also reduced at first the circulation of the work of Joyce and Lawrence.

The features discussed above which make modernist writing challenging sometimes continue to be thought to make it inaccessible or 'highbrow'. Modernism has been variously criticised for this supposed elitism, sometimes on specifically political grounds (see Chapter Two). This state of affairs contrasts strangely with the Victorian period, when serious literary novels, even those seeking to advance the novelist's grasp of technique and subject, were often also a substantial success with the public. Perhaps it is not surprising, therefore, that the more popularly successful novelists of the early twentieth century were often ones who looked back to the Victorian period for their method and inspiration. Walpole, for example, praises the methods of Trollope as an alternative to the modern novels he deplores. Similarly, Galsworthy talks of 'looking back on the Victorian era, whose ripeness, decline, and "fall-off" is in some sort pictured in *The Forsyte Saga*'. James was quick to note that Wells's comic style clearly resembles Dickens's:[25] the same might be said of J.B. Priestley's style and subject in a popular novel published in 1930, *Angel Pavement*.

Such conservative influences survived strongly until 1930 and beyond. Though Woolf was right to see the greatest successes of Bennett, Wells, and Galsworthy as belonging to the Edwardian period, around 1910, these novelists by no means disappeared after the war. They continued to publish in the twenties, and certainly continued to be admired. It is significant, for example, that one contemporary study of the novel, Gerald Bullett's *Modern English Fiction* (1926), despite its title, mentions Joyce, Woolf, Lawrence, and Dorothy Richardson only in a last chapter devoted to 'Eccentricities'. Bennett, Wells, Galsworthy, Conrad and E. M. Forster each merit a main chapter. Bullett's priorities are a useful indication of the general state of opinion, not only in the mid-twenties but probably for some time thereafter: the modernists did not enjoy an immediate ascendancy over their contemporaries, least of all in popular opinion.

It is worth pausing, however, to question this division of authors of the early twentieth century into 'modernists' and 'contemporaries'. Several successful novelists of the period are not easily accommodated in either category, and Bullett's inclusion of a chapter on E.M. Forster is a reminder of the reputation of one of these. Forster has been confidently claimed by various critics as the first of the modernists; or, on the other hand, as an arch-Edwardian; or even as the last of the novelists of the nineteenth century. It is more accurate to acknowledge that, as Forster's career as a novelist falls into two distinct phases, he belongs in part to each of these areas. His early novels, *Where Angels Fear to Tread* (1905), *The Longest Journey* (1907), *A Room with a View* (1908), and *Howards End* (1910), were all written before the War. Each seems to demonstrate some belief that problems confronting individuals or society in general might be solved by a modification of outlook or imagination—by acquiring, for example, the faculty to connect one's own experience with that of other people which is so strongly advocated in *Howards End*. Such sentiments, and the novels in which they appear, belong firmly to the heyday of British liberalism in the period from 1906 to 1914. After the war Forster's liberal imagination, in *A Passage to India* (1924), seems much more uncertain, perhaps perplexed by the 'crack across the table of history' which appears as such a chasm in the work of his contemporaries. The hollow 'ou-boum' resounding in the Marabar Caves in *A Passage to India* seems almost a further, desolate echo of the explosions of 1914-18. At any rate, the novel is as a whole less optimistic than Forster's early phase, showing the individual confronted by an alien society and an indifferent universe which teases and finally eludes attempts at understanding or connection.

Like E.M. Forster, Aldous Huxley is difficult to categorise. In *Point Counter Point* (1928), he employs an unusual narrative strategy, sustaining several different 'counterpointed' stories supposedly occurring simultaneously and presented in successive blocks of narrative in his text. This creation of a new sort of narrative style seems to belong with the urge for technical innovation which characterises the work of the modernists, but the rest of Huxley's fiction is structurally and stylistically more conventional, and he is perhaps most appropriately considered as a satirist and social commentator. In works such as *Crome Yellow* (1921) and *Antic Hay* (1923) he presents with witty acuteness the new social, sexual and intellectual fashions of the bright, cynical jazz age which surrounded him in the post-war years.

Part-satirist and part-fantasist, Ronald Firbank is similarly hard to define. He made an impression on the twenties with strange novels such as *Valmouth* (1919), *Prancing Nigger* (1924), and *Concerning the Eccentricities of Cardinal Pirelli* (1926). These portray societies both peculiarly permeated by Catholicism and yet exquisitely, perversely decadent in ways which look back to Oscar Wilde and the eighteen nineties. Yet in his talent for presenting a certain sordidness amid glittering social pretensions, and in his heavy reliance on dialogue rather than authorial report, Firbank also looks forward. His writing anticipates in style and interest many satirists and novelists of high society who follow in the thirties and thereafter.

The work of writers such as Forster, Firbank and Huxley is a worthwhile reminder that there are limitations to any division of authors into schools. Nevertheless, at least in general terms, it is clear that a central feature of the early decades of the twentieth century was the development of an innovative modernist fiction which defined itself in deliberate antithesis to the more traditional, formally conservative work of authors such as Bennett, Galsworthy, and Wells. Though Woolf's *The Waves* (1931), and Joyce's most challenging novel, *Finnegans Wake* (1939; see Chapter Five), were published later, by 1930 this modernist initiative was largely complete. Later novelists were confronted by the need to come to terms with the possibility of divergence from traditional forms and styles which it had created. Though Pound suggests in commenting on *Ulysses* that in some ways the modernist novel was inimitable and unrepeatable, he also goes on to remark of Joyce's work that 'it does add definitely to the international store of literary technique'. Whether or not *Ulysses* or any other modernist novel could be 'duplicated', later novelists inherited from the early twentieth century an incentive to exploit or experiment with a great many new possibilities and techniques for fiction—new methods of concentration upon subjective consciousness; of re-ordering the novel's episodes independently of their chronology; or, more generally, of breaking and re-shaping the language or conventions of fiction to fulfil particular needs or beliefs about the nature of art.

On the other hand, through the formal conservatism of the Edwardians, and other contemporaries of the modernist movement opposed to its innovations, there survived at least as far as 1930 conventions of story-telling which belonged to a main line of development of the British novel, reaching back to the great popular and literary successes of the nineteenth century. Many authors in the early decades of the twentieth century remained, as Gerald Bullett describes Hugh Walpole, 'undaunted pedestrian[s]' who 'plodded along the main road of English fiction'.[26] The work of such novelists—of Bennett, Wells, Galsworthy, Walpole, Priestley and others—has been overshadowed by the originality of modernism, and has partly faded from critical esteem as a result. It would be a mistake, however, to overlook their continuation into the twentieth century of the traditional strengths of fiction which Walpole valued in his *Letter to a Modern Novelist*. Neither the omniscient narrator nor the chronologically episodic form of story, for example, were by any means eclipsed by modernism.

Faced both by this continuing strength of tradition, and by a challenging modernist counter-movement, the position of the novelist in 1930 and since has been perplexing but full of potential. Possibilities existing for the novel form by 1930 may have been puzzling in their heterogeneity, but the range of stylistic choice had been extended perhaps further than ever before by the work of earlier decades. Modernism encouraged exploitation of diverse new opportunities, and opened up a possibility of synthesising these new techniques with older conventions. 'The main road of English fiction' also remained open. Perhaps encouraged by this extended sense of opportunity, Virginia Woolf concludes her essay on 'Mr. Bennett and Mrs. Brown' with a 'surpassingly rash prediction... we are trembling on the verge of one of the great ages of English literature'.[27] The following pages consider whether subsequent developments in fiction have justified Woolf's optimism, and assess how far later authors have succeeded in continuing, ignoring, or combining the style of the modernists and of the other novelists working in the early decades of the twentieth century.

2
In the Thirties

Between the Acts: Politics and Literature in the Nineteen Thirties

Looking back in 1940, Virginia Woolf suggests that the decade just completed had not fulfilled the hopes for a great literary future she entertained in 1924. In her essay 'The Leaning Tower' she indicates some of the factors which in her view inhibited literary developments in the thirties:

> In 1930 it was impossible—if you were young, sensitive, imaginative—not be to interested in politics; not to find public causes of much more pressing interest than philosophy. In 1930 young men...were forced to be aware of what was happening in Russia; in Germany; in Italy; in Spain. They could not go on discussing aesthetic emotions and personal relations...they had to read the politicians. They read Marx. They became communists; they became anti-fascists. [1]

One of the young contemporary novelists Woolf might have had in mind was George Orwell, whose essay 'Inside the Whale', also written in 1940, reaffirms her view of recent developments. He records that

> During the past ten years literature has involved itself more and more deeply in politics...the younger writers have 'gone into politics'...the movement is in the direction of some rather ill-defined thing called Communism. [2]

As Woolf and Orwell suggest, a central feature of nineteen-thirties fiction is its development away from the 'aesthetic emotions and personal relations' which had concerned the modernists, towards a more direct reflection of the political events and public causes of the period. Two principal factors encouraged this change of interest. The first and simplest of these was the critical, threatening nature of public affairs at the time, virtually impossible, as Woolf suggests, for writers to ignore. The collapse of the Wall Street stock market late in 1929 helped create an economic depression which quickly dominated British affairs: by 1931, the pound had been devalued; the Labour Party ousted by a National Government created to deal with the emergency; and unemployment had reached a scale which provoked hunger marches and riots. Similar crises abroad forced the British public to 'be aware of what was happening in Russia; in

Germany; in Italy; in Spain'. The effects of the depression in Germany allowed Hitler to seize power in 1933: in Italy, another fascist dictator, Mussolini, had been in control since 1922. By 1936, Italy had overrun Abyssinia and Hitler had reoccupied the Rhineland from which Germany was supposedly excluded by the Treaty of Versailles. These foreign developments were made still more immediate for British people by the founding in 1932 of Sir Oswald Moseley's British Union of Fascists.

Contemporary anxieties were particularly focussed by the Spanish Civil War which followed General Franco's right-wing revolt against the Republican government in 1936. The war in Spain, eventually involving German, Italian, and Russian forces, and many British volunteers, deeply affected opinion at the time, especially among artists and writers. They saw in it evidence of an intensifying conflict between politics of right and left, fascist and communist, which seemed to make a wider war inevitable. Graham Greene's *The Confidential Agent* (1939), for example, suggests that the Spanish Civil War would not be long in spreading to the rest of Europe. Recollection of the First World War also added to current anxieties: Greene's *A Gun for Sale* (1936) and Evelyn Waugh's *Vile Bodies* (1930) present an expected Second World War in terms of memories of the First: by the time George Orwell came to write *Coming up for Air* (1939), this expectation had hardened into certainty. Throughout the decade, however, the 'vision of Europe, bristling with guns, poised with planes' created a sense of being trapped between wars, with 'the doom of sudden death hanging over us... no retreating and advancing', as Virginia Woolf expresses it in her novel *Between the Acts* (1941).[3] One of the leading poets of the decade, Stephen Spender, likewise remarks 'from 1931 onwards, in common with many other people, I felt hounded by external events', adding 'the 1930s were a perpetual state of emergency for those aware that there was an emergency'.[4]

A second common factor in the outlook of thirties writers was their distinctive preparedness to be 'aware that there was an emergency'. This disposition is partly retraceable to the public-school experience shared by many of them at the time of the First World War. Orwell remarks in 'Inside the Whale' 'nearly all the younger writers fit easily into the public-school-university-Bloomsbury pattern' (p.560). In his critical study *Reading the Thirties* (1978) Bernard Bergonzi lists many of the novelists who emerged during the decade—Christopher Isherwood, Edward Upward, Evelyn Waugh, Graham Greene, George Orwell, Anthony Powell, Cyril Connolly, Henry Green—among authors who attended public school and (with the exception of Orwell), Oxford or Cambridge University.[5] Far from insulating these writers from the shock of the First World War, the exclusive atmosphere of their educations may in some way have sharpened its impact on their minds at a most impressionable age. Anger against the ruling class and their responsibility for the carnage of 1914-18 was widespread during and after the war. Public schools, traditional bastions of English social structure, offered an immediate encounter with the establishment values which seemed implicated in the conduct of the war, and hence profoundly corrupt to many members of the younger generation at the time. Christopher Isherwood, for example, recalls in his autobiography *Lions and Shadows* (1938) a mixture of guilt at being a non-combatant and outrage at the system of authoritarian values he encountered at school. This view of schooldays is confirmed by other commentators such as Cyril Connolly, and by Isherwood's friend W.H. Auden, the most representative poet of the decade, who remarked in 1934 'the best reason I have for opposing Fascism is that at school I lived in a Fascist state'.[6] As Auden suggests, the early experience of the ex-public schoolboys of the thirties made them particularly prepared for the threatening developments of their times, unusually ready to reject the establishment, 'read Marx', and 'become anti-fascists'. For many contemporary writers, 'the red flag was intertwined with the old school tie', as the critic W.W. Robson remarks.[7]

Their youth at the time of the First World War, and the political outlook which resulted, underlie thirties writers' departure from modernist styles. For the modernists, the First World War came as an interruption, a 'crack' or 'chasm' on the previously smooth road of their historical experience in the Edwardian period.[8] The strategy of much of their fiction, with its intense reliance on memory, may be seen as partly directed by a desire to recover or escape back into the benign atmosphere of these pre-war years. Such refuge in the past was inaccessible to younger writers, unequipped with adult memories of life before the First World War. They were more disposed as a result to confront the 'nightmare' of history not through imaginative or aesthetic transformations which partly denied or tried to escape its processes, but through direct, political attitudes which sought to transform reality and historical process themselves.

These attitudes made modernist emphasis on memory, individual consciousness, 'aesthetic emotions and personal relations' seem irresponsible and self-indulgent, especially to the more politically-committed of thirties commentators. For example, in *The Novel Today: Studies in Contemporary Attitudes* (1936)—described by George Orwell in a review as 'a survey of the contemporary novel from a Marxist standpoint'—Philip Henderson suggests that 'the novel today...could scarcely have a nobler function than that of awakening man to a consciousness of his destiny as a social being'. This function he considers absent from the work of the modernists, whom he accuses of 'compromise and evasion...pure aestheticism and social indifference...more than an element of decadence'; and of having 'lost touch with the basic realities of the world'.[9] Modernism was likewise rejected at the time by another communist critic, Ralph Fox, whose study *The Novel and the People* (1937) dismisses authors such as Joyce and Proust for their 'false outlook on life', advocating instead a 'new realism'.[10] Such opinions are representative of hostility to modernism expressed by left-wing criticism: this receives its most articulate summation later in 'The Ideology of Modernism', an essay by the Hungarian Marxist Georg Lukács. Like Henderson and Fox, Lukács dislikes what he calls the modernists' 'anti-realism', and criticises their work for its 'rejection of narrative objectivity' and the 'surrender to subjectivity'.[11]

Similarly negative views of modernism were sometimes expressed by thirties novelists. George Orwell, for example, suggests of the modernists

> ...what is noticeable about all these writers is that what 'purpose' they have is very much up in the air. There is no attention to the urgent problems of the moment, above all no politics in the narrower sense... when one looks back at the twenties...in 'cultured' circles art-for-art's sake extended practically to a worship of the meaningless. Literature was supposed to consist solely in the manipulation of words.
>
> ('Inside the Whale', p.557).

J. B. Priestley likewise looks back to Virginia Woolf's 'Modern Fiction' essay and suggests that the novelist may find that

> If his fiction is concerned with men in a particular society, and with the character of that society, then this highly subjective, interior monologue, halo-and-envelope method will not serve his purpose at all. In the unending dazzle of thoughts and impressions, society disappears.[12]

Unimpressed by the dazzle of modernist innovation, inappropriate for their social concerns, thirties novelists were often disposed to return to 'the main road of English fiction' which Chapter One suggested continued undeviatingly in the early decades of the century in the work of Bennett, Galsworthy and Wells. This preference for the models modernism rejected is neatly encapsulated by Philip Henderson, who dismisses in his turn Woolf's rejection of Arnold Bennett in her essay 'Mr. Bennett and Mrs. Brown'. Henderson returns to Woolf's imagined meeting with a hypothetical character on a railway journey to London, but suggests that in the thirties

> ...we begin to look away from old Mrs. Brown, sitting opposite in her respectable poverty, and glance out of the window at the street upon street of hovels converging upon London.[13]

As Henderson suggests, Woolf's urge to 'look within' is often replaced in the thirties by an inclination to 'glance out' at external reality and social being, a change which adds to the oscillation of styles and priorities in fiction in the first forty years of the twentieth century and beyond. In his account of the literary situation in 1938, *Enemies of Promise*, Cyril Connolly refers to this 'perpetual action and reaction' and concludes

> ... the realists had it their way in the years before the war; from 1918 to 1928 ... Joyce, Proust ... Woolf ... and Aldous Huxley ... ruled supreme, while from 1928 to 1938 the new realists have predominated ... Realism, simplicity, the colloquial style, would appear to have triumphed everywhere at the moment.[14]

New Realism and the 'Mild Left': Christopher Isherwood, George Orwell, Graham Greene

Many features of thirties writing are illustrated by the career of Christopher Isherwood, who remained close to the decade's developments through friendships with its leading authors, particularly W.H. Auden, with whom he collaborated in the writing of several verse plays (*The Dog beneath the Skin* (1935); *The Ascent of F6* (1936); and *On the Frontier* (1938)). Isherwood's novels particularly exemplify the 'action and reaction' Connolly recognises. His first novel, for example, *All the Conspirators* (1928), demonstrates some of the additions made by modernism to 'the international store of literary technique'.[15] Isherwood later admitted to a 'fatal facility for pastiche' which almost overburdened *All the Conspirators* with 'echoes' of authors whom he admired at the time, particularly E.M. Forster, Virginia Woolf, and James Joyce.[16] Isherwood's debts to Forster contribute to a tone of urbane, ironic understatement which is a feature of much of his fiction: Forster's influence also appears in the figure of Victor, based on Henry Wilcox in Forster's *Howards End* (1910). Victor embodies many of the establishment values mistrusted since schooldays by Isherwood's generation: his conflict with the novel's more sensitive hero, Philip, participates in what Isherwood describes as support for 'My Generation — right or wrong!'[17] This bias is also incorporated in the novel's technique: Victor and the parental generation are described with conventional objectivity, whereas Philip and other younger characters are favoured by more inward dramatisation through a variety of modernist devices. Interior monologue often predominates over conversation or action in a way which 'echoes' Virginia Woolf: there are also sections of randomly associating thoughts more indebted to the stream-of-consciousness method of Joyce. Isherwood's partly-autobiographical account of Philip's struggle to overcome restrictions of family and circumstance and establish himself as a writer further recalls Joyce's *A Portrait of the Artist as a Young Man* (1916): description of his friend Allen's painting sometimes resembles Woolf's account of Lily Briscoe's art in *To the Lighthouse* (1927).

Though Isherwood's next novel, *The Memorial* (1932), still shows some of the 'excessive reverence for Mrs Woolf'[18] which he believed limited *All the Conspirators*, it is much more successful in integrating modernist techniques, rarely used as mere echoes of novelists he admired. Interior monologue, for instance, is used to illustrate ironic disparities of outlook between characters often unable to communicate their thoughts to each other. For example, in presenting the dedication service for the war memorial from which the novel takes its title, the narrative first concentrates on the sad memories of a war-widow, then switches suddenly to her sister-in-law's banal anxieties about cooking and shopping for the weekend. Many such disjunctures appear in *The Memorial*, dramatising in a wide cast of characters an isolation which both reflects and is deepened by the fragmentation of their post-war society as a whole.

Isherwood records that *The Memorial* was written to show 'not the War itself, but the effect of the idea of "War" on my generation'.[19] Like Evelyn Waugh and Aldous Huxley, Isherwood examines the brittle gaiety and general disillusionment communicated by the war to a

> ...new generation, so eager for new kinds of life and new excitement,
> with new ideas about dancing and clothes and behaviour...so certain to
> sneer or laugh at everything...liked and enjoyed in nineteen hundred.[20]

The novel also examines the feelings of an older generation who survived the war to find themselves 'living on in a new, changed world, unwanted', and tormented by memories of 'the old safe, happy, beautiful world' of the Edwardian era (pp.46, 58). Isherwood communicates their sense of loss and of the collapse of history by means of a chronologically disorderly narrative, frequently dramatising reminiscences more vividly than accounts of a tawdry actuality. The novel is divided into four parts, headed 1928, 1920, 1925, and 1929: each of these sections is punctuated by recollections, within the interior monologues of various characters, of a more splendid, stylish life before the First World War. Such techniques share the modernists' reliance on individual consciousness and memory as alternatives to historical chronology and to external life and events in general. Division of *The Memorial* into non-chronologically ordered sections, full of obsessive memories, is very similar to a late American product of modernism, William Faulkner's *The Sound and the Fury*, first published in Britain the year before Isherwood's novel. Deferred explanations and flashbacks also resemble Ford Madox Ford's methods in *Parade's End*. Isherwood seems to act upon Ford's suggestion that 'to get...a man in fiction you could not begin at his beginning...you must...work backwards and forwards over his past'. He explains in *Lions and Shadows* that in *The Memorial* he attempted 'to start in the middle and go backwards, then forwards again...time is circular, which sounds Einstein-ish and brilliantly modern'.[21]

Isherwood's 'brilliantly modern' techniques and their moving dramatisation of the effects of the war make *The Memorial* an outstanding novel, deserving fuller critical attention than it has usually received. Like *All the Conspirators*, it is also worthwhile for its demonstration of the strength of modernist influence in the early thirties; Isherwood himself appearing at least until 1932 a version of the difficult, innovative author to whom Hugh Walpole's *Letter to a Modern Novelist* was addressed in that year. This early phase, however, is rapidly and completely abandoned in favour of 'new realism' as the thirties go on. The opening scene of Isherwood's next novel, *Mr Norris Changes Trains* (1935), is an appropriate introduction to this change of style: it is set in a railway compartment, like Philip Henderson's and Virginia Woolf's competing versions of the task and priorities of the novelist. In one corner of Isherwood's compartment, however, is not the genteel Mrs Brown of Woolf's essay, but a half-criminal exotic, Mr Norris; while in the other sits the narrator, William Bradshaw, not exactly a novelist, but a partly-autobiographical projection of the author, whose full name is Christopher William Bradshaw Isherwood.With some of Arnold Bennett's concern for objectivity and visual detail, Bradshaw records Norris's appearance and strange demeanour. As Henderson might have wished, his report is colloquial and uncomplicated, largely abandoning the subjective concentration and interior monologue of earlier novels. The chronological complexity of *The Memorial* is likewise absent from Bradshaw's account of progressive acquaintanceship with Norris, traced from their meeting on the train taking them to Berlin until Norris's eventual flight to South America at the end.

The straightforwardness of Bradshaw's narrative is representative of his character. He fails to perceive the significance of one of his earliest observations of Norris—'His smile had great charm. It disclosed the ugliest teeth I had ever seen'.[22] Bradshaw's ingenuousness delays his recognition of the ugly corruption beneath Norris's undoubted charm: the obvious limitations of his assessment provide an incentive to readers to exercise their own judgements. This highlights a particular need to penetrate lies and deceit, for Norris is in part an analogue of Hitler, whose superficial appeal to Germans, and to many people in Britain in the early thirties, Isherwood is determined to expose. A clever liar himself, Norris nevertheless feigns indignation about Hitler, suggesting 'it is indeed tragic to see how, even in these days, a *clever unscrupulous liar* can deceive millions' (p.188). His ironic indication of the powers of deception is part of an urgently admonitory quality in Isherwood's Berlin fiction, a warning against the threat of Hitler which emerges particularly unpleasantly in the closing pages of *Mr Norris Changes Trains*.

This threat permeates Isherwood's *Goodbye to Berlin* (1939) even more oppressively than it does the earlier novel. Its narrator remarks 'I am a camera with its shutter open, quite passive, recording, not thinking'. This neutrality forces readers, as in *Mr Norris Changes Trains*, to judge for themselves the dangers emanating from a city seductive yet unstable; sexually liberated but bitterly violent and corrupt. Isherwood's 'loosely-connected sequence of diaries and sketches',[23] as he calls it, presents a broad spectrum of Berlin's life and citizenry, ranging from the rich, Jewish Landauers to the destitute Novak family. The disconnected form of the novel and the fragmentary quality of the life it presents dramatise the narrator's reluctance to commit himself to a defining structure for his experience: it also emphasises the collapse of a decadent city, ready and often willing to fall before the Nazi threat.

Several factors may have contributed to Isherwood's abandonment of earlier complexity in favour of the more objective view of circumstances created by his detached narrators in the Berlin novels. Experience of the sexual, and homosexual, licence of Berlin may have released him from the self-protective persona of 'Isherwood the Artist'—in favour of 'brilliantly modern' techniques—which is ironically surveyed in his autobiography *Lions and Shadows*. Brief employment as a film writer may have encouraged the production of simple scenes and clear dialogue. Isherwood also records in *Lions and Shadows* the way in which his fascination for 'the flicks' made him 'endlessly interested in the outward appearance of people' (pp.40, 52-3): cinema is a significant influence on other writers of the thirties, its technique of cross-cutting, for example, perhaps contributing to the rapid alternation between short scenes in Evelyn Waugh's *Vile Bodies* (1930) and Graham Greene's *It's A Battlefield* (1934). Perhaps the greatest incentive, however, to Isherwood's abandonment of the modernist manner of *The Memorial* was simply the nature of the political circumstances he discovered in Berlin, developments in the city seeming so threatening as to demand communication in a documentary style as lucid and objective as possible. Isherwood's changing technique thus exemplifies not only the manner but some of the reasons for the drift away from modernist styles in the thirties. The political significance of the Berlin novels at the time and the colloquial clarity with which this is expressed also made him in the view of one commentator 'the voice...most willingly listened to in the 1930s'.[24] Especially since the film *Cabaret* (1972) dramatised the 'Sally Bowles' episode in *Goodbye to Berlin*, that novel and *Mr Norris Changes Trains* have remained

Isherwood's most popular and admired fiction, though some of his early success continues in the American phase of his career in novels such as *The World in the Evening* (1954), *Down There on a Visit* (1962) and *A Single Man* (1964).

Cyril Connolly suggested in 1938 that 'in England the ablest exponents of the colloquial style among the younger writers are Christopher Isherwood and George Orwell, both left-wing and both...superlatively readable'.[25] They are also comparable in relying in various ways on what Orwell's biographer Bernard Crick calls 'a confusion or fusion of autobiography, fiction and documentary'.[26] Orwell's early novels are largely based on the experience he summarises in his essay 'Why I Write' (1946):

> First I spent five years in an unsuitable profession (the Indian Imperial Police, in Burma), and then I underwent poverty and the sense of failure. This increased my natural hatred of authority and made me for the first time fully aware of the existence of the working classes, and the job in Burma had given me some understanding of the nature of imperialism: but these experiences were not enough to give me an accurate political orientation. Then came Hitler, the Spanish Civil War, etc.[27]

His first novel, *Burmese Days* (1934), develops Orwell's 'unsuitable' imperial experience and his understanding of the evil nature and effects of British rule. Much of the indignation of *Burmese Days* extends into his next two novels, *A Clergyman's Daughter* (1935) and *Keep the Aspidistra Flying* (1936). These reflect his period of 'poverty and the sense of failure'—also charted in his autobiographical *Down and Out in Paris and London* (1933)—and the growing awareness of 'the existence of the working classes' which resulted. All three novels show a talent for exact, journalistic observation which develops a detailed context for examination of social questions. *A Clergyman's Daughter*, for example, is as precise as *Down and Out in Paris and London* in documenting its heroine Dorothy's progressive impoverishment below the breadline: every price and transaction is recorded as her experience 'brought home to her...the mysterious power of money'. This 'meticulous descriptive quality', as Orwell calls it, his 'pleasure in solid objects and scraps of useless information', shows his fiction sharing like Isherwood's in the 'new realism' of the thirties.[28] As one contemporary reviewer comments,

> ...with Mr Orwell we reach the complete realist. He is one of those fortunate writers for whom, like Arnold Bennett, any object at all, by its mere existence, thereby acquires a vivid and exciting nature.[29]

Orwell's stylistic resemblance to Bennett is one aspect of his continuation on 'the main road of English fiction': an admiration for another of the authors modernism rejected, H.G. Wells, also appears in several of his novels. Like Wells's endowment of his hero with sudden wealth in *Kipps* (1905), for example, Dorothy's loss of her memory in *A Clergyman's Daughter* is an arbitrary device created to assist examination of social questions within fiction. Dorothy's strange descent to the life of the down-and-out, through various adventures of tramping, hop-picking and sleeping rough, allows Orwell to investigate a range of social strata and their problems. His observations sometimes extend into overtly sociological discussions of the events portrayed. During a description of Dorothy's gruelling time as a teacher in a private school, for example, Orwell introduces apparently casually an analysis of the inadequacies of private education by remarking 'there are, by the way, vast numbers of private schools in England' (pp.211-12). Their deficiencies, the 'facts about private schools' (p.213) are outlined throughout several succeeding paragraphs.

This sociological, documentary material illustrates a concern with 'public causes' typical of thirties fiction: it has led at least one critic, however, to conclude that 'Orwell was primarily an essayist'.[30] Much of Orwell's best writing is in the form of essays, and the tone of this material, the voice of the essayist, is never wholly absent from his fiction—for that matter, some of his ostensible essays, such as 'Shooting an Elephant' (1936), read rather like short stories. The success of Orwell's best novel, *Coming up for Air* (1939), results from a particularly effective synthesis of his methods as essayist and novelist. The sections of opinion which sometimes seem awkward appendages in his other fiction are a more integrated part of *Coming up for Air* as they are all spoken in the distinctively-characterised voice of a narrator, George Bowling. Throughout his first three novels Orwell had developed the easy, colloquial style which Connolly admired in 1938: this is used to its best effect in Bowling's frank, direct language in *Coming up for Air*. His slangy familiarity is established from the novel's opening sentences:

> The idea really came to me the day I got my new false teeth.
> I remember the morning well. At about a quarter to eight I'd nipped out of bed and got into the bathroom just in time to shut the kids out. It was a beastly January morning.[31]

As well as characterising George, this everyday language and his ostentatious common sense are used to create a complicity with readers, further drawn into sharing Bowling's opinions by frequent rhetorical questions and his insistent address to 'you':

> Who's afraid of war? That's to say, who's afraid of the bombs and the machine-guns? 'You are', you say. Yes, I am, and so's anybody who's ever seen them. (p.149).

The vision of contemporary life presented through this perspective is further particularised by Bowling's nostalgia and the narrative structure which it establishes. Parts One and Three show him oppressed by a tawdry society, threatened by impending war. Part

Two follows his return in memory to the tranquil security of his Edwardian childhood in Lower Binfield, and his recollection of the First World War which turned this 'settled period...into a sort of ghastly flux' (pp.107, 109). Part Four gives Bowling's account of an attempt to 'come up for air' before the expected Second World War, returning in actuality to a Lower Binfield which he discovers really exists only in memory. Overtaken by the shabby urbanisation of the inter-war years, it has grown as unpleasant as everywhere else, and George is scarcely sorry to return to his monotonous London job and tedious marriage. This four-part structure affords an opportunity for what Bowling calls 'looking at two worlds at once' (p.178), employed by Orwell to develop satirical contrasts between an idealised British past and an ugly, meretricious present. *Coming up for Air* is a bitter portrayal of the general collapse in standards of a society corrupted by its commercialism; blind to the threat of Hitler; lacking permanent values or understanding of its position. Orwell ironically suggests that the anticipated war has already been lost to these self-destructive tendencies, a point made forcefully at the end of the novel when the bomb which falls on Lower Binfield turns out to have been dropped not, as everyone surmises, as the first part of Hitler's onslaught, but accidentally by the RAF.

Coming up for Air also indicates some of Orwell's wider political convictions. Guilty about his attempted escape to Lower Binfield, Bowling half believes he is being pursued on his way there by

> ...the people whom you've never seen but who rule your destiny all the same, the Home Secretary, Scotland Yard, the Temperance League, the Bank of England, Lord Beaverbrook, Hitler and Stalin on a tandem bicycle, the bench of Bishops, Mussolini, the Pope—they were all of them after me. I could almost hear them shouting:
> 'There's a chap who thinks he's going to escape! There's a chap who says he won't be stream-lined! He's going back to Lower Binfield! After him! Stop him!' (pp.173-4).

This image of the single man pursued by a hostile crowd resembles the scene in 'Shooting an Elephant' in which the collective expectations of a huge crowd of Burmese—'their two thousand wills pressing me forward'—compel Orwell to destroy a probably-harmless elephant.[32] These images are representative of Orwell's general fear of threats to individual autonomy; of attempts to 'rule your destiny'. During the thirties, these feelings developed into a particular hatred of the totalitarian dictatorships of Hitler, Stalin and Mussolini which threatened to rule the destiny of the whole decade. Orwell commented in 1946 'every line of serious work that I have written since 1936 has been written, directly or indirectly, *against* totalitarianism and *for* democratic socialism'.[33] This motive appears directly in *Coming up for Air* in Bowling's expectations of

...the world we're going down into, the kind of hate-world, slogan-world. The coloured shirts, the barbed wire, the rubber truncheons. The secret cells where the electric light burns night and day, and the detectives watching you while you sleep. And the processions and the posters with enormous faces, and the crowds of a million people all cheering for the Leader till they deafen themselves into thinking that they really worship him, and all the time, underneath, they hate him so that they want to puke (p.149).

These fears of an impending 'hate-world' are further developed in Orwell's best-known novel, *Nineteen Eighty-Four* (1949). Like Aldous Huxley's *Brave New World* (1932), *Nineteen Eighty-Four* is a prophetic fantasy: Huxley, however, shows the possible dangers of aspects of scientific progress, whereas Orwell is more concerned with projecting into an imaginary future Britain his continuing political anxieties. Fears of 'an age of totalitarian dictatorships' in which 'the autonomous individual is going to be stamped out of existence'[34] were not dispelled even after the war against Hitler had been won: Orwell also warns of their threat in *Animal Farm* (1945), a political fable satirising the betrayal of the Russian revolution under Stalin's totalitarian rule.

Orwell at one stage considered calling *Nineteen Eighty-Four* 'The Last Man in Europe', a title which summarises a primary concern for the 'autonomous individual' which informs both his fiction and his essays. Many of the latter reproduce the stylistic features of *Coming up for Air*. Rhetorical questions, direct address to the reader as 'you'; matter-of-fact tone and a plain, colloquial style cajole the reader into sharing Orwell's opinions, creating an impression of straightforward frankness. This quality was the principal feature of his work fixed upon by Cyril Connolly in 1938, and 'the honesty of Orwell' as he calls it is invariably referred to by critics who have followed.[35] Though this 'honesty' is principally an aspect of Orwell's style, it is seen as characteristic of his career in general: the mixture of fiction, documentary and autobiography noticed by Crick has made Orwell's whole experience contribute to the impression of his integrity. An old Etonian concerned about the evils of imperialism; prepared to go down and out to add to his social understanding; to fight in Spain on behalf of the ideals he learned; and in general to chart and resist the pressures of his age, Orwell has always seemed an admirably autonomous individual, one whose experience and expression offer a clear insight into the character of contemporary life. Christopher Isherwood's career exemplifies some of the stylistic developments of the thirties: George Orwell's life and writing can be seen to provide a touchstone for the political consciousness which was such a feature of his age.

Orwell indicated the politics of his contemporary Graham Greene by suggesting that he was 'a mild Left with faint C.P. leanings'. He also adds

> I have even thought that he might become our first Catholic fellow-traveller... If you look at books like *A Gun for Sale*, *England Made Me*, *The Confidential Agent* and others, you will see that there is the usual left-wing scenery.[36]

Despite his own pleas to the contrary, Greene is usually assessed as a Catholic novelist: as Orwell suggests, his fiction shows at certain stages an allegiance to left-wing politics, sometimes ignored by critics, as well as to Roman Catholicism. Political and humane concerns check or balance religious faith, even within single novels: a dual commitment underlies the conflict of the priest and the lieutenant in *The Power and the Glory* (1940), for example, and reappears in the debates between the priest and the communist ex-mayor which occupy much of *Monsignor Quixote* (1982). The predominance of one or other area of his commitments, however, generally divides Greene's career into distinct phases. Converted to Catholicism in 1926, he remarks

> ... no one had noticed the faith to which I belonged before the publication of *Brighton Rock*... by 1937 the time was ripe for me to use Catholic characters. It takes longer to familiarise oneself with a region of the mind than with a country.[37]

Greene's career and his Catholic novels following *Brighton Rock* (1938) are fully assessed in Chapter Three. As he points out, most of his thirties fiction shows little concern with religion apart from a few suggestive passages: politics and the expression of 'mild left' feelings predominate in the novels Orwell lists and in *It's a Battlefield* (1934).

Shared among other contemporary authors, such feelings create a common landscape in the literature of the time, a background of what Orwell calls 'the usual left-wing scenery'. As Bergonzi suggests in *Reading the Thirties*, both fiction and some of the poetry of the period present similar descriptions of the conditions of life in the depression; of the new industrialisation and tawdry housing which appeared between the wars, for example.[38] Several authors extend Orwell's attention to

> ... houses, houses everywhere, little raw red houses with their grubby window-curtains... and blokes walking up and down, and women shaking out mats, and snotty-nosed kids playing along the pavement. (*Coming up for Air*, p.179).

Greene shares both Orwell's depressive vision and a faculty for detailed observation, perhaps developed during his work as a newspaperman in Nottingham in the late twenties. Unlike Orwell, however, whose fiction often finds in the countryside some relief from the desolation of towns, Greene's descriptive powers are unswervingly directed on the squalor of city life. A particular characteristic in his writing is the closeness with which it connects the shabbiness of these urban domains and the spiritlessness or misery of the characters who inhabit them. His vision in *It's a Battlefield*, for example, equates 'the hate and the pain and the sense of guilt and the sound of crying in the greying room and the sleeplessness and the walls shaking as the early morning lorries drove out of London'.[39] Represented in a flat, enwearied prose, this disconsolate setting is often considered a permanent feature of Greene's writing, and critics have coined the term 'Greeneland' to describe it. It provides an appropriate background in *It's a Battlefield*, for example, for Greene's examination of an inequitable society run by 'kings and priests and lawyers and rich men'; an infernal London whose miserable lives highlight questions such as 'do you believe in the way the country is organized? Do you believe that wages should run from thirty shillings a week to fifteen thousand a year?' (pp.97, 189).

As well as showing Greene's 'mild left' interests, *It's a Battlefield* suggests some of the influences on his fiction. The dutiful, weary attempts of the Assistant Commissioner to understand fragmentary city life recall Joseph Conrad's police chief in *The Secret Agent* (1907): there is even a character in *It's a Battlefield* named Conrad, after a merchant seaman. Like Conrad or Robert Louis Stevenson, Greene uses a strong, exciting story (often in his later fiction set in some distant corner of the world) as a basis for the examination of moral issues and the development of character in psychological depth. Some of the excitement of his stories also derives from exploitation of popular genres of detective or spy fiction: almost all of his thirties novels fit into one or other of these 'thriller' categories. Greene, however, talks of an 'ambition to create something legendary out of a contemporary thriller',[40] and often counterpoints his narratives against the expectations usually associated with this sort of fiction. His hero D. in *The Confidential Agent* (1939), for example, is a distinctly unconventional secret agent; a shy, gentle ex-lecturer in Medieval French whom the exigencies of the civil war have forced into acting as an emissary for Republican Spain. Greene's exploration of the stresses which result investigates characters, morals and relationships much more fully than most spy fiction: a particular achievement of his early work is this creation of a new depth and seriousness for the 'thriller' form.

D.'s character and experience are developed not only by counterpoint with conventional spy fiction, but occasionally by means of a further comparison of his story with the Medieval French legend of Roland and Oliver, the Berne manuscript of which was the subject of his earlier research. This technique of using a more traditional or conventional story-within-the-story as a touchstone for his own narrative is one Greene uses repeatedly (see also Chapter

Three). In *The Confidential Agent* it highlights the seediness of the contemporary world and its disasters in contrast to the romantic, idealised atmosphere of *The Song of Roland*. D. reflects of his experience:

> People were united only by their vices... He had been too absorbed in the old days with his love and with the Berne MS. and the weekly lecture on Romance Languages to notice it. It was as if the whole world lay in the shadow of abandonment.[41]

Secondly, comparison to the extravagant heroism of *The Song of Roland* emphasises the more human scale of D.'s own courage and integrity in the grey, mundane world of the thirties. He emerges as a likeable victim of the Spanish Civil War, a sympathetic vehicle for Greene's final vision of the political conflicts of the decade, and for his anticipation of the wider European war which would shortly bring them towards some sort of conclusion.

These conflicts Greene envisages from a 'mild left' standpoint which is largely shared by Isherwood and Orwell. Though all three authors are clearly committed to the left, none of them, however, offers much evidence for Woolf's conclusion that the young men of the thirties 'read Marx' and 'became communists'. Greene was a member of the Communist Party for only four weeks, while a student at Oxford, and his 'C.P. leanings' thereafter, as Orwell indicates, were slight. As his biographer Brian Finney explains, Isherwood was 'a life-long left-wing liberal', one who remarks in a letter to Stephen Spender in the thirties 'I'm through with the Communists. All politicians are equally nasty'. Orwell describes himself as a 'Tory anarchist' as late as 1935.[42] Though he moved towards 'democratic socialism' thereafter, encouraged by the journey into the Northern working class recorded in *The Road to Wigan Pier* (1937), the experiences of the Spanish Civil War described in *Homage to Catalonia* (1938) prejudiced him permanently against communism. 'Mild left' feelings of his sort were widely shared at the time: there were also, however, as Woolf suggests, many young English writers who were strongly attracted to the Communist Party. Two of these, Rex Warner and Edward Upward, are discussed in the next section.

Fantasy, Marxism and Class: Rex Warner, Edward Upward, Walter Greenwood, Lewis Grassic Gibbon

Cyril Connolly suggested in 1938 that 'the novelists who feel their responsibilities are also searching for something deeper and more universal than superficial realism and are finding it in the allegory'.[43] Comparable in their Marxist commitments, Upward and Warner also exemplify the movement away from 'new realism' which Connolly identifies. Warner remarks, for example, 'I do not even aim at realism':[44] in his allegorical first novel, *The Wild Goose Chase* (1937), like Orwell in *Nineteen Eighty-Four*, he projects fears and convictions about the political present into an imaginary, fantastic world. Though this is strangely warped by Einstein-ish versions of space and of time, which 'depends on the person',[45] many of the political concerns of the thirties remain recognisable. The novel concludes in Marxist wish-fulfilment, with a communist state magically created out of the ruins of the relativistic kingdom: earlier, satirical versions appear of Moseley's fascists; of the British government's policy of appeasement and of its failure to rearm; and of the consequences of the General Strike, for example. Book reviewers, the contemporary art world, and educational systems are also attacked: final confirmation of the lasting effects of schooldays on the thirties generation is amusingly offered by a dying revolutionary who finds it possible, despite a wretched life, to forgive everyone except his senior classics master. *The Wild Goose Chase* is often funny: like Henry Fielding's *Tom Jones* (1749), however, which its hero admires, its humour is diffused through a long, bizarre series of adventures, making Warner's novel seem shapeless and over-ambitious. His fantasy is more pointedly concentrated in *The Aerodrome* (1941), which contrasts a lively, disorderly village with the soulless organisation of the air force stationed nearby. This conflict between 'ordinary life and...perfect efficiency...iron compulsion'[46] summarises some of the threats to worthy, ineffectual democracy posed by the streamlined fascism of the thirties. An imaginative vision of the violent divisions of its age, *The Aerodrome* was very popular in the early years of the war.

Warner acknowledges the influence on his fantasy and allegorical methods of the Czech novelist Franz Kafka, of whom he remarks

> ... no other author has been more successful in expressing the doubt and uncertainty, the pervasive guilt which...marks the modern man...all the time at the mercy of abstract forces, economic, political or psychological.[47]

Kafka's fiction began to appear in English translation in 1930: four of his novels were published in Britain in the following decade. Though his nightmarish parables are more metaphysical and less political and economic than Warner's remarks suggest, there are signs that they immediately interested several novelists in the thirties. C. Day Lewis, for example, takes his epigraph from Kafka in *Starting Point* (1937), a novel which clarifies the source of thirties political commitments during schooldays and at university. Graham Greene, in *The Confidential Agent*, adopts Kafka's habit of naming his protagonists by the single letter K.—one of the adversaries of Greene's hero D. is called 'Mr K'. Unlike Warner, however, neither Greene, Day Lewis, nor many other contemporary authors followed Kafka in style or manner. Other incentives to depart from the 'new realism' of the thirties were similarly limited in their effect. Though the Surrealist exhibition in London in 1936 seemed as disturbing as the Post-Impressionist exhibition had to a previous generation in 1910, the Surrealists were often dismissed as politically irresponsible, a further indication of the extent to which realistic, conventional methods were felt during the thirties to be essential to the expression of social concerns.

It is typical of such feelings that Edward Upward's first novel, *Journey to the Border* (1938), one of the most successful of thirties employments of fantasy, actually offers an account of how fantasy can and should be renounced. Christopher Isherwood records in *Lions and Shadows* how — and why — he and his friend Upward developed in the first place a talent for fantasy and a 'special brand of...surrealism' (p.43) while they were still students at Cambridge. Disaffection with the establishment ethos they found at university encouraged their joint creation of an alternative world: this dream-domain, Mortmere, Isherwood describes as a

> private world...deliberately created for ourselves, a world which was continually expanding, becoming more absorbing, more elaborate, sharper and richer in detail and atmosphere, to the gradual exclusion of the...personalities, social and moral obligations, codes of behaviour and public amusements which formed the outward structure of our under-graduate lives. (p.40)

Mortmere can be considered along with the fantasies of other university men such as Lewis Carroll, C.S. Lewis and J.R.R. Tolkien (see Chapter Three), perhaps also created as alternatives to intellectually-exacting, socially-restricting Oxford and Cambridge life. Isherwood describes Mortmere as a 'cult of romantic strangeness...a luxury for the comfortable University fireside' (p.168) which Upward found it hard to renounce when he left Cambridge:

> He was to spend the next three years in desperate and bitter struggles to relate Mortmere to the real world...to find the formula which would transform our private fancies and amusing freaks and bogies into valid symbols of the ills of society and the toils and aspirations of our daily lives...[he] did at last find it...clearly set down, for everybody to read, in the pages of Lenin and of Marx. (pp.168-9)

Upward's difficult transition is reflected in *Journey to the Border*. In the course of a day at the races, 'the tutor' (the central character has no other name) undergoes a journey to 'a sort of no-man's-land'[48] between reality and fantasy, sanity and insanity. He begins to see other characters in terms of Mortmere fantasy, as 'freaks belonging to the same order of reality as the characters in a Grimm's fairy story or a cinema film' (p.10). His deteriorating mentality is strongly communicated by Upward's confinement of the narrative to his interior monologue—sometimes even interior dialogue—depriving readers of referents to external reality and of any clear perception of what is going on. The tutor, however, retains just enough sanity to realise that he is in a hallucinatory state of 'cowardly fantasies' (p.256) created by his mind's lazy evasion of the realities which confront it. He reasons that the only way to regain reality is to 'get in touch with the workers' movement...there is no other way of dealing *successfully* with the real external problems' (pp.213, 215).

This propagandist type of conclusion reappears in Upward's later fiction. Another partly-autobiographical novel, *In the Thirties* (1962), has a similar story to *Journey to the Border,* as Upward explains in his introductory note:

> *In the Thirties*...describes the experiences of a young man whose failure to live as a poet leads him to make common cause with the unemployed and with others frustrated by the social and economic conditions of the time, and to join the Communist Party of Great Britain.

Like Isherwood and Orwell, Upward mixes documentary with his fiction. Presenting the political development of the failed poet, Alan Sebrill, he also shows in detail the mass demonstrations of the thirties; the large pacifist movement which grew up in response to the threat of war; and the activities of rambling clubs, sometimes associated with organisations such as the Left Book Club, which grew very popular at the time. Stephen Spender describes *In the Thirties* as 'the most truthful picture of life in that decade':[49] Upward's broad presentation of 'the social and economic conditions of the time' is the most rewarding aspect of a novel of uneven style and uncertain tone.

Alan Sebrill shares with the tutor in *Journey to the Border* and with Upward himself a 'social condition' which particularly troubled thirties writers. In seeking to join the workers' movement, the tutor worries 'my upbringing, my education, my social origin—won't these tell against me?' (p.213): many authors at the time likewise found that their 'public-school-university-Bloomsbury' backgrounds inhibited attempts to 'make common cause with the unemployed', making them exiles from the class their writing and politics sought to support. Two writers of the period, Walter Greenwood and Lewis Grassic Gibbon, particularly benefit from their exemption from such difficulties. Greenwood's clasic account of the depression, *Love on the Dole* (1933), for example, is warmer and less abstract than Warner and Upward in its support for the poor and unemployed, benefiting from first-hand knowledge of the depressed Northern industrial community portrayed. This especially contributes to Greenwood's creation of a fluent dialectal idiom for the novel:

> 'Mornin', Joe. Heigh, hei, ho. More rain, more rest', said the copper.
> 'N' rest f' t' wicked, lad, 'cept them as is bobbies, an' they ne'er do nowt else...how thee and thy mates have cheek to hold hand out for wages just f' walkin' about streets...N' wonder folks call it a bobby's job'.[50]

Enlivened by this language, the warmth and resilience of

Greenwood's characters are counterpointed against the deadening effects of their poverty and the depressed industrial landscape they inhabit. This background contains much of the 'left-wing scenery' found in other thirties novels such as Orwell's. Greenwood's realistic description is likewise comparable to Arnold Bennett's:

> The houses remain: streets of them where the blue-grey smoke swirls down like companies of ghosts from a million squat chimneys: jungles of tiny houses cramped and huddled together, the cradles of generations of the future. Places where men and women are born, live, love and die and pay preposterous rents for the privilege of calling the grimy houses 'home' pp. 12-13).

The purposelessness of struggle against this monstrous environment is emphasised by the circularity of the narrative, beginning and ending before dawn on a miserable Monday morning; rain, darkness and poverty the only unchangeable conditions of existence.

A more wide-ranging presentation of working life appears in Lewis Grassic Gibbon's trilogy *A Scots Quair*, which requires extended discussion both for its broad summation of the political consciousness of the age, and for the unusually effective way in which this is presented. Gibbon's heroine Chris Guthrie's progress is in part an analogue for general demographic changes since the industrial revolution: she moves from the agrarian life of Kinraddie detailed in *Sunset Song* (1932), through the squalid mill town of Segget in *Cloud Howe* (1933), ending in the industrial city of Duncairn in *Grey Granite* (1934). Specifically, however, Chris's story develops a bitter version of events from around 1911 until the mid-thirties. This concentrates on the First World War in *Sunset Song*; the failure of the General Strike in *Cloud Howe*; and the consequent hardening of political attitudes into the communism of the thirties, which informs Gibbon's vision in *Grey Granite* of 'capitalism falling to bits everywhere, or raising up classes of slaves again, Fascism coming, the rule of the beast'.[51]

Like Greenwood, and like D.H. Lawrence, whose work *A Scots Quair* sometimes resembles, Gibbon was born in the class and country he came to write about, growing up among the farmers and agricultural labourers of North-East Scotland. Gibbon's familiarity with this working community appears like Greenwood's in his development of a pungent dialect which makes lively and intimate his presentation of ordinary people. This is also much enhanced by his unusual use of a second-person form of narrative to reflect his characters' thoughts. Chris Guthrie's feelings for her home and parents, for example, are presented in this way:

> You saw their faces in firelight, father's and mother's and the neighbours', before the lamps lit up, tired and kind, faces dear and close to you, you wanted the words they'd known and used,

forgotten in the far-off youngness of their lives, Scots words to tell to your heart. (*Sunset Song*, p.32).

Gibbon develops in this way a range of interior monologues, particularly those of Chris and her son Ewan. The second-person form also has a choric function, however, creating a collective voice not specifically located in any one individual, but freely alternating between many different sections of the community. In successive paragraphs, for example, first the poorer, working folk and then the rich farmers reflect on their reasons for abandoning religious faith after the First World War:

> Why the hell should you waste your time in a kirk when you were young, you were young only once, there was the cinema down in Dundon, or a dance or so, or this racket or that... To hell with ministers... they were aye the friends of the farmers, you knew...
> ... you would take the mistress a jaunt instead, next Sunday like or may be the next, up the Howe to her cousin in Brechin that hadn't yet seen the new car you had bought, or maybe you'd just lie happed in your bed... to hell with ministers... they were aye the friends of the ploughmen, you knew. (*Cloud Howe*, pp.15-16).

As in Orwell's fiction and essays, the 'you' form makes particular demands on attention, challenging readers of *A Scots Quair* to judge almost without the need of authorial comment a wide range of characters whose personalities are expressed in their own voices.

Gibbon's familiarity with the North-East of Scotland also appears in Chris Guthrie's feelings for the land she works in her youth and to which she returns at the end of the trilogy. Closeness to this rural landscape contributes to her vision of its eternal integrity:

> The wet fields squelched below her feet, oozing up their smell of red clay from under the sodden grasses, and up in the hills she saw the trail of the mist, great sailing shapes of it, going south on the wind...
> And then a queer thought came to her there in the drooked fields, that nothing endured at all, nothing but the land she passed across, tossed and turned and perpetually changed below the hands of the crofter folk since the oldest of them had set the Standing Stones by the Loch of Blawearie... the land was forever, it moved and changed below you, but was forever, you were close to it and it to you. (*Sunset Song*, p.117).

Frequent references to these Standing Stones emphasise Gibbon's belief in 'golden hunters of the Golden Age', an ancient, ideal state of human society which 'fell' when 'gods and kings and culture and classes' first appeared in the world. The landscape and the Stones which have dominated it since this fall provide a larger context, sometimes a contrast, for Ewan's growing conviction that 'if there was once a time without gods and classes' there could be that time again. In *Grey Granite* this belief develops into 'a stark, sure creed that will cut like a knife'; a communism which makes Ewan determined to initiate historical progress towards a better future himself. He talks of 'LIVING HISTORY ONESELF, being it, making it', and dreams of 'the chariot of Time let loose on the world roaring down...haughs of history into the shining ways of tomorrow'.[52]

This faith in historical progress is sustained alongside the timeless ideal represented by the Standing Stones by means of the adroit structure of *A Scots Quair*, which relies on successive flashbacks, 'as though Time turned back'. Chapters are circular, beginning at a moment in time later than the events they go back to describe, ending with the story advanced again to the moment with which the chapter began. Always envisaged in retrospect, from a more aloof point of view, even the most urgent events of the 'living history' which concerns Ewan are subordinated in this way to a larger pattern of vision, counterpointing transience and eternity. This technique is especially successful in the elegaic presentation in *Sunset Song* of the stable way of life of the 'Last of the Peasants, the last of the Old Scots folk',[53] destroyed by the First World War. The memorial for those killed in the war, carved into one of the Standing Stones, recalls the earlier loss of the immemorially distant Golden Age; a juxtaposition of Gibbon's dual visions of history and eternity, of immediate grief and infinite perspective, which makes the conclusion of *Sunset Song* exceptionally moving.

Like the familiarity with which he presents the rural community, Gibbon's view of time and landscape may owe something to his particular background. The 'great sailing shapes' of mist and the rocky bleakness of much Scottish scenery are more suggestive than mellower English contours of a geological scale of time beyond the human dimension of history. A degree of separateness from the mainstream of English society may also have affected Gibbon's writing in other ways, contributing (as it did for many of the modernists) to freedom from conventional narrative styles and structures. Gibbon shows a greater readiness than his middle-class English contemporaries to develop new techniques specifically adapted for expression of the political convictions of the time. The use of 'Scots word to tell your heart', for example, gains entrance to the thoughts and feelings of ordinary people less accessible to authors writing standard English. The second-person form of narrative is also unusually egalitarian, developing the consciousness not only of a few principal characters but of the community as a whole. The chronology of *A Scots Quair* is likewise expressive of contemporary concern with current events directed by desire for a politically ideal future far beyond them. In such ways, Gibbon's structure and his communism of insight and utterance create an exact formal reflex for the left-wing ideology of the age. Despite the didacticism and melodrama which mar *Grey Granite*, this provides *A Scots Quair* with a good claim to being the outstanding novel of the nineteen thirties, though this has not often been recognised. Although in *The Novel Today* Philip Henderson calls it 'one of the most remarkable achievements of that time' (p.272), he was predisposed by his own Marxism to admire Gibbon's work. Separateness from the English context, actually a source of its strength, has perhaps deterred other critics from appreciating the place of *A Scots Quair* in the literature of the period. Other outstanding novelists in the Scottish literary renaissance of the time, notably Eric Linklater and Neil Gunn, have suffered from a similar neglect.

Satire and the Right Wing: Wyndham Lewis and Evelyn Waugh

George Orwell suggests in 'Inside the Whale': 'as early as 1934 or 1935 it was considered eccentric in literary circles not to be more or less "left"' (p.561). Evelyn Waugh and Wyndham Lewis are thorough-going eccentrics in Orwell's terms, both firmly committed to right-wing views. Lewis, in fact, deliberately cast himself in the role of 'eccentric' throughout much of his career; 'The Enemy', as he calls himself, not only of political developments but of many of the dominant artistic modes of time. Like the hero of his early novel *Tarr* (1918), he based his own artistic priorities firmly on his work as a painter. This made him more interested in visible surfaces than in the internal states of consciousness presented by the modernists, to whom he remained hostile throughout the twenties and beyond. Lewis also disliked modernist manipulation of the narrative dimension of time, and attacked in *Time and Western Man* (one of the enormous cultural critiques which he called 'pamphlets') what he saw as the pervasive influence on his age of Bergson, Einstein and other thinkers. He concentrates the literary focus of his hostilities in *Time and Western Man* (1927) on James Joyce, resuming this attack in satirical and parodic form in his fantasy *The Childermass* in 1928 (see Chapter Three).

Lewis's *The Apes of God* (1930) mocks the pretensions of the Bloomsbury art world in London between the wars, rather as *Tarr* had earlier satirised the painters quartered in Paris before the First World War. It also puts into practice some of Lewis's own artistic preferences, with less than complete success: rigidly exclusive of internal consciousness, his observational, painterly style is unwieldy and fails to sustain interest in his characters throughout the great length of the novel. Lewis himself felt a need to defend his methods, arguing for their validity for satiric purposes in another pamphlet, *Men Without Art* (1934), which also attacks Virginia Woolf. Lewis's preferences left little sympathy for Woolf's techniques: like other novelists and commentators in the thirties, he took particular exception to her advocacy of attention to internal consciousness in essays such as 'Mr. Bennett and Mrs. Brown'. *Men Without Art* also includes critiques of several other contemporary authors, completing Lewis's attack on modernism: he had already disposed of D.H. Lawrence, among others, in *Paleface* (1929).

Another of Lewis's 'pamphlets', *The Art of Being Ruled* (1926), discusses Mussolini admiringly and suggests that society should be controlled by 'the most powerful and stable authority that can be devised',[54] rather than democratically. Though he later realised his error, Lewis also published a sympathetic account of Hitler in 1931. Such political feelings, as well as artistic issues, figure in his dislike of the views of his contemporaries in the thirties. Lewis was hostile not only to their left-wing ideas but to the pretentious way he felt these were being flaunted at the time. *The Revenge for Love* (1937) returns to the phoney art world of *The Apes of God*, examining political as well as artistic affectation and in particular what Lewis presents as a false, fashionable response to the war in Spain. His central figure Victor Stamp is a failed artist who makes a living painting counterfeit Van Goghs before being lured with the communist 'hero' Percy Hardcaster into a gun-running mission to Spain. Other London artists have little more talent than Victor. They have the further disadvantage of being 'salon-reds...Oxford and Cambridge "pinks"'[55] who pretend like Hardcaster to violent political convictions which they are careful to keep at a safe distance from the front line. Such affectations are typical of a world dominated by falsity and counterfeit. Lewis's original title was 'False Bottoms': from the food basket brought to Hardcaster in jail at the begining to the gun-running car used by Victor and Margaret Stamp at the end, everything in the novel has a false bottom of one sort or another—a Spaniard describes his nation and England generally as 'two countries going rotten at the bottom' (p.6).

Lewis's stylistic quirk of painterly concentration on the appearance and observable behaviour of his characters provides an appropriate medium for presenting this hollow world. His external method, however, is also complemented in *The Revenge for Love* by a more inward transcription of the unspoken thoughts of some of his characters, creating an inner voice shared with the author. This sustains interest in characters more fully developed than in *The Apes of God*. It is especially successful in communicating the only emotion in the novel exempt from pervasive artificiality, Margaret's love for Victor: the purposelessness of their death in the Pyrenees at the end bitterly exemplifies the destructive effects Lewis felt to result from the political allegiances of his contemporaries. This moving conclusion and the combination of internal and external perspectives, unusual in Lewis's fiction, contribute to the critical opinion that *The Revenge for Love* is the best of his novels.

Like *The Revenge for Love*, Evelyn Waugh's newspaper-satire *Scoop* (1938) mocks English communists as 'University men',[56] parodies speeches on behalf of the proletariat, and obliquely satirises the support extended from Britain to Republican Spain. Like Lewis, Waugh was firmly antipathetic to the left-wing feelings of many of his contemporaries: he indicated support for General Franco in 1937, and *Waugh in Abyssinia* (1936) shows some approval of Mussolini's fascists and their ambitions in Africa. Waugh, however, is a very different sort of satirist from Lewis; less overtly interested in politics; more concerned with social rather than intellectual or artistic life; and generally much lighter and wittier in tone. His style and methods are comparable to those of Ronald Firbank: though a precise observer of society, Waugh like Firbank exaggerates for comic effect the amoral qualities of his characters and situations, sometimes making them eccentric and grotesque. This almost fantastic enlargement, however, is sustained in an understated style: like Firbank's, Waugh's satiric wit functions economically, through ironic implication rather than statement. Readers are never told, for example, of the awfulness of Mr. Prendergast's 'little joke about soles and souls'[57] in *Decline and Fall* (1928), but can hardly fail to guess for themselves.

Decline and Fall, a very popular first novel, indicates the milieu of Waugh's satire as well as some of its methods. His attention is directed upon the smart, rich social world of the time: members of his cast of 'Bright Young People'[58] reappear in *Vile Bodies* (1930); some even survive into *Black Mischief* (1932). Frivolous and cynical, they inhabit a hedonistic society in fashionable, self-indulgent rebellion against conventional morality. Like Aldous Huxley, Waugh shows in the life of the twenties a sophisticated decadence, a continual 'decline and fall'. Many of its phases are illustrated in Waugh's first novel by the erratic progress of his central figure, Paul Pennyfeather, a character as lightweight as his name suggests, mistakenly sent down from Oxford and driven hither and thither by abominable public school teachers, white slave traders, upper class buffoons, deranged architects and other menaces in the social life of the times. Waugh admits in the novel to this use of Paul as a revealing cipher:

> The shadow that has flitted about this narrative under the name of Paul
> Pennyfeather...would never have made a hero, and the only interest
> about him arises from the unusual series of events of which his shadow was
> witness (pp.122-3).

Like several of Orwell's characters, Paul finds his movement through several layers of contemporary society turns out to be circular: he ends up back in the peaceful seclusion of his Oxford college. The main leason he learns from his bizarre experience is of the virtue of this seclusion and withdrawal. He is persuaded partly by a modernist architect, Otto Silenus, who compares life to 'the big wheel at Luna Park':

> You pay five francs and go into a room with tiers of seats all round, and in the centre the floor is made of a great disc of polished wood that revolves quickly...Lots of people just enjoy scrambling on and being whisked off and scrambling on again...But the whole point about the wheel is that you needn't get on it all, if you don't want to. People get hold of ideas about life, and that makes them think they've got to join in the game, even if they don't enjoy it (p.208).

The purposeless, centrifugal energy suggested in Silenus's metaphor appears throughout Waugh's early fiction, also expressed, for example, in the nightmare of a character in *Vile Bodies* who

> ...thought we were all driving round and round in a motor race and none of us could stop, and there was an enormous audience composed entirely of gossip writers and gate crashers...all shouting at us at once to go faster, and car after car kept crashing until I was left all alone driving and driving. (pp.187-8)

Paul's conclusion that he need not join in the contemporary whirl is also widely shared. The British Legation in Azania in *Black Michief* cherish their inaccessibility at the end of an unmade road leading to the chaotic capital they are supposed to serve. Tony Last in *A Handful of Dust* (1934) and William Boot, the unlikely foreign correspondent of *Scoop*, each seek secluded emotional autonomy in their respective country mansions.

Waugh himself seems to share his protagonists' urge to withdraw from contemporary life. The ironic precision of his humour results from an aloof, dispassionate authorial perspective, as if he had retired to mock from the safe distance of the 'tiers of seats' which surround the chaotic revolutions of contemporary life. Authorial judgement or comment on this life is generally omitted: a sense of moral vacuity is heightened by the insubstantiality of his characterisation. Like Paul in *Decline and Fall*, most of his figures have a feather-light or hollow quality. Waugh's fiction presents only animated surfaces, rather like a cartoon—highly coloured and mobile, and often very funny, but lacking in substance, depth, or human feeling with which readers might sympathise: even death is used only for throwaway comic effect in *Decline and Fall* and *Vile Bodies*. As a result, it is difficult to be much involved in 'the unusual series of events' which his shadowy characters witness, and this diminishes the satiric effect of his novels. The shallow aspect of Waugh's fiction has preoccupied several of his critics: Malcolm Bradbury, for example, suggests that Waugh

> ...does not 'press upon us the full complexities of life'...his novels do not create that sense of human largeness and possibility we associate with the great liberal strain in the English novel. He has few characters to whom we feel very close or who represent striking, endearing or responsible systems of value.[59]

Waugh might be defended by analogy with many satirists who employ shallow caricatures as an effective accentuation of their criticisms. The absence of an asserted authorial morality, like the reticence of William Bradshaw in Isherwood's *Mr Norris Changes Trains*, can also be seen to encourage readers' own judgements. In any case, although the criticisms outlined above never wholly cease to be applicable to Waugh's fiction, they grow less relevant as his styles and interests develop during and after the thirties. The successs of *A Handful of Dust*, for example, which some critics think Waugh's best novel, is partly owed to the fuller development of its central figure. Tony Last is a much more rounded character than Waugh's earlier protagonists, with an emotional nature evolved in sufficient detail to attract and sustain readers' sympathy. Waugh's satire is sharpened as a result. Partly because it is seen though Tony's response, the soulless London society portrayed in *A Handful of Dust* seems more genuinely evil and corrupting than in earlier novels, especially after the accidental killing of Tony's son, affecting in a way quite absent from the deaths in *Decline and Fall* and *Vile Bodies*. The London society presented has itself changed slightly: as one of Waugh's characters remarks, due to the depression 'everyone's got very poor and it makes them duller'.[60] This offers less promising material for Waugh's earlier form of satire: comic anarchy fades from his later fiction, in which his own values begin to be developed more explicitly.

Brideshead Revisited (1945), for example, presents with more obvious approval the sort of ancestral country mansion which had seemed to William Boot, Tony Last and Paul Pennyfeather 'something enduring and serene in a world that has lost its reason'. Waugh also indicates another aspect of his allegiances, almost for the first time, by defining his theme in *Brideshead Revisited* as 'the operation of divine grace'. There are hints of his Catholicism in Waugh's early work: generally, perhaps, in its presentation of a society whose 'unredeemed squalor' may result from its loss of 'faith either in religion or anything else'.[61] Just as Graham Greene's religious interests were scarcely visible in his fiction before 1937, however, the faith to which Waugh was converted in 1929 is not examined directly until *Brideshead Revisited*. Now that his own values, ironically withheld in some thirties novels, begin to be reintegrated into the fiction, Waugh for the first time uses a first-person narrator, Charles Ryder: his complex emotional involvement in the events he presents never allows the aloof, disdainful cynicism of the authorial voice in earlier novels.

Religious views and a less wildly comic style also extend into some of Waugh's subsequent work, including the *Sword of Honour* trilogy (see Chapter Three). Waugh's reputation as a serious novelist is mostly based on this later phase of his fiction: his first novels, however, are still among his most widely read. Among twentieth century humourists, he is rivalled in popularity only by P.G. Wodehouse, whose comedy relies on brilliantly ingenious plots rather than the elegant style and distinctive, cruel wit of Waugh's early satire.

Politics and Beyond: Compton Mackenzie, L.H. Myers, Ivy Compton-Burnett, John Cowper Powys, Malcolm Lowry, Rosamond Lehmann, William Gerhardie

Evelyn Waugh's combination of Catholicism with right-wing attitudes seems a curious contrast to Graham Greene's left-wing position as a 'Catholic fellow-traveller', as Orwell defined it. Orwell also suggests in 'Inside the Whale', however, that thirties inclinations to political and religious faiths, of whatever variety, are comparable in their answering of a 'need for *something to believe in*'; a need for 'an orthodoxy, a discipline' as an antidote to the threatening developments of the time (pp.564-5). The political interests of another Catholic convert, Compton Mackenzie, are not even confined to left or right-wing views. In *The Four Winds of Love* (1937-45), he eventually concentrates his attention on Scottish Nationalism, though he also includes anxieties about Hitler; an encounter with Italian fascism; and discussions of communism and Catholicism. *The Four Winds of Love* is a huge, eight-volume extension of the *bildungsroman* style of *Sinister Street* (1913-14): Mackenzie attempts to cover the range of adventures, beliefs and personalities encountered by a single character, John Ogilvie, from the early part of the twentieth century almost until the outbreak of the Second World War. Despite the great scale of action, however, opinions and discussion, often political, occupy such a large proportion of Mackenzie's attention that they overwhelm the narrative, whose interest is further restricted by the amorphous nature of its hero.

A combination of religious and political interests also appears in a novel-sequence much admired in the thirties, L.H. Myers's tetralogy *The Near and the Far (The Near and the Far* (1929); *Prince Jali* (1931); *The Root and the Flower* (1935); *The Pool of Vishnu* (1940)). Myers remarks in his preface:

> This is not a historical novel, although the action is placed in the time of Akbar the Great Mogul...in choosing sixteenth-century India as a setting, my object was to carry the reader out of our familiar world into one where I could—without doing violence to his sense of reality—give prominence to certain chosen aspects of human life, and illustrate their significance. It has certainly not been my intention to set aside the social and ethical problems that force themselves upon us at the present time.

As Myers suggests, despite its distant, romantic setting, *The Near and the Far* remains concerned with several of the 'social and ethical problems' of the thirties: its remote context is sometimes used to help establish an objective perspective for their assessment. The complex struggle for power between Akbar's sons Daniyal and Salim raises general questions about the ethics and process of government, for example. Myers also demonstrates in particular a version of the communist ideal of the thirties, showing in *The Pool of Vishnu* a state which has redistributed its resources among the peasants and is run as a co-operative commune. Contemporary interests are further extended in *Prince Jali* and *The Root and the Flower*, which satirise some of the artistic pretensions also attacked by Wyndham Lewis in *The Apes of God:* Prince Daniyal sets up a perverse colony of aesthetes, a 'Pleasance of the Arts' whose portrayal parodies some of the affectations Myers himself encountered in Bloomsbury in the twenties and thirties.

Renunciation of material interests in the communist state in *The Pool of Vishnu* is endorsed by the teaching of a Guru: his discussions add to Myers's investigation of spirituality and its relation to life in the everyday world. This theme is also followed in the life of Rajah Amar, a Buddhist ruler determined to renounce his worldly responsibilities in favour of withdrawal into a contemplative life. Religion preoccupies many of Myers's other characters, and the various claims and problems of Buddhism, Hinduism and Christianity are debated at length. These discussions and investigations of abstract issues are added to a complex plot, full of action, intrigue, suspense and puzzle: part of Myers's achievement is his creation of such an extensive panorama of historical life and colour in an almost wholly imaginary sixteenth-century India. There is also a symbolic function in many episodes and scenes, such as Prince Jali's witnessing of a snake's self-destructive rage at intransigent circumstance in the novel's opening pages. This symbolic quality helps to connect Myers's philosophic speculation with his proliferating intrigues: the latter, however, still seem at times desultory and unresolved. Jali discovers the difficulty of 'correspondence between outward things and the inner landscape of his mind'. Many other characters encounter this problem of adjusting 'the near'—the everyday world of appearance—and 'the far'—the world of spirit which underlies the veil of Maya, of appearance and illusion. Myers's fiction itself seems likewise to present some of its action as only 'the complications of the world...artificialities painted over the true forms of life'[62]—forms revealed only in abstract thought or debate.

Though this gap between action and reflection has perhaps been responsible for deterring later generations of readers, it is in part the consequence of an actual strength of Myers's fiction—the seriousness of its interest in 'the true forms of life', in spiritual integrity beyond immediate existence. The predominance of abstraction and discussion over action is less of a problem than in Mackenzie's *The Four Winds of Love*, for example: in some ways it contributes to the 'depth of interest' which leads W.W. Robson to conclude that *The Near and the Far* belongs 'among the few philosophical novels in English that can stand comparison with Mann's *The Magic Mountain*'.[63] *The Near and the Far* is also one of the few thirties novels successful in projecting political issues beyond the immediate realities of their time: *The Pool of Vishnu* provides a much more persuasive, attractive Marxist vision than Rex Warner's *The Wild Goose Chase*, for example.

Myers's extension of political interests into sixteenth-century India further indicates the pervasiveness of their hold on contemporary consciousness. A few thirties authors, however, remained apparently uninterested in political or other developments in their era. Ivy Compton-Burnett, for example, who published five novels during the decade, incuding some of her best work, remarks 'I do not feel that I have any real or organic knowledge of life later than 1910'.[64] Her methods as well as her interests were shaped before the decade began, and continued mostly unchanged long after its end: her fiction remains consistent from her first novel, *Pastors and Masters* (1925), throughout the eighteen others which followed. Her technique is well described in the words of Cyril Connolly: it was

> ...to write in dialogue...Narrative prose as opposed to dialogue is used only for vignettes of places or descriptions of characters when they first appear. It is the most brisk and readable form of writing, making demands on the reader's intelligence but none on his eye or ear... dialogue—not as a set-piece in the texture of the novel, as are the conversations of Wilde and Meredith—but as the fabric itself. (*Enemies of Promise*, p.48).

Connolly's remarks actually refer to Ronald Firbank: though Compton-Burnett presents a darker, more serious world than Firbank, there is sufficient resemblance between their styles to make his comments almost equally applicable to each. Like Firbank, Compton-Burnett observes claustrophobic groupings of characters with an acuteness and wit which rely on implication, and often entirely on dialogue.

Though this dialogue is often 'brisk and readable', it does make unusual 'demands on the intelligence'—or the patience— of readers more familiar with novels which present and explain their situations conventionally through expositional narrative. The reader is forced to deduce for the characters intricate motives implied—or sometimes disguised—in the stream of conversation. A character in *Pastors and Masters* remarks 'I find that I only like wickedness and penetration',[65] and this comment could be taken as a motto for Compton-Burnett's work as a whole. A good deal of penetration is required to reach behind the façades of what is actually said, and the task is made more urgent by the wickedness generally involved. This ranges from petty jealousies in *Pastors and Masters* to loathing and murder in *A House and its Head* (1935), for example. Such wickedness, however, is carefully contained in the respectable, apparently trivial, domestic life of late Victorian or Edwardian upper-class families, usually dominated by a cruel, tyrannical parent. Compton-Burnett's minute, subtle examination of character in this prosperous setting occasionally resembles the work of Henry James as well as Ronald Firbank: the idiosyncrasy of her style and subjects, however, make her almost a unique figure in English fiction. Dialogue form and her interest in cruel family struggles for power at times place her work closest to the Greek tragedy she studied and admired.

John Cowper Powys is also a unique figure, with an equally long career, including twenty novels among his dozens of publications. Like Ivy Compton-Burnett, he published some of the best of his fiction around the thirties in novels such as *Wolf Solent* (1929), *A Glastonbury Romance* (1932), *Weymouth Sands* (1934), and *Maiden Castle* (1936). Each is set in Wessex: Powys himself grew up in Dorset and Somerset and dedicated his first novel, *Wood and Stone* (1915), to another Wessex novelist, Thomas Hardy, equally committed to the primordial life and values of the country. Powys, however, is concerned not only with the natural world: as one recent critic suggests, his novels are 'huge, prolix and digressive amalgams of Dorsetism and supernaturalism [and] his assumed and flaunted celticism".[66] Powys's prolix style and amalgam of natural and supernatural, physical and metaphysical, are illustrated in the extraordinary opening sentences of *A Glastonbury Romance:*

> At the striking of noon on a certain fifth of March, there occurred within a causal radius of Brandon railway-station and yet beyond the deepest pools of emptiness between the uttermost stellar systems one of those infinitesimal ripples in the creative silence of the First Cause which always occur when an exceptional stir of heightened consciousness agitates any living organism in this astronomical universe. Something passed at that moment, a wave, a motion, a vibration, too tenuous to be called magnetic, too subliminal to be called spiritual, between the soul of a particular human being who was emerging from a third-class carriage of the twelve-nineteen train from London and the divine-diabolic soul of the First Cause of all life.

Some of the causes whose operation Powys investigates are entirely earthly: despite its magical dimensions, *A Glastonbury Romance* is in some ways quite closely connected to the thirties, envisaging at one stage a struggle between capitalists and communists, for example. As the passage quoted suggests, however, much of Powys's interest is in the infinite 'divine-diabolic' factors his hero encounters in a walk to

Glastonbury and Stonehenge. The attempt to present all such forces—spiritual, magical and secular—as they work upon men's lives and souls is undertaken on an enormous scale, taking up twelve hundred pages of complicated plot and introducing around fifty oddly-named characters. Critics have found this sort of work not only 'huge, prolix and digressive', but altogether over-ambitious, clumsy and muddled: twenty years after his death, Powys's literary reputation remains very uncertain. The supernatural and celtic elements of his fiction, however, have a continuing minority appeal. There is also an unusual depth of vision in Powys's attempts, like L.H. Myers's, to discover 'the true forms of life' behind the everyday, and to relate spiritual, physical and psychic aspects of human experience. Such qualities have attracted several admirers: the novelist Angus Wilson, for example, suggests that Powys will 'stand with James, Lawrence, and Joyce in the eyes of future literary critics'.[67]

Powys's extraordinary family background has also added to the interest of his work: seven of his brothers and sisters were published authors. Llewelyn Powys was a distinguished essayist and novelist: another brother, T.F. Powys, was a more concise and less clumsy writer than John and may eventually acquire a securer reputation, though his fiction is equally unusual. His best-known work, *Mr Weston's Good Wine* (1927), for example, is a homely allegory in which God turns up as a wine salesman in an English village. Despite its whimsical theme, the story is rarely sentimental, achieving transitions between natural and supernatural with an ease and imaginative power unusual in English literature. Imagination is itself one of T.F. Powys's central concerns in the novel, which suggests that God 'possessed in a very large degree a poet's fancy, that will at any moment create out of the imagination a new world'.[68] Among its other visionary material, *Mr Weston's Good Wine* introduces subtle analogies between divine and literary creation of a sort which continue to interest later twentieth-century novelists such as Muriel Spark and Graham Greene.

John Cowper Powys's concern with the forces behind the immediate surface of life inevitably involves attention to the depths of his characters' consciousnesses: one of the limitations of his fiction, however, is the awkwardness with which this is presented. Though Powys published a study of Dorothy Richardson in 1931, like several of his contemporaries he seems to have rejected modernist methods of transcribing characters' thoughts. Modernist influence, however, does continue to appear elsewhere during the thirties, even in the work of some of the authors already discussed whose social or political interests generally made them favour a 'new realism'. Graham Greene, for example, alternates in the early part of *England Made Me* (1935) between the first-person narratives of two characters, whose thoughts are sometimes briefly presented in stream of consciousness. This form appears again, along with some other unusual devices, in Greene's short story *The Bear Fell Free* (1935). In *A Clergyman's Daughter*, also published in 1935, George Orwell develops Dorothy's experience of a destitute, freezing night in Trafalgar Square in dialogue form, complete with stage directions, songs and surreal remarks. Though generally hostile to the modernist mood of the twenties, Orwell records an admiration for Joyce amounting to an 'inferiority complex',[69] and he clearly bases his presentation of Dorothy's nocturnal adventures on Joyce's methods in the 'Nighttown' section of *Ulysses*. The inclusion of such features in Greene's and Orwell's otherwise conventional fiction indicates the continuing interest of the modernists' example in the mid-thirties, just as Isherwood shows its appeal at the start of the decade.

Other nineteen-thirties novelists attempted more thoroughgoing adoption of the methods added by modernism to 'the international store of literary technique'. One such is Malcolm Lowry, who includes in *Ultramarine* (1933) a range of interior monologues, stream of consciousness, excursions into memory, changes of perspective, and polyglot Joycean wordplay. Some of these devices are successful in communicating the loneliness of a rather cerebral, confused young man 'as homeless, as exiled as the ship itself' during his first voyage as a merchant seaman.[70] His story, however, is almost overwhelmed by its complex diversity of styles, some borrowed from Joseph Conrad, Herman Melville and Conrad Aiken as well as Joyce. Lowry's best fiction appears later in *Under the Volcano* (1947: see Chapter Three).

Rosamond Lehmann's writing shows a more modest inheritance of the methods of modernism, and a better integration of them for her own purposes. This is particularly evident in her third novel, *The Weather in the Streets* (1936), a sequel to *Invitation to the Waltz* (1932). *The Weather in the Streets* resembles *Ultramarine* in changing from the third-person authorial perspective used in Parts One, Three, and Four to the first-person narrative of her heroine Olivia Curtis in Part Two. This tactic particularly heightens the immediacy with which her relationship with Rollo Spencer is presented, at a stage when their affair has itself achieved maximum intimacy and happiness. Olivia's emotional experience, however, is highlighted throughout: Lehmann subordinates action to reflection, establishing 'an intensely concentrated inner life of thought and feeling',[71] as it is called in the novel, and creating a distinctive register for Olivia's thoughts. Her imagined acceptance of Rollo—'Yes, I'll say...Yes. Anything you say. Yes.' (p.143)—is similar to Molly Bloom's contemplation at the end of *Ulysses*, but her occasional stream of consciousness rarely displays the random associativeness with which Joyce presents Molly's mind. Instead, Olivia's half-conversational inner voice, musing in well-formulated, reflective phrases, shows Lehmann as one of the first of many later women novelists to employ a form of the 'feminine prose' developed by Dorothy Richardson and by Virginia Woolf.

The modernity of Lehmann's technique is generally matched by the nature of the story she tells, though in some ways this is disappointingly conventional: tales of love between a poor, unhappy girl and a rich sophisticate are as old-fashioned as *Cinderella*. Olivia's life, however, is eventually less rewarding; always more complex; and seemed shockingly immoral to some of the first readers of *The Weather in the Streets*. The affair is adulterous, involving an abortion and a defection by Rollo, and ending with the suggestion that at best things may drag uneasily on. The bruised emotions involved in these developments are compellingly communicated by concentration on Olivia's perspective. Rarely envisaged independently, through his own mind or thoughts, Rollo appears a familiar yet ultimately inscrutable figure for readers as well as heroine. The secrecy of their liaison also leads to some ironic, often funny, contrasts between Olivia's inner voice and her respectable conversation. Lehmann's technique and the frankness with which it highlights a range of disturbed emotions make *The Weather in the Streets* seem ahead of its time, one of the outstanding novels of the thirties.

Few other successful novelists during the decade were concerned as deeply as Lehmann with love and emotional affairs. Among her contemporaries, only William Gerhardie matches her examination of these areas. In his best novel, *Of Mortal Love* (1936), he shows in the relationship of Walter and Dinah something of Lehmann's sense that even after the greatest intimacies 'we don't, *can't*, come near each other; we are talking to each other's phantoms'[72]—almost throughout, Dinah remains for her lover as elusive as Rollo often appears in Lehmann's novel. Like *The Weather in the Streets*, *Of Mortal Love* traces a relationship (also adulterous) through a very wide range of its fluctuating emotions, leading to Dinah's death and the conclusion that 'the deeds and thoughts of living beings were as nothing besides their griefs' (p.299).

Gerhardie's outlook, however, is not wholly tragic. A Russian emigré, he wrote the first study in English of the Russian dramatist Anton Chekhov, particularly popular in Britain between the wars: something of Chekhov's mixture of comedy and sadness appears in much of his own fiction, creating a tone sometimes almost incongruously light for the events portrayed. *Of Mortal Love* also moves away from feelings of tragic loss through Walter's vision of Dinah's life as whole, eternal, ultimately resolved by her death:

> He saw of a sudden the whole long road of that life which was
> herself...the final seal of a life which was her true being...She had not
> died, because the Dinah he had visualized a little at a time had in fact
> never lived save as a shadow in the tarnished and obscuring mirror of his
> mind. (p.299)

This benign, concluding vision develops from Walter's opinion that

> Time was an illusion...in the real and timeless world everything which is
> to be has been...memory is the sixth sense, a faculty whose rightful
> function is to apprehend the eternal aspect of things. It should work here
> and now to supplement our time sense and make us see each moment as
> containing all the things we so lamentably fail to see at the time. (pp.192,
> 30, 59-60)

Gerhardie's unusual narrative technique sometimes extends this interest in time and memory, which he shares with the modernists: emphasis on memory as a shaping, liberating recovery of past life particularly resembles Marcel Proust's *Remembrance of Things Past (A la Recherche du Temps Perdu* (1913-27)). Such interests make *Of Mortal Love* deeply felt and imagined as well as entertaining. Gerhardie's unusual tone, his mixture of humour and seriousness, have continued to appeal to later novelists, notably Olivia Manning, C.P. Snow and William Cooper.

Conclusion: the Literary Budget

George Orwell concludes part of his assessment in 'Inside the Whale' by remarking

> On the whole the literary history of the thirties seems to justify the
> opinion that a writer does well to keep out of politics...no decade in the
> past hundred and fifty years has been so barren of imaginative prose as the
> nineteen-thirties. There have been good poems, good sociological works,
> brilliant pamphlets, but practically no fiction of any value at all. From
> 1933 onwards the mental climate was increasingly against it. Anyone
> sensitive enough to be touched by the *zeitgeist* was also involved in
> politics. (p.568)

In *The Thirties: A Dream Revolved* (1966) the novelist Julian Symons likewise suggests that poetry and other forms predominated in the literature of the time.[73] Much of the interest in politics which Orwell sees as limiting thirties fiction, however, also appears in its poetry, equally affected by a *zeitgeist* apparently present everywhere in the life of the age. Auden, Spender, Louis MacNeice, C. Day Lewis and other poets share the generally left-wing outlook of contemporary novelists, and their poetry is often similarly involved in documenting the harsh realities and social concerns of their era. Other spheres of the life and literature of the thirties show the effects of the same 'mental climate'. Writers committed to the left were prominent in America, and the work of novelists such as John Steinbeck and John Dos Passos is sometimes stylistically as well as ideologically comparable to that of their British contemporaries. The 'new realism' of fiction also appeared in thirties cinema. Some of the outstanding British films of the decade were documentaries, made by

John Grierson and others in the GPO film unit, formed in 1934, which produced such classics as *Night Mail* (1936), with commentary by W.H. Auden. A stranger manifestation of contemporary interest in documentary appeared in 1937 in Mass-Observation, led by a communist poet, Charles Madge, and an anthropologist, Tom Harrisson. This organisation attempted to heighten social and political consciousness, creating the 'anthropology of ourselves' by means of the 'observation by everyone of everyone, including themselves'.[74] Mass-Observation eventually involved thousands of volunteers, who collected great quantities of documentary material—incidentally providing Graham Greene with a crucial plot device in *The Confidential Agent*, in which a Mass-Observer spots a detail which identifies a murderer.

Greene is one of several contemporary novelists who intersperse 'observation of themselves', documentary, and travelogue with their fiction. His records of a difficult West African trip in *Journey without Maps* (1935), and of Mexican religious persecution in *The Lawless Roads* (1939), can be compared to Orwell's description of more domestic journeys into poverty and the working class in *Down and Out in Paris and London* (1933) and *The Road to Wigan Pier* (1937). Like Orwell in *Homage to Catalonia* (1938), several other authors at the time give personal accounts of travels to troubled parts of the world: Auden and Isherwood of a joint visit to China in *Journey to a War* (1939); Waugh of African conflict in *Waugh in Abyssinia* (1936). Especially since Isherwood describes all his novels as 'a kind of fictional biography',[75] even his *Goodbye to Berlin* and *Mr Norris Changes Trains* can be considered part of this group of accounts of private experience in areas of political instability. The threats emanating from these areas help to explain the tenuous separation of fiction and autobiography in the work of Isherwood and several of the other novelists mentioned above: as Virginia Woolf suggests, their interest in themselves was

> ...forced upon them by their circumstances. When everything is rocking round one, the only person who remains comparatively stable is oneself. So they wrote about themselves—in their plays, in their poems, in their novels. No other ten years can have produced so much autobiography as the ten years between 1930 and 1940...their autobiography is so much better than their fiction.[76]

Commitment to politics, documentary, autobiography, and realistic method, shared by the authors mentioned above and many others at the time, has encouraged a view of the thirties and its literature as exceptionally uniform in outlook and attitude. Orwell recognised this uniformity at the time, suggesting of his contemporaries in 'Inside the Whale' that

> ...when one compares these writers with the Joyce-Eliot generation, the

immediately striking thing is how much easier it is to form them into a group. Technically they are closer together, politically they are almost indistinguishable. (p.560)

Recent studies such as Samuel Hynes's *The Auden Generation* (1976), Bernard Bergonzi's *Reading the Thirties* (1978), and Richard Johnstone's *The Will to Believe* (1982) have also tended to form thirties writers into a group, concentrating on Isherwood, Greene, Orwell, Upward, Warner and Waugh among the novelists, and highlighting similarities in technique or politics. Each critic is careful to indicate elements of selectiveness in his approach, and Hynes warns of possible distortions in any 'myth by which a complex, confused, often contradictory time has been simplified in order that it might be comprehended'.[77] Nevertheless, the very success of their studies, undoubtedly accurate in general terms, tends to contribute to a dominant critical scheme of the decade; a 'myth' which sometimes obscures significant though less central developments. In particular, though one of the clearest trends of the age was to reject modernism in favour of realism and political commitment, the modernists themselves did not simply cease to write in 1930. Their initiatives are extended, even partly redirected, in Virginia Woolf's *The Waves* (1931), for example, and in Joyce's *Work in Progress*, eventually published as *Finnegans Wake* in 1939. The readiness shown by Rosamond Lehmann and Malcolm Lowry to adopt modernist technique also appears in the work of a number of other writers— Elizabeth Bowen, Jean Rhys, Samuel Beckett, Lawrence Durrell, and Flann O'Brien, for example. Each had published at least a first novel by the end of the thirties: though their significance was not always immediately apparent, their work can be seen in retrospect to add to the diversity of the decade, and to its promise.

Less homogeneous in fictional technique than Orwell supposed, the thirties may also have been less 'barren of imaginative prose' than he suggests. One of the distractions of the 'myth' of the decade is that it has tended to install as the major figures of the period its most representative writers, rather than necessarily those most accomplished. The representative quality of certain contemporary authors is in some ways actually connected to limitations in their work. Concentration on the immediate experience of the age in some of the fiction of Isherwood, Upward and Orwell, for example, rather narrowly restricts imagination to fact and self, as Woolf suggests. Writers who move away from realism and documentary are at times equally limited: Warner and Upward, as the latter recognised, sometimes work on a level of fancifulness and abstraction which obscures or trivialises the political realities they seek to elucidate. None of these novelists, of course, offers much warrant for Orwell's suggestion that the decade produced 'practically no fiction of any value at all'. Yet only Lewis Grassic Gibbon wholly refutes his conclusion that in order to be successful a writer must 'keep out of politics'—and Gibbon is often omitted from assessments of the age. Some re-reading of the thirties is required, taking fuller account not only of Gibbon's *A Scots Quair* but also of other unusual, outstanding contemporary fiction—Myers's *The Near and the Far;* Lehmann's *The Weather in the Streets;* even the novels of John Cowper Powys; as well as the work of the authors mentioned above who followed on from modernism. If this material is added to the 'new realist', politically-concerned fiction on which criticism has usually concentrated, a more accurate and also a more promising picture is created of the range of the novel at the time, and of its potential for the future.[78]

Cyril Connolly provides significantly varied assessments of this potential. His first and only novel, *The Rock Pool* (1936), portrays what it calls 'the central concept of the nineteen-twenties—futility'[79]: an equally gloomy view of the next decade appears later, in Connolly's *The Modern Movement* (1965). In this study he follows Woolf and Orwell in describing the thirties as

> ... the disastrous decade. Infiltration of literature by destructive influences of Surrealism ... and politics (exhaustion of talent in lost causes like anti-fascism, popular fronts, etc.)[80]

When Connolly first wrote about the thirties, however, before its 'myth' had formed, he viewed the period more optimistically. In *Enemies of Promise* (1938)—another autobiographical study—he sometimes indicates a fruitful diversity in the writing of the time. He suggests, for example, that although no longer in the ascendant, the potential of modernism had not been lost, but survived as part of the 'perpetual action and reaction' of innovative and traditional styles:

> What I claim is that there continue action and reaction between these styles, and that necessary though it were and victorious as it may appear, the colloquial style of the last few years is doomed and dying. Style ... is a relationship between a writer's mastery of form and his intellectual or emotional content. Mastery of form has lately been held, with some reason, to conceal a poverty of content but this is not inevitably so ... Now all seems favourable. Experiment and adventure are indicated, the boom of the twenties has been paid for by the slump of the thirties; let us try then to break the vicious circle by returning to a controlled expenditure, a balanced literary budget, a reasoned extravagance. (p.94).

Connolly's remarks and the example of some of the writers mentioned above indicate continuing promise in the situation of the novelist, modernist 'mastery of form' and the opportunity to integrate it with more conventional styles still providing a range of possibilities for writers at the end of the thirties. Connolly's conclusion in *Enemies of Promise* offers a further version of the 'surpassingly rash' hopes for the future of literature which Woolf proposed in 1924: contemporary politics, however, seemed to conspire to postpone fulfilment of such hopes once again. Like every other sphere of life, literature was hugely affected by the war which began so soon after Connolly's remarks were made, dominating British consciousness for the next decade and beyond. The next chapter assesses the developments in the novel which resulted, and how far they satisfied hopes for 'a balanced literary budget'.

3

War and Post-war, 1940-1956

The Wartime Scene: George Orwell, Arthur Koestler, C.S. Forester, J.B. Priestley, Alexander Baron, Evelyn Waugh

'As I write, highly civilised human beings are flying overhead, trying to kill me'. Orwell's dramatic opening to *The Lion and the Unicorn* (1941) indicates the extent of the challenges to writing, and to civilisation in general, which seemed to contemporary novelists to overwhelm their work in the war and post-war period. During the war, Orwell suggested 'the *impossibility* of any major literature until the world has shaken itself into its new shape': writing immediately afterwards, in 1946, Rosamond Lehmann complained that

> There has so far been no great war novel, no one to make a story, adequate in moral, emotional and intellectual weight, out of the experiences of the last six years.[1]

Later, in 1951, the novelist P.H. Newby suggested in his useful study, *The Novel 1945-1950*, that 'it is debatable…whether so overwhelming and universal a catastrophe as the late war can be reckoned the sort of experience out of which an artist can create. What…can he do with it?'[2] Another novelist, Robert Liddell, still felt in 1953 that writing fiction was

> …probably now, for several reasons, as difficult as it has been at any time…the chief difficulty today is caused by the crushing impact of public affairs.[3]

This sort of 'impact', which had so conditioned writing in the thirties, seemed as a result of the war to threaten to crush literature out of worthwhile existence altogether, and the gloomy views of Liddell and his contemporaries have often been substantiated in later estimations of the period. Cyril Connolly confirmed that the war destroyed his hopes, quoted at the end of the last chapter, for a 'balanced literary budget': he later described the decade which followed the optimism of *Enemies of Promise* in 1938 as 'the frustrated 'forties, five years of total war and five more of recrimination and exhaustion during which the Modern Movement unobtrusively expired'.[4] Other critics have followed Connolly in suggesting that a null, drab period in the development of literature resulted from the war. W.W. Robson, for example, suggests that 'The 1940s were one of the worst periods of English literature', adding that 'perhaps it is remarkable that any literary life went on at all'. Robert Hewison concludes his useful study of the conditions of wartime writing, *Under Siege* (1977), by remarking simply that 'the war was a depressing time...the next years were to be worse'.[5] In surveying the fiction written during and in the years following the Second World War, the present chapter will eventually suggest that this may have been a less depressing time for the novel than has often been supposed. The opinions quoted, however, indicate what were obviously grave and genuine problems for the authors of the period. These must be considered first, along with some of the means authors used in trying to overcome them and 'make a story' out of the six years of 'overwhelming and universal catastrophe'; the extraordinary years of the war itself.

Some of the frustrations for novelists in wartime were simply practical. As Hewison records, publishers were hampered both by a serious shortage in the supply and quality of paper, much of which was needed for official purposes, and also by extensive destruction of their stock of books in the course of German bombing raids on London, the Blitz of 1940-41. As a result, it was more difficult to publish new novels, and also to keep others in print. As the novelist Elizabeth Bowen sadly explained in 1948, this meant that in addition to their other difficulties, many authors found that their earlier work had entirely ceased to be available, depriving them both of the financial support of royalties, and of any continuity of public attention.[6] This attention may also have seemed likely to be distracted from literature by the 'impact of public affairs' and the priorities of the war. In C.S. Forester's wartime novel *The Ship* (1943), for example, the view is expressed that 'poetry was something that did not matter...a torpedo into a German submarine's side was worth more than all the sonnets in the world',[7] and there were other contemporary indications that fiction may have seemed no less irrelevant than poetry to the circumstances of war. A critic in the *New Statesman*, for example, suggested in 1940 that 'there can have been no moment, since the invention of novels, when fewer people wished to read them'.[8]

In fact, as the war progresed, this view proved quite misleading. In his account of the desert war, *Alamein to Zem Zem* (1946), Keith Douglas is one of several contemporary authors who record the demand for reading material in the armed forces and elsewhere. Evelyn Waugh's novel of wartime, *Sword of Honour* (1952-61) likewise suggests that 'It was in miniature a golden age for the book-trade; anything sold; the supply of paper alone determined a writer's popularity'.[9] This 'golden age', however, did not necessarily encourage good contemporary fiction. Rosamond Lehmann suggested in 1946 that wartime readers had 'nearly all...gone back to the great nineteenth century novelists'.[10] The audience which remained for new publications may not always have looked beyond the flood of lightweight adventure stories fostered by war experience. These 'Dunkirk books...RAF books...Blitz books' were unkindly but firmly dismissed as a 'cataract of tripe' by Tom Harrisson, a founder of Mass-Observation who claimed to have read 'literally every book which has anything to do with the war' for a review in Cyril Connolly's journal *Horizon* in 1941.[11]

As well as having to face such practical difficulties in securing a reading public and a publisher with sufficient paper to reach it, authors were sometimes further perplexed by the political uncertainties of the period. Events leading up to the outbreak of war in 1939 undermined the ideology which had informed much of the literature of the nineteen thirties. The fall of Barcelona and the final victory of General Franco in the Spanish Civil War in 1939 were severe disappointments to the many left-wing writers who had supported Republican Spain. Some of their likely feelings at the start of the Second World War are summarised by Samuel Hynes, who suggests in *The Auden Generation* (1976) that

> ...for the 'thirties generation, the battle had already been fought and lost...the appropriate response to the end of the 'thirties was silence...it was not really their war...not...a cause, but a consequence of a cause that had already been lost.[12]

The silence Hynes mentions was deepened by the departure in January 1939 of two of the leading figures of the 'thirties generation', Christopher Isherwood and W.H. Auden. Their apparent desertion to the refuge of America slightly shocked contemporary opinion, and made them an easy satirical target for Evelyn Waugh, who presents them as the escapist poets Parsnip and Pimpernell in *Put out More Flags* (1942).

Later in 1939, in August, came a much greater shock, the Non-Aggression Pact signed between Russia and Germany. To the 'thirties generation', who had often seen Russia as an ideal socialist state and a bulwark against the expanding threat of fascist Germany, this development seemed especially disturbing. Disillusion with Russian socialism was heightened by the appearance in 1940 of Arthur Koestler's *Darkness at Noon*, written in German but first published in English translation. A Hungarian by birth, Koestler, like Orwell, had had first-hand experience of Communist politics, and in *Darkness at Noon* sets out to explain the Moscow trials of the thirties in which Stalin had bewildered the world by purging members of his own ruling party. Koestler records in his dedication 'the characters in this book are fictitious. The historical circumstances which determined their actions are real', and his intentions are at least partly documentary. His demand for revised understanding of the Russian Revolution anticipates Orwell's satiric version of Russian history in *Animal Farm* (1945) and also some of his vision of the totalitarian manipulation of language, truth and consciousness in *Nineteen Eighty-Four* (1949). Koestler's hero, N.S. Rubashov, is a former party leader imprisoned and executed ostensibly for disloyalties which he is brainwashed into confessing, but really because his utopian socialism cannot be adjusted to the inhuman demands of political pragmatism and of Stalin's autocratic rule. His dilemma is presented convincingly and largely without bias: Koestler's confrontation of political expediency and natural human feeling does not conclude wholly in favour of the latter, and their conflict is successfully dramatised through careful concentration on the uneasy workings of Rubashov's mind. Koestler's technique has some of the strengths of Kafka's vision of an isolated individual menaced by an incomprehensible society, and also of Dostoevsky's treatment of mental suffering, doubt and guilt in confinement.

Though the novel which results, like Orwell's *Homage to Catalonia* (1938), strongly challenged some of the assumptions of the 'thirties generation', much of the uncertainty to which Koestler may have contributed was dispelled in June 1941 by the German invasion of Russia. An article in *Horizon* in October 1941, signed by Connolly, Koestler, Orwell, Stephen Spender and others, remarks

> When war broke out, many writers were hesitant. They did not see the issues as clearly as they had seen the Spanish Civil War...or the last European War...With the invasion of Russia, feeling has crystallised.

Orwell himself was one of the authors who contributed to this crystallisation of socialist feelings in a war against fascism. In *The Lion and the Unicorn*, a patriotic political study of the state of wartime Britain, he suggests that 'only Socialist nations can fight effectively...with its present social structure England cannot survive...We cannot win the war without introducing Socialism'.[13] The advocacy in *The Lion and the Unicorn* of a socialist future, and the wish often expressed at the time for a better and more egalitarian Britain to succeed the war, show a continuity of some of the political aspirations of the nineteen thirties. These were eventually partly fulfilled by the election in 1945 of the reforming Labour government which created the Welfare State.

Despite the wartime difficulty of establishing a political alignment, or simply of finding a supply of paper and readers, by far the greatest problem affecting contemporary writers was neither practical nor ideological but imaginative. The novelist and critic Walter Allen suggested in 1941 in the wartime journal *Penguin New Writing* that 'the war dominates us like a physical fact... and to write of anything that does not deal with the war or throw light on the immediate situation is almost impossible'.[14] Yet the violent, extraordinary experience of the war seemed to offer impossibly intractable material for the novel, material perhaps more appropriate for poetry, or for 'journalism rather than for art', as Allen goes on to suggest. In the first place, fiction almost seemed to have been made redundant by fact. The weirdness of London and other cities ruined in the Blitz created the feeling mentioned by many observers that—without the help of any author—the war had itself fantastically transformed actuality into and beyond the domain of fiction. The American journalist Negley Farson, for example, records in his documentary account of the Blitz, *Bomber's Moon* (1941) 'In these early weeks of the heavy bombing raids there was a certain dream-like quality to the life on the land. You just didn't believe it'. The novelist Henry Green likewise remarks that experiences in London at the time existed on 'a frontier of hopes or mostly fears' beyond 'a web of dreams'; and in *Alamein to Zem Zem* Keith Douglas similarly presents in the context of the desert war 'the impression of having walked through the looking-glass which touches a man entering a battle'. He goes on to discuss the resulting feeling of emerging into 'an illimitably strange land, quite unrelated to real life, like the scenes in "The Cabinet of Doctor Caligari"'.[15]

If this fantastic, dream-like intensity in actual life did not make fiction seem altogether redundant, it at least made its structuring, its shaping of reality, unusually difficult. Knowing at first hand the chaos of the Blitz, the novelist and short-story writer William Sansom suggested that the war offered 'experience... too violent for the arts to transcribe'.[16] Tom Harrisson likewise concludes in his review that 'books pale into stupidity beside the real thing', adding that

> So far, this has been overwhelmingly a war for superficial writers and journalists... the drama now is total, colossal, more than Ibsen or Gogol could contain... ordinary writers therefore find the reconstruction and rearrangement of life's events (literature) taken over, as it were, by the more powerful and less manageable pressures of gigantic war. It is difficult... to work it into the familiar patterns. (pp.435, 436)

The fabulous nature of contemporary reality, and the difficulty of transcribing it into the 'patterns' of literature, may account for contemporary interest in a form of 'journalism rather than... art'—documentary. The profusion of diaries, documentary accounts of war experience, and Mass-Observation reports at the time is also partly explained by Angus Calder's suggestion in his excellent history of the period, *The People's War* (1969), that 'people... assumed that anything which happened to anyone at this time was of intrinsic interest'.[17] Oddly, given the penchant for travelogues and documentaries shown in the thirties, fairly few of the factual accounts of the time are the work of novelists, though several wrote autobiographies during the war. Some of the unearthly strangeness of the Blitz is recorded in a journal Graham Greene kept at the time and later included in *Ways of Escape* (1980), and in the accounts of his work in the A.F.S. (the Auxiliary Fire Service) which Henry Green contributed to *Penguin New Writing*.[18] But probably the best of many contemporary documentations of war experience appears in the restrained and minutely-detailed observation of *Alamein to Zem Zem*, the work not of a novelist but of one of the best of the Second World War poets.

Novelists at the time may have redirected into their fiction some of their interest in documentary, for something of its form and tactics appears in several novels dealing with the war. As is partly suggested by its subtitle, 'A Close-Up of a Modern Naval Action', C.S. Forester's *The Ship* (1943) was accurately described by a contemporary reviewer, Jack Marlowe, as an 'imaginative documentary'[19]—a change of style from Forester's earlier historical fiction and romantic sea adventures. Interspersed with objective accounts of the action supposedly rendered in 'The Captain's Report', Forester examines in successive chapters the character and function of various members of the crew separately at work in different parts of the ship. Though the method is comprehensive in illustrating the organisation of a cruiser, it largely removes the possibility of significant interaction between the characters. The ship itself, a 'huge marine animal' (p.20) in Paymaster Jerningham's vision, is more vital and interestingly-developed as a central character than any of the humans aboard. Concurrently, perhaps, with Jerningham's opinion of the relative merits of poetry and torpedoes, quoted earlier, *The Ship* is not a literary novel but 'war propaganda of the soundest and most unexceptionable sort', as Jack Marlowe recognised at the time.

Forester's 'imaginative documentary' style nevertheless usefully illustrates a technique which appears in several other novels of the period. J.B. Priestley stresses in a prefatory note to *Daylight on Saturday* (subtitled 'A Novel about an Aircraft Factory') that 'this is a work of fiction, not a piece of reporting', but his strategy strongly resembles Forester's. Priestley initially moves attention around the factory by concentrating on a single character and describing him until his work leads him to meet another, then treated in the same manner. Employing the attractively direct, almost conversational address to the reader which enhances much of Priestley's work, *Daylight on Saturday* (1944) is eventually rather fuller than *The Ship* of interesting characters, relationships and conflicts. Priestley's development of some of these conflicts and of the ideas associated with them also makes his novel representative of some of the issues of its times. In particular, just as Rex Warner contrasts village and airfield in *The Aerodrome* (1941), Priestley resumes some of the ideological antitheses of his era in the struggle between a drunken but good-hearted works manager and his eventual boss, who is inclined to a fascistic, Futurist preference for machines and inflexible organisation as an antidote to the inefficiencies of humanity. *Daylight on Saturday* also echoes popular sentiment in criticising the British leadership which let the war develop and then muddled its early conduct, and Priestley continues some of the socialist sentiments of the thirties in the novel's approval of Joint Production Committees and working-class resistance to capitalist industrialism. Russian socialism is also occasionally discussed in a favourable way.

A popular novelist and dramatist before the war, Priestley probably reached the height of his fame during it, in his series of postscripts to evening radio news bulletins. Like Orwell, he offered in these talks visions of a more egalitarian Britain emerging from current conflicts, and *Daylight on Saturday* further expresses this sort of socialist optimism. The title, which might even be intended as an answer to Koestler's *Darkness at Noon,* refers at one level to the weekend release from long shifts under the factory's artificial lights. It also indicates, however, a more general hope and expectation about the future, a 'new kind of Britain' of 'socialism and engineering' which will succeed the darkness of the war.[20] Part of a trilogy of novels 'of—and for—wartime', *Daylight on Saturday* is typical of Priestley's grasp of popular feeling during this period. It also occasionally shows the interest in the nature of time and in 'man's ultimate deliverance and freedom...his home-coming among the stars' (p.108) which appears at other stages in his career, especially in his popular plays.

Some of the documentary technique of *The Ship* is also employed in Alexander Baron's *From the City, from the Plough* (1948). His account of an infantry battalion's training and its combat during and after the Normandy D-Day landing moves informally among a wide range of characters and social types found in the battalion. Unlike Forester and Priestley, however, Baron largely avoids telling the reader about his characters by means of direct introductions, and shows them in action and conversation instead, keeping explanation and authorial comment to a minimum. This technique contributes to the 'freshness about the telling' which P.H. Newby praises in *The Novel 1945-1950:* it is also successful in heightening the immediacy of Baron's presentation of violent military action. Encountering a stream of rapidly successive and barely explained events, the reader shares some of the bewilderment of the participants. *From the City, from the Plough* thus seems to present some of 'the more powerful and less manageable pressures of gigantic war' with unusual clarity and apparent objectivity, though Baron's dispassionate treatment of his story does occasionally lapse into a kind of sentimentality. As Newby suggests, too often he puts 'the best complexion on his material'.[21] For the most part, however, the novel's emotions are firmly located in the responses of its characters. With most of the battalion eventually wiped out in action, these feelings among those left alive develop into an overwhelming sense of exhaustion with the endless casual slaughter. By the novel's conclusion, anticipated in its first chapter, its feelings of loss and futility reach a level which recalls Erich Maria Remarque's classic account of the First World War, *All Quiet on the Western Front* (1929).

Writing in 1951, P.H. Newby adjudged *From the City, from the Plough* 'probably the best English novel about the war and nothing else but the war to appear since the fighting ended'.[22] Most later critics, however, have considered Baron's novel surpassed by one which began to appear in the year after Newby made his judgement—Evelyn Waugh's *Sword of Honour.* Cyril Connolly and Anthony Burgess, for example, concur with W.W. Robson in finding that '*Sword of Honour*... is Waugh's finest work, and the best English novel inspired by the Second World War'.[23] Both the length and subject matter of Waugh's trilogy (*Men at Arms* (1952), *Officers and Gentlemen* (1955), and *Unconditional Surrender* (1961)) invite comparison with the outstanding English novel of the First World War, Ford Madox Ford's tetralogy *Parade's End* (1924-28). Like Ford's Christopher Tietjens, Waugh's partly-autobiographical hero Guy Crouchback is a rare attempt at the portrayal of an exceptionally good man. Like Tietjens, Crouchback remains committed to his honour despite the manifest readiness of the wartime world to reward most highly the least honourable action. Like Tietjens, he finds the chaos and disturbing immorality of this world made painfully immediate by the spectacular, sustained infidelities of his wife.

Crouchback, however, initially approaches the war optimistically. Unlike the 'thirties generation' of writers, he finds the Russo-German pact of 1939 a starting point, an incentive to honourable action:

> News that shook the politicians and young poets of a dozen capital cities brought deep peace to one English heart... now, splendidly, everything had become clear. The enemy at last was plain in view, huge and hateful, all disguise cast off. It was the Modern Age in arms. (p.11)

After many rebuffs, Guy's enthusiasm for the struggle against this enemy leads him to join an infantry regiment, and to an unsatisfying progress through several stages of training; various postings; a dubious action on the coast of Africa; a disastrous retreat from Crete; and disturbing work among refugees in Yugoslavia. His experience steadily convinces him of the ineptitude of his initial idealism and the naïveté of his belief that 'this terrible time of doubt, danger and suffering…was a time of glory and dedication' (p.49). In the latter part of the trilogy, he develops a less idealistic understanding, recognising the need to sustain his personal beliefs independently of the decline of the civilisation which surrounds him. This opens the way for a conclusion in *Unconditional Surrender* whose qualified affirmation of security and possible future happiness in Guy's life further recalls *Parade's End*.

Like Tietjens, Guy responds to his disagreeable circumstances with resilient patience and an independence initially prepared to discount challenges to his principles. This spirit shows him sharing 'a certain remote kinship…a common aloofness' (p.259) not only with one of his fellow soldiers, but with his author: Guy's independence sometimes extends towards the sort of distantly ironic, superior standpoint of Waugh's thirties fiction (see Chapter Two). This aloofness is also related to 'the indefinable numbness which Guy recognized intermittently in himself' (p.483): it makes him an occasionally unsympathetic character, and sometimes simply a dull one. One of his subordinates aptly compares him to a 'feather in the vacuum' (p.439): his numb, inert disengagement from his society leaves him too rarely in illuminating conflict with the moral vacuity which surrounds him. Principled passivity is obviously one of his virtues, but it does restrict intensity and significant action in Waugh's novel, at least until Guy is eventually redeemed from his inertia by realising the errors in his ideas of honour.

A further problem in *Sword of Honour* is created by Waugh's presentation of his hero's progress alongside extended stories of his bizarre friend Apthorpe, the fate of his cherished portable toilet, and other farcical developments. These stories of Apthorpe, and the later absurb adventures of other minor characters, help to show the repellent nature of a world adrift from secure moral principles, emphasising in counterpoint Guy's dedication to older, more permanent values. Various repeated jokes and references to such stories also enlarge the scale of *Sword of Honour*, contributing to its portrayal of military life in a wide theatre of war. But Waugh's penchant for absurdity at times trivialises and distracts from Guy's crusade against 'the Modern Age in arms': it creates an ambiguous tone, a strange combination of the seriousness of *Brideshead Revisited* (1945) and the farce of Waugh's thirties novels.

No Directions: James Hanley and Henry Green

Lacking the structural and stylistic sophistication of Ford's novel, *Sword of Honour* does not benefit from comparisons with *Parade's End*. It is perhaps significant that Robson describes Waugh's trilogy specifically as the best *English* novel 'inspired by the Second World

War'. As Anthony Burgess has suggested, the violent action of the world between 1939 and 1945 has been much more successfully treated by American novelists. It is hard to find English fiction to compare with works such as Norman Mailer's *The Naked and the Dead* (1948), Joseph Heller's *Catch-22* (1961), or Thomas Pynchon's *Gravity's Rainbow* (1973). Dealing partly with the British experience of the Rocket Bomb attacks on London in 1944-45, the latter in particular comes closer than any other novel to expressing what Tom Harrisson called in 1941 'the real character of this war, its multiple mass mechanizations, the random mathematics of its death'.[24] As Burgess suggests, among its other merits, *Gravity's Rainbow* is 'the war book to end them all'.[25]

P.H. Newby complained in 1951 that for English writers the war was 'too near, too general an experience...to control',[26] and American fiction at the time may have benefited from the further removal of the USA from some of the war's immediate impact. The historical distance separating Heller and Pynchon from the conflict is also likely to have enhanced objectivity and control. Their novels in any case avoid some of the difficulties of dealing with 'experience too violent for the arts to transcribe' by renouncing any attempt to 'work it into familiar patterns'. Their unconventional styles and techniques offer the reader an experience in its own way as unsettling and unprecedented as some of the unfamiliar events portrayed.

Comparable tactics on a more modest scale are employed by two British novelists who communicate some of the extraordinary impressions of war. Both James Hanley and Henry Green examine one of the the strangest of wartime experiences, the Blitz which turned the comfortable, familiar landscape of London into an arena of danger and ruin, a tangled 'web of dreams'. James Hanley's *No Directions* (1943) shows the effects in a London tenement of a single night of the Blitz. Its dream-like experience is excellently expressed in the 'hectic impressionism' which Henry Reed suggests in his study *The Novel since 1939* (1946) is characteristic of this prolific novelist. Hanley's 'impressionism' is created by omitting authorial explanation —there are almost 'no directions' to the reader—and presenting most of the events in the tenement through the disturbed minds of its various occupants. As the American novelist Henry Miller remarks in his introduction to *No Directions*, 'The style which Hanley employs to register this fantastic *dégringolade* is superbly suited to his needs. One feels that the author is not merely in the seemingly meaningless suite of events which are piled on one another pell-mell but in the débris and bric-à-brac of the mind itself'.[27] Hanley's characters have little leisure for reflection or more than the hastiest formulations of their alarming experiences. Their disorderly impressions are often made more chaotic by fear, drink, or the feeling that during raids 'you couldn't even think, mind's doors closed up' (p.135). Swiftly alternating among confused, contradictory responses, the novel presents with unusual immediacy the experience of the Blitz, its 'welter and frenzy of shapes...the city rocked with outrageous power' (pp.61,135). Hanley challenges readers' comprehension in a manner at least partly analogous to the shock of the Blitz to the understanding of immediate observers.

The bizarre effects of the air raids and their challenge to imagination are also part of Henry Green's subject in *Caught* (1943), which Walter Allen considers 'the best novel we have of London during the phoney war and the early days of the blitz'. Its hero Richard Roe joins the Auxiliary Fire Service, as Green himself did. He initially experiences in his station the wearisome inactivity of the quiet early days of the war, described in Evelyn Waugh's *Put out More Flags* as 'that odd, dead period before the Churchillian renaissance, which people called at the time the Great Bore war'.[28] Like Waugh's novel, the early part of *Caught* gives an extended picture of the peculiarity of this 'Phoney War'; of the oddly menacing first experiences of the Blackout, for example. The unfamiliar darkness is referred to by one of Roe's fellow firemen as 'a conga night', a description Green explains by adding that

> ...this man had seen 'King Kong', the film of an outsize in apes that was twenty foot tall...the experience had had a lasting effect on his adjectives... 'conga', he used to cover almost everything.[29]

Green's presentation of wartime experience through this analogy with a monstrous cinema fantasy recalls Keith Douglas's use of the surreal film *The Cabinet of Doctor Caligari* as an appropriate comparison for his experience of battle. After the first air raids have brought the Great Bore war to an end, Roe himself confirms the appropriateness of this sort of analogy, suggesting 'What will go on up there tonight, in London, every night, is more like a film, or that's what it seems like at the time...everything seems unreal' (p.174).

Significantly, Roe finds this 'unreal' experience very difficult to communicate to his sister-in-law, despite urgent attempts to do so while recuperating in the country from the shock of a near miss by a bomb. His efforts produce only an 'inadequate description' which she finds 'very dull', and Roe admits that 'the point about a blitz is this, there's always something you can't describe' (pp.177, 179-80). Green emphasises this point by juxtaposing Roe's explicit version of events with his inward, unspoken recollections and thoughts which appear throughout the novel enclosed in parentheses:

> 'The first night', he said, 'we were ordered to the docks. As we came over Westminster Bridge it was fantastic, the whole of the left side of London seemed to be alight'.
> (It had not been like that at all.. the sky in that quarter, which

happened to be the east...was flooded in a second sunset, orange and rose, turning the pavements pink...) (p.176).

Roe's difficulty in giving an account of the air raids, and the disparities Green demonstrates between his narrative and his actual visual memory, exemplify the problems encountered by wartime writers in turning into fiction experience already 'unreal', film-like, or 'too violent for the arts to transcribe'. As well as illustrating these difficulties, however, Green adroitly circumvents them by presenting violent action, like Hanley, through the consciousness or narration of a character whose disturbance by the events he witnesses helps to communicate their oddity. The ingenuity of *Caught* in overcoming some of the particular difficulties of writing in the war contributed to its appeal for Rosamond Lehmann. She concluded in 1946 that *Caught* was 'one important exception' to her view that 'no great war novel' had appeared. She added that Green had 'succeeded in coming to terms with the times...succeeded in translating fresh experience, the direct result of war, into an adequate pattern'.[30]

Caught, however, is more than simply a 'translation' of the experience of the Blitz, which only really appears in its last chapter. Green himself is not only a wartime novelist, but one of the outstanding English writers of the twentieth century: other aspects of his career require some further assessment. The scenes in Roe's fire station during the idle, enervating days of the phoney war, for example, show his general talent for dialogue, and his equally characteristic skill in expanding the novel's grasp of the apparently dull, daily lives of ordinary people. Green is especially adept throughout his career in showing arrays of emotions and tensions, affections and suspicions, within a group of such people 'caught' together in a situation of work or leisure. The routines and rituals through which they interact, negotiate and balance their relationships are a central concern of his fiction, successfully realised as early as his second novel, *Living* (1929). In it Green concentrates on a small group of ordinary workers, their everyday lives at home and in the factory, and the complex progress of their various relationships and aspirations. Walter Allen calls *Living* 'the best English novel of factory life':[31] it is certainly a much better novel than *Daylight on Saturday*.

Like *Caught*, *Living* is based partly on Green's own experience. Like George Orwell, his near-contemporary during public school days at Eton, Green felt guilty about his social status, and went as an ordinary worker to his father's factory in Birmingham. This move and his concentration on working-class life in *Living* led him to be initially included, rather misleadingly, among the writers of the 'thirties generation'. Though Green does anticipate some of their interests, his unusual narrative organisation and extraordinary language differ widely from the straightforwardness of thirties fiction, which *Living* surpasses in conviction and effectiveness. In particular, by frequently deleting pronouns, conjunctions and adjectives from the novel, Green creates a language partly representing the spoken idiom of its characters, sometimes approximating to the sort of Free Indirect Discourse employed by D.H. Lawrence and discussed in Chapter One. The jagged repetitions and occasional awkwardness of this language make it especially appropriate to the harsh conditions of factory life, enhancing the immediacy with which the workers are portrayed:

> Two o'clock. Thousands came back from dinner along streets...
> Thousands came back to factories they worked in from their dinners...
> Noise of lathes working began again in this factory. Hundreds went along road outside, men and girls. Some turned in to Dupret factory.
> Some had stayed in iron foundry shop in the factory for dinner. They sat round brazier in a circle.[32]

Green's unusual style has often been the subject of critical comment. G.S. Fraser, for example, discusses his 'extraordinary powers of narrative organisation through a prose which makes much use of asyndeton'.[33] As Fraser suggests, a form of asyndeton—the omission of conjunctions—is a feature not only of Green's prose, but of his narrative organisation in general. A distinctive oddity of his fiction, partly responsible for the 'kind of opacity' Fraser finds in it, is the absence of authorial indications of how different sections within novels relate to one another, or of how connections should be made between various potentially significant elements. Particularly in *Loving* (1945) and *Concluding* (1948), Green juxtaposes separate scenes in a way suggestive of mutual significance which nevertheless remains unstated. More generally, Green's fiction often seems pregnant with symbols and latent meanings without firm indication of how, or to whom, these symbols might be connected. In *Caught*, for example, the reader must work out how or whether Roe's family relations are comparable to those of his chief Pye; and how far the novel's many references to bright lights, colours, and fires should be connected with one another, or held to be symbolic at all. As Frederick R. Karl has remarked in his *Reader's Guide to the Contemporary English Novel* (1963), 'Green forces the reader into "making" the novel himself, by bringing together the various bits and *quanta* that the narrative throws out'. Green himself suggests that 'life is oblique in its impact upon people', adding that the novelist should 'communicate obliquely with his readers'.[34] The absence of direct, clearly-indicated connections between its various elements or 'quanta' helps his writing to communicate obliquely—perhaps opaquely—a feeling of some of the awkward and puzzling actuality of life itself, as if the more familiar processes of fictional organisation had scarcely been involved in shaping the vision presented. Though the wartime novel *Caught* perhaps raises most clearly the issue of how experience can be 'worked into the familiar patterns of art' or even of understanding, this question is directed at the reader throughout Green's fiction.

In 'forcing the reader' to make his own deductions in this way, Green partly resembles the modernists, who sometimes similarly require the reader to reconstruct events obliquely rendered in their narratives. They also share Green's interest in forging fresh fictional languages (see Chapters One and Five). His enigmatic style, however, really makes Green almost a unique figure in English literature. His talent for including inexplicable details in his novels, and for frustrating conventional expectations of pattern or meaning, makes his work more easily comparable to a recent development in French fiction, the *nouveau roman* (see Chapter Five). Significantly, one of its leading practitioners, Nathalie Sarraute, has recorded a particular admiration for Green's technique.[35]

Perhaps it is Green's puzzling, opaque quality which has been responsible for debarring him from general popularity. The difficulty of his fiction, however, is balanced by a consistent humour and an affirmation of living and loving which belong to a specifically English tradition. As Fraser suggests, Green's work sometimes presents 'a strange air of remote pastoral comedy'.[36] Some of the contrasts in *Concluding*, for example, particularly resemble the divisions between city and country in Shakespearean comedy. Green juxtaposes a rigidly organised state academy, recalling some of the atmosphere of Orwell's *Nineteen Eighty-Four*, alongside the more anarchic, natural world of an old scientist who lives in its grounds. While *Concluding* recalls Shakespearean comedy, the strange, almost magical vision of *Back* (1946) partly resembles Shakespearean romance. Though its hero Charley returns wounded from the war, he overcomes some of the pain of his recent experience, compensating for the death of his lover Rose by means of an affair with her half-sister Nancy. Physically similar to Rose, under the pressure of Charley's obsessive, wandering memory, Nancy comes to be almost wholly identified with her in a mysterious restoration of Charley's lost past which makes *Back* one of the least pessimistic of contemporary visions of the effects of war.

Innocence and Experience: Henry Green, Rosamond Lehmann, Elizabeth Bowen, L.P. Hartley, P.H. Newby

Green's earlier skill in 'coming to terms with the times' makes *Caught* not only a successful wartime novel in itself, as Rosamond Lehmann suggests, but, incidentally, an excellent paradigm for some general developments in fiction in the forties and early fifties which can be seen to result from the influence of the war. Roe's struggle for effective communication of his strange, unreal Blitz experience aptly exemplifies the sort of difficulties which encouraged some contemporary authors towards a directly documentary approach, while influencing others — Hanley, Green himself, and in some ways Alexander Baron — to seek specific techniques and unfamiliar patterns to encompass the unusual imaginative challenges of wartime action. *Caught*, however, also interestingly indicates a direction followed by other contemporary fiction which, depicting neither Blitz nor battle, can nevertheless be seen as strongly related to the war's impact. When Richard Roe has leave from his exhausting duties as a fireman, he goes to visit his young son and generally recover in a country house outside London. On some of these visits, he finds its 'wild garden...reminded him of so many small events he had forgotten out of his youth'. (p.178). Roe's occasional retreat into a country garden, and into memories of his youth, is of a sort which apparently appealed strongly to several contemporary authors, and which was clearly encouraged by the war. John Lehmann, editor of *Penguin New Writing*, remarked in 1941, for example:

> War makes us uneasy; and when among the vast possibilities of our lives we find ourselves confined to stratagems of killing and avoiding being killed, we feel instinctively how important it is to be able to keep our delight in the world of childhood and nature.

His sentiments were echoed in 1946 by his sister Rosamond Lehmann:

> For the present most novelists are likely to turn back to the time when, the place where they knew where they were — where their imaginations can expand and construct among remembered scenes and established symbols, just as they mostly did during the period [of the war]. They will look to their youth...or they will invent allegories and fantasies.

P.H. Newby similarly explained the urge to write about childhood — also apparent in contemporary poetry — remarking in 1951

> ...for most people who were beginning to write at this time experience could be divided into two halves: childhood and adolescence on the one hand and war on the other. Unless one wandered off into fantasy or allegory these were the inescapable themes and of the two childhood probably proved the more attractive.[37]

As discussed in Chapter Two, George Bowling's escape to the scene of his youth in Lower Binfield, first in memory and later in fact, gives evidence of the attractiveness of remembered childhood as an alternative to threatening present circumstances even on the eve of the Second World War, in Orwell's *Coming up for Air* (1939). The strength of this sort of attraction during the war itself is confirmed in a minor novel of desert warfare, *The Desolate Market* (1948) by John

Cousins. When Cousins's hero goes missing in combat, it is discovered that in spare moments during his active service he has been writing a novel, an autobiographical account of his innocent early childhood. Though *The Desolate Market* is now largely forgotten, it is a significant indication of the way the stresses of wartime experience encouraged appreciation for the uncomplicated life of early youth, and fostered an inclination to seek in memory relief from the unpleasantness of actuality. Some further evidence of this tendency appears in *From the City, from the Plough*. When the soldiers engage in literary discussions, it is the early chapters of Dickens's *David Copperfield* (1850), portraying the hero's innocent boyhood, which meet with most approval. Treatments of the same sort of theme in contemporary novels were equally well received. *Young Tom*, for example, Forrest Reid's idyllic, rather idealised story of rural childhood, though it seems a slight work nowadays, nevertheless won the James Tait Black prize for the best novel of 1944.

A novel published in that year which seems to have survived better than *Young Tom* is Rosamond Lehmann's *The Ballad and the Source*, which, as she remarks, also 'sprang...from childhood memories'.[38] Its narrator Rebecca Landon, who reappears in Lehmann's later novel *A Sea-Grape Tree* (1976), is ten when she begins to learn a story she is barely equipped to understand at that age. It concerns Sybil Jardine's abandonment of her husband and daughter Ianthe in favour of a lover, and the disturbing emotional consequences for three generations of her family which arise from this action. These include Sybil's attempts to recover Ianthe, and her subsequent struggle to sustain her influence over her grandchildren. Rebecca's account of these complicated, miserable affairs is pieced together from the testimonies of three of the figures deeply involved: Mrs Jardine herself; the servant Tilly; and eventually Sybil's granddaughter Maisie, who summarises the uneasy emotional state of the family as it has developed by the beginning of the First World War. Thus equipped with at least four narrators, who admit their unreliability and preparedness to fabricate events they did not witness, *The Ballad and the Source* exhibits a 'technical excellence of...construction' which one contemporary critic particularly praised.[39]

The same reviewer, however, added that despite its sustained ingenuity, the novel was 'without real emotional significance', and it may be that the technique of *The Ballad and the Source* is less well integrated with its material than is the case in Lehmann's earlier *The Weather in the Streets* (1936; see Chapter Two). In particular, although it is made clear that Rebecca records her encounter with Mrs Jardine and her story at a much later period in her life, fairly little use is made of the resulting disparity in perspective between adult and child—between the grown-up Rebecca who records the story and the girl who first heard and pondered it at age ten. A potentially interesting ironic dimension is missing from the novel as a result. On the other hand, through the straightforward, generally uncritical recording of the experience of the child, Lehmann avoids imposing any final, controlling judgements on the material presented, making compellingly immediate the original moral dilemma of Rebecca herself. Like Rebecca, the reader must arbitrate between conflicting versions of the story, and assess the ambivalent figure of Sybil Jardine, sinned against as well as sinning. Some 'real emotional significance' does derive from the directness of this participation in Rebecca's difficult encounter with apparently endless threats to love and even sanity, passed on from generation to generation from an original corruption of emotion. As Rebecca sadly concludes,

> This same paternal threat...this thing went on and on, like a curse. Liar begot liar; and all their road, forward and back, far back, was cratered with disastrous pits of guilt, haunted by ruinous voices crying vengeance.[40]

This sense of an inherited curse also appears in another novel concerned with childhood, *The House in Paris* (1935), by Elizabeth Bowen, whom Lehmann admired. The best of Bowen's early novels, and her own favourite, *The House in Paris* resembles *The Ballad and the Source* in several respects. It presents the encounter of two children with what Lehmann calls in her novel 'a whole range of complex personal emotions, far ahead of their present capacity, alien to their experience'. (p.34). The first section of *The House in Paris* shows Henrietta and Leopold, aged eleven and nine, waiting in Naomi Fisher's Paris house for a visit from Leopold's mother, whom he has scarcely ever seen before. The second section shows why: Leopold is the unexpected result of an affair which took place between Naomi's fiancé Max and Karen Michaelis, ending in Max's suicide and Karen's expedient marriage. The novel's final part returns to the children in the house in Paris and shows the bewildering consequences for Leopold of his mother's eventual failure to visit him. Like *The Ballad and the Source*, *The House in Paris* examines the intrusion of the debilitating effects of the past, with its guilty entanglements, upon the innocence of a subsequent generation of children: the effect of this intrusion is adroitly emphasised by Bowen's insertion of a section of past experience into the middle of the novel's development of a day in the present. This tripartite division into sections entitled 'The Present', 'The Past', 'The Present', also rather resembles the structure of Virginia Woolf's *To the Lighthouse*. Both Bowen and Lehmann admired Woolf, whose influence further appears in *The House in Paris* in Bowen's extensive interior monologues, carefully dramatising 'the you inside you...reflections...memories'. This creates for her characters some of the 'intense inner existence' whose presence in Virginia Woolf's fiction Bowen saw as a particular strength.[41]

Techniques Bowen may have learned from Virginia Woolf are amalgamated in her next novel, *The Death of the Heart* (1938), with some which originate in the work of earlier authors. Like Jane Austen, Bowen concentrates upon the complicated interaction of motives, explicit and suppressed, which animate the relationships of a small, self-contained, group of refined people. Her development of this material partly through the point of view of a young girl, Portia—the novel even occasionally presents her diaries—strongly recalls the work of another author whom Bowen admired, Henry James, and especially *What Maisie Knew* (1897). Though the actual extent of Maisie's knowledge is one of the questions James's novel ingeniously raises, she is at least comparatively innocent, and her morals and motives are employed to illumine ironically those of the adults around her. Bowen's use of Portia works to similar effect. Like James's Maisie or Jane Austen's Fanny in *Mansfield Park* (1814), Portia is forced to establish for herself a place in the world—like Leopold in *The House in Paris*, she is an illegitimate child. The novel's brilliant opening scene in a frozen park anticipates the chilliness of the domain she finds: her quest for affection remains unsatisfied by her half-brother and his wife, who become her guardians. Portia's presence in their house in London, under the shade of the impending Second World War, reveals only the complicated web of suppressed emotion which exists there, the 'private obsession...each person at Windsor Terrace lived impaled upon'.[42] The novel concludes with Portia's demand—as exigent as some of Maisie's—that her guardians 'do the right thing' (p.304). This seems almost impossible in a complex, glacial world in which Portia's warm ingenuousness seems permanently out of place.

Something of the same theme reappears in Bowen's next novel, *The Heat of the Day* (1949). The existence of warm and innocent feelings is made if anything even less promising by the vicissitudes of wartime London in which the story is set. As in *The House in Paris*, Bowen also shows her characters growing increasingly aware of the betraying effect of the past on the present. Her heroine Stella Rodney's current feelings and happy memories of an affair with Robert Kelway are darkened by the revelation that he has really been acting as a German secret agent. This dramatic plot of espionage and betrayal seems to belong more to the work of Graham Greene than to Virginia Woolf, whose influence nevertheless continues to be apparent in the meticulousness with which Stella's inner life is envisaged. This sort of tension between plot and vision is part of a difficulty more widely evident in Bowen's fiction—the incongruous inclusion of violent or rather melodramatic developments in novels otherwise scrupulously concerned with the finer subtleties of mind and motive. The suicides of Robert in *The Heat of the Day* and Max in *The House in Paris*, for example, seem extravagant, part of an inconsistent, implausible feeling which particularly affects some of Bowen's male characters. Max, Robert and several others seem victims of Bowen's belief that sometimes in fiction 'characters are called into existence by the demands of the plot'.[43]

Despite such shortcomings, however, *The Heat of the Day* offers a moving and accurate portrayal of London life during the Blitz. P.H. Newby suggests in *The Novel 1945-1950* that 'no novel...was influenced so much by the fact of war as *The Heat of the Day*' (p.19), and Anthony Burgess comments 'No novel has better caught the atmosphere of London during the Second World War'.[44] The unreal, fantastic effects of the Blitz are vividly conveyed in the novel through Stella's carefully-detailed experience and memories: her recollection, for example, of

...that heady autumn of the first London air raids...the sense of death...mists of morning charred by the smoke from ruins... phantasmagoric...apocryphal...tideless, hypnotic, futureless.[45]

These recollections of the Blitz, especially in Chapter Five, show Bowen's talent for creating scenes of unusual colour and dramatic intensity. This appears intermittently throughout her writing—at the start of *The Death of the Heart*, for example, or in Max and Karen's meeting in Boulogne in *The House in Paris*. Bowen's best work, however, is probably in this earlier fiction, before *The Heat of the Day*: even P.H. Newby tempers his admiration by suggesting that although 'Elizabeth Bowen "absorbed" the war to greater effect than any of her contemporaries with established reputations...even so I cannot feel that *The Heat of the Day* is as complete a success as some of her earlier novels'.[46]

Like Bowen and many others around the time of the war, L.P. Hartley concentrates on the theme of childhood and benefits from the example of Henry James, especially *What Maisie Knew*. Hartley's *Eustace and Hilda* trilogy was his first fiction for almost twenty years. In style, structure and length it also looks back beyond James to the *bildungsroman* favoured by the Victorians. In this case, however, the novelist's attention is focused not quite so exclusively upon the development of the central figure, Eustace, but upon intense, mutually destructive relations between him and his sister Hilda. The trilogy opens with a fatal encounter of a shrimp and an anemone in a rock pool, witnessed by Eustace and Hilda as children: this scene provides a sustained comparison for the progress of their relationship. Its development is traced from the inescapably formative years of Edwardian childhood shown in *The Shrimp and the Anemone* (1944); through Eustace's days at Oxford after the First World War in *The Sixth Heaven* (1946); concluding with his happy experience of Venice between the wars, and his early death at the end of *Eustace and Hilda* (1947). This untimely death appears more tragic because it is the consequence not of any malice but of good intentions frustrated and misdirected. The profound mutual influence of brother and sister is largely innocent of explicit ill-will. Although Hilda is manipulative, she always believes she acts for her brother's benefit. Eustace, whose self-sacrificial death continues Christian overtones present throughout, is himself almost obsessively concerned with doing and being good: 'he had one aim, to increase the volume of good surrounding Eustace Cherrington and radiating from him all over the whole world'.[47]

Despite the naïveté and even selfishness of such views, Eustace remains a more sympathetic and perhaps more persuasive portrayal of a genuinely good man than Evelyn Waugh's Guy Crouchback. However, though Eustace's circumstances are generally much less threatening than Guy's, he is in the end equally rebuffed by them. Suffering from a shrimp-like weakness of body and will, and faced with the intransigence of a world which will not fulfil his innocent expectations, Eustace increasingly takes refuge in an imaginative faculty whose creations he finds 'more real to him than any actual experience' (p.111). He produces a whole idyllic novel—modelled on Henry James, he claims—as a consolatory alternative version of his sister's unhappy love affair. The imaginative strength which makes Eustace a novelist also encourages him to project around the core of actual events in his life daydreams and fantasies which often express anxiety about his conduct in society. The presentation of these hypothetical, imaginary versions of Eustace's experience creates a sort of fiction-within-the-fiction in a manner Hartley occasionally experimented with later in his career. It also offers extensive, often amusing insight into the operation of Eustace's mind: his 'interior dialogue...with himself' (p.693), as it is called, is in some ways quite an effective substitute for the interior monologue or stream-of-consciousness techniques of the modernists.

Eustace might have been speaking for his author, however, when he remarks in *The Sixth Heaven* 'Compression isn't my strong point' (p.240). *Eustace and Hilda* is very long, and sometimes seems too long. Hartley's best novel, *The Go-Between* (1953), benefits from the concision and control imparted to its material by a device Henry James approved: the use of 'an intervening first person singular'.[48] This narrator, Leo Colston, at the age of 'sixty-odd' reassembles events which took place more than half a century previously. Partly nostalgic and partly critical in looking back at his earlier self, his recollections provide a firmly-characterised perspective for the novel: they also establish a dimension of irony noticeably absent from Rosamond Lehmann's *The Ballad and the Source*.

Leo's memories concentrate upon the formative childhood

experiences which have incapacitated him, like Eustace, for sexual and emotional relations in later life. Preferring like Eustace 'the world of the imagination' to 'the world of experience', Leo invests his ideals and fantasies as a child in the figures he meets on a visit to Brandham Hall in 1900.[49] He considers them 'the substance of my dreams, the realisation of my hopes...actors in my drama... immortals, inheritors of the summer and of the coming glory of the twentieth century' (pp.19, 264). A principal 'actor' for Leo is Marian, the elegant young lady of the Hall. She is involved with a local farmer, Ted, in a clandestine affair which rather resembles the relationship of Lady Constance and the gamekeeper Mellors in D.H. Lawrence's *Lady Chatterley's Lover* (1928). The progress of Marian's affair depends on her use of Leo as a messenger: largely unaware of the nature and implications of the developments he assists, his sense of 'drama' and 'glory' is permanently, shockingly eradicated by his eventual discovery of Marian and Ted making love.

Though extreme, Leo's disillusionment is in some ways typical of the fate of the many children who appear in fiction around the time of the war. Sometimes, their disappointing encounter with the disturbing complexities of adult life is partly accidental, like Leo's. Occasionally, it is a result of inherited circumstances which confront them throughout their childhood, as in *The Death of the Heart* and *The Ballad and the Source*. In either case, it contributes to a 'harrowing impression of the contrast between experience and innocence'[50] which Henry Reed recognised in the work of Elizabeth Bowen, but which is really much more widespread in contemporary fiction. Even novels which seem to portray an ideal childhood are often concerned not solely with innocence but with its loss. Forrest Reid's *Young Tom*, for example, which seems to offer simply an idyllic escape from the stress of wartime life, actually shows the friction of innocence against the 'prosaic world' of adults which increasingly imposes itself on Young Tom's ardent imagination.[51] John Cousins's *The Desolate Market* likewise shows the child in the airman's novel discovering that in innocently 'protecting his intention and his love from the world outside' he has in the view of adults simply committed a theft and a lie.[52] Even Richard Roe's visits to his son in the country in *Caught* are not a real escape from the war. Instead, they are a reminder of the dangerous instability of his superior officer, Pye, who can neither forget that his sister once abducted Roe's son, nor keep this episode separate in his mind from doubtful recollections of an earlier sexual adventure of his own.

The nature of such contemporary portrayals of childhood helps to explain their proliferation. They appear not so much as an alternative to facing the shock of the war, but as a means of finding a context within individual experience in which to examine and come to terms with its challenge to imagination and understanding. Henry

Green remarks at the start of his autobiography *Pack my Bag* (1940) 'the war...is a reason to put down...what comes first to mind and that must be how one changed from boy to man'.[53] P.H. Newby similarly suggests that novelists during and after the war were confronted by an experience divided 'into two halves: childhood and adolescence on the one hand, and on the other...war', but it is rather misleading of him to suggest that the former simply proved 'more attractive'. Novelists generally did not retreat into childhood *instead* of dealing with the war. Rather they examine childhood innocence, jointly with its disillusioning loss, as contexts which reduplicate the coexistence in the imagination of the disparate 'halves' Newby mentions—memories of peace anomalously juxtaposed with actual experience of the war. 'The incarnated glory of the twentieth century' (p.19) in Leo's optimistic vision of 1900 could hardly have been more sharply divided from the actual experience of 'Destruction, civilisation in ruins, man's moral degradation and spiritual poverty'[54] which Newby found the legacy of the years between 1939 and 1945. Perhaps only in the contrast between childhood innocence and disillusioned adult experience could some analogy be found to help the novel encompass within the lives of individual characters the wider disasters in the progress of the twentieth century, which so insistently challenged authors at the time.

Several novels of the period make explicit their employment of this sort of connection between private and historical experience. *The Go-Between*, for example, concludes with Leo returning to Brandham after the numb, emotionless half-century which has succeeded his disillusionment. He discovers the fate of subsequent generations in the family whose expectations Marian so betrayed in the bright summer of 1900: some have been killed in the First World War, some in the Second. One lives on embittered in the present. This prospect of waste, death and emotional atrophy, the 'death of the heart' which results from the history of the twentieth century, underlies Leo's view of its development as analogous to his own. He wonders

> Has the twentieth century...done so much better than I have?...Ask yourself whether it has fulfilled your hopes. You were vanquished, Colston, you were vanquished, and so was your century, your precious century that you hoped so much of' (p.20).

The Heat of the Day similarly indicates the reflection in individual life of the broader disturbances of contemporary history. Stella Rodney feels of her experiences of the Second World War that

> The fateful course of her fatalistic century seemed more and more her own: together had she and it arrived at the testing extremities. (p.134)

Likewise, in *The Ballad and the Source*, when Maisie reflects on the final chaos of Ianthe's madness, Mrs Jardine's malign influence, and its consequences for the family, she remarks

> Talk of midsummer madness!...When I think about it now I feel as if the
> war started then—all roaring armies marching against one another and
> land mines bursting under everybody. When the real war started and
> every one else was in a state of chaos, it seemed to me a mere rumble on
> the horizon. (pp.257-8)

This tendency to envisage 'the real war' encompassed in the
conflicts and disillusionment of individual lives also appears in the
early fiction of P.H. Newby. He clarifies the congruence of his
interests with those of some of his contemporaries when he remarks
in *The Novel 1945-1950*

> ...the collision of innocence and experience...no matter how much we
> may pretend otherwise...is a collision most of us never cease to be
> involved in, though with diminishing violence, for the whole length of our
> lives. (p.9)

This theme is part of a strong moral concern which regularly
appears in Newby's many novels. It is perhaps most clearly present,
and most obviously connected with contemporary events, in *A Step
to Silence* (1952) and *The Retreat* (1953), which follow the fate of
Newby's hero Oliver Knight before and during the Second World
War. *A Step to Silence*, as its title partly suggests, is set immediately
before the outbreak of war, in a 'world...haunted because of the
ever-present possibility of violence...the worst of eventualities...
ruin, death of the young'.[55] Oliver is not a child at the time, but an
eighteen-year old entering college. His naïveté, however, is
emphasised by his feeling like 'a child in a world where adults kept
all the secrets' (p.199)—at least until his college experience and the
attempted suicide of his friend Hesketh demonstrate to him the
incompetence of innocence in a violent, dangerous world. Like his
contemporaries, Newby strongly connects this individual loss of
innocence with political and historical developments at the time.
Oliver recognises in Neville Chamberlain's optimistic belief in peace
a disturbingly exact image of the naïveté which had impeded his own
understanding of the world:

> ...having read the various speeches by the head of the British government
> since the Nazi occupation of Austria, Oliver felt he understood the man
> better than many of the people he actually knew; he understood and felt
> guilty as a result. Like himself before Hesketh's attempt at suicide,
> Mr. Chamberlain appeared to take his own character and disposition as a
> piece of information about human affairs in general...He grieved over
> him as he grieved over his own past blindness...no one, not even those in
> the highest authority, was immune to innocence. (p.193)

A Step to Silence typifies the contemporary tendency to connect the
'collision' of innocence with experience in private life and in current
historical developments. *The Retreat* is equally representative of the

related disposition to reconsider youth and earlier times in an attempt to understand how bewildering present circumstances could have come into being. Surviving the withdrawal from Dunkirk despite being bombed at sea, Oliver retreats still farther from the war, abandoning his duties as an RAF officer and returning with Hesketh's wife Jane to the Worcestershire countryside of his boyhood:

> Jane and Knight were a man and a woman with a history of feeling for each other safely behind them...They were returning to a landscape which they had once shared...the train carried Jane and Knight into the years before the war; they stood on the long, curving platform of Shrub Hill, momentarily recovered from the dream of catastrophe.[56]

Their journey into a landscape which was the setting for youthful innocence in *A Step to Silence* can be seen as partly an attempt, like Charley's in Henry Green's *Back*, to recover the earlier happiness of 'the years before the war'—to heal the 'wound' between the past and the present which Oliver finds the war's 'dream of catastrophe' has made (pp.218-19). Like Charley's, however, Oliver's motives are never wholly clear, even to himself. His flight across England with Jane, away from her husband and his own wife Helen, seems inexplicable to their relatives and at times to the reader.

The oddity of their behaviour, the disturbance of mind which underlies it, and the violent wartime events responsible for this instability, are all communicated with great conviction by Newby's unusual style. William Sansom's anxiety that the war provided material 'too violent for the arts to transcribe', was based on the view that 'The results of violence and its reflections may be written down—but never the core of the violent act itself. In the first place, language fails'. Newby apparently circumvents the problem Sansom indicates by almost allowing his language to fail at moments of violent action. The bombing of Oliver's ship off Dieppe, for example, cannot be easily followed in Newby's partially-realised, chaotic account of it. This forcefully communicates Oliver's bewildered feeling, at the time, of being

> ...detached from the world of matter. He had lost contact. There was neither hard nor soft, and there was no sound of any kind. He opened his eyes and looked up at the golden surface of the sea. Bubbles sped from his mouth and he thought that if he could but follow they would take him to Helen. (p.34)

Similar feelings of 'lost contact' frequently reappear in Newby's fiction. Most novels give the impression of being accounts of events assembled some time after their occurrence, after due authorial judgement and reflection. Newby, on the other hand, seems to present the crises which impinge on his characters as if at the moment of their perception, before there is time for reflection or assessment. The reader is thus made to share with unusual immediacy characters' difficult, sometimes unsuccessful attempts to order and make sense of their experience; even just to work out what is really going on. Oliver, for example, finds in *The Retreat* that 'a strange pattern was being presented, but no matter how quickly his eye moved the pattern never fell within his field of vision' (p.60). Likewise, in *A Step to Silence*, he feels that 'this bewilderment blew itself up into a state of mind familiar to him, that the happenings of the moment were illusion and that even his own identity was in doubt' (pp.136-7). Sharing Oliver's uncertainty and for the most part his subjective 'field of vision', the reader is often confused by the difficulty of verifying whether the 'happenings of the moment' Oliver experiences are illusory or real. In *The Retreat*, for example, there is a strong, though eventually misleading suggestion that a dead airman 'seen' by Oliver may in fact have been a hallucination.

This unsettling quality is more noticeable in *The Retreat*, where the unstable minds of the characters are more prone to uncertainty and illusion, than it is in *A Step to Silence*. It is ingeniously appropriate to Newby's presentation of people overwhelmed by the anarchy of a world unhinged by war. By refracting the turbulence of this world through the immediate perceptions of the disturbed minds which encounter it, *The Retreat* partly answers Newby's own doubts about 'whether so overwhelming and universal a catastrophe as the late war can be reckoned the sort of experience out of which an artist can create'. Like Hanley, Green, and others, Newby sustains the challenge to the imagination of wartime experience by establishing a technique specifically adapted to encompass it. This technique may have some affinity with the 'hectic impressionism' of James Hanley, and Newby's fluent incorporation into fairly short novels of serious moral issues also makes him comparable to William Golding. There is perhaps more justice, however, in Walter Allen's comparison of Newby to Henry Green, also adept at presenting 'strange patterns' which mysteriously seem just to elude the reader's 'field of vision'. Newby's creation of uncertainty about the true or illusory quality of the experience presented, and of doubts about the possible deceptiveness of his narrative, also make his work, like Henry Green's, comparable to the French 'new novel', the *nouveau roman*. The unusualness of his early fiction opened up potentialities for renewal in the English novel which have not been generally exploited since, except of course by Newby himself. *Something to Answer For* (1968), for example, reflects the chaos of another conflict, this time the Suez crisis of 1956, in the mind of a man unable to recover his mental equilibrium following an injury shortly after his arrival in Egypt. Once again, like this character, the reader is challenged by the task of differentiating reality and hallucination in a setting whose political crisis and dream-like disintegration make the two domains all the more difficult to distinguish.

Good and Evil: Graham Greene, Somerset Maugham, Joyce Cary, Philip Toynbee, C.S. Lewis

In Newby's *A Step to Silence*, after they have seen a film simulating the expected bombing raids of the Second World War, Jane tries to shake Oliver Knight out of his innocence, insisting 'You've got to know there is a real something called Evil if you want to understand the world you're living in'. Partially persuaded, Oliver remains confused by 'the imminence of war, the immanence of God, the reality of evil' (pp.80-81). The understanding of the world shown by several contemporary novelists includes assessments of the nature of good and evil and of the 'immanence of God', perhaps encouraged, like Oliver's, by the imminence or actuality of the war. Good and evil might have been considered further extensions of the 'halves' of peace and violence, innocence and experience, which Newby envisaged as the result of the war's impact on contemporary life. At any rate, the circumstances of the war particularly furthered belief and interest in the existence of 'a real something called Evil'. Britain's struggle against fascism and Nazi Germany was very frequently seen at the time, and with some conviction, as a struggle against evil and the powers of darkness. Stephen Spender, for example, remarks in *Penguin New Writing* in 1941 that 'the angels and the demons of an earlier time, have simply been suppressed in our consciousnesses, that is all'; and he adds emphatically that fascism is 'a deliberately chosen life of damnation...macabre diabolism'. Cyril Connolly, writing around the same time, suggests that Nazism was simply an 'opposite' to 'goodness and sanity'.[57] His views are exactly echoed in Guy Crouchback's summary in Waugh's *Sword of Honour*: 'the German Nazis he knew to be mad and bad' (p.11). Some of this sense of conflict between madness and sanity, good and evil, appears in Guy's own story in *Sword of Honour*—it perhaps also contributes to L.P. Hartley's view of the frustration of good intentions in a recalcitrant world in *Eustace and Hilda*.

Waugh's religious concerns were perhaps brought to the foreground by the war, appearing explicitly for the first time in his fiction in *Brideshead Revisited* (1945). The most obvious example of a contemporary author concerned with 'the immanence of God' and 'the reality of evil', however, is Waugh's fellow-Catholic Graham Greene. Such religious interests begin to appear in Greene's fiction before the war, in *Brighton Rock* (1938), but are consolidated in three novels published during or shortly after it—*The Power and the Glory* (1940); *The Heart of the Matter* (1948); and *The End of the Affair* (1951). These are often considered Greene's best work. In some ways, they are quite clearly distinguished from his earlier fiction, in

93

which drab urban settings and the political or social interests of the nineteen thirties usually predominate (see Chapter Two). Though Greene set a wartime spy story, *The Ministry of Fear* (1943) in the London of the Blitz, as his interests move increasingly into the 'region of the mind' which he saw as the domain of his Catholic faith, his novels often abandon the familiar English background of his thirties fiction in favour of distant foreign settings. *The Power and the Glory*, for example, reflects the religious persecution Greene encountered on his visit to Mexico in 1938, and *The Heart of the Matter* is set in a West African context made familiar to him by his posting there during the war. Greene's later novels often continue to be set in distant, disturbed foreign locations of this sort. His urge to escape the boredom which he claims has threatened him since his youth has often led him to visit such places at times just before or after—or sometimes during—their appearance in the world's news, later using the experience in his fiction. Thus *The Quiet American* (1955) anticipates American involvement in Vietnam; *Our Man in Havana*, an 'entertainment' set in Cuba and published in 1958, anticipates the Cuban Missile Crisis of 1962; and *The Honorary Consul* (1973) describes the activity of South American terrorists.

Greene's choice of such settings on the edge of political instability is in accordance with his statement that

> ...if I were to choose an epigraph for all the novels I have written, it would be from *Bishop Blougram's Apology*:
> 'Our interest's on the dangerous edge of things.
> The honest thief, the tender murderer,
> The superstitious atheist...'[58]

The 'dangerous edge of things' in politically turbulent parts of the world often provides an ideal context for moral dilemmas experienced by Greene's characters, both heightening and reflecting their restlessness and tension. Along with the interest expressed in the sort of contradictory figures mentioned in his epigraph, however, his choice of such apparently exotic locations may seem to invite the criticism the Catholic church made of *The Power and the Glory*, which the Vatican considered was 'paradoxical' and 'dealt with extraordinary circumstances'.[59] In fact, the most extraordinary aspect of Greene's settings is not their exoticism so much as its absence. The dreary, dispirited 'Greeneland' discussed in Chapter Two as the background of his early novels seems to continue as a homogeneous context throughout his fiction: the grim London of *It's a Battlefield* (1934) is surprisingly similar to the shabby South America of *The Honorary Consul*. Any specific sense of locale is partly subordinate to the weary feeling of waste and human failure which provides the distinctive background of all Greene's fiction—its pervasive sense of belonging in 'a dying, cooling world, of human beings who had evolved from animals for no purpose at all', as the Lieutenant envisages it in *The Power and the Glory*.[60]

This largely unvarying context of Greene's fiction is related to its religious sense. The fallen, graceless, domains in which his actions unfold are partly a reminder of how far the human sphere falls short of the divine; how far the actual world betrays the ideal. Human nature often appears similarly flawed and fallible. From *The Man Within* (1929) to *The Human Factor* (1978) Greene has repeatedly turned to the theme of betrayal, perhaps because on a human scale it re-enacts the inevitable failure of men to keep faith with their ideals, or their God. Yet Greene's depressive view of human fallibility and evil is simultaneously conditioned by the sort of faith shown by the Priest in *The Power and the Glory* in 'the convincing mystery—that we were made in God's image' (p.101). Greene apprehends with particular intensity the sordidness and corruption of the human domain. That it should be the work, even the image, of God is a 'mystery' underlying a distinctively 'paradoxical' strain which is a feature not only, as the Vatican suggested, of *The Power and the Glory*, but of Greene's fiction as a whole. Good and evil, virtue and vice, honesty and corruption, are frequently envisaged in his novels as existing simultaneously, even interconnectedly, despite their obvious antitheses. Greene's general interest in 'the honest thief, the tender murderer', for example, is specifically realised in a range of characters possessed of interdependent yet contradictory qualities. In *The End of the Affair* Bendrix records that 'hatred seems to operate the same glands as love: it even produces the same actions'.[61] The Lieutenant in *The Power and the Glory* is described as 'a little dapper figure of hate carrying his secret of love' (p.58). Elsewhere in the novel it is suggested that 'the word "life" was taboo: it reminded you of death' and that 'pain is a part of pleasure' (pp.38, 69). Perhaps *Brighton Rock* shows most clearly Greene's interconnection of moral opposites, suggesting

> Good or evil lived in the same country, spoke the same language, came together like old friends, feeling the same completion, touching hands.[62]

This paradoxical quality in Greene's writing may be retraceable to a childhood which he has indicated as an important influence on his work; in particular, to his awkward position as a pupil in a school where his father was headmaster. Greene records of the proximity of home and school:

> One was an inhabitant of both countries: on Saturday and Sunday afternoons of one side of the baize door, the rest of the week on the other. How can life on a border be other than restless? You are pulled by different ties of hate and love. For hate is quite as powerful a tie: it demands allegiance.[63]

An even earlier experience may also have helped initiate an inclination to paradox. Greene records in his autobiography *A Sort of Life* that 'the first thing I remember is sitting in a pram at the top of a hill with a dead dog lying at my feet' (p.13)—a memory which incidentally provides a perfect image of the sort of collision of childhood innocence with a world of experience and death which so often appears in the writing of the forties. The paradoxical doubleness of 'allegiance' in Greene's own fiction at this time, its interconnection of innocence and corruption, ideal and actual, may also account for the incorporation in his novels of contrasting, often more virtuous versions of their actual events. The appearance of this tactic in *The Confidential Agent* (1939) was discussed in Chapter Two: it is also a feature of *The Power and the Glory*. Greene shows his shabby whisky-priest first counterpointed and perhaps eventually synthesised in a child's imagination with a romantic story, read to him by his mother from a Catholic tract, about a priest who is more obviously recognisable as a hero and a martyr. This sort of counterpoint between conflicting versions of the same story appears most directly and extensively as an issue in *The End of the Affair*, largely the first person, supposedly autobiographical, narrative of Maurice Bendrix. He is a novelist who is afraid that any human story he tries to tell may be an inadequate version of a larger pattern; any narrative organisation of his own merely a distortion of a history already shaped and plotted by divine will.

As well as exemplifying in this way Greene's technique of narrative counterpoint, *The End of the Affair* illustrates some of the trends in fiction around the time of the war. It also provides a good example for the discussion of Greene's religious concerns, which some of his critics have found more strongly and less acceptably present in this novel than in any of his others. His last use of an English setting until *The Human Factor*, *The End of the Affair* spans the London years of the war and its drab aftermath. Bendrix's affair with Sarah Miles begins in 'one of those bright condemned pre-war summers' (p.25), and is brought to an apparent end as a result of events in the Blitz, later recollected after the war. As Greene suggests, *The End of the Affair* is 'ingeniously constructed to avoid...the time sequence'[64]: Bendrix organises his story partly in accord with his feeling that 'If I could have turned back time I think I would have done so' (p.66). Each chapter in the novel's first section opens with an account of Bendrix's life in the post-war period, then resumes part of the ended affair through his memory's association of it with present events. Like Elizabeth Bowen's retrospective method in *The Heat of the Day*, this 'ingenious construction' includes even in the presentation of the affair itself a sense of the inevitability—the fact—of its end. Like many other contemporary novels, *The End of the Affair* looks back from disturbed times to earlier happiness which the war has helped to destroy, juxtaposing this former happiness with present loss and death. Bendrix's nostalgic wish to turn back time is perhaps especially comparable to some of the feelings of *The Retreat* and *The Go-Between*, as well as *The Heat of the Day*.

The 'ingenious construction' of Greene's time sequence is complemented by a similar dexterity with the novel's point of view. This changes completely in the third section, which consists of Sarah's diaries, passed on to Bendrix by a private detective he has hired to investigate her. From these, Bendrix learns—along with the reader—that his account of events presented in the first two sections of the novel wholly misconstrues Sarah's behaviour. His version of the end of the affair in these sections has inadvertently shown almost the same talent for fictionalising as he applies to his novels. Sarah's actions have resulted not from weariness with Bendrix or a real desire to end their affair, but from a continuing love for him, though one increasingly complicated by her growing love of God. Greene's juxtaposition of her diary alongside Bendrix's narrative, each full of affection but radically divergent from the other in subjective construction of events, movingly dramatises the same sort of inevitability that ends affairs in *The Heat of the Day*. Desire for another person seems inevitably doomed by his or her habitation of a separate, subjective world. This is at most only partly accessible from the outside, though sometimes, in the bitter irony of *The End of the Affair*, it is as near as a turn of the head.

Greene records that the lessons he learned in the use of first-person narrative later proved helpful in writing *The Quiet American*, but the sort of ingenuity in chronology and perspective which helps to make *The End of the Affair* such a moving novel does not reappear in his later fiction. This generally shows a straightforwardness in construction which is an adjunct of his direct, vivid verbal style. Greene records that the structural complexity of *The End of the Affair* was partly the result of 'continual rereadings of that remarkable novel *The Good Soldier* by Ford Madox Ford', and he recalls with pleasure in *Ways of Escape* that *The End of the Affair* was particularly admired by the American modernist William Faulkner.[65] Other commentators, however, have been less generous than Faulkner in their admiration, and less interested in the novel's inheritance of an excellence of construction from the modernists. Instead, they have concentrated on its religious aspect, suggesting that it is responsible for a sense of contrivance which is apparent both in Sarah's strange promise to give herself to God if He will return Bendrix alive from beneath the debris of a bomb explosion, and in the miraculous cures which are mentioned in the novel's last section.

Neither feature need really be seen as a failure. Sarah's enactment of her promise is not unduly implausible, but largely in keeping with her character, and specifically her admission that

> I have always wanted to be liked or admired... God loves you, they say in the churches, God is everything. People who believe that don't need

admiration, they don't need to sleep with a man (p.91).

.Sarah's growing faith in the love and attention of God makes earthly admiration and contact with Bendrix superfluous for her. For Bendrix himself, the apparently inexplicable, perhaps miraculous consequences of Sarah's death are the most appropriate demonstration of the inadequacy of his secular apparatus for understanding experience. They provide final evidence that the 'story' he finds unfolding around him cannot be assimilated 'according to the rules of [his] craft' (p.7) as a novelist, and that it may have been prearranged by a more powerful 'author', the creator of the universe. In this way, though the miracles are implausible, outwith normal experience, it is exactly this quality which makes them contribute interestingly to Bendrix's dilemma, and especially his difficulties as a storyteller. Greene's inclusion of Bendrix's uneasy discussions of his 'craft' suggests that rather than simply suffering from a problematic incorporation of religion in its fiction, *The End of the Affair* is itself in some ways an attempt to come to terms with this sort of problem; an examination of the difficulties of incorporating religious belief in the secular, artificial form of the novel.

Bendrix is deeply committed in imagination and emotion, as a writer, to the earthly world of human experience, yet he is also increasingly, uneasily aware of a divine dimension beyond it. In this way, he is a 'superstitious atheist' representative of the paradoxical quality of Greene's fiction as a whole, and even to some extent of its author himself. For Greene, as for Bendrix, the Catholic religion seems a matter for anything but complacent acceptance, at least in *The Power and the Glory*, *The Heart of the Matter* and *The End of the Affair*. Each of these novels shows characters accepting rather reluctantly, or actually in conflict with, the various demands of their faith. These demands are in any case only a part of the stress which keeps Greene's characters on 'the dangerous edge of things'. The dissolution into loneliness and death of the affair between Sarah and Bendrix, for example, results not only from the complications of religion, but from the pressures of war, and of their own natures. Rather than creating the difficulties for which Greene is regularly criticised, the religious dimension of his fiction often functions partly to heighten the significance of the pain, resilience or disappointment with which an unrewarding, fallen world is encountered by his characters. Character itself, human nature, and the sort of secular emotions so sharply focused by the structure of *The End of the Affair*, are central interests of Greene's work as a whole, even when, as in that novel, Catholicism is also clearly a subject. For Graham Greene, the heart of the matter remains the human factor. The breadth, variety, and sympathy of this interest, in a career already spanning more than fifty years, has made him a pre-eminent English novelist of the later twentieth century.

Somerset Maugham, best known as a writer of plays and short stories, had a career as a novelist probably even longer than Graham Greene's, stretching back to a successful first novel, *Liza of Lambeth*, in 1897. Like Greene, Maugham has an interest in strange and distant places, which often provide the locations of his numerous short stories. Though there are few other similarities between the writers, an overlap of Maugham's interests with those of Greene and his contemporaries does occur in *The Razor's Edge* (1944), a novel concerned with religion, good and evil, and occasionally with war. Its hero Larry is made permanently mistrustful of his society by his experience of war—in this case, as an airman in the First World War. Finding that he 'couldn't understand why there was evil in the world', Larry spends his life avoiding social entanglements and trying to 'make up [his] mind' 'why evil exists' and 'whether God is or God is not'.[66] His efforts at understanding such questions lead him to eastern religion and the conclusion that 'the East has more to teach the West than the West conceives' (p.261). The teaching of the East particularly exposes the corrupting nature of Western materialism, illustrated in a variety of ways in *The Razor's Edge*. It appears particularly in Larry's desertion by a girl seeking a more securely lucrative marriage, and more generally in the behaviour of the rich American society whose habits Maugham examines and contrasts with those of Europe, rather in the manner of Henry James.

Larry's flight from this society and his preference for the East interestingly anticipates behaviour which followed in the generation after Maugham's novel appeared. Its exploration of Eastern mysticism also provides an intriguing variant on the connection of war, good, and evil, with conventional Christianity in other contemporary novels. Nevertheless, Maugham's work seems rather shallow and unsatisfactory when compared with these other novels. Graham Greene criticised him for an agnosticism which in his view made it difficult for Maugham to 'believe in the importance of a human action', leading him to 'minimise—pain, vice, the importance of his fellowmen'.[67] The narrator of *The Razor's Edge* admits to finding 'deep and genuine human emotion' chilling (p.95), and this disposition may be responsible for the shallow, 'minimising' effect Greene identifies. This is partly disguised by Maugham's attempt at a sophisticated, self-conscious construction, allowing his narrator to engage in long, urbane discussion of his organisational decisions in presenting his story. But these sections often seem repetitive and trivial if compared with the use Greene makes of Bendrix's analysis of his craft in *The End of the Affair*.

A much better realisation of some of the methods of *The Razor's Edge* appears in *Cakes and Ale* (1930), an entertaining, well-constructed novel, Maugham's own favourite among his works. Its subject is not only the bright, attractive lives of a famous author and his wife, but the disappearance of these people into a past whose true quality seems to fade beyond the reach of biographers, literary executors, even memory. Maugham dramatises this problem by ironically contrasting his narrator's own recollections with other reminiscences of these past lives. There are also extended reflections on the nature and falsification of fiction, biography, and nostalgia. The novel's consequent complexity and elaborate chronology, heavily dependent on memory, seems to benefit like Greene's *The End of the Affair* from the example of Ford Madox Ford. At any rate, *Cakes and Ale* exploits and very engagingly demonstrates the range of formal possibilities modernism had made available by the end of the nineteen twenties. As Anthony Burgess suggests, it is an outstanding novel, and deserves fuller critical recognition.[68]

Like Greene, Maugham, Newby, and many other twentieth-century English novelists, Joyce Cary was stimulated by the experience of strange foreign places and encounters with alien culture during the period of the British empire. His work as an assistant District Officer in Nigeria provided him with the setting for the best of his early fiction, *Mister Johnson* (1939). Vividly written in the present tense, this novel shows a Nigerian chief clerk, the eponymous Johnson, destroyed by the stress of his attempt to accommodate the values of indigenous culture with those imposed under British rule. After writing two novels which share contemporary interest in childhood, (*Charley is my Darling* (1940) and *A House of Children* (1941)), Cary returned to something of the theme of *Mister Johnson* in his outstanding work, the trilogy *Herself Surprised* (1941), *To Be a Pilgrim* (1942), and *The Horse's Mouth* (1944). Like *Mister Johnson*, these novels show the tension and interaction between radically disparate views of the world. As Cary explains, the trilogy

> ...was designed to show three characters, not only in themselves but as seen by each other. The object was to get a three-dimensional depth and force of character. One character was to speak in each book and describe the other two as seen by that person, [showing]...three leading persons in relation to, or in conflict with, other characters and the character of their times.[69]

In practice, this is not quite the scheme followed, as the single characters who 'speak in each book' do not keep the other two figures constantly in view. Cary's intention to examine the conflicts of these characters with each other and with their times is nevertheless forcefully realised. Like Greene in *The End of the Affair*, he is adept at juxtaposing contrasted, subjective views of the world. Each volume of his trilogy is 'spoken' in a sharply distinguished voice. The radical differences of style between these three dramatic monologues illustrate the disparity of the characters' outlooks, and the particularity of vision which often puts them into conflict with each other and with their society. The account of her life as cook, wife, and in the end domestic servant which Sara Monday gives in *Herself Surprised* is a complete contrast to the narrative of her eventual employer, Tom Wilcher, in *To be a Pilgrim*. Sara's record is engagingly straightforward and sensual, piling up details of sight, taste and touch. It is also distinguished by a talent for vigorously imaginative ideas, which project her unconstrained appreciation of life:

> ...we would sit...and watch the sun going down like a hot penny through green and yellow like snapdragon fires; you could see right through them into the sky behind, and above the sky was like a Dutch bowl, blue delf. Then the waves seemed to come up suddenly all glittering with hundreds and thousands, like cakes for Easters and birthdays...such is the bounty of providence, to pour out pleasures. [70]

Wilcher's narrative, on the other hand, is as cerebral as Sara's is exultingly sensual; precise and parsimonious where hers is open-hearted in attitude and profligate in imagination. He is as firmly concerned with problems of morality and history as Sara is with simple enjoyment of the life of the moment. Something of Sara's indulgence and unconstraint is shared by her 'husband', the impoverished artist Gulley Jimson, and reappears in his monologue in *The Horse's Mouth*. His narrative is also strongly coloured by his visual imagination, and by a nervous energy which vibrates in the rhythm of short, sharp sentences which emphatically express his observations and ideas:

> I was walking by the Thames. Half-past morning on an autumn day. Sun in a mist. Like an orange in a fried fish shop. All bright below. Low tide, dusty water and a crooked bar of straw, chicken-boxes, dirt and oil from mud to mud. The old serpent, symbol of nature and love (p.503).

Cary remarks that 'all novels are concerned from first to last with morality...All writers have, and must have...some picture of the world, and of what is right and wrong in that world'. [71] The contrasting parts of the trilogy constantly raise moral questions, forcing the reader to assess various versions of 'what is right and wrong' and to arbitrate between conflicting subjective 'pictures of the world'. Similar conflicts, unsettling any complacent certainty of judgement, are also raised by developments within each separate volume. *Herself Surprised*, for example, begins with Sara's recollection that

> The judge, when he sent me to prison, said that I had behaved like a woman without any moral sense...he said...'she is another unhappy example of that laxity and contempt for all religious principle and social obligation which threatens to undermine the whole fabric of our civilisation...' (p.9).

Though she is guilty of all the crimes for which she is brought to court, Sara's narrative in the rest of the novel diminishes the significance of this fact by showing her to be unusually likeable and affectionate; a buoyant, determined survivor like Daniel Defoe's heroine in *Moll Flanders* (1722). In the end, the official version of her morality in the court's judgement is shown to be no more valid than Wilcher's view of her as 'happy...saved...deeply religious...one of those people to whom faith is so natural that they don't know how they have it' (p.179). Wilcher's own strict concern with faith and morality, so persuasively expressed in *To be a Pilgrim*, nevertheless has to be judged in the context of his admission that he has suffered all his life from the 'curse' of material possessions, and from an emotional repression so severe that it has occasionally forced him to commit wholly immoral acts himself. Gulley Jimson is similarly hard to judge. He believes that 'he's very sane—the other people are mad', and attempts to keep living and painting in defiance of 'Governments and the People and the World, and so on' (pp.47, 696). Though this often seems entirely justified, it is also part of the anarchic selfishness which appears in his eventual murder of Sara.

Such challenges to 'moral sense' are brilliantly sustained by the vitality and variety of Cary's prose. It is astonishing that dramatic monologues as self-consistent but mutually contradictory as those of Sara, Gulley and Wilcher are all the work of a single author. Both in form and language, Cary is highly original. Just as Gulley admires the poet and artist William Blake, and tries to emulate him by living and painting independently of conventional styles and restrictions, Cary himself seems exuberantly unconstrained by conventional fictional techniques. Transcriptions of his characters' thoughts may owe something to Joyce and the modernists, and as critics have also suggested, his strong moral sense can be related to Conrad and Defoe. Cary's trilogy, however, is largely shaped by the 'really powerful release of fresh forces' for which Gilbert Phelps praised him in his study 'The Novel Today'.[72] Cary continued to write prolifically after the war, and produced another, similarly-structured trilogy (*Prisoner of Grace* (1952), *Except the Lord* (1953), *Not Honour More* (1955)). Even on the strength of the 'fresh forces' exhibited by *Herself Surprised*, *To be a Pilgrim* and *The Horse's Mouth* alone he is one of the best of modern English novelists, and certainly the most interesting to emerge around the time of the Second World War.

Phelps continues his analysis by suggesting that Cary is 'one of the few novelists to come into prominence after the war who responded deeply and imaginatively to the wider movements of contemporary history and their human implications'. Cary himself suggests that his narrators 'recall...the history of the times, as part of [their] own history'.[73] Connecting political and historical developments with personal destiny, the trilogy as a whole envisages the period from the late Victorian period until 1939—the outbreak of the Second World War effectively coincides with the final collapse of Gulley and of his art at the end of *The Horse's Mouth*. As Henry Reed points out, *Herself Surprised*, *To be a Pilgrim*, and *The Horse's Mouth* are an attempt to see 'English history, through English eyes, for the last sixty years'.[74] The 'wider movements of history', however, are the particular concern of *To be a Pilgrim*, and of Wilcher's reminiscences, which juxtapose past and present rather in the manner of *The End of the Affair*.

Aged and almost dying, Wilcher is looked after at his family's country house—to whose preservation he has virtually dedicated his life—by members of a younger generation whom he can scarcely understand. Puzzled by the actions of these young relations, Wilcher is also 'Preoccupied...with the state of the country' (p. 492), eventually under the shadow of the approaching Second World War. His memory rehearses the developments that have brought this current state of affairs into being, progressively resuming the 'turmoil of change' in the life of the house, of his family, of the nation as a whole. Some of these historical changes, such as the First World War, he sees as the result of 'the enormous power of evil...evil will' (pp.399-400). This strong and often pessimistic moral sense makes his narrative throughout an anxious elegy for the 'decline of religion' (p.492) and the shifts in public and private ethics which threaten 'the life of the spirit' (p.254) in the twentieth century. As Cary suggests, Wilcher's historical vision is shaped by a combination of 'political and religious intuition'; and his 'tragedy...is that he sees the good for ever being destroyed with the bad...virtues so tangled into evil practice that they are for ever in danger'.[75]

Wilcher's connection of 'political and religious intuition'; his concerns with good and evil; and with 'the wider movements of contemporary history', all extend in Cary's trilogy a more general pattern in contemporary fiction. Like L.P. Hartley, Cary reflects in the recollections of a rather repressed, loveless individual the dispiriting evolution of twentieth-century history. Like Leo in *The Go-Between*, or George Bowling in Orwell's *Coming up for Air*, both Sara and Wilcher look back nostalgically to earlier, happier times in the Edwardian era. In different ways, this tendency to retreat in imagination or memory into a happier past is also apparent in many other contemporary novels—*The Retreat*, or *Caught*, for example. None of these novels, however, is unreservedly nostalgic. Often by means of extended personal, family, or public histories, each connects unhappy consequences in the present with emotional or sometimes sexual complications which intruded upon the idyllic past evoked. Such investigations of what 'poisons from what far-back brews went on corroding' (*The Ballad and the Source*, p.42) have some obvious affinities with the Bible's retracing of evil to Adam and Eve's

103

original sin and loss of paradise in Eden. This story of paradise lost often figures explicitly in contemporary fiction, Cary's included. In *The Horse's Mouth*, for example, Gulley Jimson connects the Fall with his loss of innocence in adolescence, and finds that it provides an appropriate theme for his painting. Something of his vision of 'the knowledge of good and evil...apples in Eden...the curse of Adam' (p.654) also appears in P.H. Newby's *A Step to Silence*. Immediately after Hesketh's attempted suicide, Oliver Knight hears the college principal preach 'a sermon on the text out of Genesis' (p.209) connected with the consequences of the Fall. In *The Retreat*, under the stress of various experiences during the war, Jane finds herself 'thinking of Eve and the Garden of Eden' and of 'that state of grace before...the present' (pp.172, 171).

In discussing contemporary novelists' frequent interest in childhood, Henry Reed remarked in 1946 'in a world of darkness we learn to hug that memory of comparative light...It is natural to turn and attempt to recapture and understand and detail that lost possibility of Eden'.[76] As his remarks help to indicate, the war provided a powerful incentive to think of 'a state of grace before the present', and to consider how it might have been lost. Milton turned to the story of Eden shortly after the English Civil War: in several novels written during and after the Second World War, the same myth provides a paradigm for the urge to find some 'source', perhaps in earlier twentieth-century history, for the incomprehensible violence which had fallen like a primal curse upon contemporary life. At various levels, not always explicit, some sense of the 'lost possibility of Eden' often informs both the fiction and the poetry of the late forties and early fifties. Shadowy or clearly indicated, its presence is a distinctive feature of the contemporary imagination, part of its struggle to structure and assimilate the experience of the war.

Two very different novels published at the time—Philip Toynbee's *The Garden to the Sea* (1953) and C.S. Lewis's *Perelandra* (*Voyage to Venus*, 1943)—particularly confirm the contemporary relevance of the story of Adam and Eve. *The Garden to the Sea* is an experimental work, written entirely in four voices: 'The Voice of Adam' and 'The Ages of Adam: Noel, the Voice of his Innocence; Tom, the Voice of his Fall; Charley, the Voice of his Punishment'.[77] The story they tell is of a marriage whose happiness before the war is recalled in the Biblical phrase 'Eastward in Eden our garden was planted by the Lord, for me to lie or toil in' (p.8). Like the relationship in *The End of the Affair*, however, this marriage collapses partly under the strain of war. Deceived in their belief that they had 'overcome war and separation, and married innocence to experience' (p.142), the couple are exiled apparently permanently, like Adam and Eve, from their earlier happiness. Though interesting for the clarity of its illustration of contemporary connections between war, innocence and Eden, *The Garden to the Sea* is not altogether successful as a novel. Its 'voices' seem to belong more to drama than to fiction: their concentration on memory and inner conscience recalls in form, though not always in interest or subtlety, some of the plays of Samuel Beckett. Toynbee is more successful in *Tea with Mrs. Goodman* (1947), a complex, poetic novel which presents another religious vision deeply concerned with good and evil.

C.S. Lewis's immensely popular fiction has none of Toynbee's strangeness of structure, though it is, literally, unearthly in subject matter. Lewis explained that he found it convenient to set his novels on other planets because it freed his imagination and removed the requirement of plausible action. In particular, it left Lewis, a lifelong popularist of the Christian faith, freer to develop his fiction as allegory, a mode which had earlier interested him as a critic of the poetry of Edmund Spenser. Set on Venus, *Perelandra* is a quite undisguised re-creation of the story of Eden. The planet is envisaged as still in a primal state of unsullied, Edenic beauty, long since lost on Earth, and threatened on Venus by the temptation of its first woman by the devil. In this version of the Genesis story, however, the devil is foiled by an earthling, Ransom, transported to Venus by the spiritual guardians of the solar system. The appropriately-named Ransom sacrifices himself to a terrifying physical struggle with the devil, consoled by the thought that citizens of his home planet are simultaneously enduring worse torments in their comparable struggle against Adolf Hitler. *Perelandra*, like other contemporary fiction, is despite its distant setting concerned with the war and what the novel calls 'explanation of that fatal bent which is the main lesson of history'.[78]

Dream Worlds: C.S. Lewis, J.R.R. Tolkien, Mervyn Peake, Wyndham Lewis

Perelandra is a slight work, interesting for the allegoric clarity of its version of contemporary concern with good and evil, innocence and experience. Lewis's work is also exemplary of another trend which the war may have encouraged—contemporary novelists' interest in fantasy. In remarks quoted earlier, P.H. Newby talks of 'childhood and adolescence on the one hand and war on the other. Unless one wandered off into fantasy or allegory these were the inescapable themes'. Rosamond Lehmann also suggested 'allegories and fantasies' as alternatives to the theme of childhood, and John Lehmann, in *Penguin New Writing* in 1941, records that for readers as well as writers, the war was an inevitable incentive to 'wander off into fantasy':

> ... one school of thought ... maintains that all that people want to read

today is stories which will take them right away from the war and ideas connected with the war, which will entertain them innocuously or help them to build dream-worlds of romance and happiness.[79]

Lehmann goes on to indicate, like Newby, that such stories were certainly not *all* that readers wanted at the time, and C.S. Lewis's work shows that even 'dream-worlds of romance' were in any case not necessarily 'right away from the war and ideas connected with the war'. Like the theme of childhood, fantasy may have appealed to writers almost more as a way of coming to terms with contemporary circumstances than as a means of escaping from them: at any rate, 'dream worlds' proliferate during the war and in the decade which followed. C.S. Lewis's *Perelandra*, for example, is only one of a trilogy of interplanetary novels. The first volume, *Out of the Silent Planet* (1938) concerns Ransom's journey to Mars. Like *Perelandra*, it shows the conflict of spirit with corruption, and contains extensive ethical debate. The trilogy's final volume, *That Hideous Strength* (1945), which Lewis subtitles 'A Modern Fairy Tale for Grown-Ups', brings Ransom and the struggle between good and evil back down to earth, and to the immediate threat of destruction and war.

By far the most widely-known of contemporary fantasists is C.S. Lewis's friend J.R.R. Tolkien, whose fiction may have benefited, like Lewis's, from a thorough knowledge of the Medieval romance, and of Anglo-Saxon literature. Tolkien's trilogy *The Lord of the Rings* (*The Fellowship of the Ring* (1954), *The Two Towers* (1954), *The Return of the King* (1955)) tells on epic scale how some engagingly ordinary creatures from Middle Earth prevent the malignant realm of Mordor from exploiting the destructive power of a mysterious ring. Though the trilogy is full of the sense of an enormous conflict between good and evil, light and dark, Tolkien has denied that it has any allegorical significance. Its uncomplicated quality is one of the reasons for its universality of appeal. Tolkien's narrative has many of the strengths often associated with children's fiction—simplicity; magic; straightforward morality; a fantastic landscape populated by threatening or wonderful creatures; exciting adventures on a dangerous and eventful journey, ending in a triumph against monstrous odds. Helped by a paperback edition in 1968, *The Lord of the Rings* grew to be immensely successful in the late sixties and seventies.

This success created a demand for fantasy and revived popular interest in Mervyn Peake's earlier 'Titus Books'. Peake had intended these as a series, a fantasy *bildungsroman* following the life of his hero Titus Groan, but only three volumes were completed, the trilogy *Titus Groan* (1946), *Gormenghast* (1950), and *Titus Alone* (1959). These novels are more serious, or at any rate much darker in tone, than *The Lord of the Rings:* as Gothic, gloomy, and unpleasant as the latter is optimistic and affectionate. The centre of Peake's vision is the vast, crumbling castle of Gormenghast, acres, even miles, in extent, and remote from any recognisable country or era. Within it, 'through honeycombs of stone...there's evil afoot': 'dreams, and violence, and disenchantment...greed and cruelty and lust for power'.[80] These passions operate among a cast of characters whose strange, crooked natures are aptly indicated by Peake's extraordinary choice of names—Flay, Prunesquallor, Rottcodd, Sepulchrave, Sourdust, Steerpike, Swelter, Slagg. Eccentrics and caricatures, they are a nightmare extension of some of the characterisation of Charles Dickens. As in some of Dickens's novels such as *Bleak House* (1853), characters are shown as victims of stultifying rituals and traditions, endless and aimless reiterations. Gormenghast is above all a domain doomed to inertia and ghastly stagnancy, and Peake's imagination is at its best in describing its rotting still life. Like Joyce Cary, Peake trained as an artist, and later worked extensively as a book illustrator: static descriptions predominate in the trilogy, and are often chillingly original in their visual quality and choice of words. The account of the masquerade of monsters in *Gormenghast* (pp.658-62), for example, and the many visions of the castle throughout, are more memorable than any development of human nature or action. Described as 'like a gigantic body' (p.759), the castle itself is more vital and interesting than any of the rather shallow caricatures who occupy it, and Peake is much less successful and original when he abandons the Gormenghast world in the last volume of the trilogy. *Titus Alone* is a rather shapeless account of his hero's adventures in a soulless modern technocracy which merely reduplicates some of the anxieties of Aldous Huxley and George Orwell in *Brave New World* (1932) and *Nineteen Eighty-Four* (1949).

Two characters rebel against the melancholy round of ritual. Though the 77th Earl of Gormenghast, Titus Groan, eventually seems to escape from the castle he has inherited, he also realises that 'he carried his Gormenghast within him' (p.1022), a belief in its partly dream-like quality which he shares with the reader. The other rebel, Steerpike, is an escapee from the castle kitchens, 'a solitary Satan', monstrously egotistical and dedicated to destruction. The consequence of his lust for power may be seen, as Anthony Burgess suggests, as

> ...a season of violence and murder...if you wish, an allegory of what had been happening in Europe during the time when Peake was writing the book. But it is also pure fantasy, a totally original creation.[81]

As Burgess suggests, the nightmarish quality of the Titus books may reflect contemporary history. Peake's own experience of military life drove him to the edge of nervous collapse, and his wife recorded that his visit in the wake of the liberating Allied armies to the Nazi death camps at Belsen directly contributed to the account of the doomed people of the Under-River in *Titus Alone*. Peake's fiction may also express in general some of the sense of deadly stagnancy and exhaustion which Cyril Connolly and other contemporary commentators saw as the particular legacy of the Second World War.[82] However, as Burgess also indicates, Gormenghast is unique, and too far beyond any recognisable world to be easily connected with contemporary experience. Peake's imagination is likewise too unusual to be easily related to any other author's. Some of Charles Dickens's novels, and the fantasies of Lewis Carroll, are remotely comparable, and several critics have suggested Franz Kafka's work, especially *The Castle* (1926), as a possible influence. Though they do show some of his qualities, the Titus books do not measure up to Kafka's talent for making dream-like visions at the same time sufficiently familiar to encompass the anxieties of a whole era. Peake's imagination is more extravagant: too idiosyncratic and sour to have such general appeal.

Though the Titus books are the centre of his achievement, Peake provides an amusing alternative to the gloom of Gormenghast in a frivolous, funny fantasy, *Mr. Pye* (1953). The novel seems to show re-emerging in the figure of its hero some of 'the angels and the demons of an earlier time' which Stephen Spender considered had 'simply been suppressed in our consciousnesses' until the war. It concerns the adventures of an evangelist whose 'unnatural piety'[83] mysteriously begins to manifest itself in a set of growing angel wings. Acting on his conclusion that 'he had grown wings because he was too good for this world...to cause them to withdraw themselves...he must be bad' (p.154), he finds himself equipped instead with a set of devil's horns. Finding that 'the whole world is unbalanced' (p.103), and struggling between good and evil, Mr. Pye offers 'if you wish, an allegory', as schematic as *Perelandra*, for a world unbalanced by the war and confronted by unusually sharp, bewildering conflicts between innocence and experience, good and evil. Peake's light, whimsical tone, however, suggests that *Mr. Pye* provides at most a comic version of the wider concerns of contemporary fiction.

Angels and demons, and a conflict of good and evil on a cosmic scale also appear in Wyndham Lewis's *Monstre Gai* (1955) and *Malign Fiesta* (1955), concluding parts of his fantasy *The Human Age*. Lewis began this trilogy long before: its first part, *The Childermass*, published in 1928, is largely a satiric attack on some of the philosophies of the nineteen twenties, and on authors whom Lewis considered to employ them. One of these, James Joyce, appears thinly disguised as the central figure of the novel, James Pullman. He is one of a group of dead souls outside the 'Magnetic City', awaiting appropriate assignment to their station in the eternal life. Pullman also figures as the hero of *Monstre Gai* and *Malign Fiesta*, admitted to the Magnetic City in the former and consigned to hell and an uneasy alliance with the devil in the latter. Both *Monstre Gai* and *Malign*

Fiesta continue the free, colourful invention of *The Childermass*, and its satiric mode, though with rather different targets: the later novels are sometimes specifically concerned with the conditions and anxieties of the war and life in post-war Britain. *Monstre Gai*, for example, contains a version of the Blitz; references to fascism; a comparison of Hitler with Lucifer; and a satiric representation of some of the institutions of the Welfare State. *Malign Fiesta* describes something of the apparatus of Nazi concentration camps being used by the devil, who also shows an admiring interest in the earthly invention of nuclear weapons, which he describes with devilish cynicism as 'a technological magic which may in the end equal us in resource'.[84]

Such contemporary interests are extended in Lewis's depiction of the struggle between good and evil. This conflict is often dramatised in various oppositions between the devil and God, and in quarrels between factions of minor angels and demons in the Magnetic City. *Monstre Gai*, however, also shows Pullman realising that 'life in this city does in fact reproduce life-on-earth as near as damn it'.[85] He concludes that 'Good and...Bad dominated human life, at its deepest level', and that 'the struggle forever in progress' between these powers 'concentrated all the major disharmonies of the contemporary scene on earth' (pp.219, 220, 221). Though *Monstre Gai* and *Malign Fiesta* are set in a cosmic domain of angels and demons, they show Lewis's imagination simply, if powerfully, projecting into a fantastic realisation moral concerns of the sort often stimulated among his contemporaries by the 'overwhelming and universal catastrophe' of the war.

Self-condemned: Wyndham Lewis, Malcolm Lowry, William Sansom

The action of evil in human history and in individual life also appears as part of the subject of Lewis's partly-autobiographical *Self Condemned* (1954). Set in the period before and during the Second World War, this novel personifies anxieties about the gloomy progress of contemporary events in the figure of a professor of history, René Harding, who believes that the world 'sleepwalked its way from decade to decade, from disaster to disaster' often under 'an evil principle of unexpected virulence'.[86] Harding's disaffection with the conventional concentration of history on war and violence leads him to publish during the thirties a prophetic study called *The Secret History of World War II*, and later to resign from his job. With his wife, he retreats from the war to Canada, which proves unbearably lonely and cold: so cold that after the Harding's hotel is completely destroyed by fire, there remains around the burnt-out void a sheeted coating of ice, frozen from the water used to extinguish the blaze.

This chill image Harding comes to realise is representative of the heartless, 'glacial shell of a man' (p.407) he has become as a result of his fixation on his own ideology and interests. The 'glacial shell' perhaps also reflects some of Lewis's own self-scrutiny, and his view of an age left empty and spiritless, hollow at heart, by the recent conflagration of the war. This feeling, along with the dispirited investigation of contemporary history in *Self Condemned,* and the vision of a vast, violent struggle in *Monstre Gai* and *Malign Fiesta,* make Lewis's last novels in some ways representative of the mood of the post-war period. This typicality, as well as his assessment of the 'striking...tragic depth' of *Self Condemned,* may have encouraged Walter Allen to nominate Lewis as 'man of the decade' in his survey *The Novel Today* in 1955.[87]

A more convincing candidate for this title, however, in terms of both merit and representative quality, is Malcolm Lowry. Allen himself later describes Lowry's *Under the Volcano* (1947), set in Mexico in 1938, as 'the finest and profoundest work of fiction written by an Englishman during the decade...a great tragic novel'.[88] Like René Harding, though even more bitterly, Lowry's hero Geoffrey Firmin is 'self-condemned', tragically divided against himself and torn between love and dissolution. Firmin is perfectly aware of his nature and its potential, and assured of the love his wife Yvonne offers when she returns to him in Quauhnahuac early in the novel. Yet he is simultaneously quite unable to renounce the hugely, insanely excessive drinking which compels his life on its tragic downward course to despair and death. The 'Day of the Dead', a Mexican religious festival, provides the context for the novel's whole action. A spiritual, partly religious dimension in Firmin's self-condemnation is further established by analogies with the tragic hero Doctor Faustus, doomed in Christopher Marlowe's Elizabethan play by being unable to repeal or repent his sale of his soul to the devil. Though Firmin's demon is drink, his abuse of 'spirits' Lowry presents as 'the abuse of mystical powers'.[89] His determination to damn himself is further illustrated by his dabbling in some of Faustus's interests in alchemy and diabolism. Craving love and innocence, yet inexorably drawn to their opposites, Firmin partly realises in his own tragic progress a 'modern...version of the Faustus story'[90] of the sort which his friend Laruelle has considered making as a film. Significantly, Firmin himself lent Laruelle the copy of *Doctor Faustus* which he peruses at the start of *Under the Volcano.*

Firmin's problems are compounded by his status as a dishonoured ex-consul, made redundant by the sort of political turbulence in Mexico in 1938 which provides the background for Graham Greene's *The Power and the Glory* and *The Lawless Roads* (1939). These disturbances in *Under the Volcano* reflect the wider violence of the contemporary world, poised on the edge of war: Firmin's self-destructiveness likewise represents the progress of his era in general. Explaining the novel in a letter to his publishers, Lowry remarks

> The drunkenness of the Consul is used on one plane to symbolise the universal drunkenness of mankind during the war, or during the period immediately preceding it...and...his fate should be seen also in its universal relationship to the ultimate fate of mankind.[91]

This connection between the ex-consul's destiny and the 'the wider movements of contemporary history' is often emphasised in *Under the Volcano*. For example, when Yvonne asks Firmin's half-brother Hugh what can be done for her husband, he replies 'What's the good? Just sobering him up for a day or two's not going to help. Good God, if our civilisation were to sober up for a couple of days it'd die of remorse on the third'. (p.121). Hugh frequently connects 'history...its worthless stupid course' (p.311) with the anxieties and broken relationships he sees around him: his own despair results from events prefiguring the Second World War, particularly the war in Spain which he dreams of fighting in himself. Hugh further suffers from the frustrations of his failed attempts as a journalist at 'persuading the world not to cut its throat for half a decade or more' (p.107): Laruelle likewise considers of his own enterprise that 'he had made great films...so far as he knew they had not changed the world in the slightest' (p.15). Like Orwell, mentioning in the remark quoted at the start of this chapter the 'highly civilised' nature of men nevertheless 'trying to kill' him, the characters of *Under the Volcano* realise that neither art nor journalism nor civilisation in general avail to retard the destructive advance of history. Like Firmin, the world seeks darkness and damnation in full knowledge of the light. Thinking of the First World War, Wilcher suggests in *To be a Pilgrim* that 'we know the light and turn from it' (p.399). Stephen Spender envisaged in the war years 'humanity with its faith in moral systems and religions shaken, at the mercy of the demonic forces of a machinery which it has itself invoked'.[92] There could be no more precise or powerful extension of their vision than *Under the Volcano*.

Firmin's dilemma, its consequences and implications, are made immensely compelling by Lowry's structure and technique. *Under the Volcano* opens on the Day of the Dead, 1939, with Laruelle recalling the events exactly one year previously which form the substance of the novel after its first chapter. Foreknowledge of Firmin's compulsive self-destruction and eventual death at the hands of a group of Mexican fascists increases the novel's sense of doom and tragic inevitability. Lowry compares its division into twelve chapters, each roughly corresponding to a single hour of Firmin's last day, to hearing 'a clock slowly striking midnight for Faust'.[93] The compulsions which force Firmin onwards through this tragic progress are also made extremely immediate by Lowry's frequent location of the novel's perspective in his protagonist's disturbed mind. Laruelle's familiarity in Chapter One with events the reader has yet to encounter is unsettling enough: subsequent developments occurring in a dazzling Mexican landscape and refracted through Firmin's unsteady, often drunken consciousness continue to make the novel seem to lurch from one barely comprehensible crisis to another. This exactly reproduces Firmin's own impression of his experience as a 'whirling cerebral chaos' (p.309): as he sinks further and further into drink, the novel itself creates a sense of 'sinking into the action of the mind, and away from normal action'.[94] As this remark of Lowry's suggests, internal consciousness predominates in *Under the Volcano:* it is a bewildering, brilliant mixture of the interior monologues and streams of consciousness not only of Firmin himself but of his wife and friends. The divergences of their differing perspectives, sometimes on the same events, help to highlight the loneliness of characters trapped in individual, irreconcilable views of the world. 'Blown fragments of their memories, half afraid to commingle' (p.72) also juxtapose alongside developments in the present a previous history of confusion and sorrow—Yvonne's liaisons with Hugh and with Laruelle; her separation from her husband; his life and expanding drunkenness on his own; their mutual misunderstanding.

A distinctive feature of *Under the Volcano* is that other 'blown fragments' frequently intrude into characters' minds from their immediate experience of the world, often providing a kind of summation or commentary on the action. For example, while walking around Quauhnahuac with her husband, Yvonne repeatedly sees advertisements for a boxing match which she half-consciously associates with her own struggle with Firmin. Two significant phrases persistently impinge on his tangled consciousness: the first is a slogan scrawled on Laruelle's house, 'No se puede vivir sin amar'—'It is not possible to live without loving'. The second comes from a poster advertising a film about a mad murderer: 'Las Manos de Orlac. Con Peter Lorre'.—'The Hands of Orlac, starring Peter Lorre'. The two phrases are definitions, repeated reminders of the extremes of love and death between which Firmin is torn. They also emphasise the connection of his tragedy with the contemporary world in general: the film was made in Germany, and its star was later a refugee from the Nazis. Its showing in the local cinema along with newsreels of the war in Spain suggests both the origin and the insanity of the violence darkening the late nineteen thirties. Torn between love and destruction, good and evil, the nature of both public and private life at the time is finally summarised by another fragment of Spanish which obsessively occurs to Firmin and which he translates to himself as 'You like this garden? Why is it yours? We evict those who destroy!' (p.132, etc.). Lowry explains in his letter to his publishers that 'the allegory is that of the Garden of Eden, the Garden representing the world, from which we ourselves run perhaps slightly more danger of being ejected than when I wrote the book'.[95]

Extensively sustained in *Under the Volcano*, this 'allegory' is one aspect of its representative quality, its illustration of an unusually wide range of the fictional themes and devices of its age. The mythic retrospection on the original loss of innocence in the Garden of Eden; the general examination of love and damnation, good and evil; and the retrospective consideration at the start of the novel of how present disturbances originated in the past, are all typical of fiction written around the time of the war. So is Lowry's encapsulation of 'the wider movements of contemporary history and their human implications' in disturbed individual experience; and his presentation of Firmin's 'struggle between the powers of darkness and light'[96] in partly religious, Faustian terms of 'the angels and the demons of an earlier time'.

The great merit of *Under the Volcano*, however, is not simply the extent of its incorporation of themes and preoccupations appearing widely in contemporary fiction, but rather the ingenuity and imagination with which these are combined. As Lowry claimed, 'the book was so designed, counterdesigned and interwelded that it could be read an indefinite number of times and still not have yielded all its meanings or its drama or its poetry'.[97] Lowry's 'meanings' and any 'allegory' in *Under the Volcano* are suggestively rather than schematically developed: his moral concern and historical vision are thoroughly 'interwelded' with a dramatic setting, sustained presentation of consciousness, and succinct intensity of action. Concentration almost entirely within the compass of a single day, with chapters devoted to each of its hours, along with Lowry's success in transcribing the minds of his characters, strongly recall the strengths of Joyce's fiction. While the theme of Lowry's first novel *Ultramarine* (1933) can be compared to Joyce's *A Portrait of the Artist as a Young Man* (1916), *Under the Volcano* more generally resembles *Ulysses* (1922). Though Lowry benefits perhaps more thoroughly than any other English novelist from Joyce's example, he also incorporates it into a vision entirely his own, one whose intensity and originality probably put *Under the Volcano* closer to *Ulysses* in standard as well as style than any English novel published since. Lowry's novel has faults: Hugh's recollection of early days at sea unnecessarily reduplicates the material of *Ultramarine*, and some of the verbal extravagance which partly marred that early novel is still occasionally apparent. But there is complete justice in Anthony Burgess's assessment of *Under the Volcano* as one of 'few authentic masterpieces' in twentieth-century English fiction.[98]

The immense promise of *Under the Volcano* makes still sadder

Lowry's failure to repeat its success or to complete the intended trilogy of which he hoped it would form a part. His own life seemed to follow the pattern established by Firmin: alcoholism and eventual suicide left almost all his other work incomplete. The unfinished novels edited and published by his widow sometimes show a reflection within the fiction of the problems of 'the very act of writing itself' which interestingly shares in one of the new directions of post-war literature (see Chapter Five). Too often, however, this material seems a mixture of undigested autobiography and paler repetition of some of the concerns of *Under the Volcano*. *Dark as the Grave wherein my Friend is Laid* (1969), for example, though still preoccupied with 'the gigantic tragedy of life', self-consciously and less powerfully examines the same landscape as *Under the Volcano*, merely resuming some of the means whereby the earlier novel was made.[99]

Lowry saw the Mexico of *Under the Volcano* as both 'paradisal' and 'infernal': there could be no greater contrast to this colourful setting than the drably suburban domain of William Sansom's *The Body* (1949).[100] Sansom first came to prominence during the war with *Fireman Flower* (1944), a volume of short stories some of which are based on his experience in the Auxiliary Fire Service. (Along with Henry Green, he may have been one of the 'group of progressive novelists in firemen's uniform' satirically envisaged in Evelyn Waugh's *Sword of Honour* (p.197).) Though some of Sansom's stories in *Fireman Flower* are documentary accounts of firefighting, others show, like Rex Warner's novels, the 'progressive' influence of Kafka, whom Sansom admired. The title story, for example, is a surreal vision of a fire. It is strangely warped by the instability of its protagonist's mind; his inability to make sense of his perceptions or to envisage amid the threatening chaos of events anything that 'can be controlled...secure, rounded off'. This difficulty is perhaps a correlative of Sansom's anxiety that wartime experience was 'too violent for the arts to transcribe'. Other stories, however, unconnected with the war, show a similar interest in the difficulty and uncertainty of perception, the distortions of mind and memory, and in general in the 'brain, the unreliable agent'.[101]

Some of these concerns also reappear in *The Body*, 'a kind of confessional' by a first-person narrator, Henry Bishop, whose stability and self-control evaporate in the vacuum of an emptying middle age. He admits that his apprehensions are at times 'ludicrous, out of all sensible proportion', and that his 'nerves were wrong, all reasonable values distorted'.[102] His distortion of normality appears in a variety of ways in his narrative, noticeably in obsessively minute concentration on banal, insignificant objects. His progressive estrangement from the normal continuity of his life, even from normal perception of it, largely results from a jealous conviction that his wife is enjoying a passionate affair with a neighbour. In a way which sometimes recalls Shakespeare's *Othello*, Bishop almost seems to relish his corrosive self-torture in elaborating to himself details of an affair which is wholly imaginary, entirely the creation of the unreliable agency of his mind. The novel's confinement within this mind and its processes creates with unusual, almost unnatural clarity an impression not only of Bishop himself, but also of the seedy post-war society which surrounds him and contributes to his collapse.

Conclusion: The Death of the Heart

Despite its thoroughly different setting, *The Body* shares some affinity with *Under the Volcano* in presenting a man estranged from ordinary life and the affection of his wife by a self-defeating inner compulsion. The incapacity to accept love shown by the central figure in these novels is also typical of an idiosyncrasy more widely apparent in fiction around the time of the war. Though the affairs of the heart and their frustrations have always provided a staple theme for the novelist, the work of Sansom, Lowry, and their contemporaries is much more than usually concerned with difficulties or failures of love, and sometimes also, correlatively, with failure or disease of the heart itself. In Peake's 'Titus Books', for example, Nannie Slagg's wearisome complaints about demands on her 'poor heart' are made more understandable by the evidence that she is one of very few people in chilly Gormenghast to be moved by any normal human affection. Tom Wilcher, in *To be a Pilgrim*, complains 'my faith was as dead as my heart' (p.202): he suffers in actuality from a dangerous heart disease which is also emblematic of the repressed, rather loveless life he recollects in the novel. In Hartley's *Eustace and Hilda*, Eustace Cherrington is inhibited throughout his life by a weakened heart which results from an emotional trauma in childhood: though Leo Colston is physically healthy, like Eustace he fails to recover emotionally from a childhood shock. Graham Greene's Scobie, torn in *The Heart of the Matter* between love of God, of his wife and of his lover, appropriately chooses a 'strained heart'[103] as an attempted disguise for his suicide. Mrs Jardine's 'nervous instability of the heart' (p.28) in *The Ballad and the Source* is likewise an apt analogue for the strained, atrophied affections whose legacy appears in her granddaughter Maisie's grim declaration that 'I shall never fall in love...I got over the whole thing in July, 1914' (p.227). Waugh's hero Guy Crouchback shows a similar inclination, at least in front of his wife, to suggest that his 'heart was broken for life' (p.66). The artist in James Hanley's *No Directions* even believes that his wife has cancer of the heart. Failed marital relations are also responsible for showing René Harding that he has become a 'glacial shell', burnt-out and hollow at heart.

Such widespread appearances of 'the death of the heart', literal or metaphoric, seem indicative of the sort of contemporary anxieties Firmin summarises in *Under the Volcano* when he concludes that 'Love is the only thing which gives meaning to our poor ways on earth' but at the same time asks himself doubtfully 'what has happened to the love and understanding we once had! What is going to happen to it — what is going to happen to our hearts?' (p.45). In a war-ravaged world, authors were disposed to share Firmin's connected doubts about 'meaning' in 'our poor ways on earth' and about the apparent loss of 'the love and understanding we once had'. The repeated appearance of such feelings in so many novels otherwise differing widely in subject is a further indication of the gloomy pervasiveness of the war's influence on the consciousness of its time. The recurrence of heart-sickness; lost innocence; conflicting good and evil; uneasy retrospection on a troubled history; even of the inclination to 'wander off into fantasy and allegory', show in the writing of the period an unusual communality of imagination. Many contemporary authors share and formulate in a range of analogous ways the sort of feeling expressed in *The Go-Between* of living in a 'hideous century...which has denatured humanity and planted death and hate where love and living were' (p.279).

The continued existence of such feelings in Hartley's novel in 1953 indicates the firmness of their persistence in the 'years of recrimination and exhaustion' which Cyril Connolly saw as the legacy of the war. Walter Allen's prophecy in 1941 that the war would continue to 'dominate' literature 'for years to come, long after hostilities cease' is confirmed by several commentators in the forties and fifties. The 'deterioration of the spirit' which Henry Reed diagnosed in 1946 still seemed a problem to P.H. Newby in 1951, when he complained that 'the war seems, in spirit, to go on and on' and discussed the 'spiritual poverty' it had created. Robert Liddell, in 1953, still found 'jaded nerves of our epoch' resulting from 'the crushing impact of public affairs'.[104] Jaded, dispirited feelings were inevitably intensified and perpetuated by the austerity of post-war life, and an 'impact of public affairs' which hardly diminished even when the war ended. As G.S. Fraser later suggested,

> The moral relief of victory over the Axis was blunted by the use of the Atom bomb and the beginnings of the Cold War and the achievement of peace through a Balance of Terror. The drab English world of the war and immediately postwar scene did not lend itself to the transforming effects of the imagination.[105]

The drab life of post-war years so exactly portrayed in Sansom's *The Body* also features in other novels at the time. *The End of the Affair*, for example, is set against a similar background of spiritless pubs and shabby tea-houses in contemporary London. Henry Green's last two novels, the aptly-named *Nothing* (1950), and *Doting* (1952), show among the sort of rich, leisured people he had previously examined in *Party Going* (1939) the same enervation and emptiness Sansom diagnoses in the middle class in *The Body*. Henry Green's almost total reliance on dialogue in these later novels, rather in the manner of Ivy Compton-Burnett, aptly delineates in endless trivial small-talk the vapid feelings of the society portrayed. Perhaps inevitably, however, a rather unsatisfactory sense of emptiness is left in these novels themselves.

The new threats and anxieties Fraser mentions also appear in fiction at the time. The opening of the Cold War of political hostility between the Russian bloc and the Western powers contributes some of its chill to Guy's disillusioning experience in Yugoslavia in the last part of *Sword of Honour*, and to the gloomy vision of an eternal, irresolvable World War in George Orwell's *Nineteen Eighty-Four*. Anxieties about nuclear war frequently figure in incidental references in contemporary novels. Its threat is cynically incorporated into the advertising of the bizarre cemetery Evelyn Waugh satirises in *The Loved One* (1948); atom bombs feature in Henry Bishop's proliferating worries in *The Body*; and Malcolm Lowry emphasises his novel's 'universal relationship to the ultimate fate of mankind' by including a warning about final eviction from the Garden of the World on the last page of *Under the Volcano*. Whole novels are also devoted to the subject: Aldous Huxley's *Ape and Essence* (1948), the popular novelist Nevil Shute's *On the Beach* (1957), L.P. Hartley's *Facial Justice* (1960), and John Bowen's *After the Rain* (1958) are all imaginative projections of the fate of mankind after nuclear disaster. C.P. Snow's *The New Men* (1954) is set against a background of the wartime research which first created the possibility of atomic warfare.

By the mid-fifties, however, the Second World War itself had become of less oppressively immediate concern. It began to be possible to recognise the nature of its historical watershed, and to place its effects in the general development of the twentieth century. In 1954, for example, Wyndham Lewis looks back in *Self Condemned* to the thirties and the sort of knowledge René Harding shares with his comfortable, leisured friends that 'such men as themselves would never exist on earth again' (p.78). The disappearance of their sort of life also provides a theme for William Plomer's *Museum Pieces* (1952), its title and story an echo of Tom Wilcher's conclusion in Cary's *To be a Pilgrim* that he is 'a museum piece', 'receding into a past which was irrecoverable' (p.442). Plomer's protagonists Mrs Montfaucon and her son Toby d'Arfey are genteel, bankrupt survivors of the Edwardian age, acutely aware of the anachronism of their style and manners in the decades of change which have swept its splendours away. Toby 'really felt himself to be what he had called a "museum piece"':[106] the novel shows his growing awareness that Nazism and the other political developments of the thirties are leading to a war which will be 'the end of the world which had made him and in which he could breathe and survive' (p.152). Appropriately, both Toby and his mother die during the war, avoiding further hazards of trying to adapt to

> ...an age of community-singing, by-pass roads, bed-sitting rooms, plastic dinner-plates and...television and prefabricated houses...the one-room flatlet, the caravan, the prefabricated shack, and the concentration camp, an era in which there is often...room for the pleasures of memory (pp.76, 127).

Partly critical of luxurious gentility, and partly an indulgent elegy for its demise, *Museum Pieces* employs some of 'the pleasures of memory' as a part of its own technique. Best known as a writer of short stories, poetry, and autobiography, Plomer uses a pseudo-biographical style: his narrator suggests that *Museum Pieces* is 'a memoir in the form of a novel, or a novel in the form of a memoir...a matter of memory, of recollection' (p.5). Like many of his contemporaries, Plomer incorporates in recollections of an individual's progress a sense of the broader disturbances and transformations of the twentieth century, resuming in retrospect an extensive private and public history. This sort of construction, along with regret for the passing of the Edwardian period and its splendid creatures, strongly recalls L.P. Hartley's *The Go-Between*, perhaps especially the combined sorrows and pleasures of memory expressed in Hartley's celebrated opening sentence—'The past is a foreign country: they do things differently there'. Comparable concern with the development of what is called in *The Go-Between* 'the most changeful half a century in history' (p.269) re-appears in Angus Wilson's *Anglo-Saxon Attitudes* (1956) (see Chapter Four). Extensively interested in the nature of society around 1955, Wilson also looks back to contrast and connect it with events before the First World War.

Anglo-Saxon Attitudes, *The Go-Between* and *Museum Pieces* all show the disappearance of earlier ways of life and the radical transformation of public and private experience. Their closely-contemporary publication indicates a general realisation by the mid-fifties that irrevocable changes in the life of the first half of the twentieth century had been completed by the Second World War, and that a new kind of life had begun to emerge in the years which followed. By around the time *Anglo-Saxon Attitudes* was published, this must have been made easily and generally apparent by 'the impact of public affairs'. The Suez crisis of 1956, for example, provided final confirmation of Britain's changed role in the world, imperial power exhausted by the war and the granting of Indian independence in 1947. At home, developments such as the creation of the Welfare State fostered the 'new attitude and values markedly different from those hitherto common' which Walter Allen recognised in 1955:[107] as Orwell had predicted, society had 'shaken itself into its new shape'. Several of the novelists famous during and after the war vanished from the scene. Cary, Wyndham Lewis, and Lowry all died in 1957, and Henry Green published nothing after 1952. A generation of 'new men' began to replace them, often directly concerned with the 'new shape' of post-war society, its 'by-pass roads and bed-sitting rooms'. Though these writers—John Wain, Kingsley Amis, and others—mostly began publishing around 1953 and 1954, their interest and significance were not fully recognised until 1956, when the great popular success of John Osborne's play *Look Back in Anger* allowed them to be grouped together as 'Angry Young Men' with an apparent common cause. Neither the label nor the connection with Osborne were entirely appropriate. *Look Back in Anger* is sometimes as nostalgic for the Edwardian era as Hartley or Plomer, whereas one of the distinguishing marks of the new fiction is its general concentration on the contemporary scene, avoiding the older novelists' attempts to bridge the experience of the war by using past history as a comparison or explanation for current events.

1956, however, provides an appropriate terminus for the present chapter: the 'new men' of the mid-fifties, 'angry' or otherwise, are considered in the next. In the meantime, it is worth concluding assessment of the war and post-war years by re-examining the negative views of the era with which this chapter began. With hindsight, it is possible to revise the conclusion Rosamond Lehmann reached in 1946 that there had been 'no great war novel'. Admittedly, Henry Green's *Caught*, which Lehmann registers as an exception herself, is perhaps the only British novel before 1946 to deal successfully with direct experience of the war: even in this case, its actual violent action appears only fleetingly in the last section. And in novels published later, probably only parts of *From the City, from the Plough* and the account of the retreat from Crete in *Sword of Honour* bear comparison with the achievements of American fiction in communicating something of the nature of wartime military action. But the apparent absence of what might be called a 'great war novel' in the British context may simply be a consequence of seeking it in the wrong place. In concluding, for example, that 'comparatively few good novels came out of that real, historical, war...the Hitler war failed to stimulate novelists', Anthony Burgess explicitly, and rather improvidently, discounts the 'civilian novel', giving *The Heat of the Day* as his example.[108] In fact, an excellent clue to a better understanding of the real 'stimulus' of the war is provided in this novel when Elizabeth Bowen remarks of Robert and Stella that:

...they were not alone...their time sat in the third place at their table. They were the creatures of history...of a nature possible in no other day—the day was inherent in the nature (pp.194-95).

Just as civilians were as inevitably 'caught' as soldiers in the experience of total war, novels not directly concerned with actual military actions are as much the 'creatures of history' as those which try to present them. For contemporary novelists, the common factor of 'their time' accounts for the communality of imagination identified throughout this chapter. Its repeated expression in the same set of themes in their novels is evidence of the extent to which 'the day was inherent in the nature' of literature as well as contemporary life. The strength and particularity with which its presence affected novels of the period makes almost all of them 'war novels' in one way or another, as Walter Allen suggests:

> No rigid distinction between war novels and others is possible...Since war was the inescapable experience of everyone, civilians as much as soldiers, we find the war present throughout the fiction of the forties and the decades that follow, not necessarily shown directly but there as the ineluctable shadow under which characters and events have their being.[109]

Burgess goes on himself in *The Novel Now* (p.50) to acknowledge that 'All British novels with a 1939-45 setting were, in one sense or another, novels about the war', but this specification of 'a 1939-45 setting' is still too restrictive. The 'ineluctable shadow' Allen mentions falls upon the 'characters and events' of many novels written around the time of the war but set quite outwith its actual duration.

One of these is *The Ballad and the Source*, and it is ironic that Rosamond Lehmann should have expressed concern about the intractable nature of the 'experiences of the past six years' of the war, since she finds in this novel such an effective context for its imaginative assimilation. P.H. Newby's similar doubt that the war was perhaps not an 'experience out of which an artist can create' is likewise resolved by the inventiveness of his own work in *A Step to Silence* and particularly in *The Retreat*. Though this phase of contemporary fiction, dealing partly indirectly with the challenge of war to imagination, may not always completely satisfy Lehmann's wish for a 'great war novel', on the other hand it offers no reason to conclude that this was 'one of the worst periods of English literature'. On the contrary, as P.H. Newby remarked in 1951, 'it would be very wrong indeed to suggest that the present-day level of purely literary craftsmanship is low—in fact, it has probably never been so high'.[110] The fiction of Rosamond Lehmann, Elizabeth Bowen, L.P. Hartley and others at the time is a product of the consistent 'craftsmanship' Newby discerns. This technical competence often shows in particular a useful assimilation of some of the lessons of the master 'craftsman' Henry James, and in general, among other strengths, a readiness to exploit some of the possibilities in manipulation of chronology or point of view, and in the presentation of inner consciousness, encouraged by the innovations of modernism.

Though sometimes similar, the technical expertise of Malcolm Lowry, Henry Green and Joyce Cary is often more powerful and original, making their work generally closer to the 'great war novel' Lehmann sought. *Under the Volcano* is certainly a great novel, a genuine extension of the potential of modernism. The writing of both Green and Cary is original enough to seem more analogous to modernism than derivative from it. Green's debts to earlier experiment are few after his first novel, *Blindness* (1926). His puzzling, disconnective narrative technique, and Cary's flexible viewpoint and vibrantly imaginative dramatic monologue, are largely original additions to the resources of English fiction.

The war's challenge to the imagination can be seen, in ways suggested earlier, to have encouraged this sort of expertise in the extension of existing techniques or the creation of fresh ones. As Chapter Two suggested, the thirties' concern with 'external events' contributed to the realistic, objective style predominant in its fiction. A much graver, more violent 'impact of public affairs' in the forties demanded more ingenuity, resource and structural complexity to contain the disturbing strangeness of the time. Some of the thirties' documentary directness did survive in a few novels of the sort discussed at the start of this chapter, and William Sansom's *Fireman Flower* provides an interesting example of both recent and contemporary impulses, towards objective documentary and towards imaginative experiment, existing in a single volume. Graham Greene's fiction at the time shows a significant, partly comparable division of technique. In the thirties and really throughout his long career Greene's fiction is generally straightforward in style and structure, but when presenting some of the experience of the war in *The End of the Affair* he employs for almost the only time a technique which derives as he suggests himself from the modernist example of Ford Madox Ford. Evelyn Waugh, likewise, makes in *Brideshead Revisited* an unusual departure from straightforward chronology in order to contrast more sharply an idyllic past and the shabby present circumstances the war has created.

Alongside developments in style and structure, there appears in contemporary fiction an outlook substantially altered from that of the previous decade. Whereas Orwell saw religion and politics, Catholicism and Communism, as the dual interests of the nineteen thirties, politics fades from fiction during and after the war. It is replaced by a greater concentration on some of the moral and religious questions, even some of the methods of presenting them, which characterise Victorian novels. The realistic detail and extended concern with childhood, individual development, and personal relations in Hartley's *Eustace and Hilda*, for example, make it seem more like a late nineteenth-century novel than anything published since. Such questions of individual morality and good and evil in society do not appear only in formally conservative novels, such as *Eustace and Hilda*, however. The strength of the fiction of Lowry and Cary, and to some extent of Henry Green and others, is that its structural and stylistic ingenuity is so specifically used to focus a moral sense and a broad view of the contemporary world. Formally complex, and simultaneously deeply concerned with the ethics of the historical period it envisages, such fiction is largely immune to the sort of criticism Henderson, Lukács, and other commentators (quoted in Chapter Two) directed at modernism for what they took to be its 'denial of history'.[111] Some of the fiction of the forties even seems to exhibit something of the 'balanced literary budget'—the amalgamation of old and of new, modernist techniques —which Cyril Connolly hoped for in 1938. Rather than having altogether expired, as he suggests, 'the Modern Movement' both survives in the forties and shows signs of synthesis with some of the styles and concerns of conventional fiction since the Victorian period.

This process continues in later decades of the twentieth century and will be further considered in the next chapter. Finally, however, it is worth emphasising that such processes of combination may have been particularly encouraged, even initiated, by simultaneous incentives to moral, historical and technical interests created by the experience of the war. Rather than having been only the negative influence indicated by contemporary and many later commentators, the war may thus have contributed a certain strength to the work of some of the best novelists of the period. Significantly, far from having 'failed to stimulate' these novelists, it seems to have made some of them more prolific: both Green and Cary published more during its course than at other times in their careers, and Lowry records it as an incentive to the completion of *Under the Volcano*. Perhaps because, as G.S. Fraser suggests, the drab world of war and post-war did not *lend* itself to the imagination, it actually provoked, in some cases, the imagination to develop and rearrange some of its resources. The result is a fiction whose quality does not always merely reduplicate the drabness or spiritlessness of the experience it encompasses. Perhaps only Cary, Green, and Lowry (and the latter only in a single novel) come close to rivalling the major figures of the nineteen twenties. But if their work is seen, as Newby suggests, as part of a generally high level of 'literary craftsmanship', and if it is recalled that Samuel Beckett (see Chapter Five) was also writing at the time, the war and post-war years seem by no means an impoverished period in the developing history of the novel.

4

Recent and Contemporary: the Novel since the Nineteen Fifties

'The Angry Decade': William Cooper, Kingsley Amis, John Wain, John Braine, Stan Barstow, Alan Sillitoe

'We are all of us, directly or indirectly, caught up in a great whirlwind of change', remarked Doris Lessing in 1957. As Chapter Three suggested, Britain experienced in the post-war years considerable alterations both in international role and in domestic organisation. In the latter area, new attitudes and values resulted from the effects of the war; the creation of the Welfare State; and a moderate redistribution of the nation's affluence. These factors helped to lower traditional barriers between classes, creating some sense of possible social mobility. Changes of this sort encouraged many authors in the fifties towards renewed interest in class, conduct and manners: this appears in one form in William Plomer's *Museum Pieces* (1952), discussed at the end of the last chapter. The older generation of novelists, however, such as Plomer, looked back at least half-regretfully to the disappearance of earlier ways of life in the war, whereas the new authors who emerged in the fifties welcomed change. They also often suggested that new developments had gone only far enough to reveal how much had not yet been achieved. John Wain, for example, recalls 'looking for profound changes and not finding them'; wanting 'old conventions, particularly class-distinctions, to be swept away'; and feeling, typically of young people at the time, generally 'dissatisfied with...the shape of English society'.[1] Doris Lessing likewise suggests that despite the 'whirlwind of change', 'British life is at the moment petty and frustrating'.[2] Developments since the war were felt to have contributed not to the social revolution that at first seemed promised by the Labour government of 1945, but to a modified stasis, in which even the two leading political parties seemed to have grown indistinguishable. Much of Jimmy Porter's energy in John Osborne's play *Look Back in Anger* (1956), for example, goes into complaints about the difficulties of being a rebel in this bland atmosphere, in which there seemed to be no 'good, brave causes left'.[3]

His feelings of frustration and disappointment effectively summed up a general mood at the time, and led to the habitual designation of Osborne and several other contemporary novelists and playwrights as 'angry young men'. According to *The Angry Decade*, Kenneth Allsop's contemporary study of the period and its literature,

> ...the phrase Angry Young Man carries multiple overtones which might be listed as irreverence, stridency, impatience with tradition, vigour, vulgarity, sulky resentment against the cultivated.[4]

Allsop adds that there was an element of indiscriminacy in the phrase's application, and that 'dissentient' rather than 'angry' might have been a better description of the sceptical, disaffected mood of the period. He concludes, however, that the label 'Angry Young Man' 'illuminated for large numbers of people a new state of mind in Britain of the Nineteen-Fifties', identifying some of the sense of 'futility' in Britain since the war (pp.9, 10, 19).

Aspects of this new state of mind are reflected in fiction as early as 1946, in Philip Larkin's *Jill*. They are more strongly apparent in *Scenes from Provincial Life* (1950): its author, William Cooper, Allsop considered a 'pathfinder' (p.27) for later writers. Though the novel is set in 1939, the demeanour of its narrator shows some of the 'irreverence' and 'impatience with tradition' typical of the fifties. Joe Lunn is 'rootless and...unconforming'[5]: he is a sceptical observer of his society, and mildly unconventional in his private affairs. The latter illustrate both the increasing liberality and some of the continuing restraint of the period. Though Joe enjoys a fairly free sexual relationship with his girlfriend, like the heroes of many later fifties novels he is made extremely anxious by the possibility of her pregnancy, and responds to her desire for marriage with an evasiveness which greatly complicates their affair. Joe is similarly evasive of the demands of his job: the mild cynicism with which he undertakes his work as a teacher is apparent from the opening sentences of his narrative:

> The school at which I was science-master was desirably situated, right in the centre of the town. By walking only a few yards the masters and boys could find themselves in a café or a public house.

Sustained throughout *Scenes from Provincial Life*, this cynical tone amusingly communicates Joe's disdain for traditional values. It also makes entertaining a story of quiet daily life which might otherwise seem, as Joe himself admits, 'discouragingly undramatic' (p.75).

Scenes from Provincial Life, however, is almost more significant for its anticipation of later trends than for its actual achievement. A mildly mocking comedy and a colloquial, sceptical tone help other writers of the period to establish 'dissentient' angles of vision on contemporary society. Everyday lives in Stan Barstow's *A Kind of Loving* (1960), for example, and in John Braine's *Room at the Top*

(1957) are dramatised by means of highly-characterised first-person narratives rather like Joe Lunn's in Cooper's novel. John Braine remarks of *Scenes from Provincial Life* 'this book was for me—and I suspect many others—a seminal influence'.[6] As he suggests, Cooper was admired and followed in theme or strategy by many of the writers who emerged as major figures in the fifties—C.P. Snow, John Wain, and Kingsley Amis, among others.

Amis's first novel, *Lucky Jim* (1954) was one of the most popular works of the decade. Its hero Jim Dixon was a 'symbol...a figure to be identified with...an archetypal figure, the hero of a generation', as Walter Allen suggests.[7] Jim embodies several of the new attitudes Allsop suggests were typical of the 'new state of mind' of the fifties, such as 'irreverence...impatience with tradition...vulgarity, sulky resentment against the cultivated'. Like Cooper's Joe Lunn, he is a teacher (though in a provincial university): his scepticism about the job he has to perform occasionally drives him to pull hideous faces or engage in mutinous, muttering rages. His resentments, however, mostly emerge in a kind of engaging clumsiness, leading him through drunken disasters with bedclothes and with the delivery of a lecture. In the end he is rescued from the confusions of his academic life, ironically by a member of the moneyed classes he professes to despise, and departs with an ideal girl for a remunerative job in London. This happy ending and the innocuous quality of his actions throughout make *Lucky Jim* seem in retrospect much more simply a comedy than the social criticism of an angry young man it was often considered at the time. Jim's farcical adventures and the ludicrous characters who menace him are too insubstantial to function as vehicles for satire or anger: his 'luck' at the end of the novel also exemplifies a tendency towards reconciliation with society, rather than any real desire to reform it, which is present even in those nineteen-fifties novels which appear most angry or dissentient. Unconforming rebels or angry young men settle for compromise and social acceptance: this disposition is even indicated by the titles of later parts of William Cooper's trilogy, *Scenes from Metropolitan Life* (1951) and *Scenes from Married Life* (1961).

Tension between rebellion and conformity is also a feature of John Wain's *Hurry on Down* (1953). After leaving university, Wain's hero Charles Lumley immediately shows his determined dissentience from normal social expectations by spurning a professional career and choosing employment as a window-cleaner instead. There is an odd appropriateness in the fact that this job makes him carry a ladder with him everywhere he goes, for he embarks on a rapid but steady descent of the social scale, almost rung by rung, in a variety of unpromising jobs. Even Charles, however, is not allowed to hurry down too far: like Jim, he is rescued in the end by a well-paid job and a desirable girl. He does continue to assert his 'neutrality', however, claiming that

> ...the running fight between himself and society had ended in a draw; he
> was no nearer, fundamentally, to any *rapprochement* or understanding with
> it than when he had been a window-cleaner.[8]

In *Room at the Top*, John Braine's hero Joe Lampton seems engaged
in a 'running fight' with society aimed at total victory; at an ascent of
the social ladder as rapid as Charles's hurrying down. Joe's appetites
are sharpened by a meticulous eye for status, class, and material
value: this produces in his narrative a constant register of prices and
possessions:

> ...The ownership of the Aston-Martin automatically placed the young
> man in a social class far above mine...
>   At last, I thought, feeling her body against me, soft and scented, clean
> all over, above all, *expensive*.[9]

Despite his rampant material ambition, Joe shows like Jim Dixon
and Charles Lumley some ambivalence in his attitude to
contemporary manners and morals. As his narrative suggests, he is
'not very fond of abstract thinking' (p.33); yet he retains certain
scruples about his complicity with a newly affluent, materialist
society, or at least a recognition of 'the muck one's forced to wade
through to get what one wants' (p.8). Along with undiminished
enthusiasm for material success, such awareness leads at times to a
sort of schizophrenia: after the suicide of a lover abandoned for a
better match, Joe talks of himself, with disgust, in the third person.
    Such tensions in Joe's character, however, are clumsily presented
in *Room at the Top*. In particular, Braine ignores the opportunity for
judgemental irony offered by Joe's retrospective narrative, looking
back from the time of his success on his younger self. *Hurry on Down*,
likewise, is rather naïvely written, as Wain acknowledges in his
introduction: both novels may be of most lasting value for the
accuracy of their reflection of the social climate at the time. Wain
partly suggests in his introduction that in *Hurry on Down* he was
interested in using fiction as a vehicle for social commentary: some of
his characters are referred to as 'an interesting sociological study'
(p.166), and Charles himself envisages 'allegorical elements' in his
'Social and Economic Maladjustment' (p.233). *Room at the Top* is
similarly indicative of social and economic factors contributing to
the 'new state of mind' of the fifties: Joe's ambitions particularly
illuminate the period's new shapes of class and conduct; its rising
affluence and materialism; and some of the changes and continuing
restrictions in its sexual habits.
    Though envisaged slightly differently, contemporary social
change is also a central, problematic issue in fifties fiction more
exclusively concerned with working-class communities. In *A Kind of*

Loving, for example, Stan Barstow portrays Vic Brown's Northern town with a warmth and vividness which sometimes resembles D.H. Lawrence's *Sons and Lovers* (1913), but the novel is also very precisely located in its own time. Though Vic's community is still close and conventional enough to force him into marriage with his pregnant girlfriend, it is also increasingly influenced by the new trends of the fifties. References to immigration, growing affluence, the new mass market for television and pop records all show aspects of the change which Barstow finds 'rushes at us with alarming speed' in the modern world.[10] Barstow's interest in this as it affects ordinary working life is shared by other contemporary novelists such as Keith Waterhouse, Colin MacInnes, and Alan Sillitoe, one of the best of the authors to emerge in the fifties. Waterhouse's *Billy Liar* (1959), for example, depicts a Northern town as drab as Vic's, enlivened only by the fantasies of the protagonist. MacInnes's 'London Novels' (*City of Spades* (1957); *Absolute Beginners* (1959); *Mr Love and Justice* (1960)) show through realistic dialogue and documentary observation life among immigrants, petty criminals and the disaffected young caught up by the jazz and race riots of the later fifties.

Like Barstow, Alan Sillitoe presents the provincial working class in ways which show his admiration for D.H. Lawrence. Like Lawrence — another Nottinghamshire novelist — Sillitoe extensively transcribes the thoughts of his characters: his first novel, *Saturday Night and Sunday Morning* (1958), relies heavily on the colloquial inner voice of its hero Arthur Seton. Lawrence is also recalled by the vivid domestic detail in which Sillitoe presents Arthur's wild Christmas celebrations with his Aunt's huge family; and by the almost religious release he experiences with his girlfriend — 'as if the weight of the world had in this minute been lifted from them both... they broke through to the opened furrows of the earth'.[11] Such sections are the best of a novel which occasionally shows its origins in fragments and short stories. Reviewers at the time, however, thought it the outstanding proletarian novel since the thirties. In the meticulous detail with which he presents factory work, Sillitoe perhaps rivals Henry Green's *Living* (1929), and *Saturday Night and Sunday Morning* successfully updates the portrayal in Walter Greenwood's *Love on the Dole* (1933) of life in the poor streets surrounding industrial centres. Like Barstow, Sillitoe is sensitive to the social renewal and affluence which by the fifties had radically altered the conditions Greenwood envisaged. Memories of the depression linger, but for Arthur's father there is now

> ... a sit-down job at the factory, all the Woodbines he could smoke, money for a pint if he wanted one... a holiday somewhere, a jaunt on the firm's trip to Blackpool, and a television set to look into at home... the thousands that worked... took home good wages. No more short time like before the war (pp.26-7).

Though well-paid himself, Arthur finds it 'no use saving your money...you never knew when the Yanks were going to do something daft like dropping the H-bomb on Moscow' (pp.27-8). Instead, he is a careless spender, and a rootless hedonist, engrossed in booze, fights, and sex.

He is also one of the fifties' more genuinely angry young men; a self-conscious rebel, infuriated by 'the raw edge of fang-and-claw on which all laws were based, law and order against which he had been fighting all his life' (p.184). This sort of struggle continues and is clarified as a part of class-conflict in Sillitoe's novella *The Loneliness of the Long Distance Runner* (1959). Its narrator finds in running and in refusing to win races some freedom from the expectations of materialist society, and the system of the Borstal in which he is imprisoned. He divides the world into

> In-law blokes like you and them, all on the watch for Out-law blokes like me and us...they don't see eye to eye with us and we don't see eye to eye with them, so that's how it stands and how it will always stand.[12]

This depiction of social and class conflict is extended in Sillitoe's trilogy *The Death of William Posters* (1965); *A Tree on Fire* (1967); *The Flame of Life* (1974), which investigates working-class possibilities in revolution and in art as part of

> ...the great hundred years' war against imperialism and the established order, class war, civil war, dark and light war, the eternal conflict of them against us and us against them[13]

Sillitoe's trilogy was less well received than his early work, perhaps lacking some of its vigour and originality. A similar, often sharper decline appears in the novels of other writers discussed above: in the view of at least one critic, 'each was essentially a man of one book'.[14] The farcical humour of *Lucky Jim*, for example, dwindles to fatuity in *I Like it Here* (1958), while Amis's *Take a Girl Like You* (1960) is assessed by Bernard Bergonzi (in his study *The Situation of the Novel* (1970)) as 'heavily padded' and impaired by 'moral and artistic incoherence'.[15] As Bergonzi suggests, *Take a Girl Like You* is informed by an awkwardly divided outlook. On the one hand, there is Amis's mixture of disdain and grudging admiration for the 'free-and-easy way of going on'[16] on the edge of the sixties: this equips the seducer Patrick with charm as well as unpleasantness. On the other hand there is a distinct nostalgia for the 'old Bible-class ideas' (p.317) partly embodied in Patrick's victim Jenny Bunn. With little arbitration between these views, *Take a Girl Like You* moves uncertainly towards Jenny's rape by Patrick and the vague, lame conclusion that all this is 'rather a pity' (p.317).

This confused division of the novel's allegiance is exemplary of difficulties some fifties novelists experienced in adjusting to the temper of the next decade. The sixties greatly extended some of the social change examined in the novels of the angry young men, introducing new developments in ways which removed or made intractable central subjects of their work. So specifically concerned with changing values—social, sexual, material—of their own time, not only *Room at the Top* and *Hurry on Down* but many fifties novels may be of more lasting sociological than literary interest. Anthony Burgess talks of *Lucky Jim* as 'socially significant' and Bergonzi suggests that although *Take a Girl Like You* is

> ...an imperfect and indeed annoying novel...it is an incisive anatomy of the England of rising affluence in the late fifties...shot through with a sense of other values which are fast disappearing. [17]

Circumscribed by specific concern with its period, fifties fiction is further limited by an anger which is largely self-indulgent rather than—as was often supposed at the time—politically motivated. *Take a Girl Like You* briefly mocks 'the precious Tory Government' and its claim that 'we never had it so good' (p.11), and there is a flirtation with left-wing attitudes in *Lucky Jim* and in *Hurry on Down*. With the exception of Alan Sillitoe, however, the angry young men are seldom genuinely critical of the forces shaping contemporary life: their 'dissentience' seems little more than irritation at their exclusion from a satisfactory place in a society that had 'never had it so good'. In the case of Amis and Braine in particular, personal success largely terminated dissentience, just as their characters' rebellions are quickly annulled by the acquisition of a job and a place in the world. Gilbert Phelps summarises some of the shortcomings of this fiction when he suggests in 'The Novel Today' that its authors were

> ...often too emotionally committed to the negative values they sought to illustrate: their attitudes were ambivalent...one has the feeling that they beat against the doors not in order to destroy them, but in the confident hope that if they made enough fuss they would be let in...how little dynamic was contained in the 'anger' or 'dissentience' of the period as far as the novel was concerned is perhaps demonstrated by the disappointing later careers of many of these writers. [18]

Phelps's opinion is confirmed by David Lodge, who remarks that 'the Angry-provincial-neorealist fiction of the Fifties doesn't seem, in retrospect, a particularly glorious chapter in English literary history'. [19] Lodge's comment also helps to define the predominant style of fiction at the time: generally realist in method, it often looks back for its technique to the example of Edwardian or earlier writers. Cooper's *Scenes from Provincial Life* anticipates this as well as other aspects of the decade's developments. His 'undramatic' material is filled out with vivid documentation of town life and of the countryside around Joe's weekend cottage. Like his title, which recalls George Eliot's *Scenes of Clerical Life* (1857), Cooper's style indicates a preference for traditional nineteenth-century forms rather than the more innovative techniques of earlier twentieth-century fiction. He also remarks

> ...writing Experimental novels is a retreat from writing about Man-in-Society...a retreat into writing about the sensations of Man-alone...the Experimental Novel had got to be brushed out of the way before we could get a proper hearing.

Kingsley Amis likewise dismissed in 1958 'the idea about experiment being the life-blood of the English novel'.[20] Other contemporary authors exhibit similar urges to 'brush away' the experimental or modernist novel in favour of more plain, direct, social concern. C.P. Snow and Angus Wilson summed up this inclination in the *Times Literary Supplement* in 1958, remarking

> ...one cannot begin to understand a number of contemporary English novelists unless one realises that to them Joyce's way is at best a cul-de-sac.
>
> It is criticism of the early twentieth-century revolution in the novel that, more than any class or regional hostility, has motivated the post-war English novelists' emphasis on the social framework.[21]

Such comments, the example of *Scenes from Provincial Life* and the practice of Cooper's successors all suggest that the novel in the fifties partly follows the pattern Chapter Two suggested developed in the thirties. When society finds itself under particular stress or in 'a great whirlwind of change', novelists tend to examine 'Man-in-Society' rather than 'Man-alone', renouncing the innovations of modernism or other elaborations of technique in favour of a realistic method reflecting as directly as possible the unsettled circumstances of the time. Angus Wilson summarised in 1954 the limited interest of the modernists for his generation, referring to a touchstone for the oscillations of literary fashion, Virginia Woolf's essay 'Mr. Bennett and Mrs. Brown' (see Chapter One). He remarks:

> External observation, social setting, character set firmly in narrative and scene have once again returned. In all this, of course, Bennett is likely to gain...the teacher and mentor to whom the new generation of writers can turn as the last of the old-time school of novelists.[22]

Other contemporaries joined Wilson in admiring Bennett, Wells and Galsworthy, the novelists Woolf and the modernists rejected. The precise class-consciousness and interest in social mobility which distinguish Wells's *Kipps* (1905), for example, reappear widely in the fiction of the fifties. Wain, C.P. Snow and Amis all indicate a specific preference for Bennett's 'old-time' style rather than the modernism of Virginia Woolf. Bennett's example was perhaps especially likely to appeal to novelists such as Alan Sillitoe, John Braine and David Storey, who concerned themselves with life in the industrial regions of the north of England.

These writers' redirection of the novel's interest upon working life in the provinces is one of the genuine achievements of fifties fiction. Its realistic style also made it easy to translate into film: successful versions of several of the novels discussed above were made for the cinema. These films and the way in which writers concentrated so precisely upon the mood and issues of their time secured for them a very wide contemporary readership. This popularity and the humour and straightforward style of authors such as Amis contributed to the appeal of fifties fiction, despite its limitations, for several later writers (see the concluding part of this Chapter). The most impressive achievements to arise from the work of the period, however, were made by novelists—David Storey and Angus Wilson in particular—who were initially closely identified with the 'new state of mind' of the time, but later developed far beyond its context and restrictions.

Beyond Fifties Realism: David Storey and Angus Wilson

David Storey's first novel, *This Sporting Life* (1960), has genuine affinities with the fiction of the angry young men: its tough Northern setting resembles the context of *Saturday Night and Sunday Morning*, and Storey's first-person narrator Arthur Machin shows some of the violent, domineering manner of Arthur Seton. He also shares some of the raw, material ambition of Braine's Joe Lampton, and is likewise occasionally appalled as well as allured by the new affluence and its inert apparatus of television and cars. Machin, however, is a more complex hero than either Braine's or Sillitoe's. He suggests:

> ...I had no feelings...I'm a natural professional. What I don't get paid to do I don't bother with. If I was paid enough to feel then I'd probably make a big splash that way.[23]

Despite such cynicism, Machin is patently capable of strong emotions, such as the tenderness he tries to show his landlady. His limitation lies rather in a failure to acknowledge his emotional nature or communicate its character to others. Dissatisfied by the success he has sought as a rugby league star, and unable to recognise the causes of his life's affluent impoverishment, he is a man divided against himself in ways which elude his complete understanding. Such difficulties strongly characterise his story, in which emotion is often implied rather than stated. The result is an elusive narrative, more perplexing and often more subtle than the provincial, angry novel it was first supposed.

Some of the self-division which disturbs Arthur Machin also affects Storey's hero in *Radcliffe* (1963). Leonard Radcliffe remarks 'I think there's an element in us which refutes and condemns our understanding of ourselves'.[24] Most of the novel's tensions, however, are dramatically projected into the conflict between Radcliffe—sensitive, frail, and refined—and his grossly physical, vital, lover, Victor Tolson. Their struggle is partly connected to the renewed class-consciousness of the fifties: Tolson is resolutely down-to-earth and working-class, while Radcliffe and his family inhabit a decaying aristocratic mansion—'The Place'—on the edge of a northern town. *Radcliffe*, however, goes beyond the social issue of class. As Radcliffe explains, his struggle with Tolson is partly symbolic, even allegoric:

> Vic was my body, and I was his soul... it's the division that separates everything in life now, *everything*... the battle was so intense between us because we could see something beyond it... the split in the whole of Western society. (pp.342-5).

Even the novel's landscape is mildly allegorical, or at least, rather in the manner of Kafka, informed by psychic and emotional qualities: Radcliffe begins, for example, to 'sense the Place as an extension of his own mind... his habitation of the Place was like his habitation of his own brain' (p.111). Likewise, the industrial wilderness around the Place is often representative of the loveless despair of its inhabitants, and is often presented in visionary terms:

> ... bared luminous nerves splattered from the earth. Row after row of giant men encased in multiple sheaths of steel, heads like metal foliage on metal trunks, rose one by one and advanced, twin columns face to face, the ground spewed up in the wake of metal feet (p.134).

The nervous movement of Storey's prose, its 'confused... rootless observations' (p.128) imitate the gradual disintegration of Radcliffe's mind under the stress of his circumstances and relationships. Half-innocent and half-demented, he is referred to as a 'reluctant Messiah', and as 'the divine idiot' (pp.241, 299) and has some affinities with Dostoevsky's Prince Myshkin in *The Idiot* (1868). He ends in murder and madness: long before, however, frustrated emotions emerge in horrifying actions which keep *Radcliffe* constantly on the edge of fantasy, of Gothic gloom and nightmare. Its darkness and morbid intensity were sometimes compared to the atmosphere of Emily Brontë's *Wuthering Heights* (1847) by early critics, though they also complained of overblown prose, implausible action, and facile allegory. Such faults are occasionally in evidence: in general, however, Storey's imagination is impressively sustained, moving beyond the straightforward realism of the angry young men while remaining partly focused on their interests in class and social change.

A similar ability to project social issues into a complex imaginative dimension enhances Storey's *Pasmore* (1972). At the end of the novel, after a breakdown for which he could find 'no reason at all', Pasmore 'still dreamed of the pit and the blackness. It existed all around him, an intensity'.[25] This dream of blackness is in some ways simply Pasmore's guilty recollection of the poverty of his parents' Northern mining town, from which he has escaped into the middle class. At another level, however, it shows Storey connecting questions of social mobility with deeper existential problems of identity, role, and self. The 'blackness' of the dream is not only a memory of his father's work in the pit, but a sample of the nothingness which Albert Camus and other Existentialists (discussed in Chapter Five) see surrounding the individual in an 'era of disintegration' (*Pasmore*, p.21). Self-tortured, lonely and confused, finding 'how quickly everything drops to bits' (p.76), Pasmore's deepening personal crisis particularly recalls Camus's *The Fall* (*La Chute*, 1956). Partly consequences of social change and uncertainty in the fifties, the 'blackness' and self-division of both *Pasmore* and *Radcliffe* also indicate that Storey's fiction brings to the modern era and its disintegration, social and spiritual, a disturbing imagination of unusual strength and range.

Angus Wilson's initial identification with the angry young men, like Storey's, was at least partly justified, as his own summary of his position among contemporary writers in 1958 helps suggest:

> Most of the English novelists (perhaps all) who have arrived since the war have reflected the predominant, politically detached, social concerns of the community. This has led to a rivival of traditional, nineteenth-century forms. It has told against experiments in technique and against exploration of personal sensitivity. I belong to this reaction myself.[26]

Wilson's own 'revival of traditional, nineteenth-century forms' reflects his admiration for Zola and Dickens (he has written studies of each) and George Eliot. It is perhaps most apparent in his second novel, *Anglo-Saxon Attitudes* (1956). One of its characters remarks 'we need another Dickens' and Wilson's determination 'to convince the reader that he is seeing society as a whole', as it appears in this novel, seems part of an attempt to fulfil this need himself.[27] Like Dickens, or George Eliot in *Middlemarch* (1872) Wilson manipulates a large number of plots, drawn from and illustrating a wide range of social strata, and linked together by coincidence or tenuous interconnection. The novel establishes in this way 'complicated webs of muddled human activity' (p.290). These are shown surrounding Gerald Middleton, an aging historian, impeding his attempts to 'face the truth in life' (p.12), both in his own experience and in the field of his historical study, which has been confused and darkened for almost fifty years by a fraud committed in 1912.

Late Call (1964) resembles *Anglo-Saxon Attitudes* both in historical depth and in realistic, broadly extended satire of the changing society of the time. Another of Wilson's aging protagonists, Sylvia Calvert, retires to live with her progressive son in a new town described as a 'little microcosm' which 'reflects very accurately the country at large'.[28] It illustrates with particular clarity the new, rootless affluence of the time, 'the nice neat England we've built', furnished with 'the washing-up machine, the quick grill, the deep freeze, the cooker, the spin dryer, and all the other white monsters' (pp.157, 81). The emptiness of this shiny new world contrasts unfavourably with Sylvia's older, more secure values. Though some of the novel's satire is mildly directed against her, Wilson generally uses her perspective as a firm basis for criticism of a community heartless and confused despite the sociological self-knowledge personified in Sylvia's son. Dispirited by the town's glossy, well-planned bleakness, Sylvia is forced increasingly towards a pastoral withdrawal into the countryside around it. This allows her to return in memory to the formative earlier times of her country childhood—'The Hot Summer of 1911', for example, described at length in the opening section of *Late Call*.

Though both *Anglo-Saxon Attitudes* and *Late Call* share the 'social concerns' Wilson himself considered typical of the fifties, even before the publication of the latter, 'experiment in technique' had partly replaced his reliance on traditional forms. This is first apparent in *The Old Men at the Zoo* (1961). As Wilson acknowledges in an introductory note, 'the events described here...are utterly improbable': set in a future of threatened nuclear apocalypse and actual European war, the novel largely abandons plausible realism in favour of a fantastic fable about events in London Zoo, another 'little microcosm' of human society. The zoo's administrator, Simon Carter, faces like Gerald Middleton in *Anglo-Saxon Attitudes* 'muddled human activity', and is dispirited by the way the 'muddling, maddening, blundering of people' contributes to random violence which stalks the world like a feral beast, and to the constant nuclear threat of 'A Good Old, Rare Old, Armageddon'.[29] Carter himself, however, mixes 'misanthropy...and yet a natural liking for people' (p.51), and his narrowing, 'priggish' belief that 'Whate'er is best administered *is* best' (pp.80, 324) make him at times the inadvertent satiric target of his own narrative. This uncertain moral status contributes to the complexity of *The Old Men at the Zoo*, which develops social concerns into a strange allegory about administration and muddle, order and anarchy; the general tortuous perplexity of organising human or even animal affairs. Such issues, however, become themselves rather tenuously focused, slightly muddled, after the expansion into fantasy which follows the arrival of a version of Armageddon.

Wilson acknowledges a significant incentive to further experimentation when he remarks in the nineteen seventies 'the chief influence in my last years has been Virginia Woolf, whom I had to attack fiercely before I felt free to recognise as the very great novelist she was'. Even in 1958, when partly attacking the modernists, Wilson recognises the merit of Woolf, and adds that 'to combine depth with breadth seems to me the principal problem that must preoccupy the contemporary English novelist'. This combination he considers might be assisted by

> ...a re-examination of the interior monologue form to see how its artificiality may be more happily combined with the direct effects of dialogue and action. This last problem...may be solved by the use of multiple voices.[30]

Wilson attempts his most ambitious combination of 'depth with breadth' in *No Laughing Matter* (1967), a huge novel whose 'multiple voices', are recorded in a variety of interior monologues whose form demonstrates his admiration for Woolf. *No Laughing Matter* opens with Wilson's protagonists, the six children of the Matthews family, watching one another in distorting fairground mirrors: the scene aptly introduces the novel's reflection and refraction of its material through the distinctively individual minds of these characters. Following their development through six decades of the twentieth century, *No Laughing Matter* frequently alternates not only between transcriptions of the Matthews family's various inner voices, but also between other wholly different narrative techniques. Large sections, for example, are entirely in the form of dramatic dialogue, sometimes parodying the work of playwrights such as Ibsen, Shaw, and Chekhov. Certain sections also allude to *Macbeth* and to Aeschylus, and the children's indulgence in 'The Game'—a semi-surreal imitation of their bizarre parents—approximates to the 'Nighttown' section of Joyce's *Ulysses*. This stylistic plurality is further complicated when one of the children takes over the narrative in the form of the thinly-disguised stories of her family on which she has based her success as a writer. She often discusses formal or technical problems identical to Wilson's own: along with his extensive use of parody and interior monologue, this self-consciousness contributes to a strongly modernist element in *No Laughing Matter*.

Wilson's modernist techniques, however, are employed principally to enhance presentation of broadly social concerns, 'Man-in-Society' rather than 'Man-alone'. *No Laughing Matter* combines some of the methods of modernism with a continuing interest in issues central to the fiction modernism rejected. *The Forsyte Saga*, for example, is often mentioned: rather like Galsworthy, Wilson is concerned with the development of solidly middle-class family life and its implication in the wider life of the times. Each of the Matthews children is placed in a different area of public affairs: following their various successful careers, Wilson establishes a very broad view of British society between 1912 and 1967. Disillusioned by the First World War, Quentin, for example, develops into an Orwellian liberal widely concerned with politics and contemporary commentary, while Rupert, a successful actor, and Marcus, a homosexual connoisseur of painting, are both involved in the progress of the arts. Their lives, and those of their sisters, intersect with many of the century's cultural and historical developments—'the very harsh unpalatable things that historical inevitability had in store'. These include the decline of the middle-class in the depression; the war in Spain; fascist marches in thirties London; Suez; the shifting, stifling, class system of Britain; and the eventual appearance of a new group of children who discover in their turn that 'no young generations do like their elders'.[31] The turbulence of these public developments is reduplicated in the inner tensions of the family's life—its bitter squabbles, the 'stale rows leading nowhere; intimacy that did not signify'[32] which Wilson presents throughout his fiction with sharp, distinctive humour. The Matthews's loneliness, lovelessness, and emotional conflict make them appropriate representatives of the wider history of their time. If *No Laughing Matter* seems occasionally rambling and eventually inconclusive, this is perhaps only a part of Wilson's demonstration that it may be the fate of the family, and of the century itself, to find no stability to set against a sense of disconnection in society and lost wholeness in the self. The range of social, moral and historical issues examined in the novel, and its almost equally successful attention to individual life, confirm Wilson as a novelist of breadth as well as depth; of historical vision and technical expertise. As Malcolm Bradbury suggests, 'to many people he stands as the most developed and impressive novel-writer of his generation'.[33]

By retracing to 1912 the determining forces which have subsequently shaped public and private lives, Wilson repeats the pattern of *Late Call*, showing Sylvia Calvert's loss of pastoral innocence in 1911, and of *Anglo-Saxon Attitudes*, concerned with a literal corruption of history originating in 1912. This retrospective scrutiny of sources of the century's disturbance associates Wilson's work with several writers such as Plomer, Hartley and Orwell discussed in Chapter Three: in its sense of the decline of England and of liberal values, *No Laughing Matter* perhaps particularly resembles Joyce Cary's *To be a Pilgrim* (1942). Historical development of comparable depth, and sometimes comparable pattern, also appears in more recent fiction, in even fuller sagas of individual life and times unfolded by the novel-sequences of Anthony Powell, Henry Williamson, and C.P. Snow.

Chronicles: C.P. Snow, Anthony Powell, Henry Williamson

The eleven volumes of C.P. Snow's *Strangers and Brothers* (1940-1970)[34] cover much the same period (1914 to the end of the sixties) as Wilson's *No Laughing Matter*. Snow's narrator Lewis Eliot is involved, rather like the Matthews children, at least as an observer of many of the significant developments of the century—the disaffected aftermath of the First World War (*Strangers and Brothers* (1940)); the drift towards the Second (*The Light and the Dark* (1947)); *The Masters* (1951)); the development of the atom bomb (*The New Men* (1954)); shocking murder trials at the end of the sixties (*The Sleep of Reason* (1968)). Like Simon Carter in Wilson's *The Old Men at the Zoo*, many of Snow's figures are bureaucrats or public men facing the dilemmas of administration in a century of shifting values and pervasive violence. In his title *Corridors of Power* (1964), Snow added to the English language a catch-phrase which also defines the interest of his sequence as a whole. He is especially concerned throughout with the relation of public power and private morality; the conflict of ambition with integrity and responsibility. In *The New Men*, for example, Lewis Eliot remarks

> ...when any group of men chose anyone for any job...put your ear to those meetings and you heard the intricate labyrinthine and unassuageable rapacity, even in the best of men, of the love of power...you have heard it in colleges, in bishoprics, in ministries, in cabinets.[35]

Individual volumes of the sequence concentrate on 'colleges... ministries...cabinets': *Strangers and Brothers* is probably at its best, as in *The Masters*, for example, when Snow restricts his examination of conflict and 'rapacity' to a single institution, in which the larger, more 'labyrinthine' operation of power in the wider world may be reflected. Setting *The Masters* in a Cambridge college in the late thirties provides a context as conveniently confined as the country house was for earlier generations of novelists. Within it, the electoral struggle between Crawford and Jago for Mastership of the college both shows an intimate intrigue corrupting some of 'the best of men', and also incorporates wider implications. The dons find 'war hysteria'[36] generated by the election: rather like another novel of the period, P.H. Newby's *A Step to Silence* (1952; see Chapter Three), *The Masters* shows conflict within an academic institution mirroring a wider world poised on the edge of war. Frequent talk of the war in Spain or of the approaching World War confirms the wider significance of *The Masters*: Snow also incorporates some of his own concerns about the relation between science and the humanities in the twentieth century, the issue he discusses in *The Two Cultures and the Scientific Revolution* (1959). Crawford is cold but politically sound and an excellent scientist; Jago an English don with 'a disinterested interest in other people: magnanimity: a dash of romantic imagination' (p.93), but a rather uncertain character. Protractedly unresolved, their struggle is implicated with great complexity in the lives and issues of the novel. It generates considerable suspense: Snow's almost claustrophobic concentration makes the potentially unpromising material of college life surprisingly interesting.

Though some of the same issues and the same confinement within a small group of characters continue to be employed in the next volume of the sequence, *The New Men*, this novel also reveals some of the weaknesses of Snow's methods. Several of these arise from the nature and use of his narrator. Knowing other characters largely from the outside, any narrator is likely to be more limited than an omniscient author in recording thoughts and feelings other than his own: in this way, Lewis Eliot's closest confederates sometimes seem 'strangers' rather than 'brothers'. But Eliot also appears curiously distanced even from his own feelings: the complications of power emerge with much more conviction than any inner emotions, and the public face of experience strongly predominates over interest in the private sphere. In the invention of nuclear warfare in *The New Men* or the murders in *The Sleep of Reason*, there is also a depth of horror which particularly reveals the inadequacy of Eliot's 'admirable detachment'[37] and his bland, equable narrative. Broadly interested in society, and shallow in presenting individual consciousness, Snow's sequence shares some of the characteristics, and the limitations, of the Angry-provincial-neorealist novels which his work as a reviewer in the fifties did much to promote. *Strangers and Brothers* extends the range of fictional subject-matter: few twentieth-century authors are as well-prepared as Snow—scientist, civil servant and politician—to examine the effects of 'the scientific revolution' or the structures of power in Britain. But Snow is limited in method and lacking in strong or original imagination: as Bergonzi concludes, the many volumes of *Strangers and Brothers*

> ...contribute to the contemporary novel as an ongoing sociological activity: what is far from being the case is that they add anything to the power of the novel to grasp and transform our experience.[38]

The public world which interests C.P. Snow figures less centrally in the twelve volumes of Anthony Powell's *A Dance to the Music of Time* (1951-1975):[39] though sensitive to general changes in twentieth-century experience, Powell is more concerned with private life and affairs. Examining the period from the end of the First World War up to the end of the nineteen-sixties, he follows a complicated evolution of personality, relationships and manners in a wide range of upper middle-class characters. This is a context which Powell established long before *A Dance to the Music of Time* began to appear. His first novel, *Afternoon Men* (1931), is set among the moneyed, leisured post-war generation whose brittle gaiety Powell exposes rather in the manner of Evelyn Waugh. *Afternoon Men* also has some of the understated subtlety in presenting character and relationship through conversation which distinguishes the work of

Ronald Firbank, whom both Powell and Waugh admired. Powell's aloof, elegant narrative voice directs a cool irony over his characters: though the result is often very funny, it is in some ways also grimmer than Waugh or Firbank—Powell's 'bright young things' are distinctly tarnished, and sometimes scarcely young.

Afternoon Men establishes Powell's milieu: some of his methods also remain similar in *A Dance to the Music of Time*, though they are modified by the introduction of Nicholas Jenkins as a narrator. He is generally an unprejudiced observer, reserved, even embarrassed about intense (especially sexual) feelings, his own in particular: his reticent narrative, retaining some of the aloofness of *Afternoon Men*, stimulates readers into making some of their own judgements about him as well as the world he presents. Jenkins's equanimity and restraint also make him an appropriate foil, a touchstone of rather fastidious integrity, set against the tortuous relationships, unstable marriages, and freakish personal ambitions which unravel and reform around him, making up much of the substance of *A Dance to the Music of Time*.

Jenkins occasionally mentions his own development as a novelist: his tendency to see the world in terms of painting or artistic pattern is particularly counterpointed against the outlook of an alter-ego, a character as awkward and obtrusive as his name, Widmerpool. Though a figure of 'innate oddness…almost…monstrosity', 'almost too grotesque to take seriously', Widmerpool nevertheless emerges as the sequence's central figure—at least its leading eccentric— especially towards the end. Widmerpool is strongly distinguished by his 'complete absorption in his own activities, and also in his ambition', and by his 'determination…to live by the will alone'.[40] His character and intrigues incorporate into *A Dance to the Music of Time* some of the 'unassuageable rapacity…the love of power', which concerns Snow. Widmerpool, and other figures such as Quiggin who resemble him, are determined to create for themselves room at the top of the social ladder, regardless of conventional values or restraints. They partly belong to the 'new state of mind in Britain of the Nineteen-Fifties', the new sense of social mobility: their appearance among Powell's more genteel characters is 'a landmark in the general disintegration of society in its traditional form'[41]—a process of interest in the sequence as a whole. Widmerpool also reveals the elitism of Powell's world: for all his faults, he is shunned partly on the grounds of his indifferent background and lineage.

Frequent, almost magically coincidental reappearances of Widmerpool in various parts of Jenkins's life also create a rhythm of repetition and variation which contributes to the unity of *A Dance to the Music of Time*, and to its developing illustration of 'the complicated pattern life forms'.[42] Jenkins considers that:

... existence fans out indefinitely into new areas of experience, and that almost every additional acquaintance offers some supplementary world... As times goes on, of course, these supposedly different worlds, in fact, draw closer, if not to each other, then to some pattern common to all... nearly all the inhabitants of these outwardly disconnected empires turn out at last to be tenaciously inter-related...[in] that extraordinary process that causes certain figures to appear and reappear in the performance of one or other sequence of a ritual dance.

(*A Buyer's Market*, pp.168, 183)

His reflections about 'pattern' and 'ritual dance' resume the sequence's opening, controlling image of

Poussin's scene in which the Seasons, hand in hand and facing outward, tread in rhythm... The image of Time brought thoughts of mortality: of human beings, facing outward like the Seasons, moving hand in hand in intricate measure... in evolutions that take recognisable shape: or breaking into seemingly meaningless gyrations, while partners disappear only to reappear again, once more giving pattern to the spectacle. (*A Question of Upbringing*, p.6)

Jenkins's remarks reflect Powell's means of structuring the mass of material of *A Dance to the Music of Time*. He relies on social occasions such as dinners and parties to draw together characters of 'outwardly disconnected' experience: their subsequent disappearances and reappearances create a pattern of acquaintanceship on a large scale, held together by various fortuitous encounters and coincidences.

Such acquaintanceship is made more plausible by its confinement to the metropolitan, ex-public school nexus of affluence and privilege which provides Powell with nearly all his characters. Nevertheless, his concentration on this coterie world contributes to the problem Anthony Burgess indicates when he talks of conflict between the 'epic scale' of the sequence and the 'smallness of scope' in Powell's vision.[43] Some 'smallness of scope' also appears in consequence of Powell's emphasis on 'dance'. Though this provides a summary image for the social gyrations he portrays, it suggests an element of superficiality in their presentation; of formalised movement, to which the deeper natures and wishes of characters are subordinated. Powell's reliance on a narrator, like Snow's use of Lewis Eliot, in any case makes deeper insight into other characters problematic, especially as Jenkins believes that 'human life is lived largely at surface level' (*A Buyer's Market*, p.27) and remains fascinated by 'the shoals and shallows of social life' (*The Acceptance World*, p.128). The following passage is typical of his interests:

I was curious to know why the two of them were friends again; also to learn what was happening about Quiggin and Mona. Such information as I then possessed had come from Jean, who knew from her brother only that they had gone abroad together. At the same time, as a friend of Templer's, I did not want to appear too obviously willing to condone the fact that Quiggin had eloped with his wife. (*The Acceptance World*, p.181)

Such passages suggest, as Bergonzi remarks, that sometimes 'the appeal of Powell's work is...above all, to a love of gossip'.[44] It is significant that it is often figures who most love gossip, such as the intriguing Oxford don Sillery, who occupy central positions in *A Dance to the Music of Time*.

A certain 'smallness of scope' in the sequence also results from its apparently straightforward vision of time as simply a continuing 'music' carrying directly forward the movement of the characters. C.P. Snow suggests that 'it is only upon Anthony Powell that Proust has exerted a direct influence'.[45] Marcel Proust also interested Snow himself, but neither he nor Powell seems to have gained much from his example. Powell is much less concerned than Proust with the inner evolutions of memory or its imaginative expansion of actuality. Jenkins's vagueness about the historical moment from which his narrative looks back over the events it presents also ignores some of the ironic and structural potential Proust exploits. Though less complex or profound, Powell does, however, occasionally approach in other ways some of Proust's effects in establishing 'the timelessness of Time' (*A Buyer's Market*, p.28). The long recollection at the start of *The Kindly Ones*, for example, intermingles an account of the start of the First World War with the actual beginning of the Second; and characters' reappearances after very long intervals often strongly activate memories for Jenkins and for the reader, creating moments of peculiar illumination within the bland chronological continuity of the sequence. For example, it is remarked in *Books do Furnish a Room* that 'to enter Sillery's sitting-room after twenty years was to drive a relatively deep fissure through variegated seams of Time'.[46] Such 'fissures' appear frequently in *A Dance to the Music of Time*: Widmerpool, for example, enters the sequence running on a chilly winter afternoon at school, in the first volume, *A Question of Upbringing*, and dies, appropriately still running, in the last, *Hearing Secret Harmonies*. Jenkins likewise ends rather as he began, burning autumn leaves and reflecting on the dance of the seasons and of human beings. Such proliferating patterns and 'seams' of time contribute to the firm but narrow appeal of *A Dance to the Music of Time*, in its huge extent the most substantial English account of social life and manners in the twentieth century.

Like Powell's sequence, the fifteen volumes of Henry Williamson's *A Chronicle of Ancient Sunlight*[47] began to appear in 1951, perhaps further evidence of the need, following the shock of the Second World War, to recall and re-examine the historical progress of the twentieth century. 'Chronicle' aptly indicates the nature of Williamson's work: straightforwardly told, it is a fictionalised autobiography of an extent unrivalled except perhaps by the eight volumes of Compton Mackenzie's *The Four Winds of Love* (1937-45). Mackenzie is further recalled by the resemblance to his *Sinister Street*

(1914) of Williamson's setting, in his early volumes, in London at the turn of the century: their detailed portrayal of family life and interest in the conflict of spiritual and material values also recalls Galsworthy's *The Forsyte Saga*. Anthony Burgess considers these early volumes the best, free of the fascist sympathies which disfigure the latter part of the sequence, and have greatly inhibited its critical and public appeal. The first volume, for example, *The Dark Lantern*, vividly presents the ordinary domestic life of the eighteen nineties, shown from the point of view of the novel's hero Richard Maddison, and the several perspectives of the family into which he hopes to marry. Williamson is prolific in period detail: Maddison's tin-wheeled Starley Rover bicycle competes for space on dusty roads with the first horseless carriages; there is talk of 'present deplorable trends for the equalisation of the sexes'; and advertisements for

> Hinde's Hair Curlers, Monkey Brand Soap, the Waterbury Keyless Watch, Nixey's Black Lead, Epp's Cocoa, Liebig's Extract of Meat, Horniman's Tea, Gerandel's Pastilles.[48]

The Dark Lantern is geographically located with equal precision, set on the extreme, semi-rural edge of London, in suburbs where it is still possible to hear 'the bleat of lambs in the fold beside the dark building of the grammar school' (p.13); areas which

> ...had stood until a few years back among green fields and wooded hills, and now were enclosed in row upon row of houses extending, as the expansive years followed one another, into the counties of Kent and Surrey (p.140).

Most famous as the author of *Tarka the Otter* (1927), Williamson writes sensitively about this darkening pastoral world. Its gradual disappearance and the novel's setting on the uncertain boundary between country and city are emblematic of the changes encroaching upon a world poised between centuries—'a changing world, with the power gone from the land to the money of the towns', 'good old things... passing away, in the change that had come upon the world' (pp.396, 106). Subsequent volumes' setting in the First World War demonstrates the quick destruction of the century's early hopes of 'another generation, to do better things than the last; for experience surely must mean something, and lead to better things' (p.339).

Some imaginative control of the passage of time in this changing world and a means of linking a vanishing past with the present seem offered by a device—possibly connected to the title, *The Dark Lantern*—which Maddison

> ...to himself... called the Camera Obscura of the Mind...
> There were many scenes he revisited by this practice... able to release his imagination in pictures and scenes passing before his eyes... a sort of

THE NOVEL SINCE THE FIFTIES

luminous screen across which impressions within the mind were impelled
into vision (pp.25, 354).

Apart from the occasional expository flashback, however,
Williamson makes little use of this device to connect different
sections of the experience he chronicles. *A Chronicle of Ancient
Sunlight* is perhaps itself of most value as a means of fictional
revisitation of 'pictures and scenes' long since passed away in 'the
change that had come upon the world'. Through Richard's meeting
in *The Dark Lantern* with an ancient man, who later helps to save the
life of his son, such scenes even extend back to Napoleonic times:
Williamson's sequence presents a very wide continuum of English life
even beyond the twentieth century, containing vivid pictures of
many 'vanished summers, of faraway sunlight' (p.288).

Anthony Burgess suggests that in the post-war period 'we can no
longer expect the one big book' but instead 'fragments of an
individual vision in book after book'.[49] The existence of such long
sequences by Snow, Powell, Williamson and others, however,
suggests a survival of 'the one big book', its appeal perhaps modified
by a need to split the novelist's individual vision into several sections.
As Burgess himself suggests, such sequences show a continuation into
the twentieth century both of the massive scale of Victorian social
novels, and also, in some ways, of the serial form of publication often
favoured by their authors. Such methods and interests continue to
appear in more recent fiction: the fifteen volumes of Henry
Williamson's *A Chronicle of Ancient Sunlight* are surpassed in extent by
Simon Raven's seventeen entertainments in the *Alms for Oblivion* and
The First-Born of Egypt sequences (1964-), which chart rather in the
manner of Anthony Powell the fate of the English upper-middle
class since the war. A comparable extension of fiction into sequence
also appears in the many trilogies and tetralogies published in recent
decades. Several of these works seem to share the interest variously
shown by Snow, Powell, and Williamson in establishing a breadth of
awareness sufficient to come to terms with 'the change that had come
upon the world' in the historical upheavals of the twentieth century.

Lost Empire: Ian Fleming, Paul Scott, J.G. Farrell, Julian Mitchell

Along with the two world wars, Britain's major historical experience
in the twentieth century, beyond the domestic scene, has been the
final flourishing, later decline, and eventual loss of her empire.
Throughout the earlier part of the century, Britain's dominions
offered many novelists—Rudyard Kipling, Joseph Conrad, E.M.
Forster, Joyce Cary, Graham Greene, and others—a variety of
colourful contexts of great narrative potential. Characters in the
colonies could be confronted with friction between cultures,

challenging encounters with unfamiliar places and values, the dilemmas of government, or simply an exiled loneliness sharpening their anxious sense of themselves. Though perhaps changed in form, some of the empire's promise for novelists has reappeared in recent years: J.G. Farrell, for example, continued to find that 'the decline of the British Empire' is 'the really interesting thing that's happened during my lifetime'.[50] After the granting of independence to India, Pakistan, Burma, and Ceylon in the late forties, loss of empire and changing world role must have seemed as pressing issues as domestic social change in the decade which followed, and some of the novelists of the time might have been expected to share Farrell's interest, especially after 1956. Britain's failure at Suez in that year should have provided a final indication that her future in international terms was likely to be as an ally of America, or as an adjunct of the European Economic Community (which she eventually joined in the sixties), rather than as a wholly independent power.

Dramatists among the angry young men of the fifties were clearly concerned with such developments: John Osborne's *The Entertainer* (1957) reflects the Suez conflict, while in his *Look Back in Anger* there is some sympathy for Jimmy Porter's father-in-law and his regrets about the loss in 1947 of his role as a soldier-administrator in India. Anthony Burgess's aptly-entitled *The Long Day Wanes (The Malayan Trilogy: Time for a Tiger* (1956); *The Enemy in the Blanket* (1958); *Beds in the East* (1959)) provides an early example in fiction of interest in Britain's declining power, charting stages in Malaya's progress from Protectorate to independent state. In general, however, such concerns seem present obliquely, if at all, in fifties fiction. The shrinkage of British dominion may underlie the diminished scale of some novels of the period—the apparent absence of the single 'big book' mentioned by Burgess. It may also account for novelists' withdrawals to provincial settings and modest, everyday questions, contributing to a general sense of indeterminacy with which even these issues are examined.

Though still indirect, perhaps as strong an indication as any of contemporary consciousness of lost empire appears in the enormous popularity of Ian Fleming's James Bond stories, starting with *Casino Royale* in 1953. In C.P. Snow's *The New Men*, Lewis Eliot remarks of Britain's position after the war 'the major power...had gone: the country would have to live by its wits' (p.205), and it is very much this sort of survival of British pre-eminence, through 'wit' as well as fabulous courage and skill, which Bond illustrates. As Kingsley Amis suggests, Fleming's fiction offers 'expressions of chauvinism at once smartened up and on its last legs': its patriotic hero shows a spectacularly greater heroism than his American allies, and an easy superiority to the villains, invariably foreign, who confront him. As Amis indicates, the Bond novels are wish-fulfilments and 'collective power-fantasy'; a technological 'fairy tale' in which Britain's major power and imperial dominion enjoy a secret continuity in the world of agents and espionage.[51] In this way, though Fleming himself dismissed claims for its seriousness, his fiction is representative of some of the mood of the time: his precision with prices and brand names also resembles aspects of novels of the new affluence, such as John Braine's *Room at the Top*. Bond was also admired by several other authors concerned with the 'new state of mind' of the fifties: Kingsley Amis's remarks are taken from an extended study, in which he finds that Fleming's novels have 'just as much in them as more ambitious kinds of fiction', and Amis himself went on to write under a pseudonym a Bond novel of his own, *Colonel Sun* (1968).[52] Anthony Burgess's interest is indicated by *Tremor of Intent* (1969), a parody which inflates to overwhelming extravagance Fleming's characteristic attention to violence, food, and sex. Confronting its characters with various temptations and Catholic dilemmas, *Tremor of Intent* also partly parodies the manner of Graham Greene's thrillers: Greene has perhaps been a stronger influence than Fleming on later popular writers of spy fiction such as Len Deighton or John Le Carré. Greene's sense of shabby, limited human enterprise in grey areas of confusion and despair reappears most clearly in the novels of Le Carré. His complex, dark presentations of the Cold War's covert viciousness reflect some of the reality rather than the dream of Britain's post-imperial situation.

The imagination of 'more ambitious kinds of fiction' which eventually appeared to chart the empire's loss mostly centres on the major British colony, 'The Jewel in the Crown'—India. Paul Scott's *Raj Quartet* (*The Jewel in the Crown* (1966); *The Day of the Scorpion* (1968); *The Towers of Silence* (1971); *A Division of the Spoils* (1975)) follows the sort of process depicted in Burgess's *Malayan Trilogy*. Scott examines India's progress toward independence, starting from the 'Quit India' riots of 1942, tracing the course of violence and change which led to final retreat and partition of the country in 1947. Like many English novelists writing about India, he is often linked with the example of E.M. Forster. The central story in *The Jewel in the Crown*, which has reverberations throughout the Quartet, is of rape and subsequent wrongful accusation, as in Forster's *A Passage to India* (1924). Scott, however, views the apparatus of empire with rather more generosity than Forster: there is sometimes sympathy for officials who are as often genuinely committed as corrupt, and there is a general nostalgia for the earlier, grander days of dominion which is sharpened by their recollection in various flashbacks.

Such tactics are perhaps most successfully employed in Scott's *Staying On* (1977), a vivid, intimate portrayal of two of the minor characters from *The Raj Quartet*, Lucy and Tusker Smalley, described as 'the last surviving member[s] in Pankot...of the old

145

school of British'.[53] Beginning at the moment of Tusker's death, Scott moves freely between various 'images and recollections' (p.48) in his characters' minds. These are assembled into a nostalgic vision, both sad and very funny, of imperial and post-imperial life, and of the moment of transition between the two—Lucy remembers

> ...the evening of August fourteen, Nineteen forty-seven, down there on the parade ground of the Pankot Rifles...the flagpole lit with the Union Jack flying from it...God Save the King, and...that terrible, lovely moment when the Jack was hauled down inch by inch in utter, utter silence (pp.170-71).

A similar contrast of the imperial past with the New India appears in Ruth Prawer Jhabvala's *Heat and Dust* (1975). Like *Staying On*, her novel employs a retrospective technique, showing a girl attempting to discover the historical truth about a distant relative's romance, while partly re-enacting its circumstances in her present life. Perhaps naturally, nostalgia predominates in several recent English novels about Indian imperial experience: a similar sense of regret for Britain's supposedly more splendid days of dominion is perhaps a factor underlying the great success in the nineteen-eighties of films such as *Gandhi*, *A Passage to India*, and *Heat and Dust* itself.

A rather different, more analytic, view of Indian empire appears in J.G. Farrell's *The Siege of Krishnapur* (1973), which concerns the Indian Mutiny of 1857. Set in a much more remote historical period than any of the fiction discussed above, *The Siege of Krishnapur* neither regrets nor celebrates the past: instead, Farrell shows how the empire's loss, prefigured by the Mutiny, was partly the consequence of its flawed ethics even when at its height. His central figure, the Collector of Krishnapur, begins as an admirer of the Great Exhibition of 1851, and of the Victorian confidence in science and 'the progress of the human race' which it embodied.[54] He considers at first that 'civilisation...includes so many things, both spiritual and practical...the spreading of the Gospel on the one hand, the spreading of the railways on the other' (p.55). Gradually, however, he becomes aware that the 'practical' side of empire entirely predominates over spiritual or moral responsibility, partly because 'it is in material things that progress can be clearly seen' (p.55). Material possessions, the paraphernalia of Victorian affluence, obsess the British in Krishnapur, even when, ironically, they have to be broken up for defences or used as shot during the desperate hardship of the siege. After its 'terrible days...which were like the dark foundation of...civilised life' (p.343), the Collector realises that 'the fiction of happy natives being led forward along the road to civilisation could no longer be sustained' (p.249). He concludes of his imperial experience that 'Culture is a sham' (p.345).

Farrell includes in *The Siege of Krishnapur* a note of the historical source-material he researched for its writing: this concern for accuracy extends into his precisely objective style, powerfully descriptive of violent action. Realist in method, and full of colourful adventure, *The Siege of Krishnapur* could almost have been written at the time of the events it portrays. Farrell's authorial voice, however, also sustains a certain critical distance from his characters, transcribing their thoughts extensively and sympathetically but with a certain appraisive, modern scepticism, often very funny. It is typical of this strange, wry, humour, as well as the novel's juxtaposition of the 'spiritual' and the 'practical', that one character is shown enduring the padre's demented version of the design argument for the existence of God while actually engaged in the most slaughterous of the siege's fighting; and that later his bible is the only implement he can find to help scrape a plague of flies from the body of a naked girl. *The Siege of Krishnapur* is one of the most penetrating accounts of the imperial phase of British experience: its witty narrative also makes it thoroughly entertaining. Farrell continues his interest in empire with equal success in *The Singapore Grip* (1978), set in a period of Britain's declining power in Malaysia just prior to that examined by Anthony Burgess.

Though much diminished in the Far East, the British Empire survived into the sixties: some of the pangs resulting from liberation of the African colonies are reflected in Julian Mitchell's *The White Father* (1964). Rather in the manner of Graham Greene, its central figure, Hugh Shrieve, is a sad, faded, but likeable ex-colonial officer who has spent years 'serving a vanished ideal'[55] in Africa. He returns to London in an attempt to secure a future for the Ngulu tribe, who have been his administrative responsibility, and whose ingenuousness exposes them to many threats in the newly-independent African state. Shrieve finds 'much...had changed' in what has become only 'poor little old Great Britain' (pp.47, 152): his natural, disillusioned comparison of past and present makes him an especially revealing observer of 'modern English morals' (p.173) and the shifting shape of society in general. His most sympathetic supporter is in his own way equally dispirited by the contemporary world: Ed Gilchrist is usually an apathetic young man, disaffected with his family and society in some of the ways Mitchell charted in earlier novels such as *A Disturbing Influence* (1962). Mitchell suggests some possible comparisons between the drifting group of Ed's friends and the Ngulu: each tends, more or less innocently, towards sexual liberation, indulgence and emotional freedom; each is at the mercy of whims of international commerce and capital; each, in different ways, seems to sink into an almost fatal torpor as a result of Britain's diminished, uncertain role in world affairs. Mitchell's juxtaposition of London and Africa thus highlights a connection, which might first have been expected of fifties novelists, between dwindling dominion in external affairs and drifting indeterminacy at home.

147

The White Father also makes clear, however, that in the early sixties Ed Gilchrist already belongs to a society quite different from that presented in fifties fiction. He is lured away from the jazz which attracted fifties novelists and their characters, and towards the beginning of the rock which set the rhythm of the next decade. 'Discontented, or disillusioned, with the world their elders have made' (p.69), he and his friends in London clubs and coffee bars are inclined to more open rejection of conventional values, favouring a loose political radicalism which rediscovers some of the possibility of 'good, brave causes', such as the Ngulu, which John Osborne and his angry contemporaries thought permanently exhausted. In such ways, Ed and his circle are forerunners of the new generation, habitués of pot and the pill, who turn up at the end of Angus Wilson's *No Laughing Matter*: *The White Father* itself is an early indication of how the 'new state of mind' of the fifties gradually gave way to 'the swinging sixties, the days of liberation'.[56]

For many of the novelists who came to prominence in the fifties, such liberation had gone too far by the end of the decade. The permissive atmosphere of the time is criticised less equivocally in John Braine's *The Crying Game* (1968) or C.P. Snow's *The Sleep of Reason* (1968), for example, than it is in Amis's *Take A Girl Like You*. Even members of a younger generation of novelists found in contemporary demonstrations and agitation, often provoked by the Vietnam War, political attitudes which disturbingly over-extended a milder radicalism they had learned from Suez and the fifties. Some of these doubts figure in David Caute's *The Occupation* (1971). They also appear in the rather bewildered accounts of the student revolution in Paris in 1968, and of Bob Dylan's Isle of Wight pop festival in 1969, included at the end of Andrew Sinclair's year-by-year satirical portrait of British life since the war in *Magog* (1972).

Though restrained in its outlook, the innovative style and structure of Caute's and Sinclair's fiction illustrate the extent to which the nineteen-sixties 'days of liberation' altered not only social norms but also narrative conventions, which developed beyond the conservative style of much fifties fiction. As discussed in the last part of this chapter, increasing flexibility of technique characterises even the more orthodox fiction of the sixties and since. The latter part of the decade, and the early seventies, also saw the publication not only of Caute's and Sinclair's novels, but of many of the other experimental works examined in Chapter Five. One of these, John Fowles's *The French Lieutenant's Woman* (1969), indicates a particularly significant area of simultaneous change in contemporary social and literary forms. It describes and criticises convention both in narrative technique and in views of sexual role, especially in the way the latter affects the position of women in society. In a decade which experienced the eventual unrestricted publication of

D.H. Lawrence's *Lady Chatterley's Lover* (1928), and the general
availability of oral contraception, perhaps the most significant social
change was in the sexual conventions which had dictated certain
restraints in the life and fiction of earlier decades, particularly
troubling the characters of fifties novels. These and other
contemporary developments especially affected the role and
behaviour of women. One of the most significant areas of progress in
fiction since the sixties has appeared in new explorations of female
consciousness and the changing, often increasingly emancipated,
position of women in society. A sample of such fiction is briefly
examined in the next section.

New Women: Jean Rhys, Eva Figes, Anita Brookner, Edna O'Brien, Margaret Drabble, Doris Lessing, Emma Tennant, Fay Weldon

Some of the challenge facing women novelists is suggested in
Anthony Powell's *The Acceptance World* when Nicholas Jenkins
remarks that 'No real tradition of how women behave exists in
English writing' (p.75). Jenkins, however, is only partially accurate:
though a particular interest of recent women's fiction has been its
necessary evolution of new narrative forms, these have often been
developed at least partly on the basis of an extant 'tradition of how
women behave', or at any rate upon some already available
techniques adapted to the representation of women's consciousness.
These are present in eighteenth and nineteenth-century fiction: they
are added to by modernists such as Dorothy Richardson and Virginia
Woolf, creating in their sensitive registers of inner thoughts and
feelings what Richardson calls 'feminine prose'. Such techniques are
extended into later decades (as discussed in Chapter Three) by
writers such as Elizabeth Bowen and Rosamond Lehmann: close
attention to inner consciousness is also sustained with particular
subtlety in the work of Jean Rhys.

Her *Good Morning, Midnight* (1939) concentrates on the inner life
of a lonely heroine, Sasha Jensen, uncertain of her independence,
threatened by an unfeeling world around her, exhausted by the
'pawings' and 'pryings' of men, concluding 'God, it's funny, being a
woman!'[57] Sasha is an abandoned member of Hemingway's 'lost
generation', dominated by her uneasy memories when she returns to
Paris, a city familiar and emotionally significant to her in the past.
Her uncertainty of mind is communicated by the way her thoughts
flit from subject to subject: her narrative also alternates frequently
between present-tense transcription of immediate thought or
experience, and recording of disorderly memories, sometimes in the
present tense, sometimes the past. This disruption of chronological
order, and mixing of musing interior monologue, memory, and

stream of consciousness, shows the continuity in Rhys's work of techniques developed by modernist authors whom she met in Paris in the nineteen twenties. Though her manner of presenting randomly associating, unfolding thoughts is at times close to Joyce's, the subtlety of her language also shows an extension of modernist technique entirely her own:

> ...That's the way it is, that's the way it goes, that was the way it went...A room. A nice room. A beautiful room. A beautiful room with bath. A very beautiful room with bath. A bedroom and sitting-room with bath. Up to the dizzy heights of the suite...A beautiful room with bath? Swing high, swing low, swing to and fro...This happened and that happened...
>
> And then the days came when I was alone. (pp.29, 118)

Rhys's admirer Francis Wyndham suggests in an introduction to her work that her novels were

> ...ahead of their age, both in spirit and in style...the novels of the 1930s are much closer in *feeling* to life as it is lived and understood in the 1960s than to the accepted attitudes of their time.[58]

Like several other innovative novelists, Rhys found little to encourage her work in the forties and fifties, and published nothing after *Good Morning, Midnight* until *Wide Sargasso Sea* in 1966. This reconsiders the character of the first Mrs Rochester, the mad wife who appears in Charlotte Brontë's *Jane Eyre* (1847). In Rhys's version, concentrating on her early days in the West Indies, she appears like Sasha 'afraid...of nothing, of everything',[59] her sensitivity recoiling and collapsing in the face of perverse harshness in her experience in general, and her new husband in particular. As in *Good Morning, Midnight*, her mind's unhinging is represented with great sensitivity. Though Rhys thought the novel's success had come too late for her own career, its re-creation of interest in her work as a whole established in the sixties an example of technical expertise in representing inner consciousness directly inherited from the modernists, and specifically adapted to the presentation of loneliness and uncertainty in women's lives.

Whether discovered independently or through intermediaries such as Bowen, Lehmann or Rhys, the example of Virginia Woolf's interior monologue continues to interest several contemporary women writers. One of these is Eva Figes, author of an influential feminist tract, *Patriarchal Attitudes* (1970), as well as several novels whose experimental forms illustrate her belief that

> Mainstream English fiction is locked in the social realist tradition of the nineteenth century...unable or unwilling to shake off the shackles of that prescriptive structure. For me the old forms are hopelessly inadequate.[60]

Figes's debts to Virginia Woolf are clearest in her novella *Waking* (1981), written shortly after re-reading *The Waves* (1931), which it closely resembles. It presents seven moments of awakening consciousness during its heroine's childhood, adolescence, pregnancy, post-marital affair, and other widely-separated stages of her life. It is at times as close to Woolf in style as in structure—in the reflective movement of the language which develops, for example, moments of

> Revising French verbs and thinking how life, like a dome of many-coloured glass, stains the white radiance. As we lie, books forgotten, grass tickling the backs of our knees, squinting into the sunlight and feeling how the world revolves under our backs as the clouds move overhead.[61]

The heroine's doubtful speculation on 'whether a good life was possible, by which we meant love, relationships with men' (p.71); her experience of pregnancy as a domestic imprisonment; or of the affair as 'the last summer...after which come the dark nights, snow and death' (p.55) all indicate the sad disparity between the sensitive inner reflectiveness exemplified in the passage above, and an unsatisfactory external life. Repeated scenes of lying in bed, listening with varying unease for sounds of wakefulness in the rest of the house, emphasise with unhappy clarity the mind's preference for its own space, away from the world which unfurls around it but so often fails to fulfil its desires.

Anita Brookner sometimes examines a comparable disparity between sensitive inner life and intractable social reality. In *Providence* (1982), for example, this disjuncture is emphasised by variations in narrative technique. The novel sometimes explores its heroine Kitty Maule's mind in a series of first-person transcriptions of her thoughts: elsewhere, however, it sustains a distant, firmly objective narrative voice which gives an account of Kitty's life at times almost cynically perfunctory. Such contrast between inner and outer vision partly corresponds to some of the division in Kitty's personality: half-English and half-French, she is perplexed by several warring elements within herself. For example, she is torn between her emotional nature and the life of the mind; between desire for her lover and her wish for autonomy; between the life-style of her flighty friend Caroline—obsessed with men, clothes, appearance—and her 'even lonelier' colleague Pauline, 'what is called a liberated woman'[62] in Kitty's view. Kitty's work is no refuge from such conflicts. A lecturer in a small provincial university, she finds her allegiance divided between a Classical need to 'put her own life into some sort of order' (p.84), and the more anarchic disposition of the Romantic tradition which forms the basis of her study. She is also perplexed by conflicts between her lover's ideas of 'providence' and her own intermittent belief in 'nothing...truly in an existentialist world' (p.91). The campus setting of *Providence*, and its frequent humour, recall some of the novels of David Lodge and

Malcolm Bradbury (see the last part of this chapter): Brookner, however, is unusual in the precision with which ideas which are the currency of university teaching are attached to the moral and emotional dilemmas of the protagonists. One of the ironies of *Providence*, for example, (and an aspect of its self-conscious speculation about the relation of fiction to life) appears in Kitty's failure to realise until too late how closely aspects of the novel she teaches parallel and anticipate her own fate, eventually betrayed by her lover. This betrayal and the frustration of her desire for both secure selfhood and emotional fulfilment make *Providence* a sad novel as well as a witty and elegant one. Kitty's problems and self-division illustrate how 'liberation' and the wish for independence may exact a certain price in loneliness, distorting or even demanding the sacrifice of certain parts of the self.

Kitty envisages her friends Caroline and Pauline—'the one so stupid, the other so intelligent, and both so bereft'—as 'casualties of the same conflict, as losers in the war' (p.84). Edna O'Brien is similarly concerned, in *Casualties of Peace* (1966), with women either lonely prisoners of their independence or victims of wretched thraldom to men. Her heroine Willa, an artist in glass, has built

> ...between her and the world...sheet upon sheet of coloured glass so that when she looked out or they looked in the gestures were all distorted and the voices barely heard. Some thought they knew her but they were deceived...No one would ever catch her again.[68]

Less lonely but no happier, Willa's housemate Patsy tries in vain to escape her husband Tom and continue her affair with another man. Guilty, frustrated relationships are presented throughout: *Casualties of Peace* begins with Willa's tangled dream of death and ends with her actual murder in error by Tom. O'Brien's general omission of authorial comment and exposition adds to the confused atmosphere: the novel is envisaged darkly, as if through one of Willa's panes of coloured glass. The impression of its characters' unhappiness is further heightened by frequent entry into their disconnected thoughts, represented in short, telegrammatic sentences: some Joycean influence from O'Brien's Irish background is apparent in her narrative style. This also benefits from rapid pace and occasional sharp humour. Despite an underlying sadness, her novels are entertaining and have always had a wide readership, perhaps partly on account of a mildly sensational explicitness about women's sexual desires which is a feature particularly of her early fiction.

Margaret Drabble's fiction enjoys a similar popularity, though it is only in its earlier phase that it shares something of O'Brien's interest specifically in the dilemmas of women. Drabble's third novel, for example, *The Millstone* (1965) shows an educated, intelligent heroine, Rosamund Stacey, forced to struggle rather like Brookner's Kitty

Maule against many difficulties and counter-attractions in an attempt to achieve a full independence. She succeeds partly through the stability created by a love for her baby daughter Octavia which she describes as 'the first of my life'.[69] Especially intense during the child's dangerous illness, this newly-discovered emotion is communicated with unsentimental immediacy by her first-person narrative: its direct, half-conversational style is typical of the lucidity of Drabble's fiction as a whole. Rosamund's love for Octavia is also exemplary of a frequent central interest of women's writing in relations between mother and child rather than between sexual partners. Illustrative of some of the differences in outlook between men and women novelists, *The Millstone* also typifies developments in attitude between the fifties and the sixties—Rosamund's unexpected, extra-marital pregnancy, eventually so welcome, is of just the sort which appalled the heroes of Cooper's *Scenes from Provincial Life*, Sillitoe's *Saturday Night and Sunday Morning*, and Barstow's *A Kind of Loving*.

Drabble has suggested

> ... my books are I think mainly concerned with privilege, justice, and salvation. Equality and egalitarianism preoccupy me constantly, and not very hopefully. None of my books is about feminism, because my belief in the necessity for justice for women (which they don't get at the moment) is so basic that I never think of using it as a subject. It is part of a whole.[70]

Though centred upon Rosamund's problems, *The Millstone* is also more widely concerned with questions of 'privilege and justice'. Rosamund shares her author's tendency to envisage society in terms of 'justice, guilt and innocence...sociological pity' (p.84): her narrative is critically observant of class-distinction, poverty in the streets, and the shortcomings of the National Health Service. Drabble's later fiction sometimes amplifies such concerns at the expense of specific attention to women's problems, moving away from concentration on a single heroine to broader interest in a range of interconnected characters. In *The Ice Age* (1977), for example, each character is a 'weed on the tide of history',[71] in whom the wider crisis in contemporary society is represented. Sketched in a series of brief flashbacks and histories, Drabble's figures are 'casualties of slump and recession' (p.14), dragging out anxious lives in great rotting cities, the work of corrupt or stupid property speculators and planners. *The Ice Age* gives a grim picture of 'the spirit of the age... the state of the nation' (pp.34, 65) in the impoverished years following the oil crisis and economic decline, which doomed the 'days of liberation' of the previous decade. Drabble's broad attention to social issues, to 'the state of the nation' as a whole, represented in a web of interconnected characters, makes this phase of her fiction rather resemble Charles Dickens's. Like her heroine Rosamund Stacey, and many of the 'new men' of the fifties discussed above, Drabble is in style at least 'at heart a Victorian'.[72] Her admiration for Arnold Bennett further associates her with fifties novelists. Though more sophisticated in showing the inner thoughts of its characters, her recent fiction shows a continuity in a later age of the social commentary which was the special concern of the 'Angry-provincial-neorealist' writing of the fifties.

Gilbert Phelps suggests:

> It could be argued...that the forces that make for division and injustice in the relationship between men and women are those, endemic to our society, that make for the fragmentation of human values in general.[73]

This is the same sort of reasoning as underlies Drabble's dual interest in 'privilege and justice' in general and 'belief in the necessity for justice for women' in particular. It is an argument also developed with great force and variety throughout Doris Lessing's long, outstanding literary career. Among her earliest novels, for example, the *Children of Violence* series (*Martha Quest* (1952); *A Proper Marriage* (1954); *A Ripple from the Storm* (1958); *Landlocked* (1965); *The Four-Gated City* (1969)) examines, Lessing suggests, 'the individual conscience in its relations with the collective'. The series follows the experience of Martha Quest, a girl who grows up in the sort of African colony where Lessing also spent her early years: it examines not only the position of women in a man's world, but also the nature of black experience under white rule, and the validity of the left-wing politics which have been a matter of sustained interest for Lessing herself. She suggested in 1958 'one believes artists should be committed', also remarking

> For me the highest point of literature was the novel of the nineteenth century...the work of the great realists...the realist novel, the realist story, is the highest form of prose writing.[74]

Admiration for nineteenth-century realism and a concern for social issues associate her early work, like Drabble's later fiction, with the 'Angry...neorealist' manner of the fifties, and Lessing was often bracketed with the angry young men at the time. Though she had some sympathy for their initiatives, she also complained in 1958 that their work was constrained by the very 'pettiness and narrowness' it protested against. Her own commitment is on a much larger scale, politically based and unconfined by exclusive interest in British society. *Children of Violence* also moves beyond the realism of its early volumes, ending in fantasy and apocalypse in *The Four-Gated City*—a change of style representative of more general rejection or modification of conventional forms in British fiction in the sixties.

Before completing *Children of Violence*, Lessing had published her outstanding work, *The Golden Notebook* (1962), also an example, though a very early one, of growing interest among sixties novelists in experimentation and self-conscious examination of narrative technique. Lessing explains in a preface the extraordinary shape of *The Golden Notebook*:

> There is a skeleton, or frame, called *Free Women*, which is a conventional short novel, about 60,000 words long, and which could stand by itself. But it is divided into five sections and separated by stages of the four Notebooks, Black, Red, Yellow and Blue. The Notebooks are kept by Anna Wulf, a central character of *Free Women*. She keeps four, and not one because, as she recognises, she has to separate things off from each other, out of fear of chaos, of formlessness—of breakdown... In the inner Golden Notebook, things have come together, the divisions have broken down, there is formlessness with the end of fragmentation—the triumph of the second theme, which is that of unity.[75]

Anna's need to divide her life into the areas the Notebooks examine results from the diversity of her activities as 'free woman', socialist, private being, and writer; and from the problematic nature of her experience in each area. The Blue Notebook, which 'tries to be a diary' (p.462), is full of the sadness of failed love and relationships, of unrewarding encounters with variously egotistical men. The Red is an account of the promise and later disillusion of Marxist politics. Though partly 'to do with Anna Wulf the writer' (p.462), the Black Notebook is largely a narrative of early experience in Africa, similar to Martha Quest's and equally fraught with tension between white and black. The Yellow Notebook is also appropriately named: Anna Wulf considers that the urge to 'make stories out of... experience' (p.462) which it demonstrates may be a cowardly retreat into an unreal order created to escape the menace of an intractable world. She remarks 'literature is analysis after the event... turning everything into fiction—must be an evasion... a means of concealing something from myself' (pp.231-2).

This anxiety about the relation between literature and disorderly reality underlies the fragmentary form of *Free Women* and of *The Golden Notebook* as a whole. Anna records throughout the possibility that

> ... everything's cracking up... the world is so chaotic art is irrelevant... the novel has become a function of the fragmented society, the fragmented consciousness... the novel... has been claimed by the disintegration and the collapse (pp.25, 60, 79, 124).

Anna's concern with this 'disintegration and collapse' develops into a 'writer's block' (p.582), a reluctance or incompetence—at least until the Golden Notebook—to make herself responsible for any final ordering of the heterogeneous constituents of her experience. The 'blocked' enterprise of her writing makes *The Golden Notebook* much more complex even than Lessing's introductory explanation suggests. It contains fragments of short stories; synopses and reviews of novels; comments on the style of other Notebooks and notes of deletions from them; reflections on the nature of fiction; and extended collections of the newspaper headlines Anna uses at one point to paper the walls of her home. These pieces of 'the inchoate world mirrored in the newspapers'—a 'record of war, murder, chaos, misery' (pp.624, 251)—further contribute to her fear of 'chaos... formlessness... breakdown'.

Many of these various fragments are themselves entertaining or revealing, though some are loose and unnecessarily long. Lessing's assemblage of them, however, creates a 'novel' whose main interest and ultimate success develop not so much from its constituents as from its extended demonstration of the difficulties of writing; of a 'grasping out for... wholeness' (p.79) which can accept both formlessness and the final, golden possibility of 'the second theme... that of unity'. One of the novel's many synopses of short stories concerns 'a man whose "sense of reality" has gone; and because of it, has a deeper sense of reality than "normal" people', and a character in this story remarks

> ... my sense of reality shivered and broke. But something very clear was there, all the same, a sort of illumination, though it would be hard to say what (p.520).

Likewise, it is actually because the conventional sense of form is shivered and broken in Lessing's novel and the usual sense of reality absent that it offers such a 'very clear... illumination' of the nature of life in the middle of the twentieth century, when 'war, murder, chaos, misery' so resolutely resist assimilation into the orders of art. The form of *The Golden Notebook* as a whole, and Anna's self-conscious discussion and demonstration of limits to the sense of reality fiction conveys, also communicate a timely challenge to straightforward realism—the 'neo-realism' of the fifties, for example, scarcely competent to apprehend the era's crises of ideology, historical conflict and consequent personal stress. In such ways, *The Golden Notebook* concurrently fulfils the wishes Lessing states in her preface: 'to give the ideological "feel" of our mid-century', and to 'comment about the conventional novel' (pp.11, 14). Lessing has rightly recorded her disappointment that *The Golden Notebook* has been so often considered only as 'a tract about the sex war' (p.10). A principal statement about the conventional novel may be of the need for women to collapse and re-create conventional narrative forms as part of their rejection of a conventionally-allotted place in society; and *The Golden Notebook* does record and demonstrate at length the possibility that 'the real revolution is, women against men' (p.218). It is entirely characteristic of Lessing's writing, however, that such issues are combined with wider interests in the '"feel" of mid-century', the nature and problems of the times.

Since the nineteen sixties, Lessing's fiction has continued 'grasping out for wholeness' in a variety of unusual forms which often reject realistic reflection of the chaotic surface of life. *Briefing for a Descent into Hell* (1971), for example, moves largely into fantasy, suggesting that in any case no valid apparatus exists for defining the limits of reality, or of sanity. Described by its author as 'inner-space fiction',[76] *Briefing for a Descent into Hell* is concentrated within the mind of Charles Watkins, in whom Lessing develops the possibility originally suggested in *The Golden Notebook* of 'a man whose "sense of reality" has gone; and because of it, has a deeper sense of reality than "normal" people'. His visions are of a beauty and moral clarity which may indicate a greater validity than the drab rationalism of his medical treatment for amnesia:

> A head, at last the body of the land,
> Fretted and worn for ever by a mothering sea
> A jealous sea that loves her ancient pain.

> Nurse: Why don't you go and sit for a bit in the day room? (p.34).

Watkins's visions of 'the Earth hung in its weight, coloured and tinted here and there, for the most part with the bluish tint of water' (p.94) seem derived from the outer space pictures NASA missions began to bring back in the late nineteen sixties. Lessing expands in Watkins's mind a similar facility for envisaging human affairs from a vastly remote point of view. Rather like C.S. Lewis's *Perelandra* (1943), *Briefing for a Descent into Hell* includes images of the Garden of Eden; distantly objective, synoptic versions of human history; and contact with the remote deities who supervise and occasionally descend to intervene in the progress of earthly events. In such ways, its 'inner-space fiction' anticipates Lessing's later development in the seventies and eighties as a writer of space or science fiction in the *Canopus in Argos: Archives* series of novels—allegorical, mythic accounts of creatures whose manoeuvrings in the distant cosmos influence the unfolding of human fate.

Lessing's next novel, *The Summer before the Dark* (1973) returns to terrestrial matters and to her characteristic combination of wider social concerns with the specific issue of women's freedom: the 'dark' of the title threatens both the wider world and the personal affairs of Lessing's heroine Kate Brown. Her son believes that 'the end of civilisation was close':[77] during her free summer of international employment and travel, Kate likewise finds decent existence everywhere threatened by strikes, pollution, extreme right-wing politics, and a streamlined, heartless anonymity throughout the conduct of modern life. She also contemplates her personal crises of encroaching middle age and dwindling significance within her family—her husband politely unfaithful, her children grown up beyond their need for her. Sensitivity to her precarious personal attractiveness equips her with an aptitude for objectivity about herself, for confronting her effect on others and seeing herself as they must see her. She learns to

> ...switch a sight on herself from across the room, as these men were seeing her. She saw, as she had in so many mirrors, a woman with startling dark-red hair, a very white skin and the sympathetic eyes of a loving spaniel... It was really extraordinary! There she sat, Kate Brown, just as she had always been, *her* self, *her* mind, *her* awareness, watching the world from behind a façade... It was a matter only of a bad posture... and people did not see her... she might have been invisible. Yet she needed only to put on the other dress, twist her hair so and so — and she would be drawing glances and needs after her at every step (pp.42, 44, 176).

'A rage, it seemed to her, that she had been suppressing for a lifetime' (p.207) results from Kate's realisation that she exists for others, men in particular, only through her 'posture' and physical appearance rather than '*her* self, *her* mind, *her* awareness'. She cuts off her 'startling dark-red hair', before returning to her family in a shape she has at least chosen for herself.

This gap Kate discovers between inner self and perceived existence is highlighted by variations in Lessing's technique. *The Summer before the Dark* alternates between careful attention to its heroine's inner thoughts, and a distantly objective perspective which presents Kate anonymously, simply as 'a woman', in several sections of the novel. This divided style resembles Brookner's tactics in *Providence*, or Margaret Drabble's alternation between first and third person narrative in *The Waterfall* (1969). Such techniques give evidence of a wider tension underlying recent women's fiction. This arises from the irony that employment of a sensitive subjective register develops exactly the aspects of female characters' 'self... mind... awareness' which their society is most likely to ignore. Many of these characters share the 'suppressed rage' of Kate's realisation that looks rather than sensitive self entirely conditions effect on others, even determining whether their existence is recognised at all. In Jean Rhys's *Good Morning, Midnight*, for example, Sasha Jensen recalls working in Paris dress-shops and

> ...watching those damned dolls, thinking what a success they would have made of their lives if they had been women. Satin skin, silk hair, velvet eyes, sawdust heart — all complete... Isn't there something you can do so that nobody looks at or sees you? Of course, you must make your mind vacant, neutral, then your face also becomes vacant, neutral — you are invisible (pp.16-17).

Eva Figes's heroine in *Waking* looks at herself in the mirror in later life and considers

> I am doomed to drag about this other body who fills me with disgust... Eyes in the street... slide away, glance past or look straight through me as though I did not exist (p.70).

This gap between 'heart' and 'skin', between the inner self and the woman the world sees, creates a kind of schizophrenia, perhaps first apparent in the need Anna discovers to divide up her experience in *The Golden Notebook*. Characters in later novels sometimes find, like Kate Brown, their sense of self-division especially accentuated by seeing or imagining themselves in mirrors: the heroine of *Waking* admits 'I do not feel completely one and the same person on such occasions' (p.26). Kitty Maule likewise finds in *Providence* that when she dresses up to amuse her friend Caroline

> ...a cynical, capable, and utterly French other self had emerged, and this self was not the sort of woman who gave lectures or aspired to the unity of a simple life... This was a face that belonged to a woman who knew how to please (p.159).

A problematic relation with the 'other self' also troubles Emma Tennant's heroine Jane in *The Bad Sister* (1978): rather like Kitty Maule, she finds that 'a woman who thinks must live with a demented sister'. She adds, however, 'often the two women war, and kill each other'. *The Bad Sister* is a more extreme, disturbing treatment of the 'two-women-in-one', projecting into fantasy and Gothic vision the sense of the 'double female self', 'the inherent "splitness" of women'.[78] Jane is perhaps 'a schizophrenic with paranoid delusions', driven beyond sanity or the 'desire for the old magic of wholeness' (p.137). *The Bad Sister* is itself split between prosaic opening and closing sections written by an 'editor', and Jane's intervening journal. This records how, like Kate Brown, she cuts off her hair, becoming 'invisible' even to her lover, and mysteriously enters a life of crime, magic, and demonic possession, at the end of which she is invisible in mirrors even to herself. This may be madness, fantasy, or more sinisterly authentic contact with spirits and demons: *The Bad Sister* moves with great facility between realistic vision of contemporary society and a dimension of dreams and illusion beyond it.

Tennant's work is in this way representative of a movement towards fantasy and dream more widely apparent in recent British fiction. Like Tennant, or Lessing in *Briefing for a Descent into Hell*, Christopher Priest shows in *The Affirmation* (1981) a seamless, schizophrenic intermingling of fantasy and reality. Other authors share Jane's interest in 'translating the known into the unknown' and letting 'the old magic that people had known... pour back into the world again' (p.73). Angela Carter's *The Infernal Desire Machines of Doctor Hoffman* (1972), for example, shows a hero divided like Jane between 'a barren yet harmonious calm and a fertile yet cacophonous tempest'; between 'the drab, colourless world' and 'the fragile marginalia of our dreams'.[79] A particular strength of *The Bad Sister*, however, is that its juxtaposition of 'the drab, colourless world' and the dimension of dreams is used to develop specific criticisms of the former, and of women's place within it. Tennant's fantasy contributes to a strongly satiric purpose. Jane's unease is shown to be heightened by the aridity of the consumer society around her, which exacerbates her potential paranoia by denying her any medium in which her imagination can be easily freed. Even when she embarks on one of her visionary excursions, the narrative continues to delineate sharply her uncongenial environment—the grotesque advertising hoardings, for example, which thrust conventional roles upon her:

> ...fluorescent reds and yellows, the prayers and exhortations to eat and sleep and breathe for the sake of the manufacturers alone...the housewife suspended in the vapours of her pie, her smile moistened in the wreaths of animal fat coming up at her like winter breath (p.38).

Through Jane's schizophrenic response to this unfeeling society, and Tennant's mixture of fable, fantasy, and satire, *The Bad Sister* illuminates with particular clarity the divided vision which has become a frequent feature of women's writing. Other concerns, of course, have also developed in recent years, as Tennant herself recognised when she remarked in 1978

> ...the trembling sensitivity of Jean Rhys...seem[s] to have disappeared. Picaresque heroines, pregnant with twins, abandoned by shits, [struggle] along the Moll Flanders highway in conflicting moods of bitterness and optimism.[80]

Fay Weldon's *Down Among the Women* (1971) exemplifies the sort of trend Tennant mentions. Though narrated partly in the first person and partly in the third, it is less interested in demonstrating inner tensions or splits within women's experience than with showing the simple awfulness of lives at the end of which they may have 'cooked a hundred thousand meals, swept a million floors, washed a billion dishes'. 'Down among the women' there is

> ...that other terrible world, where chaos is the norm, life a casual exception to death, and all cells cancerous except those which the will contrives to keep orderly; where the body is something mysterious in its workings, which swells, bleeds, and bursts at random; where sex is a strange intermittent animal spasm; where men seduce, make pregnant, betray, desert: where laws are harsh and mysterious, and where the woman goes helpless.[81]

These horrors are illustrated in the lives of three generations of women. Rather like Defoe's heroine Moll, they lurch fairly cheerfully from one dispiriting misadventure to another, their lives warped and ruined not only by men but by the malignancy of circumstance and the vagaries of their own natures. Tumbled from one representative situation to the next, they are in another way victims of their author's urgency in showing social processes and problems, from the difficult days after the war until the more promising possibilities of women's liberation in the sixties. Episodic and colloquial, Weldon's present-tense narrative is perfunctory in plausible characterisation and at its best in the witty, sociological sections which open each chapter, breaking the illusion of the fiction. *Down Among the Women* is as much a statement· as a novel, representative of sometimes simultaneous interests, among women writers of the sixties and seventies, in journalism and ideology as well as the novel.

Many other women writers are considered elsewhere in this and other chapters. This section provides only an illustrative sample of particular ways in which women's writing has developed in the past two or three decades. In its panorama of changing conditions since the war, *Down Among the Women* indicates the extent to which women's experience at this time has offered new attitudes, problems and possibilities for the attention of novelists. The appearance of this fresh experience, and of the particular fictional techniques and visions discussed above, evolving for its development, make women's writing both a distinctive and a promising area in the recent history of the novel. Emma Tennant suggests 'women's English' is a separate language: the novelist Ian McEwan adds, of its potential, 'women writers seem best placed now to use the novel seriously to open out relatively unexplored areas of individual and social experience'.[82] Since such experience may be in some ways summary or representative of a contemporary 'fragmentation of human values in general'—as Gilbert Phelps suggests and Margaret Drabble and Doris Lessing help to show—its treatment should ensure a continuing and expanding interest in women's writing. Its future is further assured by the support of publishers such as Virago Press, which has also re-created an audience for important women writers from earlier in the twentieth century, such as Rebecca West, Storm Jameson, Rose Macaulay, May Sinclair and Stevie Smith.

The Ineluctable Shadow: Susan Hill, Paul Bailey, Olivia Manning, Richard Hughes, Gabriel Fielding, D.M. Thomas

The last chapter quoted Walter Allen's prediction that the Second World War would continue to dominate literature 'for years to come, long after hostilities cease'. Even although, as that chapter suggested, the immediacy of the war's impact began to fade from fiction in the fifties, what Allen calls its 'ineluctable shadow' remains apparent in the decades that follow, an important factor in the outlook of the writers discussed in this section and in the next. Certain recent novelists, however, also envisage more widely the historical

161

disturbance of the twentieth century, concentrating on the First World War rather than only the Second. In Paul Bailey's *Old Soldiers* (1980), for example, one of the central figures still suffers from a kind of extended shell shock, a residual effect of the trenches underlying an uncertainty of identity, almost an insanity, lasting for more than half a century. The novel's other protagonist also retains traumatic memories of the 1914-18 war, revivified by the death of his wife. Bailey's development of these memories is typical of his fiction, which frequently adds to present action extended recollections of earlier events. In *Old Soldiers*, this technique locates within a wider history of loss and decline his old soldiers' meeting and their subsequent acquaintanceship amid the increasing squalor of contemporary London. A slight but elegantly-structured novel, *Old Soldiers* extends in the nineteen eighties the pattern of some of Angus Wilson's fiction, and of some of the novels discussed in Chapter Three, looking back beyond the Second World War to early decades of the century as a possible source of present disturbance and uncertainty.

An odd acquaintanceship between soldiers also provides the subject of Susan Hill's *Strange Meeting* (1971). Her title is taken from the poetry of Wilfred Owen: *Strange Meeting* presents the First World War largely in terms made familiar by Owen's work. It appears as a gruesome, purposeless slaughter, redeemed only occasionally by the intensity of personal emotions—in this case, shared by Hill's protagonists Barton and Hilliard. The latter realises, for example, that

> ... nothing mattered except Barton and what he felt for him: that he loved him, as he loved no other person in his life... the war was irrelevant, something for them to get through. Nothing else could be truly important again.[83]

His feelings are illustrative of an occasional interest in close male relationships which appears in Hill's fiction: this contributes in *Strange Meeting* to a moving account of love in a senseless world, intricately presented from the point of view of both protagonists. Like *Old Soldiers*, *Strange Meeting* indicates the continuing imaginative challenge and narrative interest of the Great War: it remains for several recent novelists—Richard Hughes, Henry Williamson, and Angus Wilson, as well as Hill and Bailey—a central part of historical awareness of the developing twentieth century.

The Second World War occupies a substantial place in the chronicles and novel-sequences already discussed. Though Angus Wilson covers the events of 1939-45 fairly quickly in *No Laughing Matter*, Anthony Powell devotes three volumes of *A Dance to the Music of Time* to Nicholas Jenkins's war experience. The Second World War and its consequences also figure largely in C.P. Snow's *Strangers and Brothers*, and in Henry Williamson's *A Chronicle of*

Ancient Sunlight, though Williamson is more vivid and expansive in his account of 1914-18 in earlier volumes, *A Fox under my Cloak* (1955); *The Golden Virgin* (1957); *Love and the Loveless* (1958). Hitler's war is treated on a scale to rival Snow, Powell, and Williamson by Olivia Manning in her six-volume sequence beginning with *The Balkan Trilogy*, which some critics see as one of the best novels of the sixties, a unique record of the war in Europe. It concentrates on the relationship of Guy and Harriet Pringle, 'married, hurriedly, under the shadow of war' and 'a long way from home, alone together in a warring world'.[84] Though eventually forced by the Nazis to move to Athens (*Friends and Heroes* (1965)), the first two volumes (*The Great Fortune* (1960); *The Spoilt City* (1962)) show them living in Bucharest, where Guy works as a teacher for an organisation strongly resembling the British Council. Physically short sighted, Guy has an equally indistinct view of mankind in general; his idealistic belief in human goodness makes him a frequent, though cheerful, victim of 'the blade of reality' (p.608) in wartime. His generosity of spirit, continued adherence to the left-wing politics of the thirties, and occasional puzzled disillusion with 'defaulting humanity' (p.654), make him partly a representative of British attitudes at the time, disturbed by 'fascist savagery...a new thing in the civilised world' (p.345).

Guy's character, however, increasingly distresses his new wife, who watches with dismay his dissipation of energy on public duties rather than private responsibilities. His obsessive determination to mount a production of Shakespeare's *Troilus and Cressida*—rather an appropriate play in a Bucharest beset by Nazis—she sees merely as an example of his 'expending himself like radium', making him 'profligate of life. The physical energy and intelligence that had seemed to her to be a fortune to be conserved and invested, would be frittered away' (p.823). Guy and Harriet, profligate and parsimonious, are interestingly contrasted, but their relationship remains static, developing only in Harriet's gradual realisation of its nature, which is rather repetitively stated. Concentration on Harriet's restrained, detached point of view—though there are occasional excursions into Guy's—also tends to exclude strong or deep emotions from the narrative. Guy and Harriet eventually become substantial figures simply through the range and variety of their appearance in the trilogy. They are less successful, however, than Manning's wide cast of minor characters; in particular the eccentric Yakimov, an aristocratic sponger who seems to embody personally some of the tumbledown history of his century itself—he always appears dressed in a mangy fur coat, which he repeatedly claims was 'once worn by the doomed, unhappy Czar of all the Russias' (p.903).

Guy's circle of acquaintance includes many such figures; diplomats, teachers, and their local associates. This equips Manning with an extended context through which to examine Rumania's disastrous decline towards subordination to the growing Nazi threat. The novel follows the effects of this process upon the daily existence of the Pringles and their circle; their lives in the streets and shops of the city, beneath the obliterating snows of winter or the humid summer sun. The strength of *The Balkan Trilogy* lies in the range and profligacy of detail with which it presents this ordinary life in an extraordinary, disintegrating foreign civilisation, warped by war and politics which make 'the only thing certain...that nothing is certain' (p.82). The precision of the novel's observation and its setting in a doomed community recall Christopher Isherwood's *Goodbye to Berlin* (1939), though the greater extent of *The Balkan Trilogy* makes familiar a wider, fuller world. Like many long novels, it is eventually able to resume and recollect a range of its own characters and events wide enough to suggest a complete grasp of a place and a phase of history. This breadth of scope partly compensates for the trilogy's limitations in point of view and sense of individual human depth, contributing to its straightforward success as an adult adventure story. The saga is continued in *The Levant Trilogy* (*The Danger Tree* (1977); *The Battle Lost and Won* (1978); *The Sum of Things* (1980)), set in the developing desert war in Egypt, where the Pringles have fled from the continuing Nazi advance.

The novels reflecting the war discussed in Chapter Three mostly concentrate on specifically British experience of it, often on the Home Front. Manning is one of several later writers in whose longer perspective there also appears a more general interest in the conflict beyond the British context. While *The Balkan Trilogy* provides a chronicle of events in the Eastern sector, two other novels published in the early sixties—Richard Hughes's *The Fox in the Attic* and Gabriel Fielding's *The Birthday King*—concentrate on developments within Germany, examining the forces underlying the war and its origins.

Richard Hughes's reputation was for many years based almost entirely on his first novel, *A High Wind in Jamaica* (1929). Its unconventional material and perspective may indirectly reflect uncertainty and shifting values in the period following the First World War. Hughes's narrative presents even the most shocking events with dispassoniate objectivity and unusual visual clarity, adding force to the story's inversion of conventional expectations. While sailing to England, a group of children are abducted by pirates, who turn out to be good or at least rather likeable men: despite apparent innocence, one of the children, Emily, is responsible for murder. She also connives at the shifting of blame for this crime onto the pirates. Naturally, the court which tries them is more disposed to suspect pirates than children. Its error illustrates the incompetence of conventional moral expectations, and also shows the difficulty of objectively determining truth. This problem also troubles the narrator. He suggests 'the novelist...is concerned with facts',[85] but frequently interjected phrases such as 'I believe', or 'I suppose that' suggest the uncertainty even of his own factual, neutral presentation. He finally acknowledges 'I can no longer read Emily's deeper thoughts...henceforth we must be content to surmise' (p.169). Despite this admission, *A High Wind in Jamaica* is distinguished by the unusual extent of its entry into children's consciousness and modes of feeling, which are shown to be alarmingly excluded from norms of adult conduct.

Hughes admitted he was 'a slow writer'.[86] *The Fox in the Attic* (1961) is only his third novel. It resumes several of the concerns of *A High Wind in Jamaica*: the difficulty of determining moral questions; the repeated conflict of innocence and experience. Such issues are given particular emphasis by the novel's setting in 1923, with most of the characters suffering from 'Memory of the Fallen... for that 1914 War had been a holocaust...that impact had been from the first on British minds something unique in history'.[87] This impact and other factors contribute to a conclusion reached by Hughes's hero Augustine that

> ...a gulf divided his own from every previous generation...his own generation really was a new creation, a new kind of human being, *because of Freud*! (pp.21, 71)

Augustine's reflections on psychology are related to the novelist's assessment of the First World War itself as a 'war "dream"', at least in part a projection of some deep emotional upheaval such as compulsive Freudian dreams...are born of'; part of a primal urge to divide the world into 'them' and 'us' which 'seems to be one of the abiding terms of the human predicament' (p.99).

Hughes suggests that 'in England the ending of the war had come like waking from a bad dream: in defeated Germany, as the signal for deeper levels of nightmare' (p.117). In an afterword he claims historical accuracy for his presentation of this 'nightmare': it is certainly both detailed and imaginative. Hughes shows Germany's rampant inflation; Hitler's abortive Munich 'putsch'; and even Hitler himself as a character equipped with a plausibly-developed inner voice. These various legacies of Germany's war experience, growing threats to European stability, are highlighted by Augustine's innocent incapacity to apprehend them during a visit to distant relations, the von Kessens. The attic of their castle strangely harbours a pet fox and Wolff, a renegade from the Baltic wars: their hidden presence is partly emblematic of the way memories of the First World War lurk as a suppressed fury within the German mind. Augustine, however, is quite unaware of their existence. His ingenuousness accentuates contrasts between England and Germany

—between his sister's sunny home and the von Kessen castle, full of half-wild children; between the machinations of Hitler and the complacency of Augustine's home country, whose quiet liberalism makes '*shooting* politicians...inconceivable' (p.145).

Such contrasts contribute to an ambitious study, psychological and political, of the impulses underlying the European conflict which erupted again in 1939. *The Fox in the Attic*, however, is almost more of a study than a novel, its equilibrium as fiction slightly upset by the extent of its theoretical speculation, Freudian and historical. A pallid hero and rapid movement between tenuously connected characters further disrupt interest and unity. Possibly Hughes's form would have been clarified had he completed what he planned as '*The Human Predicament*...a long historical novel of my own times culminating in the Second World War',[88] of which *The Fox in the Attic* forms the first part. Though a second was published (*The Wooden Shepherdess* (1973), centred on Hitler's 'night of the long knives') and a third exists in manuscript, Hughes died before completing his project.

Like *The Fox in the Attic*, Gabriel Fielding's *The Birthday King* (1961) examines the origins of the Second World War in the 'inflation, ignominy, and influenza'[89] which in Germany followed the First. This is briefly summarised, however: Fielding's principal concern is with the place of the Nazi regime within the German state of mind as it develops between 1939 and 1945. Historical figures appear only in the background of a story which concentrates on struggles within a rich family of factory owners. The Waitzmanns are determined to sustain their individual empire within the new power structures of Hitler's Germany: the novel shows one of the family's sons, the selfish opportunist Ruprecht, usurping managerial control which rightly belongs to his brother Alfried. Alfried is a spiritual, almost saintly character, who experiences in terms of the agony of Christ, as a 'petty Calvary' (p.154), the sufferings to which Ruprecht and his own passive resistance to Hitler consign him.

By examining war-time Germany through a few contrasting characters in a family power-struggle, Fielding makes manageable —almost natural—the larger horrors of the age; even slave labour, even Alfried's torture and experience of Dachau concentration camp. Such outrages, sometimes supposed unimaginable, are presented as merely the cumulative result of petty sins or connivance; of fairly understandable moral choices. *The Birthday King* offers in this way an unusual depth of insight into a society gradually dehumanised by its selfish toleration of Hitler, welcomed at first because in the Weimar Republic Germans find 'when you fall into a cess-pit...you grab at anything that shows signs of floating' (p.18). Rather like Malcolm Lowry in *Under the Volcano* (see Chapter Three), Fielding carefully shows the allure as well as the horror of such Faustian pacts with human history: his narrative tone—empty of comment and as objective as Hughes's in *A High Wind in Jamaica*—forces upon readers responsibility for judging historical processes. The significance of some of these continues beyond the end of the war. Fielding shows the liberating Americans seeking to diminish the impact of the death camps on world opinion, in favour of re-creating Germany as a strong capitalist ally against communism. This leads to the novel's uneasy conclusion on a note of collective responsibility, suggesting that where Dachau, Belsen or other concentration camps are concerned 'even the guiltless aren't so guiltless as they wanted to be...no one can dissociate themselves... not Germany nor Europe nor America' (pp.318, 320).

As the war itself fades from immediate memory, the concentration camps remain as a continuing nightmare in contemporary consciousness—a torment for the hero of Julian Mitchell's *The Undiscovered Country* (1968), for example, or for the character in Fay Weldon's *Down among the Women* who talks of 'this year of Our Lord 1950, or rather P.B.5, which means Post Belsen Five' (p.21). After *The Birthday King*, however, few British novels attempt at any length to take up the concentration camps' intractable challenge to the imagination, until D.M. Thomas's *The White Hotel* (1981). Rather like Hughes, Thomas envisages his material partly in terms of 'a new creation, a new kind of human being, *because of Freud*'. Thomas calls Freud 'one of the dramatis personae'[90] of his novel, which presents a series of letters, case histories, and journals relating to Lisa Erdman-Berenstein, or 'Frau Anna' as Freud calls her. Following Freud's analysis of her case, Thomas builds up through the novel's various texts complex, sometimes competing conclusions about her psyche and its disturbance, creating for *The White Hotel* an absorbing sense of unfolding discovery, almost the excitement of a detective story. Entirely engrossed in Frau Anna's rich, confused inner life, it is a complete shock when the novel in its penultimate section shows her murdered by the Nazis at Babi Yar, alongside, eventually, a quarter of a million others. The intensity of earlier concentration on Frau Anna gives some emotional basis for an apprehension, or at least a reasoned incomprehension, of the scale of the slaughter:

> ...the soul of man is a far country, which cannot be approached or explored. Most of the dead were poor and illiterate. But every single one of them had dreamed dreams, seen visions and had amazing experiences... their lives and histories were as rich and complex as Lisa Erdman-Berenstein's. If a Sigmund Freud had been listening and taking notes from the time of Adam, he would still not fully have explored even a single group, even a single person. (p.220)

Thomas's approach to the general by means of the absolutely particular is the basis of a strategy, like Fielding's, at least nearly sufficient to assimilate material often thought beyond the grasp of fiction. Though *The White Hotel* is nevertheless not entirely free from some suspicion of sensationalism, its explicit treatment of sex, for example, is partly connected to a wider vision; to the novel's suggestion of the sources of historical conflict and destruction. Lisa records 'thinking about sex...thinking about death...sometimes both at the same time' (p.77): Freud concludes she is 'someone in whom an hysteria exaggerated and highlighted a *universal* struggle between the life instinct and the death instinct' (pp.116-17). Lisa's disturbed mind also goes beyond the range of Freud's analysis or imagination into a dimension of clairvoyance. Through this faculty, she intuits an exact coincidence of sex and death in her own fate, prefigured in the novel in various ways which further heighten its developing excitement of expected discovery. Her mind's participation in 'a *universal* struggle between the life instinct and the death instinct', and her anticipation of this struggle's massive manifestation in Holocaust and war, also show Thomas following *The Fox in the Attic*: like Hughes, he suggests that the twentieth century's wars and annihilations, its movements towards madness and meaninglessness, may be emanations from deep within the European consciousness itself.

Old Conflicts and New Syntheses: William Golding, Iris Murdoch, Anthony Burgess, Muriel Spark

D.M. Thomas indicates another aspect of conflict within the European mind when Lisa remarks in *The White Hotel* 'what torments me is whether life is good or evil' and talks of 'good and evil coupling, to make the world' (p.171). This uncertainty about whether life is good or evil is representative of some recurrent interests which appear in fiction since the war, perhaps as its consequence. Something of a 'universal struggle' between good and evil underlies Richard Hughes's scrutiny of moral concerns, and Gabriel Fielding's depiction in *The Birthday King* of conflict between the absolutely selfish Ruprecht and the saintly Alfred. Similar interests figure in the work of other writers discussed above. Set in the nineteen thirties, C.P. Snow's *The Light and the Dark* (1947), for example, shows another stage in the life of one of the dons from *The Masters*, concurrently perplexed by the rise of the Nazi party and by his discovery in his academic research of a Manichean sect—a group of heretical early Christians who believed the universe precisely divided between equal forces of good and evil, light and dark. This division also appears in Wyndham Lewis's *Monstre Gai* (1955) and *Malign Fiesta* (1955, see Chapter Three), and is continued in more recent fiction in Doris Lessing's *Canopus in Argos: Archives* series, which shows powers of good and evil brooding in deep space over the fate of the earth.

Similarly divided moral forces also figure distinctively in the fiction of Iris Murdoch, William Golding, and Anthony Burgess, who have emerged as among the outstanding writers of recent decades, and whose work demands extended discussion. Each lived through the war, which may be connected to their various subsequent visions of 'good and evil coupling, to make the world'. When discussing some of the war's effects on fiction in *The Novel Now* (1971), Anthony Burgess quotes Jean-Paul Sartre's view that

> ...we have been taught to take Evil seriously...Dachau and Auschwitz have...demonstrated to us that Evil is not an appearance, that knowing its cause does not dispel it, that it is not opposed to Good as a confused idea is to a clear one.[91]

Chapter Three suggested that the war stimulated novelists fairly immediately to examine the nature and relation of good and evil, innocence and experience, God and Devil. Burgess's quotation and the various examples of Hughes, Thomas and Fielding suggest that such concerns are extended into later decades by the sustained challenge of the concentration camps' memory; the developing legacy of the war's impact on imagination. Golding provides a figuration of these continuing interests in recent fiction, and of their likely wartime origins, in his opening to *Darkness Visible* (1979). It depicts an innocent child, Matty, walking out of the fiery centre of war in the London blitz, as if 'born from the sheer agony of a burning city'.[92] One half of his face is light, the other burned dark. The novel shows him going on to enter a strange, 'universal struggle' between powers of good and evil, half-spiritual, half-earthly.

Walter Allen remarks of Golding's fiction

> ...great gifts of imagination and narrative...force us to accept, as part of the truth about man and his nature, the realities summed up in our time in the hysterical nastiness of Nazism and concentration camps.[93]

Depressing truths about 'man and his nature' are presented throughout Golding's work. They are already apparent in his first novel, still his most popular, *Lord of the Flies* (1954), which demonstrates what the novel defines as 'the end of innocence, the darkness of man's heart'.[94] Like several of the authors discussed in Chapter Three, Golding develops this theme in loose analogy with the Bible story of original sin in the Garden of Eden. In the course of some future war, a group of boys are abandoned on a largely paradisal desert island, but rapidly fall away from civilisation into barbarism and an allegiance to 'The Lord of the Flies'—a name for the devil. An officer from the naval cruiser which rescues them on the novel's last page forlornly remarks 'I should have thought that a pack of British boys...would have been able to put up a better show than that', adding that their situation seems 'like the Coral Island' (pp.222-3). Golding's novel is partly based on R.M. Ballantyne's *The*

Coral Island (1857), some of his characters even sharing the names of Ballantyne's. But *Lord of the Flies* belongs to a more disillusioned age, distanced from the Victorian optimism in Ballantyne's story of castaways' enterprising re-creation of British society in the wilderness. Like Richard Hughes's *A High Wind in Jamaica*, *Lord of the Flies* denies even the hope—which consoled many of the authors discussed in Chapter Three—that human innocence exists in children.

Golding's next novel, *The Inheritors* (1955), also examines 'the end of innocence, the darkness of man's heart', but on a still larger, more nearly mythic scale. The innocence lost is of Neanderthal man, eradicated in prehistory by the darkness at the heart of Homo Sapiens, a new species shown to be 'endowed with possessions...skill and malice...a people of the fall'.[95] Its members are intelligent, equipped with reason and art, but their simultaneous capacity for hatred, crime, and superstition alienates them from nature and even from each other, making them seem a sad alternative to their predecessors. Like Lewis Grassic Gibbon in *A Scots Quair* (1932-4), Golding envisages the Neanderthal age as one of Edenic simplicity, loving community trust and immediacy of communion with the natural world. These qualities are compellingly dramatised by general restriction of point of view to the Neanderthal community, and by Golding's creation of a language—simple, declarative, and vividly perceptual—which attempts to represent consciousnesses barely able to distinguish dream, memory, imagination and actuality. Typically of Golding's fiction, this language compels readers— sharing the superior discrimination of Homo Sapiens—to make connections and reach conclusions about events barely comprehensible to the participants themselves.

The language of *The Inheritors* is also particularly effective in its description of primitive, natural settings, registered in smells, sound and touch as much as sight. This linguistic facility is characteristic of Golding's work as a whole. It is a particular feature in his third novel, *Pincher Martin* (1956), which presents with great sensual immediacy man in an elemental relation to nature: Christopher 'Pincher' Martin is a 'poor mad creature clinging to a rock in the middle of the sea',[96] following the torpedoeing of his destroyer. His distress is deepened by tormenting memories. These zigzagging flashbacks move across an earlier existence of voracious selfishness, culminating in an attempt to murder his saintly friend Nathaniel, ironically at the moment their destroyer was sunk. Pincher's struggle for survival, however, is more complicated even than it at first appears. Rather like *The Inheritors*, whose last section dramatically switches to the perspective of Homo Sapiens, the conclusion of *Pincher Martin* offers a radically different perception of all that has preceded it. Washed ashore, Pincher's body shows he 'didn't even have time to kick off his seaboots' (p.208), when the ship sank. The reader has shared in Pincher's creation of a wholly fictional future for himself, a refuge on 'a rock in the middle of the sea' constructed out of dissolving fragments of his consciousness at the moment of death. The qualities of selfishness which warped Pincher's life contribute to this mental refusal of personal annihilation, and to his choice instead of a self-created purgatory, 'The sort of heaven we invented for ourselves after death, if we aren't ready for the real one' (p.183). Wicked, doomed, but hugely resilient, the greedy clinging of Pincher's mind to the remotest stirrings of its consciousness indicates 'an extraordinary capacity to endure' (p.71), but also an inescapable implication of evil and selfishness within exceptional strength of individuality.

The Inheritors, *Lord of the Flies*, and *Pincher Martin* show something of the origin of evil within the species, its inherent presence within 'civilised' man, and its inevitable connection with individual will. Set in contexts remote in time and space from everyday life, each is essentially a fable, illustrative of a particular facet of 'the truth about man and his nature'. As John Wain pointed out in 1962, in his early phase

> William Golding...is not a novelist...he is an allegorist. He has certain perceptions about the human condition which he...goes ahead and creates an allegory to represent.[97]

Golding is sometimes praised in such terms, though also criticised for 'gimmickry'[98] in his structures and endings, or for a supposed lack of human substance in novels over-schematised by moral issues. After *The Spire* (1964), he published little fiction until *Darkness Visible* (1979). Divided between fable and closer attention to everyday reality, it shows some of the difficulties as well as the strengths of his methods.

Its first part shares the 'allegorical' style of Golding's earlier writing, showing Matty as 'a human shape or...a bit of flickering brightness' (p.15). Like Nathaniel in *Pincher Martin*, he is an awkward saint, whose experience is often described in Biblical language and is half-comically approximate to crucifixion and a passage through the underworld. Part Two, 'Sophy', contrastingly examines evil, sometimes envisaged on a cosmic scale in terms of

> ...the voice of the darkness between the stars, between the galaxies, the toneless voice of the great skein unravelling and lying slack...
> Running-down. Dark (p.173)

Sophy sees this entropic 'running-down' to darkness as part of 'the "Of Course" way things sometimes behaved...as if the whole world was co-operating' (pp.108, 126). Even the narrative voice of the novel seems to 'co-operate' in her vision, often adding with glib certainty the words 'Of Course' to descriptions of evil or human failure. However, despite its suggestions of 'magic' and 'the darkness between the stars', Part Two is predominantly neither fable nor allegory, but mostly concerned realistically with life in the shabby streets and supermarkets of contemporary Britain, 'the Liberal club closed for repairs, graffiti on every available surface' (p.202).

Part Three of *Darkness Visible*, indicatively entitled 'One is One', attempts to show 'the world of spirit' (p.233) of the novel's first section entering and informing the mundane, everyday area of the second. Matty dies as he was born, in fire, miraculously rescuing first a child from Sophy and her terrorists, and then in the novel's concluding, poetic, moment, returning to retrieve the soul of its shabbiest character. This connection of spiritual with secular is central to the novel's vision: evil and general 'running down' are a matter 'of course' in contemporary life, too debased and dispirited to redeem itself, so a revitalising intrusion from the spirit world Matty seems to inhabit is essential. This intrusion, however, requires an awkward coalescence of the methods of the first and second parts of the novel. This is ambitiously attempted, but it stretches the reader's imagination uneasily between fable and realism. The unity claimed for Part Three is imperilled as a result: despite the emotive power of its last pages, *Darkness Visible* is one of the most challenging and least certain of Golding's achievements.

His particular strengths are better integrated in *Rites of Passage* (1980); concentrated again in the sort of unusual, isolated context successfully employed in earlier novels. Confinement to a ship sailing to Australia provides *Rites of Passage* with 'a separate world, a universe in little',[99] inhabited by 'men at sea who live too close to each other and too close thereby to all that is monstrous under the sun and moon'. The narrative is further confined to the point of view of Edmund Talbot, as it is set down in his journal. Partly in imitation of the style of near-contemporary eighteenth-century novelists such as Laurence Sterne, Talbot confesses to 'the limitations of such a journal' (p.28). These are dramatically illustrated by its decline from cheerful orderliness to confused uncertainty and persistent disparity from other versions of events recorded, for example, in Parson Colley's letter to his sister. Talbot's journal also reveals a naïveté and short-sighted conceit which makes him incompetent to understand or communicate things 'monstrous under the sun and moon'. He is innocently unaware, for example, of the true nature of the Parson's decline into disgrace and death. This ingenuousness creates a narrative which—as in *The Inheritors*—operates subtly, by implication rather than statement: Talbot's 'limitations' are a stimulus to readers' own judgements. Like *A High Wind in Jamaica*, *Rites of Passage* is an initiation, a journey for reader and character into less optimistic assessment of man's nature. In the naïveté of Talbot's journal Golding also illustrates, like Richard Hughes, how conventional, consoling assumptions interfere with truth. Eventually more mature in moral awareness, Talbot admits his letter of condolence to Colley's sister 'will be lies from beginning to end' (p.277).

This final, misleading letter recalls Marlow's reassuring, lying version of Kurtz's death for the benefit of his 'Intended' in Joseph Conrad's *Heart of Darkness* (1902). Both in its general vision of 'the darkness of man's heart', and perhaps especially in the 'sea-story' (p.277) *Rites of Passage*, Golding's novels often resemble Conrad's fiction. Like Conrad, Golding is concerned with the frailty of man's morals, understanding, or control of self and environment; asking 'philosophy and religion—what are they when the wind blows and the water gets up in lumps' (*Rites of Passage*, p.16). Golding is at his best when, like Conrad, he approaches such questions in distant settings, showing men struggling to survive at the limits of an imagination isolated from the support of society. Representative of 'realities in our time' made more sharply challenging by 'Nazism and concentration camps', the darkness these elemental struggles reveal is made immediate, as Walter Allen suggests, by 'great gifts of imagination and narrative'. Rather than being limited by his fable form, Golding's moral questions are precisely and specifically focused by narrative strategies often entirely different in separate novels, and highly original in themselves. Perhaps especially in *Pincher Martin*, concluding redefinitions of the way a novel's vision has been created challenge some of the conventions of imagination and fiction. Golding's Nobel Prize was perhaps awarded not only for such variety and inventiveness, but also for a humane quality in his fiction. Though he has been accused of providing only a depressing view of ineradicable and primary evil, of not showing 'if the line of darkness had an ending' (*The Inheritors*, p.233), *Darkness Visible* at least indicates 'hope struggling with a natural pessimism' (p.24); spirits of good as well as evil surrounding and superintending mankind and its confused affairs.

Iris Murdoch remarks 'we have not recovered from two wars and the experience of Hitler', adding that 'it is curious that modern literature…contains so few convincing pictures of evil…in spite of Hitler'.[100] Rather like Golding's novels, some of her own fiction offers 'pictures of evil', sometimes in conflict with its opposite. *A Fairly Honourable Defeat* (1970), for example, contains a thoroughly developed characterisation, a convincing picture of evil, in the figure of Julius. Having 'spent the war in Belsen'[101] he has emphatically not 'recovered from the experience of Hitler', but extends its malignant shadow into his conduct and opinions in contemporary life. He believes with fathomless cynicism in the rottenness of human nature and its capacity merely to flatter itself with ideas of goodness or self-respect. He claims, for example,

…good is dull. What novelist ever succeeded in making a good man

173

interesting? It is characteristic of this planet that the path of virtue is so unutterably depressing that it can be guaranteed to break the spirit and quench the vision of anybody who consistently attempts to tread it. Evil, on the contrary, is exciting and fascinating and alive. It is also very much more mysterious than good. Good can be seen through. Evil is opaque. (p.223)

His comments set a challenge to the novel itself, one which Murdoch takes up in the figure of Tallis, a successful attempt to make a character both generally interesting as well as good. Despite a past as traumatic as Julius's, Tallis remains 'the only person about the place with really sound instincts' (p.433), and the one most likely to combat Julius's dark intentions.

Since one of Tallis's peculiarities is an occasional vision of 'principalities and powers...demons' (p.209), and Julius is described as a 'magician', 'really...a *god*' (pp.414, 170), there is some suggestion that their conflict belongs to the sort of spiritual dimension which appears in parts of *Darkness Visible*, and that they are as sharply contrasted figures of good and evil as Matty and Sophy. The nature of their conflict, however, is better indicated by Sartre's comment that 'Evil...is not opposed to good as a confused idea is to a clear one'. The confused, well-meaning squalor in which Tallis generally lives makes it difficult to prefer him unreservedly to his suave adversary. It is responsible, instead, for creating exactly the dimension of complexity and particularity which makes him such an interesting fictional character. Particularity of this sort makes him and Julius plausibly good and evil men, rather than 'allegorical' figures. *A Fairly Honourable Defeat* is much less a moral fable than some of Golding's fiction: as in much of the rest of Murdoch's work, its moral investigation is combined with sustained attention to the details of ordinary, everyday life. Though Tallis is tempted, for example, to explain the misery around him rather like Golding in terms of original sin, he rejects this idea in favour of a more mundane view of a 'disastrous compound of human failure, muddle and sheer chance, so like what it was all like' (p.443). The length and diversity of *A Fairly Honourable Defeat* show this compound complicatedly at work upon a range of interconnected characters: their failures and muddles combine disastrously with Julius's ability to 'mystify people and make them act parts' (p.396). His belief in the vacuity of moral values is vindicated, and Tallis 'defeated' when one of their friends, Rupert, is driven to despair, perhaps suicide, despite a 'deep age-old confidence in the power of goodness' (p.359), and an almost-completed work of amateur moral philosophy.

Narrated in the third person, *A Fairly Honourable Defeat* relies heavily, at times exclusively, on dialogue, in the manner of Ivy Compton-Burnett or the later Henry Green. Dramatising conflict in conversation and action, this technique is an improvement on Murdoch's earlier fiction, in which first-person narrators sometimes

THE NOVEL SINCE THE FIFTIES

dissipate tension in over-extended sections of reflection or self-analysis. This tendency is occasionally present in Murdoch's first novel, *Under the Net* (1954), for example, though it is checked by colloquial humour and tremendous pace of action; perhaps also by the gradual realisation on the part of the narrator, Jake Donaghue, that 'life. Ragged, inglorious and apparently purposeless'[102] overtakes any reflection or analysis of it. Rather 'ragged and purposeless' himself, Jake is a shiftless outsider, 'a sort of professional Unauthorized Person' (p.140): his insouciant, sexy adventures on the fringes of London's underworld encouraged early reviewers to group Murdoch with the angry young men of the fifties. Rather than seeming over-reflective or philosophic, *Under the Net* does at times resemble John Wain's *Hurry on Down*, or, more closely, J.P. Donleavy's *The Ginger Man* (1955), popular at the time more for its bawdy tale of Dublin drunkenness—'women, drink and...general chaos'[103]—than for the occasional Joycean vigour of its language and technique.

Murdoch, however, is funnier than either Wain or Donleavy, and also more profound. Jake keeps a copy of Samuel Beckett's *Murphy* (1938): his thoughtful disdain for conventional society often makes him resemble Beckett's hero. *Under the Net* as a whole, as Murdoch has explained, is indebted to her admiration for Beckett and for some of the ideas of freedom and self-determination in the philosophy of Jean-Paul Sartre (see Chapter Five). Murdoch was for many years a university teacher of philosophy, and her novels, like Sartre's, strongly exhibit the shape and influence of philosophical interests. Her approval, for example, of Simone Weil's idea that morality is 'a matter of attention'[104] is developed throughout her fiction. In *A Fairly Honourable Defeat*, for example, Rupert indicates the dangers of 'some general view which makes you blind to obvious immediate things in human life' (p.222). Jake similarly realises through his study of language

> All theorizing is flight. We must be ruled by the situation itself and this is unutterably particular. Indeed it is something to which we can never get close enough, however hard we try as it were to crawl under the net. (p.82)

Jake also has to realise the nature of the 'net' he has cast over reality himself. He acknowledges in the end that in certain judgements he had 'got it all the wrong way round...this was all a hallucination' (pp.228, 230), a recognition which allows him to accept that a former lover 'really existed now as a separate being and not as a part of myself'. This new, clear, knowledge is 'one of the guises of love' (p.239), and of the 'attention' described by Weil which Murdoch sees as an important component of goodness.

Many of Murdoch's characters, like Jake, go through an enlightening process of the renunciation of 'hallucination'. One such is Martin Lynch-Gibbon, though he and the other characters in *A Severed Head* (1961) also have to learn the particular lesson that they 'cannot cheat the dark gods'.[105] Despite the restraints of intellect and the sophistications of psychiatry, their attempts to live entirely rationally are a vain denial of the darker forces of their emotional natures. Explicitly concerned in this way with the relation of ideas and intellect to the fullness of lived experience, *A Severed Head* also reveals indirectly some of Murdoch's comparable difficulties in integrating philosophy into fully realistic fiction. Her demonstration of the operation of 'the dark gods' requires a swapping of sexual partners on a scale so comprehensive as to seem at times dance-like or operatic rather than plausible. The narrator actually remarks at one stage 'what happened next may seem a little improbable, but the reader must just believe me that it did occur' (p.112). To some extent, this 'improbable' quality can be excused as part of a novel of psychological rather than ordinarily realistic interest, almost an adult fairy-tale. It does also illustrate, however, the element of contrivance often considered a serious limitation in Murdoch's fiction. Rather like William Golding, she is criticised for an apparent readiness to sacrifice character or the human substance of her fiction to the creation of some illustrative pattern, fable or myth: Murdoch herself admits to 'giving in to the myth'[106] in this way in *A Severed Head*. Such 'giving in' raises the paradoxical possibility that some of her fiction suffers from the very tendencies it specifically warns against—creating patterns which, like Jake's in *Under the Net*, warp and falsify reality; ignoring Rupert's warning in *A Fairly Honourable Defeat* about 'some general view which makes you blind to the immediate things in human life'. A self-conscious awareness of this possibility appears in Murdoch's work: several novels show characters in flight from an enchanter—a wicked figure who imposes false patterns on reality or reduces people to puppets—who is also in some way an artist. Julius, for example, simply claims in *A Fairly Honourable Defeat* 'I am an artist' (p.431).

A comparable enchanter and 'artist' appears in *The Sea, The Sea* (1978). Its narrator, Charles Arrowby, is 'in favour of illusion...the trickery and magic of art...the never-never land of art...filling us with false hopes and empty dreams'.[107] Though initially manipulative of his friends and acquaintances, Charles shows himself, unlike Julius, capable of change and improvement. Rather like Jake Donaghue and Martin Lynch-Gibbon, in fact, he learns in the course of the novel the dangers of self-delusion, concluding

> I have been in a state of illusion and caused much fruitless distress...what a 'fantasist' I have been myself. I was the dreamer, I the magician...
> reading my own dream text and not looking at the reality. (pp.339, 499)

This realisation also helps him to renounce his selfish hold over his friends: he accepts that 'the last achievement is the absolute surrender of magic itself...goodness is giving up power' (p.445). Such realisation, and his wish to 'abjure magic' (p.2) are particularly appropriate in a former actor and theatre director whose success has included being 'a good Prospero' (p.38). Murdoch's admiration for Shakespeare appears in many further analogies between Charles and Shakespeare's hero, and between *The Sea, The Sea* and *The Tempest* as a whole. The house to which Charles has retired from the stage is almost surrounded by the sea, infinitely changeable and the 'image of an inaccessible freedom' (p.263). Its vast formlessness provides for him, rather as it does for Prospero, an element perfectly antithetical to any urge to project patterns upon reality.

Like Shakespeare, Murdoch also uses the 'illusion...trickery and magic' of her hero partly as a means of artistic self-examination; of investigating the relation between literature and life, form and disorder. Charles comments extensively on 'writing my life...as a novel' (p.153), making clear the nature and allure of narrative's potential to distort actuality:

> ...if one had time to write the whole of one's life...as a novel how rewarding this would be. The pleasant parts would be doubly pleasant, the funny parts funnier, and sin and grief would be softened by a light of philosophic consolation. (p.99)

Creation of such a 'dream text...not looking at the reality', however, is part of the 'trickery and magic of art' which Charles eventually learns to abjure. His journal in the end accepts that:

> ....life, unlike art, has an irritating way of bumping and limping on, undoing conversions, casting doubt on solutions, and generally illustrating the impossibility of living happily or virtuously ever after...Human arrangements are nothing but loose ends and hazy reckoning, whatever art may otherwise pretend in order to console us. (p.477)

A character in Golding's *Rites of Passage* remarks 'life is a formless business...literature is much amiss in forcing a form on it' (p.265). Like Golding, Murdoch successfully confronts and overcomes this problem in 'some kind of sea-story' and the journal of a first-person narrator. Charles's discussions of the process of his writing make explicit in Murdoch's fiction an element of technical self-consciousness, an illustration of the nature and mechanics of illusion, sufficient to neutralise dangers to 'our sense of reality' which Murdoch recognises arise from the 'sense of form, which is an aspect of our desire for consolation'. Such self-consciousness in her work shows Murdoch developing beyond the problems of 'forcing a form' which appear in *A Severed Head* and other early fiction. *The Sea, The Sea* offers instead evidence for her conclusion that 'through literature we can re-discover a sense of the density of our lives'. This results not only from Charles's exposure of the way literature risks warping the world, but also from the breadth and detail of the world Murdoch presents. She remarks that 'a respect for the contingent, is essential to imagination as opposed to fantasy',[108] and qualifies her admiration for Sartre's work partly because in her view it lacks sufficient attention to the ordinary stuff of everyday existence. Elaborate recipes for Charles's meals, or gratuitous but poignant descriptions of tombstones in the village churchyard, for example, are typical of an attentiveness to the 'immediate things in human life' which is a distinctive feature of her own work as a whole. Though this broadly-based realism and her committed communication of a philosophic 'general view' occasionally work against each other, they are successfully mutually adjusted—as in *The Sea*, *The Sea* and *A Fairly Honourable Defeat*—often enough to make Iris Murdoch one of the foremost of contemporary novelists.

Like *The Sea*, *The Sea*, Anthony Burgess's *Earthly Powers* (1980) raises self-conscious questions about 'the capacity of literature to cope with human reality'.[109] Its narrator is a successful popular writer, Kenneth Toomey (often thought to be Burgess's fictional portrait of Somerset Maugham). He is aware from the first page of his 'cunning' and 'contrivance', and intrigued by their effects in transforming reality. Discussions of such technical issues also figure as part of Toomey's acquaintanceship with Joyce, Wyndham Lewis, Ford Madox Ford and Rudyard Kipling: intimate portraits of these and other writers add to the literary self-consciousness and sometimes to the humour of *Earthly Powers* as a whole. Like Murdoch, however, Burgess also has much wider interests and moral concerns. Toomey is personally familiar not only with distinguished literary figures, but also with some of the people and events generally significant in the developing history of the century. Though he occasionally enjoys indulgently enough the fruits of his popular success, lifelong homosexuality makes him at various stages an exile from conventional society: driven into an itinerant, eventful existence, he sometimes finds himself close to 'Hitler...Mussolini and the rest of the terrible people this terrible century's thrown up' (p.639). He meets, for example, 'nearly everybody who counted in the Nazi party' (p.386), and he visits the concentration camps shortly after they are liberated in 1945.

Toomey also describes his lifelong acquaintance with Cardinal Carlo Campanati, eventually Pope Gregory, a churchman of determinedly liberal views who seeks to 'transform Christianity' with a vision of 'divine good to oppose to the growth of evil in our time' (pp.364-5). Though Campanati is apparently one of the strongest moral opponents of 'the terrible people this terrible century's thrown up', Toomey is suspicious of his belief that man is inherently good and corrupted only by the devil and various of his agents such as Adolf Hitler. He parodically summarises this conviction in suggesting that 'man was not really bad...everything could be blamed on a kind of moral virus that had landed in Eden in a spaceship' (p.575). When he visits the concentration camps, Toomey also remarks

> I wanted to have Carlo with me there to smell the ripe gorgonzola of innate human evil and to dare to say that mankind was God's creation and hence good. Good, that's what I am, sir, it was the devil made me do it. Man was not God's creation, that was certain. God alone knew from what suppurating primordial dungheap man had arisen (p.458).

Toomey finds the denial of human responsibility for evil a corruption of morality grave enough to make Campanati not the saint he is often supposed but an '*advocatus diaboli*' (p.640), an inadvertent agent of the devil he seeks to oppose. The web of horrors eventually shown to surround Campanati's life and actions partly vindicates Toomey's opinion, though his own lonely vision of man, meaningless offspring of the 'primordial dungheap', is shown to be equally limiting.

Toomey's conflict with Campanati and the material of *Earthly Powers* as a whole illustrate Burgess's belief that 'literature...can make clearer the whole business of moral choice'. He adds 'I believe that good and evil exist, and that evil has to be resisted.' Rather like William Golding in *Darkness Visible*, or C.P. Snow in *The Light and the Dark*, Burgess envisages a conflict between good and evil sharp enough to divide the whole universe into opposing forces: he suggests 'duality is the ultimate reality...life is binary...this is a duoverse'.[110] This Manichean 'universal struggle' is elaborately dramatised, in its earthly effects, by the unfolding historical span of Toomey's recollections. His narrative stretches back over six decades of the twentieth century to the First World War. The extended period of public life and history envisaged makes *Earthly Powers* comparable to Angus Wilson's *No Laughing Matter* and to the other long chronicle novels discussed in this chapter, or to some of the retrospections on the century's development discussed in Chapter Three. Though Burgess was quoted earlier suggesting 'we no longer expect the one big book' he also considers that 'novels should be about the whole of a society':[111] like *No Laughing Matter* and other chronicles, *Earthly Powers* is an ambitious attempt at a 'big book' bringing together the 'fragments of an individual vision' into a whole view of the twentieth century. Like some of the fiction of Golding and Murdoch, it is partly limited by subordination of characters and their histories to schematic development of moral issues. This illustrates all the more openly, however, the connection variously made by all three novelists between moral questions and 'two wars and the experience of Hitler.' Linking Eden and Belsen, Satan and Hitler, *Earthly Powers* is one of the clearest of recent visions of 'good and evil coupling, to make the world'; of evil's action in human experience and its Manichean conflict with opposing 'principalities and powers' as the force underlying the unruly progress of the twentieth century.

A concise and in some ways more successful treatment of some of the themes of *Earthly Powers* appears in *A Clockwork Orange* (1962), one of the most popular of Burgess's many novels, especially since Stanley Kubrick's spectacular film. Campanati remarks in *Earthly Powers* 'God gave his creatures the most tremendous endowment, the thing most like his own essence—I mean freedom of choice' (p.555). Emphasised by the brisk, repeated question, 'What's it going to be then, eh?' which opens each of the novel's three sections, this freedom of choice and, its moral consequences are the central interests of *A Clockwork Orange*. Like Sophy in Golding's *Darkness Visible*, Burgess's narrator Alex stresses that his delinquency is entirely a matter of free choice of evil, of deliberate self-assertion:

> ...badness is of the self, the one...But the not-self cannot have the bad, meaning they of the government and the judges and the schools cannot allow the bad because they cannot allow the self. And is not our modern history, my brothers, the story of brave...selves fighting these big machines?...what I do I do because I like to do.[112]

Alex's murderous violence in the first part of the novel is partly validated as a deliberate, if monstrously self-indulgent, act of rebellion against an especially numbing social 'machine'. *A Clockwork Orange* is set in a soulless, technological future Britain of advanced urban decay, unrestrained sale of drugs, 'more space-trips and bigger stereo TV screens and offers of free packets of soapflakes' (p.35). There is also, more sinisterly, an Orwellian aspect of authoritarian social control. Part Two shows Alex being brainwashed by new penal techniques, including sickening films of Nazi violence, which leave him 'committed to socially acceptable acts, a little machine capable only of good' (p.122)—a 'clockwork orange' as mechanical as the society which conditions him. Though he recovers in Part Three, his ultimate fate is left unusually unresolved: later editions of *A Clockwork Orange* follow Burgess's deletion, for the film, of a final section showing Alex contemplating marriage and a settled life, ending instead with a full and violent renewal of his joyful choice of evil.

The contrast, however, between his phase of automatic goodness and his earlier nature, free and evil, establishes with more than sufficient clarity the novel's central questions (recalling some of Milton's interests in *Paradise Lost*): 'Does God want goodness or the choice of goodness? Is a man who chooses the bad perhaps in some way better than a man who has the good imposed upon him?' (p.76). To communicate such questions effectively, the 'man who chooses the bad' must be presented in a way which avoids simply repelling readers' sympathy. Disapproval of Alex and his 'ultra-violence' is partly checked by his vitality, more admirable than his society's inertia, and by his constant assertion of complicity with his readers, addressed in his narrative as 'my brothers' or 'only friends'. He also benefits greatly from the novel's most interesting feature, Burgess's creation of a language which reflects both Alex's violent energy and the stylishness which appears in his fastidious love of elegance and preference for classical music. Alex's teenage language is also sufficiently peculiar to keep readers distanced from the immediate impact of horrors which follow from his choice of 'the bad':

> Pete and Georgie had good sharp nozhes, but I for my own part had a fine starry horrorshow cut-throat britva which, at that time, I could flash and shine artistic. So there we were dratsing away in the dark, the old Luna with men on it just coming up, the stars stabbing away as it might be knives anxious to join in the dratsing... and, my brothers, it was real satisfaction to me to waltz — left two three, right two three — and carve left cheeky and right cheeky, so that like two curtains of blood seemed to pour out (pp.16-17).

Such language is at times almost too successful in formalising or romanticising Alex's violence, occasionally disrupting the sort of moral response it should help to direct upon issues of freedom, evil, and choice. Nevertheless, its language makes *A Clockwork Orange* one of the most impressive of Burgess's prolific range of novels. Its verbal inventiveness may be related to the multilingual facility its author developed as a teacher in Malaya, and Alex's fascination for reproducing patterns of sound perhaps reflects Burgess's lifelong interest in music and its composition. Probably the major source of the novel's linguistic ingenuity, however, is the example of 'the exact use of language' for which Burgess praises Joyce.[113] Joyce's influence appears variously throughout his fiction: he has also edited an abbreviated version of *Finnegans Wake*, as well as publishing a critical introduction to Joyce's work, *Here Comes Everybody* (1965) and a study of his language, *Joysprick* (1973).

Burgess's admiration for Joyce connects him more clearly than either Golding or Murdoch with the work of the modernists. All three writers, however, depart to some extent from the socially-concerned 'neorealism' predominant when their work began to appear in the fifties. Though Golding's precise, rich observation was perhaps responsible for encouraging contemporary commentators to group him with the angry young men, his powers are developed in fables and 'allegories' of greater imaginative scope and originality of construction than appears in their work. Setting *Pincher Martin* entirely in a man's mind at the moment of death, for example, significantly extends the attention to inner consciousness and the flexibility of chronology which distinguish modernist writing. Iris Murdoch's fiction shows a comparable tension between realism and other more elaborate, self-conscious ways of writing. Murdoch suggests in her essay 'Against Dryness' (1961):

> ...the twentieth-century novel is usually either crystalline or journalistic; that is, it is either a small quasi-allegorical object...or else it is a large shapeless quasi-documentary object, the degenerate descendant of the nineteenth-century novel.[114]

The 'quasi-allegorical', philosophic mode of her own fiction combines some of the conventions of the nineteenth century, which she thinks 'the great era of the novel',[115] with the 'crystalline' qualities of the twentieth century. The latter also appear in a Joycean interest in language in *Under the Net*, for example; in the self-reflexive mode of novels such as *The Black Prince* (1973); and in the self-scrutinising commentary on techniques and limitations of writing in *The Sea, the Sea*.

Similarly self-conscious narrators are employed in *Rites of Passage* and in *Earthly Powers:* each of these novels shows its author sharing some affinity with the more radically experimental, self-reflexive writing discussed in the next chapter as the direct descendant of modernism. The appearance of such innovative traits suggests that Anthony Burgess might have been speaking for Murdoch and Golding as well as himself when he remarked 'we must welcome experiment in the novel...but it would be a pity to throw overboard all that the novel has learned throughout the slow centuries of its development.'[116] Golding, Burgess and Murdoch each incorporate within 'lessons learned throughout the slow centuries of its development' some of the new technical possibilities added to the novel's resources by modernism and subsequent literary experiments of the twentieth century. Their work is connected not only by conventional concern with the old conflict of good and evil: they are also associated by their various attempts at synthesis of 'journalistic' and 'crystalline' styles.

Muriel Spark shares with Burgess, Golding and Murdoch some concern with good and evil. She is also committed, simultaneously and often much more firmly, to experiment in technique. Her first novel, *The Comforters* (1957), for example, shows her heroine Caroline struggling to come to terms with her conversion to Catholicism, and with some sharp experiences of the conflict of good and evil, in various forms including a black mass. Caroline is simultaneously perplexed, however, by literary questions which go some way beyond her critical study, *Form in the Modern Novel*. Like Maurice Bendrix in Graham Greene's *The End of the Affair* (see Chapter Three), she begins to feel analogies between the relations of self to deity and fictional character to author. She considers 'it is as if a writer on another plane of existence was writing a story about us...there's an attempt being made to organise our lives into a convenient slick plot".[117] Her suspicions are peculiarly confirmed by a persistent faint sound of typing: eventually, she is able to overhear and even dispute the controlling voice of a novelist. Determinedly asserting 'I'm not wholly a fictional character. I have independent life' (p.160), she decides to write her own novel about 'characters in a novel' (p.202), though this seems merely to resemble the novel in which she figures herself.

A novel about writing a novel about writing a novel, as Spark calls it, *The Comforters* is to some extent simply an example—partly the result of Spark's early awareness of the French *nouveau roman*—of the sort of experimental, self-reflexive style discussed in Chapter Five. Caroline's religious problems, however, also exemplify Spark's characteristic employment of innovative narrative forms to direct attention upon moral or psychological issues. A concern with forces affecting individual destiny, for example, is developed by several other figures in her novels who assert that they are not 'wholly fictional characters' but have 'independent life'. *The Driver's Seat* (1970), for example, anticipates almost from its opening the ultimate fate of its heroine, Lisa, as a victim of murder, yet she achieves a bizarre measure of 'independent life' by taking over within the story complete responsibility for arranging her own death. Installing herself and her decisions as the determining, driving force of the plot, she challenges like Caroline conventions of authorial organisation and control. A sense of mysterious, unstable connection between authorial intention, individual will and destiny results. This is heightened by the provisional quality of present-tense narrative, and by a tone as rigorously objective as any in the *nouveau roman*, allowing at most only speculation about Lisa's inner life and the driving forces of her personality.

The exercise of moral or psychological power and control over destiny is further examined in Spark's best-known novel, *The Prime of Miss Jean Brodie* (1961). One of 'the progressive spinsters of Edinburgh'[118] in the thirties, Brodie is a schoolteacher whose sinisterly powerful influence over her girls, 'the Brodie set', leads to comparisons with some of the contemporary dictators whom she ardently admires:

> Mussolini stood on a platform like a gym teacher or a Guides mistress...
> the Brodie set was Miss Brodie's fascisti...all knit together for her
> need...in unified compliance to the destiny of Miss Brodie, as if God had
> willed them to birth for that purpose (pp.30-31).

One of her girls, Sandy, reflects that Brodie 'thinks she is Providence...she thinks she is the God of Calvin, she sees the beginning and the end' (p.120). Like *The Driver's Seat*, *The Prime of Miss Jean Brodie* contains many anticipations of later events, allowing the reader to 'see the beginning and the end' simultaneously and late the effect of Brodie's 'Providence' in the subsequent lives of girls. She is partly responsible, for example, for accentuating some significant contradictions in Sandy's character. Her 'Christian morals' (p.125) oppose Brodie's egocentric idea of herself as 'Providence': Sandy eventually betrays her to authorities suspicious of her 'progressive' methods. Nevertheless, Sandy is the most imaginative as well as the most moral of the Brodie set, repeatedly envisaging life around her in terms of fiction. This makes her not only an opponent but a secret sharer of some of Brodie's priorities; a reluctant admirer of her attempts to impose her will, even her identity, on her girls:

> Sandy was fascinated by this method of making patterns with facts, and was divided between her admiration for the technique and the pressing need to prove Miss Brodie guilty of misconduct. (p.72)

Torn between ethics and imagination, Sandy eventually retires into an uneasy life as a nun, but still retains some fame for her 'odd psychological treatise on the nature of moral perception, called "The Transfiguration of the Commonplace"' (p.35). Her 'odd' subject is actually an entirely appropriate one. In their diverse ways, Brodie and Sandy are each involved in 'the transfiguration of the commonplace'—Brodie by shaping the lives of her set, Sandy more loosely in art and imagination. Both try to 'organise...lives into a convenient slick plot': like Sandy's treatise, *The Prime of Miss Jean Brodie* examines the 'moral perception' involved in such processes. The oppositions and analogies between its complex characters contribute to Spark's most thorough examination of relations between moral responsibility and transforming imagination; between artistic order, destiny, and freedom.

Contemporary Gothic: Muriel Spark, Beryl Bainbridge, Ian McEwan, William Trevor, Martin Amis.

The Prime of Miss Jean Brodie is thoroughly entertaining as well as complex. Its humour often derives from an aloof, dispassionate tone characteristic of Muriel Spark's fiction: rather like Ivy Compton-Burnett, or Evelyn Waugh, Spark presents with apparent equanimity the gravest moral disturbance and degeneracy, even murder, despair or death. This disparity between grotesque developments in characters' lives and an orderly elegance in their exposition creates a suggestively ironic—sometimes very black—sort of humour, as in descriptions of Brodie's final betrayal and death, or, in *The Driver's Seat*, of Lisa's begging for death in four languages. Though Spark's precise, remote vision is to some extent distinctively her own, comparable mixtures of horror and levity also appear in the work of several novelists who gained prominence in the seventies. Combining wickedness and perversity with a persistent sort of ghastly humour, writers such as Beryl Bainbridge, Martin Amis, Ian McEwan and William Trevor are sometimes as close to the 'Gothic' novels popular in the late eighteenth century as they are to Spark.

Beryl Bainbridge is like Spark and Waugh a Catholic convert: faith in an orderly spiritual dimension beyond the wickedness of the world may encourage the sort of detached tone which appears in *The Bottle Factory Outing* (1974). It opens with Bainbridge's heroine Frieda an enthusiastic spectator of a grim urban funeral: before long, she is herself accidentally killed by one of her workmates. Her large, awkward corpse is stuffed into an empty wine barrel and despatched to likely oblivion with only a plastic tulip for company. Though dismayed by her death, her workmates are thus pragmatic rather than conventionally sentimental in their attitudes: Bainbridge's narrative is likewise depleted of emotion. The confused lives of her characters and their dispiriting urban environment are reported objectively and with an element of dryly ironic humour.

A similarly detached tone distinguishes Ian McEwan's first novel, *The Cement Garden* (1978), also concerned with the disposal of an embarrassing corpse. Helped by his brother and sisters, the novel's adolescent narrator, Jack, buries his mother's body gruesomely in cement in the cellar: he calmly remarks, however,

> ...nor could I think whether what we had done was an ordinary thing to do...or something so strange that if it was ever found out it would be the headline of every newspaper in the country.[119]

Surprise or revulsion are felt only by readers: like children in Richard Hughes's novels, Jack seems unconcerned by moral or other conventions. His juxtaposition of nightmare and death with everyday domestic detail creates a narrative in which, rather in the manner of Kafka, unconscious or sexual forces are interfused with otherwise ordinary scenes or events. Jack's memories, dreams, visions of his mother, accounts of his sexual awakening or simply of daily domestic life commingle in a narrative often unusually compelling despite its morbid subject. Nevertheless, though there is some sense of progress in the revelation of Jack's psyche, McEwan's central situation remains disappointingly static, the family set in its various mutual attitudes as firmly, until the conclusion, as its mother is in cement. This shows an insufficient extension in the scope of McEwan's excellent short stories. Like *The Cement Garden*, many of these are partly limited as well as enhanced by narration from a child's or adolescent's point of view, uneasily scrutinising an adulthood half-shunned and half-desired.

McEwan acknowledged in 1978 'adolescent narrators have been for me a very useful rhetorical device,' adding 'I'd like what I do next to be larger, more complex, taking into account the adult world, adultly observed.'[120] His second novel, *The Comfort of Strangers* (1981) is concerned with an apparently adult subject, what the novel calls

> ...the politics of sex...how the imagination, the sexual imagination, men's ancient dreams of hurting, and women's of being hurt, embodied and declared a powerful single organising principle, which distorted all relations, all truth.[121]

McEwan does not altogether succeed, however, in presenting 'the adult world, adultly observed'. The 'dreams of hurting' which murderously impinge on a couple's European holiday are still shown, at length, originating in the murderer's troubled childhood. Elsewhere in the novel, adult characters are rather tenuously developed by external observation: McEwan's abandonment of first-person narrative sacrifices the subjective intensity and warping view of the world of earlier short stories and *The Cement Garden*. Objectivity, however, creates a peculiar quality of its own. Like Bainbridge, McEwan sustains a precise, economic prose, disturbingly aloof from the black events it presents. The result is at times an almost beautifully exact, stylish account even of blood and the macabre: the narrative warps normal responses into 'dreams of hurting...which distorted...all truth', communicating the sense of what the novel calls 'fantasy...passing into reality' (p.114). Though both *The Cement Garden* and *The Comfort of Strangers* suggest that McEwan remains limited in the range of his material, his unusual vision and the precision of its expression confirm a position as one of the more promising of younger British writers.

Like Bainbridge and McEwan, William Trevor often presents a mingling of fantastic and macabre events in everyday life. Though *The Children of Dynmouth* (1976), for example, offers a broad view of ordinary life in a quiet enough seaside town, it also follows the plans of Timothy Gedge, a child as strange as any in the fiction of Ian McEwan. Gedge finds Tussaud's gallery of murderers 'comic...you definitely had to smile'[122] and dreams of winning television stardom with a comic act based on the 'brides-in-the-bath' murder case. To one of the other children, this wish 'to glorify the violence of murder' suggests 'he was possessed by devils' (p.151). To the town's vicar, however,

> ...possession by devils was just a form of words...the boy had become what he was while no one was looking. The boy's existence was the horror he spoke of...[a] reminder of waste and destruction. (pp.166, 178-9)

As the vicar suggests, Gedge's dark nature is the product of its disorderly environment. The lonely child of a fractured family, his entertainment comes mostly in the form of vacuous, violent television programmes. Gedge has also 'witnessed terrible things' (p.66) among the people of Dynmouth and its neighbourhood—all the petty adulteries, corruptions, perversities of daily life, as well as possible suicide or murder. Such vices seem unopposed in Dynmouth by shared values or any firm moral centre, a sense of lost coherence heightened by the range and disconnection of Trevor's various perspectives on local people and the 'waste and destruction' inherent in their lives.

In the face of 'all this ugliness, like a slime around them' (p.134), the emergence of a black humorist among the children of Dynmouth seems almost a natural consequence of experience of the town's life: Timothy Gedge's darkening imagination is in this way also representative of more general movements in contemporary fiction. Unnatural acts and the numbed quality of the narrative in *The Cement Garden* show a similar response to a decaying environment, a depressive city background in which

> ...twenty-storey tower blocks...stood on wide aprons of cracked asphalt where weeds were pushing through...all down their concrete sides were colossal stains, almost black, caused by the rain. They never dried out. (p.22)

Similarly depressing landscapes appear elsewhere in contemporary fiction. Malcolm Bradbury's *Rates of Exchange* (1983), for example, records in passing

> ...a time of recession and unemployment, decay and deindustrialisation. The age of Sado-Monetarism has begun...the bombs explode in Ulster, the factories close...vandalism marks the spaces, graffiti the walls, where the council pulls down old substandard housing, to replace it with new substandard housing...rain falls over factories which stand empty with broken windows.[123]

Like McEwan and Bradbury, several other recent novelists follow Margaret Drabble in *The Ice Age* in grimly depicting urban and social decay in 'a time of recession'. In such an era, with 'all this ugliness, like a slime around them', certain novelists' black humour and Gothic vision may be a response to contemporary social conditions as direct as Timothy Gedge's in *The Children of Dynmouth*.

Such dark visions, however, though especially characteristic of recent fiction, are also a feature of novels in earlier decades, especially in the aftermath of the Second World War. There can be few comedies blacker, for example, than Evelyn Waugh's *The Loved One* (1948); or novels more Gothic than Mervyn Peake's *Titus Groan* (1946) and *Gormenghast* (1950). Peake's vision is said to have been shaped by his experience of the war and his visit to Belsen: several more recent novelists may continue to be influenced similarly, if less directly. A macabre quality distinguishes the work not only of McEwan, Bainbridge, and Trevor, but also in various ways many of the other novelists mentioned in this chapter, such as Emma Tennant, Angela Carter, Edna O'Brien, Fay Weldon, D.M. Thomas,

Paul Bailey, and David Storey. Having grown up as 'children of violence' during or in the years just after the war, many of these novelists might be considered to belong rather like the hero of *The Loved One* to 'a generation which enjoys a vicarious intimacy with death.' Beryl Bainbridge talks of

> ...the generation who came after, who were still in short trousers when the war ended, though vividly retaining memories of barrage balloons and absent bananas and blitzkrieg nights spent under dining-room tables.[124]

Her ironically-entitled novel *A Quiet Life* (1976) reflects in darkly comic terms aspects of this generation's childhood: various other characters also discuss

> ...the effect of war on the younger generation...fears...dreams... symptoms of one sort or another...changing times...the old standards swept away by the war.[125]

Such changes and challenges are inevitably reflected in later writing. The loss of 'the old standards,' in particular, contributes to a sense of moral insecurity and emptiness which appears in recent fiction. In novels such as Trevor's, fears and dreams advance largely unchecked: no accepted framework of values exists to resist disorder. This outlook is not confined to fiction in the post-war period. In the plays of Joe Orton, or in some of the 'absurd' drama of Samuel Beckett, Harold Pinter, and others popular since the fifties, there appears a sense of contingency, and a mixture of grimness and farce, comparable to the dark vision and black humour of many recent novelists. Such 'symptoms of one sort of another' suggest that the ineluctable shadow of the war may be responsible not only for the moral concerns of older authors such as Burgess, Golding and Murdoch, but also for a distinctive darkness in the work of novelists emerging in the past two decades; a Gothic gloom lately deepened by recession and continuing world violence.

One of the most admired of these new novelists is Martin Amis, who indicates the presence and contemporary provenance of black humour in his own work when he remarks 'my books are playful literature. I'm after laughs,' but also explains

> I use all the absurd, intimate and pathetic things I see around me... looked at seriously, of course, my books are ghastly...there is an enormous shabbiness and misery around these days.[126]

Such concerns, and other aspects of Amis's fiction, often lead to comparison with Ian McEwan: in *Other People: A Mystery Story* (1981), for example, there is a sense not only of 'enormous shabbiness and misery', but also, as in McEwan's *The Comfort of Strangers*, of 'fantasy...passing into reality'. Dreams and reality are initially indistinguishable for Amis's heroine Mary Lamb, apparently an amnesiac whose regained consciousness at the beginning of the novel seems almost a rebirth. Her subsequent vision is characterised by the sort of nursery innocence her name suggests. She is wholly uninitiated; bereft of any perceptual habit; unable even to recognise that clouds are not aerial animals, for example, or to recall a previous existence she may have had under the name Amy Hide. A similarly thorough disorientation is forced upon the reader by the novel's indecipherable time-scheme and by a narrator who sustains as peculiar a relationship with the characters as any in the novels of Muriel Spark. His attitudes are mysterious and sinister; his identity largely uncertain. He could be close to the policeman who tries to help Mary and suggests her connection with Amy Hide, or he may be the man who attempted to murder Amy. He could even be some superintendent devil in a purgatory or hell to which Amy has been consigned: Amis's title and Sartre's suggestion 'Hell is other people'[127] help to indicate this latter possibility.

Though the true identity of character and narrator remains unsure, and Amis's elegant, engrossing puzzles eventually irresolvable, there is no uncertainty in the novel's demonstration that metaphorically at least, 'life is hell, life is murder.'[128] Vulnerably open to all experience, Mary's consciousness is reflected in prose of intense lucidity: this provides an exceptionally sensitive register for her encounters with 'other people...the lost, the ruined, the broken, the effaced' in the 'clinks and clinics and soup-queues...hostels and borstals and homes full of mad women' (pp.70, 100) in contemporary London. While Mary remains disjunct in mind and spirit from this tawdry urban context, the narrator is wholly familiar with its various perversities and depravities, presenting these with gleeful conviction, almost relish. The combination of their perspectives focuses with particular clarity Amis's satirical vision of 'enormous shabbiness and misery around these days'.

Conclusion: Martin Amis, David Lodge, Malcolm Bradbury

Martin Amis has explained

> I can imagine a novel that is as tricksy, as alienated and as writerly as those of, say, Robbe-Grillet while also providing the staid satisfactions of pace, plot and humour with which we associate, say, Jane Austen. In a way, I imagine that this is what I myself am trying to do.[129]

Other People is a successful realisation of the sort of novel Amis imagines. Fractured time-scheme, detective-story format, and weird lucidity of vision all recall the innovative novels of Alain Robbe-Grillet (see Chapter Five); while realistic description and strong, satiric basis in contemporary London simultaneously incorporate much longer-established strengths of fiction. Amis provides in this way a later, more radical example of the coalescence of journalistic and crystalline styles which appears in the fiction of Murdoch, Golding and Burgess. This combination is a distinctive development of recent fiction, and its presence has been indicated in the work of several other authors discussed in this chapter, such as Doris Lessing, or Angus Wilson, who combines in *No Laughing Matter* admiration for Virginia Woolf and for George Eliot, for experiment as well as tradition. As Wilson's work helps to show, and as he explains himself, the fifties' renunciation of modernist innovation and technical flexibility in favour of 'angry-provincial-neorealism' was 'only a temporary rejection of...devices still rich in promise'.[130] Other writers and critics have commented on the tendency which has since emerged either to attempt a recovery of some of the 'promise' of modernism, or, more often, to combine it with continuing reliance on more conventionally realistic narrative modes. In the fiction of the sixties and seventies, in the work of Spark, Lessing, Burgess and others, David Lodge, for example, discerns a trend

> ...in the direction of formal experiment and formal self-consciousness...
> Realism is not rejected, but it is not employed naively, innocently,
> either...realism is played off against other modes of writing.[131]

Lodge's own fiction further illustrates the trend his criticism identifies. In discussing his work, he talks of a need for

> ...a way of reconciling a contradiction, of which I had long been aware,
> between my critical admiration for the great modernist writers, and my
> creative practice, formed by the neo-realist, anti-modernist writing of the
> 1950s.[132]

As Lodge suggests, his 'creative practice' is clearly connected to the fiction of the fifties: he and Malcolm Bradbury are the principal English novelists to follow Kingsley Amis's *Lucky Jim* in comically depicting campus life, a subject which has also been very popular in recent American fiction. In a postscript to *The British Museum is Falling Down* (1965), for example, Lodge acknowledges the effects of a 'distillation of the post-Amis campus novel'.[133] Following Amis in humour and context, *The British Museum is Falling Down* also continues to examine some of the problems of sexual relations and unwanted pregnancy which beset fifties heroes. Such difficulties extend for Lodge's protagonist Adam even into the era of easily available contraception—he is the father of an alarmingly expanding Catholic family, tortured by moral dilemmas involved in trying to restrict its size.

Such problems, however, are lightened by Lodge's witty tone, and by an element of literary playfulness: Adam is a research student in English literature, and frequent parodies of the fiction he studies illustrate his theory that

... there've been such a fantastic number of novels written in the last couple of centuries that they've just about exhausted the possibilities of life. So all of us ... are really enacting events that have already been written about in some novel or other. (pp.118-19)

Various events in Adam's life are narrated in the styles of the modernist writers whom Lodge admires—Virginia Woolf, Franz Kafka, Joseph Conrad, and Henry James, among others. Compression of the story into the space of a single day and a long concluding interior monologue closely imitating *Ulysses* also indicate Lodge's particular respect for James Joyce. In combination with continuing 'faith in traditional realism'[134] and admiration for Kingsley Amis, these parodies create in *The British Museum is Falling Down* a sort of lightweight, comic version of the synthesis between prevalent tradition and 'other modes of writing' which its author sees as a trend in recent fiction.

Lodge wrote *The British Museum is Falling Down* while on an academic fellowship in the United States. Its occasional departures from 'traditional realism' may have been encouraged by what he calls 'the generally stimulating and liberating effect of the American experience' (p.163). Some such effect also appears in Malcolm Bradbury's *Stepping Westward* (1965), and may have motivated the more radical fictional experiments (discussed in Chapter Five) undertaken in the late sixties and early seventies by other visitors to America such as David Caute, Julian Mitchell, and Thomas Hinde. Lodge himself shows the 'stimulus and liberation' of America more directly in *Changing Places* (1975), which extends some of the narrative inventiveness of *The British Museum is Falling Down*, contrasting the disrupted cultural assumptions of an English and an American academic on exchange in each other's universities.

Petworth, protagonist of Malcolm Bradbury's *Rates of Exchange* (1983), is asked while on an academic visit to an imaginary East European state if he knows 'a campus writer Brodge? ... who writes *Changing Westward*?' (pp.268-9). Though Lodge and Bradbury are not as indistinguishable as these questions suggest, there are substantial similarities in life and work: both men are distinguished university teachers and excellent critics of recent fiction. And Lodge might almost have been speaking for Bradbury both when he remarks 'as an academic critic and teacher of literature with a special interest in prose fiction, I am inevitably self-conscious about matters of narrative technique,' and also when he adds 'my novels belong to a tradition of realistic fiction.'[135] Though some of Bradbury's novels include self-conscious or modernist techniques, these appear fairly modestly and intermittently: like Lodge's, it is mostly to the realist tradition that his work belongs. His best-known novel, *The History Man* (1975), for example, is a satire whose only substantial departure from conventional narrative technique is its extended use of the present tense. This contributes to a rapid narrative pace which helps to dramatise the confusion of views and values centred on university life in the rebellious late sixties and early seventies, when the conflicts of Vietnam and Ulster burned in the background. 'A radical sociologist', Bradbury's protagonist Howard Kirk occupies 'a wide intellectual constituency'[136] which allows for some precise, slick social observation of the chic pretensions which sometimes disfigured the permissiveness and political conscience of the period.

Bradbury also uses the present tense in *Rates of Exchange*, where it creates a feeling of impressionistic proximity to Petworth's colourful experience. This is sometimes presented with the sort of self-consciousness about matters of narrative technique which Lodge mentions, wittily and playfully expressed. Petworth, for example, is said to possess

> ...an idiolect—composed of many fascinating terms, like *idiolect* and *sociolect*, *langue* and *parole*, *signifier* and *signified*, *Chomsky* and *Saussure*, *Barthes* and *Derrida* (p.33)

Descriptions of several of Petworth's adventures suggest that Bradbury is equally—and sometimes satirically—aware of recent developments in linguistic, structuralist, formalist and other narrative theories. Bradbury's narrative is also very inventive linguistically, sketching a whole imaginary East European language and even its speakers' standard errors in tackling English. *Rates of Exchange*, however, enters only occasionally what is called in the novel 'the garden of forking paths, where the narratives divide and multiply' (p.238). Technical self-consciousness is generally subordinate to the preferences which made Bradbury one of the firmest admirers of William Cooper's *Scenes from Provincial Life*. Though very much more sophisticated and intelligent, *Rates of Exchange* even remains comparable to Kingsley Amis's *I Like it Here* as a comic, half-travelogue account of strange encounters with foreign customs and manners.

Bradbury's mixture of tradition with some 'other modes of writing' makes his fiction technically quite similar to the work of Burgess, Murdoch and Wilson, in which realist method remains a predominant element even within an expanding, often increasingly adventurous repertoire of narrative forms. Perhaps because his creative practice participates in the sort of synthesis of old and new styles most frequent in recent fiction, Bradbury is like Lodge an unusually enthusiastic, perceptive critic of such developments. He comments extensively on the attempt 'in a number of contemporary writers...to make realism and fictiveness co-exist', and sees

> ...a generation of writers the best of whom have taken the British novel off into a variety of experimental directions...which have challenged and reconstituted the mimetic constituents of fiction while not dismissing its realistic sources entirely.

The diversity and promise of such movements Bradbury considers to have left 'the novel now...in a profitable ferment', a state too often obscured by 'a depressing and outdated folklore'—narrowly based on the conservatism of the fifties—which states that the English novel is predominantly and dully conventional.[137]

As the next chapter suggests, the English novel may be less committed to experiment than some of Bradbury's remarks suggest, and, as he sometimes acknowledges, when experiments or formal developments do appear, they have often had to be imported from abroad. Nevertheless, Bradbury's analysis and its optimistic conclusion are in most ways justified. The dates chosen for Rubin Rabinovitz's study *The Reaction Against Experiment in the English Novel, 1950-1960* (1967) are significant. In the sixties, especially towards the end of the decade, and in the early seventies, 'angry-provincial-neorealist' writing was gradually replaced by a more wide-ranging, sophisticated fiction, whose promise extends to the present day. Recent novels have sometimes integrated particularly fruitfully moral awareness partly engendered by the war and technical resourcefulness partly learned from modernism. In such ways, the English novel in the past two decades has probably come closer than at any previous stage of the century to combining the various strengths of conventional and of innovative fiction which have been available at least since 1930. Despite the notable achievements of Golding, Burgess, Murdoch, Spark, Lessing, and Wilson, the full potential of such a combination may still remain to be realised. The experimental fiction considered in the next chapter, a direct extension of the initiatives of modernism, ensures that a maximum possibility of formal development is kept open. The various potential of the novelists mentioned above; of the new women writers of the sixties and seventies; and of other younger novelists such as McEwan and Martin Amis, suggests that development will certainly occur. Despite the continuingly problematic and gloomy history such writers envisage, perhaps because of it, there seems little reason to share the fear of an American critic that 'the English novel, like the country itself, will constrict to a tight little island.'[138]

5

Modernism and Post-modernism: the Experimental Novel since 1930

The Autonomy of Language: James Joyce and Samuel Beckett.

— A day of dappled seaborne clouds.
The phrase and the day and the scene harmonized in a chord. Words. Was it their colours?...No, it was not their colours: it was the poise and balance of the period itself. Did he then love the rhythmic rise and fall of words better than their associations of legend and colour? Or was it that, being as weak of sight as he was shy of mind, he drew less pleasure from the reflection of the glowing sensible world through the prism of a language many-coloured and richly storied than from the contemplation of an inner world of individual emotions mirrored perfectly in a lucid supple periodic prose?[1]

Stephen Dedalus's preferences are interestingly indicative of the movement, outlined in Chapter One, of modernist writing towards increased concentration on the 'inner world' at the expense of the 'reflection of the glowing sensible world' predominant in the realistic fiction of the Victorian and Edwardian periods. Stephen's comments, quoted above from Joyce's *A Portrait of the Artist as a Young Man*, (1916), also indicate another development of modernist fiction, and of Joyce's especially, which has continued to inform experimental and innovative writing since the nineteen twenties. In the manner Stephen suggests, 'the poise and balance...the rise and fall of words' occasionally preoccupy modernist writing, partly at the expense of words' 'association'—their actual meaning and significance in communicating the 'glowing sensible world'; the 'inner world of emotions'; or the other material of the story. This interest in the nature and operation of language participates in the self-consciousness about art, and the processes whereby it is created, which Chapter One identified as one of the features of modernist fiction. The concerns of Lily Briscoe, for example, incorporating Woolf's own artistic self-consciousness in *To the Lighthouse* (1927), include an anxious awareness of language's limited capacity to represent either the 'inner world' or the objective, 'sensible world'. She reflects that 'Words...broke up the thought and dismembered it...words fluttered sideways and struck the object inches too low'.[2] Something of the same concern also appears in the American context in the work of Ernest Hemingway, who demonstrates the incapacity of language and narrative to represent the experience of the First World War, for example.[3] In this way his fiction indicates the sort of connection suggested in Chapter One between the apparently increasing disorder of the 'sensible world' and writers' increasingly self-conscious examination of their means of representing it in orderly form in their novels.

Investigation of the stress between word and world, and the examination of literary form and language, are most comprehensively and influentially undertaken in the work of James Joyce. The sustained parody, stylistic imitation, and linguistic inventiveness of *Ulysses* (1922) constantly scrutinise the nature and validity of existing fictional forms, indirectly installing language, style, and fictional technique as subjects of the novel. Although in *Ulysses* such interests never altogether predominate over the story of Bloom and his Dublin day, the 'sensible world' and the element of story are much more thoroughly subordinate to linguistic and formal concerns in Joyce's later writing. This began to appear in the Parisian journal *transition*, as 'Work in Progress', in 1927, and was eventually published entire as *Finnegans Wake* in 1939. Since it creates a highly-wrought, inventive language to express the dreaming mind of H.C. Earwicker, the sleeping Dublin publican at the novel's centre, *Finnegans Wake* has sometimes been seen as simply an attempt to develop beyond *Ulysses* the transcription of an 'inner world', creating a sort of 'stream of unconsciousness'. For example, in *Our Exagmination Round his Factification for Incamination of Work in Progress* (a book of essays defending Joyce's methods against contemporary hostility and bewilderment), one of the editors of *transition*, Eugene Jolas, argues that Joyce's creation of a 'real night language', though peculiar, is essential to his attempt 'to describe that huge world of dreams'.

Jolas adds, however,

> The real metaphysical problem today is the word. The epoch when the writer photographed the life about him with the mechanics of words redolent of the daguerrotype, is happily drawing to its close. The new artist of the word has recognised the autonomy of language.[4]

As Jolas's comment suggests, Joyce's real interest in *Finnegans Wake* is less with 'photographing', 'reflecting', or representing anything, even 'the huge world of dreams', than with the 'problem' of the word. His language in *Finnegans Wake* is at least as much a prolonged examination and celebration of itself, an enormous extension of the literary self-consciousness of *Ulysses*, as it is a communication of any world, inner or outer. For example, one of the many minor stories which proliferate in the novel begins:

The Mookse and The Gripes

Gentes and laitymen, fullstoppers and semicolonials, hybreds and lubberds!

Eins within a space and a wearywide space it wast ere wohned a Mookse.[5]

Far from being meaningless, as some early critics complained, such language is almost overfraught with wayward significances. These, however, do less to communicate the story which seems to be promised than to direct attention self-referentially at Joyce's means of expression. 'Eins within a space', for example, by parodying the traditional opening 'once upon a time', emphasises Joyce's distance from narrative convention; establishing a sort of equation of space and time, and reinforcing this idea through Joyce's use of the German 'eins' with its half-suggestion of Einstein. In such ways, the density and playfulness of language in *Finnegans Wake* continually direct attention to the nature and relationships of words, to linguistic issues such as phonetics and etymology, rather than to the traditional subjects of the novel. Character, for example, the gents and ladies to be found in conventional fiction, are converted in the above extract to 'fullstoppers and semicolonials'—features of punctuation, aspects of language. Concentrated partly self-referentially on its own words and methods in this way, *Finnegans Wake* achieves the sort of 'autonomy of language' Jolas recognised. As Samuel Beckett explains in his opening essay in *Our Exagmination Round his Factification for Incamination of Work in Progress* (1929), 'here form *is* content, content *is* form…His writing is not *about* something; *it is that something itself*.'[6]

The 'autonomy' which Jolas and Beckett recognise in *Finnegans Wake* makes it a transitional work, both a great extension of the incipient self-consciousness of the modernist idiom of the nineteen twenties, and an antecedent for the frequently self-conscious, self-referential 'experimental' writing which has followed. Samuel Beckett is one of the first and still probably the best of authors in this new idiom. A great admirer of Joyce, as his essay in *Our Exagmination* shows, and his friend in Paris in the twenties, Beckett redeploys some of Joyce's methods in his own fiction, which also extends some of the other developments of modernism. The hero of his first novel, *Murphy* (1938), for example, shows a preference for the 'inner world' much fiercer than Stephen Dedalus's. Murphy resents the 'complacent scientific conceptualism that made contact with outer reality the index of mental well-being', and devotes his ingenuity to achieving the state of complete physical inertia and dissociation from 'outer reality' which allows him to 'come alive in his mind, as described in section six'.[7]

Murphy thus continues both modernism's interest in the 'inner world', and also some of its self-consciousness, suggested by references such as the one quoted to the novel's own section six. Beckett's development in directions established by Joyce is clearest, however, in the novels he considers central to his writing as a whole—the trilogy *Molloy* (1950), *Malone Dies* (1951) and *The Unnamable* (1952). Unlike *Murphy,* each of these novels is written in the first person. Each is a monologue whose associative fluidity loosely resembles Joyce's techniques, but amplifies his stream of consciousness into whole floods of speech, often sustained without pause or paragraph-break to relieve their intensity. Interruptions of other sorts, however, do occur very frequently. Narrators repeatedly contradict themselves, entangle themselves in their syntax, struggle for apt expression, or pause to discuss the effectiveness of their language. Each of Beckett's aging narrators is a sort of portrait of the artist as an old man, concerned, like Stephen Dedalus, with 'words...their colours...poise and balance'—their aesthetic worth or simply their efficiency. Molloy and Moran, for example, interrupt their narratives at various times in *Molloy* with comments such as

> I began at the beginning, like an old ballocks, can you imagine
> that?...This should all be re-written in the pluperfect...mostly I shall
> use the various tenses of the past...I speak in the present tense...when
> speaking of the past. It is the mythological present, don't mind it...I
> apologise for these details, in a moment we'll go faster...That last
> sentence is not clear, it does not say what I hoped it would...All is
> tedious, in this relation that is forced upon me...I weary of this invention
> and others beckon to me...in order to blacken a few pages, may I say I
> spent some time at the seaside...I'm lost, no matter.[8]

An occasional feature of *Molloy,* such reflections on the limitations of narrative and language are greatly expanded as the trilogy progresses, occupying paragraphs rather than sentences in *Malone Dies.* Malone's discussion of his difficulties in producing his text even extends to description of the actual physical problems of writing it—the dwindling of his second-last pencil; its occasional disappearance, along with the exercise book in which he writes, among the bedclothes or beneath the bed in which he is confined. Far from simply introducing a diversion from the narrative as they sometimes seem to in *Molloy,* such reflections are as substantially a part of *Malone Dies* as the stories Malone attempts to tell. Rather than only impeding or redirecting his narrative, they contribute to its momentum and to the sense of urgency and struggle in his attempted articulation.

This growing self-consciousness about language and the narrative act is still further extended in *The Unnamable.* Its narrator remarks simply that 'it all boils down to a question of words...all words, there's nothing else' (pp.308, 381). He demonstrates and discusses almost continuously the impossibility of language representing or helping to define 'outer reality', or even of its finding a term for its own nameless progenitor. In the trilogy as a whole, and increasingly as it continues, Beckett thus develops in his own terms the 'autonomy of language' Jolas recognises in the later Joyce. In *The Unnamable* in particular, Beckett creates a language chiefly concerned with its own devices and difficulties; what Stephen Dedalus might have called a 'prism of a language', though one whose reflection is internally directed upon itself, focused upon its own shape and operation.

The unnamable narrator of the trilogy's final part concludes 'in my life, since we must call it so, there were three things, the inability to speak, the inability to be silent, and solitude' (p.365). One of the paradoxes of the trilogy is that 'the inability to speak'—the constant negotiation with the unreliability of their language which Beckett's narrators impose upon themselves—does not diminish an irresistible urgency in their speaking. This 'inability to be silent' is partly a condition of their solitude. Like the unnamable, the other narrators find they 'have to go on... the discourse must go on' (pp.268-9). In each case, this 'discourse' is an essential, if barely effective, distraction from their own progressive debility and the great loneliness and sadness of their circumstances. *Molloy* is set in an inhospitable, largely rural context, recognisable as loosely reflecting Beckett's Irish background; *Malone Dies* takes place in an isolated room in a building as mysterious and unspecific in function as some of the settings of Kafka's stories; while *The Unnamable* inhabits a dim, amorphous domain, whose delineation is one of the problems confronting narrator and reader. The increasing vagueness of the novels' settings is partly a correlative of the dwindling ability of the narrators to explain, comprehend, or even move around the areas they inhabit. Molloy is crippled, as eventually is his counterpart Moran; Malone is bedridden and increasingly debilitated; the unnamable is scarcely in command of physical existence at all. Increasingly immobilised in uncertain, twilit worlds, each narrator engages compulsively in speech to try to order and define his experience, or simply to pass the time of his wearisome entrapment in himself. Reminiscences form an important part of their discourse, especially in the first two novels: one of Beckett's earliest published works was an essay on Marcel Proust, and his narrators often show an interest analogous to Proust's in inhabiting imaginatively times made more coherent and congenial through the shaping of art and memory.

Stories, however, are the principal distraction for Beckett's narrators. Molloy remarks early in the trilogy 'what I need now is stories' (p.14) and Malone likewise looks forward to the stories he will use to divert himself. Such stories provide variously satisfactory alternatives to an uncongenial actuality, distracting from the empty certainty that '*Nothing is more real than nothing*' (p.177), and from the experience of the 'old void' which the unnamable finds 'hems me round' (p.275). As a character in Beckett's playlet *That Time* (1976) remarks, stories are 'just one of those things you kept making up to keep the void out just another of those old tales to keep the void from pouring in on top of you'.[9] Beckett's narrators discover, however, that their attempt to 'keep the void out' through the device of narrative is limited by their eventual impotence to sustain an imaginative dimension wholly separate from their own sad circumstances. An indication of their failing powers, of the way in which they 'finish dying' (p.9), appears in the tendency towards fusion of their imaginative stories and their actual lives. Though Malone, in particular, chooses fresh, separate, circumstances for his narrative, it becomes increasingly concerned with a man, almost exactly like himself, apparently confined in a sort of asylum. As Beckett's fiction advances, it introduces comparable doubts about the status and stability of its own imaginative creation. Figures assumed to have a firm existence in earlier parts of the work are progressively revealed as perhaps only figments and devices of subsequent narrators. Thus Moran, who may himself be a narrative contrivance of Molloy, mentions Murphy as part of the 'rabble in my head...stories, stories' (p.126). Malone, likewise, is aware of 'Murphys...Molloys, Morans and Malones' (p.217). The unnamable extends this progression, perhaps towards the ultimate author, Beckett himself, by remarking

> All these Murphys, Molloys and Malones do not fool me...their pains are nothing, compared to mine, a mere tittle of mine, the tittle I thought I could put from me, in order to witness it. Let them be gone now, them and all the others, those I have used... these creatures have never been, only I and this black void have ever been (p. 278).

The progressive admission that each narrator is only another means whereby a subsequent figure distracts himself from the 'black void' creates in the trilogy a kind of 'autonomy of fiction' or imagination, extending the 'autonomy of language' created by its continuously self-questioning discourse. Beckett's novels reveal themselves as fictions about the creation of fiction. The massive self-scrutiny and continuous creative hesitation of *The Unnamable*, in particular, almost entirely subordinates imaginative narrative to investigation of the processes of imagination and the impulse toward creativity. The novel both enacts and examines the mind's attempt to order and illumine the 'black void' around itself; to clothe consciousness in language and sense. Such attempts are seen as both essential and ultimately impossible to fulfil: the trilogy concludes with the phrase 'in silence you don't know, you must go on, I can't go on, I'll go on' (p. 382).

The paradoxical quality of this final statement aptly summarises the contradictory character of Beckett's trilogy as a whole. In a novel concerned with the insufficiency of word and expression, a principal feature is nevertheless the fluency with which Beckett's language

communicates the obsessive unravelling of his narrators' consciousnesses, incidentally providing some descriptions of unusual beauty
and adding many moments of darkly ironic humour. Though
challengingly complex and often despairingly gloomy, Beckett's
juxtaposition of word and silence, creativity and emptiness, and his
investigation of the whole enterprise of language and imagination,
brilliantly extend for his own purposes the self-reflexive 'autonomy'
of the later Joyce. In his novels and in his later drama, Beckett's
outcasts and cripples find expression for some of the sense of isolation
and exile in the mind of modern man: their solitary struggles are
envisaged with an intensity of inward vision whose profundity is
unrivalled in twentieth-century fiction.

Literary Reflections: Flann O' Brien and B. S. Johnson

A more humorous extension of Joyce's interests appears in a novel he
admired for its wit and comic spirit, Flann O'Brien's *At
Swim-Two-Birds*, first published in the same year as *Finnegans Wake*.
Its narrator is a parodic version of the Stephen Dedalus of Joyce's
Stephen Hero or *A Portrait of the Artist as a Young Man*. He is a sort of
Stephen anti-hero, lazy, mildly debauched, and inclined like
Beckett's Murphy to prefer the privacy of his mind to 'outer reality',
as he carefully explains in the novel's opening paragraph:

> Having placed in my mouth sufficient bread for three minutes' chewing, I
> withdrew my powers of sensual perception and retired into the privacy of
> my mind, my eyes and face assuming a vacant and preoccupied expression.
> I reflected on the subject of my spare-time literary activities. One
> beginning and one ending for a book was a thing I did not agree with. A
> good book may have three openings entirely dissimilar and inter-related
> only in the prescience of the author, or for that matter one hundred times
> as many endings.[10]

Appropriately for someone who finds that 'Mr Joyce' is
'indispensable...to an appreciation of the nature of contemporary
literature' (p.11), the chief result of this principal narrator's 'literary
activities' is a fantasy concerning Dermot Trellis, a Dublin publican
like Joyce's H. C. Earwicker. Whereas the material of *Finnegans Wake*
unfolds unconsciously in Earwicker's dreaming mind, Trellis,
himself an author, takes an altogether more systematic approach to
the productions of his imagination. He takes the precaution of
'compelling all his characters to live with him in the Red Swan Hotel
so that he can keep an eye on them and see that there is no boozing'
(p.35). A strange range of figures, 'most of them...used in other
books' (p.35) are so confined. Unfortunately for Trellis's system,
almost all these characters have narrative ambitions of their own.
Freed from Trellis's control while he sleeps, they drug him into a

perpetual coma, take over his story themselves, and make it into a tale of his hideous torture and mock trial, their revenge for his earlier despotic treatment.

Ostensibly controlled by a whole range of determined and competing story-tellers, *At Swim-Two-Birds* thus becomes a heterogeneous collage of narratives. Its 'examples of three separate openings' (p.9) are a relatively modest sample of what becomes an elaborate story about a man writing a story about a man writing a story about storytellers—a pattern roughly comparable to Beckett's in the trilogy. This 'autonomy of fiction' is extended by the principal narrator's inclusion of extracts from other works which interest him; explanations of his own narrative difficulties; and, occasionally, even apologies for withholding from the reader several pages of text which he has mislaid. Such interpolations emphasise 'literary activities', and the nature and practice of storytelling, as central subjects of *At Swim-Two-Birds*. Flann O'Brien's wit and ingenuity (also brilliantly extended in *The Third Policeman* (1940)) have sometimes led to *At Swim-Two-Birds* being considered no more than an excellent literary joke. Its self-consciousness, however, and its array of narrators, really offer a paradigm for subsequent developments; an influential model for later generations of authors who have scrutinised within the novel their own fictional forms. Significantly, *At Swim-Two-Birds* was much more popular when republished in 1960 than on its initial appearance in 1939.

Its influence is immediately apparent in B.S. Johnson's first novel, *Travelling People* (1963), which begins

> Seated comfortably in a wood and wickerwork chair of eighteenth-century Chinese manufacture, I began seriously to meditate upon the form of my allegedly full-time literary sublimations... one style for one novel was a convention that I resented most strongly... I concluded that it was not only permissible to expose the mechanism of a novel, but by doing so I should come nearer to reality and truth... I should be determined not to lead my reader into believing that he was doing anything but reading a novel.[11]

Most of Johnson's fiction shows his feeling of being 'besotted by Irish writers like Sam Beckett, James Joyce and Flann O'Brien'.[12] In particular, his wish to 'expose the mechanism of the novel' in order to 'come nearer to reality and truth' recalls the conviction of Flann O'Brien's narrator that the novel 'should be a self-evident sham to which the reader could regulate at will the degree of his credulity', thus avoiding the possibility that readers might be 'outwitted in a shabby fashion and caused to experience a real concern for the fortunes of illusory characters'. (p.25). In *Christie Malry's Own Double Entry* (1973), for example, Johnson dispels any 'real concern for... illusory characters' by appearing in the narrative himself, discussing its progress with its hero Christie, and conversing with him about the limitations of the novel form and of the omniscient narrative style which is parodied throughout. As Christie suggests, such self-consciousness is sustained throughout Johnson's fiction, making it 'a continuous dialogue with form'.[13] His work undertakes a variety of experiments which demonstrate his admiration for the Irish writers he mentions and illustrate the range of possibilities and interests which their work established in fiction.

Travelling People, for example, acts upon its stated resentment of 'one style for one novel' by employing a series of different methods: omniscient and first-person narratives; journals and letters; as well as various streams of consciousness and interior monologues. Several blacked-out or shaded pages show Johnson borrowing another device from earlier fiction. His suggestion that the 'most obvious of my debts was to the black pages of *Tristram Shandy*'[14] (1759-67) is a reminder of the way Laurence Sterne's work distinctly anticipates the self-consciousness of some later twentieth-century writing— Sterne includes in *Tristram Shandy* extended commentary on the nature of narrative and illusion, and on the relations between literature and life, realism and reality. Johnson's own concern with such questions continues in his second novel, *Albert Angelo* (1964), a story about a London school-teacher which remains loosely realistic until its author breaks off to assess his own technique and suggest that in the earlier part of the novel he has simply been lying. He goes on to discuss his general belief that 'telling stories is telling lies', and to explore the preference Johnson states elsewhere for writing 'autobiography... truth in the form of a novel' rather than fiction.[15]

Johnson's most unusual experiment in this sort of 'autobiography' is *The Unfortunates* (1969). It concerns his visit as a football reporter to a Midlands town which he remembers on arrival is familiar as the home of an old friend who has died of cancer. The novel demonstrates its narrator's confused juxtaposition of memory and actuality in two ways: by using a faltering stream-of-consciousness style which shows how 'the mind circles at random... at hazard, tripped equally by association and non-association'; and by its unbound, loose-leaf form. Johnson describes this as 'a physical tangible metaphor for randomness'.[16] A note on the box in which *The Unfortunates* was published adds

> This novel has twenty-seven sections, temporarily held together by a removable wrapper. Apart from the first and last sections (which are marked as such) the other twenty-five sections are intended to be read in random order. If readers prefer not to accept the random order in which they receive the novel, then they may rearrange the sections into any other random order before reading.

The unusualness of this form for *The Unfortunates*—or, to take another example, of the holes cut in the pages of *Albert Angelo* to allow readers to see into the future—has sometimes led to critical dismissal of Johnson's methods as merely trivial tricks. Johnson retorts that 'to dismiss such techniques as gimmicks... is crassly to miss the point' and he adds that

> ... where I depart from convention, it is because the convention has failed, is inadequate for conveying what I have to say... for every device I have used there is a literary rationale and a technical justification; anyone who cannot accept this has simply not understood the problem which had to be solved.[17]

A 'literary rationale' does exist for Johnson's innovations: the fragmentary form of *The Unfortunates*, for example, forces the reader to share with unusual immediacy its narrator's struggle to order his experience. The novel's loose-leaf form might also be seen as a means of overcoming one of the constraints upon modernist fiction which, despite often abandoning serial chronology in favour of more random associative memory, remains confined within the serial form of the bound book. It is not always clear, however, that the technical problems Johnson confronts justify the extremity of the solutions he discovers. Virginia Woolf once remarked of the strikingly innovative character of Joyce's fiction that it suggested the author was 'a desperate man who feels that in order to breathe he must break the windows.'[18] The tendency to excess in Johnson's unconventionality can be explained as a result of his considering himself writing in a later version of the stifling literary atmosphere Woolf's image suggests. Samuel Beckett describes Johnson as 'a most gifted writer', but he also acknowledges that he is 'deserving of far more attention than he has received up to now'.[19] Johnson's own comments suggest both disappointment at the lack of recognition of his work, and also a measure of desperation and isolation in his position as an innovative innovative writer in the post-war British context. He remarks regretfully

> ... so many novelists still write as though the revolution that was *Ulysses* had never happened... Nathalie Sarraute once described literature as a relay race, the baton of innovation passing from one generation to another. The vast majority of British novelists has dropped the baton, stood still, turned back, or not even realised that there is a race.[20]

The Game of Mirrors: Lawrence Durrell and John Fowles

As he suggests himself, Johnson is one of fairly few recent British novelists to whom 'the baton of innovation' taken up from Joyce by Beckett and Flann O'Brien has been passed on altogether directly. When the influence of Joyce and other modernists does survive, or other innovations appear, they are often rather indirectly derived, principally from intermediary French and American models. Thus

Lawrence Durrell's early writing shows him less 'besotted by Irish writers' than by Henry Miller, a Paris-based American author whose work was widely admired at the time. His *Tropic of Cancer* (1934) was praised by George Orwell, for example, in his essay 'Inside the Whale' (1940: see Chapter Two). Miller advocated a liberation of self and society through a freeing of attitudes to sex, and his influence is strongly apparent in Durrell's mildly-erotic early novel, *The Black Book* (1938). Resembling D.H. Lawrence as well as Miller, Durrell envisages England as a wintry, loveless wilderness, cut off from its deeper energies of emotion, sex, and the psyche.

Durrell later described *The Black Book* as 'a two-fisted attack on literature...the cultural swaddling clothes which I symbolised here as "the English Death".'[21] Sharing Miller's anxiety that artistic form could be a further restriction of the fullness and formlessness of life, Durrell creates a chaotic, disconnected and almost surreal narrative. His challenge to conventional 'cultural swaddling clothes' is extended by extravagantly elaborate language, which recalls Malcolm Lowry's excesses in *Ultramarine* (1933) and anticipates some of Durrell's own later writing, in which as he admits himself 'a tendency towards the baroque is always present'.[22] *The Black Book* also prefigures Durrell's later work in showing intermittently a self-referential concern with expression and fiction. One of Durrell's two narrators, Lawrence Lucifer, remarks of his story, for example,

> Frankly, all this is a little boring...The truth is that I am writing my first book. It is difficult, because everything must be included: a kind of spiritual itinerary which will establish the novel once and for all as a mode which is already past its *senium* (pp.27, 66).

Unconventional in assemblage and outlook, *The Black Book* hardly seems to belong in the thirties. Like *At Swim-Two-Birds*, Beckett's first novel *Murphy*, and *Finnegans Wake*, all published in 1938-9, it indicates that experimental writing of the post-war period has strong, distinct roots at the end of the thirties, though it took some time for these to develop after the war. Many aspects of *The Black Book* are extended in Durrell's own major work, *The Alexandria Quartet* (*Justine* (1957); *Balthazar* (1958); *Mountolive* (1958); and *Clea* (1960)). The interest shown in *The Black Book* in love and sex, for example, is enormously multiplied in *The Alexandria Quartet*. It examines a great range of intricately interconnected affairs among a leisured community of artists, diplomats and writers who drift among the exotic flotsam of Alexandrian life around the time of the Second World War. The city of Alexandria seems to encourage relationships as sterile as the desert which surrounds it, and such complex, unsatisfying affairs provoke a good deal of reflection about the nature of love and sex. In *Justine*, *Balthazar*, and *Clea*, this mostly takes the form of the narrator Darley's discussion of his own liaisons—in particular, his infatuation for Justine, a figure of sexual magnetism around whom many of the novel's affairs and political intrigues unfold.

Darley, however, also expands the sort of self-consciousness of *The Black Book* by reflecting frequently and at length on the various aesthetic paradoxes associated with distinguishing reality and illusion, or converting the one into the other in the medium of art, part of his own project as a writer. As Durrell admits of *The Alexandria Quartet* as a whole, 'the novel is only half secretly about art, the great subject of modern artists'.[23] Darley's interest is extended by Durrell's inclusion at the end of each volume of the Quartet of 'Workpoints'—fragments of narrative unused elsewhere, or statements (sometimes teasing or misleading) about technique or creative principle. Darley's own reflections on the medium and implications of writing are still further expanded by several other characters in the novel who are authors or artists.

Many of their comments refer to and help clarify Darley's literary methods and priorities, and those of Durrell himself. A successful novelist to whom Darley feels rather inferior, Pursewarden, is often especially interesting in this respect, but it is Justine who provides the most useful single description of the technique of *The Alexandria Quartet* as a whole. While 'sitting before the multiple mirrors at the dress-makers' she remarks

> Look! five different pictures of the same subject. Now if I wrote I would try for a multi-dimensional effect in character, a sort of prism-sightedness. Why should not people show more than one profile at a time?[24]

Durrell considers *The Alexandria Quartet* as 'a game of mirrors',[25] and images of mirrors and reflections proliferate in the text, representative of the sort of 'prism-sightedness' Justine mentions. The novel itself is a kind of prism: not so much the 'prism of a language' Stephen Dedalus mentions, but a continuous fracturing of perspective through the use of 'multiple mirrors'—multiple points of view on 'the same subject'. Durrell greatly expands the duality in perspective of *The Black Book* through the use of a wide range of subsidiary narrators who take over from Darley. As in *At Swim-Two-Birds*, almost all the figures in *The Alexandria Quartet* seem to be eager potential storytellers: even Justine adds to her sexier charms a masterly talent for oral narrative.

Many characters thus contribute in their own stories, or in journals, letters, extended commentaries or in other forms to Darley's (and the reader's) understanding of events. Thus while pursuing Justine in the first part of the Quartet, Darley happens upon and extensively quotes a novel ostensibly written about her by a former husband. Later, Darley's whole view of the events presented in *Justine* is radically altered again by a commentary on his narrative provided by his friend Balthazar and quoted extensively in the Quartet's second volume. The third, *Mountolive*, is entirely narrated in the third person by 'an invisible narrator' as Durrell calls him:[26] along with the inclusion of Pursewarden's journal in *Clea*, this provides an objective external view of Darley which assorts surprisingly with his subjective version of himself in the rest of the Quartet.

Other characters, and other episodes such as Pursewarden's suicide, are subject to more bewildering revolutions in significance and understanding as *The Alexandria Quartet* progresses and more versions of its action emerge. Resulting from the novel's shifting perspectives and angles of vision, such constant revisions and reversals in the reader's view of events create the impression of 'different sorts of truth...thrown down one upon the other', and of characters who appear to be 'living on several different levels at once' (pp.338, 547). *The Alexandria Quartet* itself fulfils Pursewarden's wish for a fiction with '"sliding panels"...the story...told, so to speak, in layers' (p.338). It shows Durrell extending some of the methods of Joyce Cary's trilogy, or of Graham Greene's use of the conflicting truths of Sarah's diary in *The End of the Affair* (see Chapter Three). The conflict in vision, the 'different sorts of truth' of *The Alexandria Quartet* both demand the sort of examination of illusion, art, and reality undertaken by many of its characters, and also, as in Greene's novel, heighten the sense of their inevitable subjective isolation, 'totally ignorant of one another, presenting selected fictions to each other' (p.693).

Because the first three volumes repeatedly resume 'the same subject' from different angles they remain static, giving the impression that, as Pursewarden suggests, the Quartet is 'standing above time and turning slowly on its own axis to comprehend the whole pattern. Things do not all lead forward' (p.198). Only in the last volume does time flow again and the narrative seem to progress, its emotions released from the stagnant spell of Alexandria, 'the capital of Memory' (p.152) by the genuine love shared by Clea and Darley. As Durrell explains, *The Alexandria Quartet* thus contains 'three sides of space and one of time'. He adds in his preface that his techniques are based on the Einsteinian idea of space and time as a four-dimensional continuum, and designed 'as a challenge to the serial form of the conventional novel: the time-saturated novel of the day'. Such comments, and the elaborate nature of Durrell's technique, have provoked criticism of *The Alexandria Quartet* on the grounds that it is generally too patterned and theoretically schematised; and that this particularly interferes with the interest and fullness of Durrell's characters. The presence of 'three sides of space and one of time' perhaps does make it inevitable that a sense of place dominates over development of the time-based creatures who inhabit it, and that in consequence, as Durrell suggests, 'only the city is real'.[27] Like L.H. Myers's mildly-melodramatic India in *The Near and the Far*, Durrell's evocation of the bizarre, fecund atmosphere of Alexandria—a city of 'five races, five languages, a dozen creeds' (p.17)—has a vividness sometimes absent, as critics complain, from his treatment of its people. Durrell also admits that his characters 'tend...to be dummies' as a result of his central interest in 'trying to light them from several different angles'.[28]

Durrell's development of such techniques, however, despite their attendant difficulties, remains a principal achievement of *The Alexandria Quartet*. Its 'different angles' extend the potential and diversity of narrative style in ways which constantly renew interest in its material. Durrell's challenge to the 'form of the conventional novel' is also generally integrated with some thoroughly conventional fictional strengths in *The Alexandria Quartet*—the excitement of deferred explanation and progressive revelation in what is partly a spy story; of adventure and violent action in an exotic location; and of the complex unfolding of a web of love relationships, for example. Like some of the novelists discussed in Chapters Three and Four, Durrell combines some of these more traditional virtues of fiction with new formal possibilities introduced by the innovations of the modernists. To this combination he adds the sort of self-consciousness about the nature of fiction which is a particular legacy of modernism in innovative writing since the late thirties. Such 'multidimensional' interests make *The Alexandria Quartet*—despite its occasional melodrama, 'baroque' prose and deliberate complication —one of the most ambitious and exciting of mid-century novels. Durrell's ambitions have since been extended still further, in an 'Avignon Quintet': *Monsieur* (1974); *Livia* (1978); *Constance* (1982); *Sebastian* (1983); and *Quinx* (1985). In these works, he attempts to complete the movements and interests initiated in *The Black Book* and continued in *The Alexandria Quartet*.

Like Lawrence Durrell, John Fowles began his writing career on a Greek island, which provides the setting for his first novel, *The Magus* (though this was not published until 1966, after the early success of *The Collector* (1963).) Like Durrell's Darley in Alexandria, the hero of *The Magus* is exposed to a series of paradoxical disguises of reality by illusion and pretence in an almost magical domain: the setting for the novel is often compared to Prospero's island in Shakespeare's *The Tempest*. While *The Magus* thus extends something of Durrell's investigation of the relation between art and reality, Fowles's best-known novel *The French Lieutenant's Woman* (1969) both continues such interests and also shows, like Durrell's work, a concern with liberating attitudes to sex. Published at a time when the feelings about political and sexual freedom discussed in the last chapter were at their height, but set around 1867, *The French*

Lieutenant's Woman counterpoints the liberality in outlook of the late nineteen sixties against the severe attitudes of the Victorian period one hundred years previously. Fowles successfully re-creates some of the atmosphere of this period of 'iron certainties... rigid conventions ... repressed emotion',[29] also reproducing some of the conventions of Victorian fiction, Thomas Hardy's perhaps particularly. In fact, part of the novel's popular success probably derives from Fowles's dexterity with a thoroughly conventional plot. The love-triangle between Charles, his prim betrothed Ernestina, and the mysterious stranger Sarah Woodruff provides a familiar, well-tried formula for the story, whose long-deferred climax further heightens its interest.

This apparently conventional story, however, also contributes to the novel's critique of the Victorian age. Charles's half-uneasy acceptance of contemporary 'iron certainties' and his materialistic urge to place Ernestina 'in his bed and in his bank' (p.114) are sharply challenged by Sarah. She seems to share the modernity of Fowles's own outlook, and employs an ingenious determination to free herself, with Charles's help, from conventional roles, social and sexual, thrust upon women by Victorian society. Her questioning of Victorian values is also extended by Fowles's own erudite discussion of Victorian life—smugly dismissive as this sometimes seems—and even by frequent footnotes to the story which consider, for example, the inadequacy of Victorian attitudes to contraception.

Fowles's strong story and varied attack on Victorian values are carefully amalgamated with literary discussion and experimentation with the novel form. Fowles's interest is not only in criticising the manners and society of the last century, but, concomitantly, in examining and attempting to supersede its more 'rigid conventions' for the novel. This involves him both in analyses of the nature of Victorian literature and also, like the other figures discussed in this chapter, in self-conscious discussion within his narrative of the form and technique of his own fiction. At the start of Chapter Thirteen, for example, Fowles appears in person to comment on his own work:

> ... This story I am telling is all imagination. These characters I create
> never existed outside my own mind. If I have pretended until now to
> know my characters' minds and innermost thoughts, it is because I am
> writing in (just as I have assumed some of the vocabulary and 'voice' of) a
> convention universally accepted at the time of my story: that the novelist
> stands next to God... The novelist is still a god, since he creates... what
> has changed is that we are no longer the gods of the Victorian image,
> omniscient and decreeing, but in the new theological image, with
> freedom our first principle, not authority.

In applying this belief in freedom rather than authority to literary as well as sexual conventions, Fowles seems to concur seriously in the half-ironic suggestion of Flann O'Brien's narrator in *At Swim-Two-Birds* that 'It was undemocratic to compel characters to be uniformly good or bad or poor or rich. Each should be allowed a private life, self-determination, and a decent standard of living' (p.25). Fowles attempts to create a measure of 'self-determination' for reader and characters not by presenting like Flann O'Brien 'three openings entirely dissimilar' but by offering three alternative endings to *The French Lieutenant's Woman*. In one of these, Charles imagines living more or less 'happily ever after' (p.292) with Ernestina; in another Fowles shows him happily reunited with Sarah after a long separation; in a third Sarah banishes him to an uncertain future, though one for which he is better equipped with self-knowledge and an incipient liberation from the limiting conventions of the age. Fowles suggests he would prefer to present competing versions of the novel's conclusion 'at once' (p.349) but (unlike B.S. Johnson) does not attempt to escape from the successive form of the bound book. He accepts instead that the third and last version will seem definitive, 'so strong is the tyranny of the last chapter, the final, the "real" version' (p.349).

Though Fowles's multiple endings do not altogether avoid the element of contrivance whose existence in omniscient narrative he sets out to criticise, the third ending at least seems most consonant with the novel's theme of liberation and with its epigraph from Marx: 'every emancipation is a restoration of the human world and of human relationships to man himself'. This supposed 'emancipation' from convention in Fowles's narrative is further indicated by the changing character of the author-figures whom Fowles introduces after his own first appearance in Chapter Thirteen. Chapter Fifty-Five shows Charles meeting in a railway carriage a version of his author very much in the god-like 'Victorian image, omniscient and decreeing'. By contrast, there appears in the final chapter a 'rather foppish and Frenchified' (p.394) figure, who adjusts his watch to obliterate from the fictional universe the occurrence of the second ending, and drives away, finally allowing events to unfold supposedly freely of any omniscience, decree, or authorial control.

The French Connection: John Fowles, Samuel Beckett, Nigel Dennis, Christine Brooke-Rose, Rayner Heppenstall, Giles Gordon

The 'Frenchified' character of Fowles's preferred narrator usefully indicates a source of some of the ideology and experimentation which inform *The French Lieutenant's Woman* and other recent experimental novels. French fiction in the early part of the twentieth century offers in Marcel Proust and André Gide strong examples of novelists partly (or in the case of Gide's *The Counterfeiters* (*Les Faux Monnayeurs*, 1926) almost wholly) concerned with art and the processes of its creation. Fowles himself suggests his work has close affinities with the French literature he studied at university. He makes his indebtedness to this literature more specific when in *The French Lieutenant's Woman* he mentions 'the lessons of existentialist philosophy' (p.63) and indicates 'the age of Alain Robbe-Grillet and Roland Barthes' (p.85) as one of decisive change for the form of the novel. As Fowles helps to suggest, both the 'theoreticians of the nouveau roman' (p.348) such as Robbe-Grillet, and the existentialism of Jean-Paul Sartre and Albert Camus, have been significantly connected with recent English fiction, whose experimental phase has often been distinctly 'Frenchified'.

Some of the nature of this French background is illustrated by the work of Samuel Beckett, which often parallels contemporary developments in French literature. In fact, Beckett can be considered as much a French author as an Irish or English one, as he has written almost all his plays and novels since *Watt* (completed in the early forties) first in French and only later translated them into English. Beckett has also lived almost continuously in France since the nineteen thirties: during the war he endured there like Sartre and Camus the depressing experience of the obliteration of moral and social order in the Fall of France to the Nazis. The formation of existential philosophy is almost simultaneous with the evolution of Beckett's fiction in the years around the war: the dark experience of those years may have similarly confirmed the sort of pessimism with which existentialism contends, and contributed to Beckett's austere vision of characters who fear that '*nothing is more real than nothing.*' Sartre's philosophy envisages man, like Beckett's unnamable, existing in a kind of void, a universe emptied partly by the death of God of any absolute principle of order. This absence leaves man in a state of freedom so radical that it is an anguishing, uncertain responsibility as well as a condition of enormous potential: even individual identity, for example, becomes a matter of difficult self-determining choice. Such 'lessons of existentialist philosophy' contribute to understanding of some of Beckett's vision (especially in his later plays): they are also an influence on a number of English authors. As discussed in Chapter Four, Iris Murdoch has a long-standing interest in Sartre's work, while Fowles's central concern with 'freedom... not authority' in *The French Lieutenant's Woman* relates to an admiration for existential thinking which he further clarifies in his 'self-portrait in ideas', *The Aristos* (1965).

Existentialist thinking was popularised in Britain in the fifties by Colin Wilson's semi-philosophical *The Outsider* (1956), which enjoyed a great vogue at the time. Some of Sartre's ideas are also apparent in Nigel Dennis's *Cards of Identity* (1955), a satirical fantasy in which several individuals demonstrate a sort of existentialist fluidity of identity, totally changing personality under the powerful influence of an organisation known as the Identity Club. The novel is largely taken up with this club's bizarre conference, which studies the contemporary failure of public life to provide a sustaining framework for individual identity, made increasingly fragile by a world of rapid social change. The conference suggests 'all the old means of self-recognition have been swept away, leaving even the best people in a state of personal dubiety'.[30] Dennis's satiric examination of such changes in British public life, its class system and political ideologies in particular, led to his being grouped at first with the satirists and 'angry young men' of the fifties (see Chapter Four). *Cards of Identity*, however, is really an ingenious amalgam of some of the social observation of the period with more philosophic responses, Sartre's included, to post-war depression. The novel also exhibits Dennis's interest in the psychologist Alfred Adler's belief that personality is a kind of fiction fabricated by the individual. Like so many of the novels discussed in this chapter, *Cards of Identity* thus shows a partly self-referential concern with the nature of illusion and reality, and with fiction itself. Complex, witty and sometimes profound, *Cards of Identity* provides an unusually sharp insight into the mood of the fifties, and was one of the most widely admired novels of its period. It remains an outstanding literary eccentricity, though one whose success Dennis was not able to repeat.

Sartre's influence was naturally strongest in the French context, and is apparent in the fiction of Alain Robbe-Grillet and other 'theoreticians of the nouveau roman'—principally Nathalie Sarraute and Michel Butor. The radical freedom which Sartre sees as an aspect of the human condition Robbe-Grillet also examines in its relation to the object world. Part of the hero's uneasiness in Sartre's *Nausea* (*La Nausée*, 1938) is brought on by a queasy sense of the autonomy of the inanimate things around him: Robbe-Grillet extends this sense of objects existing in stubborn separateness, empty of certain significance. In his essay 'Towards a New Novel' ('Pour un Nouveau Roman', 1956) he discusses both this view of the problematic nature of objects, and certain concomitant difficulties which confront attempts to make sense of life in general. He suggests that it is misleading to envisage any sort of human meaning inherent in the inanimate, since in general 'the world is neither significant nor absurd. It *is* quite simply'. Such views also make him more generally suspicious of the literary urge to create coherence, significance or 'control' for 'the world around us':

> ...We had thought to control it by assigning it a meaning, and the entire art of the novel, in particular, seemed dedicated to this enterprise. But this was merely an illusory simplification...We no longer consider the world as our own, our private property, designed according to our needs and readily domesticated.[31]

Robbe-Grillet's suspicion of attempts to domesticate or 'impose a conventional order'[32] appears in his own fiction's frustration of conventional expectations of 'assigned meaning', pattern or significance. In his first novel, *The Erasers* (*Les Gommes*, 1953) for example, unresolved conflicts between different versions of the same experience, and the impossibility of discovering a plausible chronology, wholly deny the usual satisfaction of a rational solution to a detective story. As Robbe-Grillet suggests, such fiction makes 'the movement of the writing'[33]—the novel's own language and technique—of more rewarding interest than its indecipherable plot.

Several English novelists have been stimulated by Robbe-Grillet's fiction and theories, perhaps especially in the early sixties, after his visit to Britain with Nathalie Sarraute in 1961. The possibility of developing a *nouveau roman* in English was perhaps especially likely to appeal to Christine Brooke-Rose, a bilingual teacher of English at the University of Paris who translated Robbe-Grillet's *Dans le Labyrinthe* (1959) into English in 1968. Her own fiction remains relatively conventional until *Out* (1964), which is partly modelled around Robbe-Grillet's *Jealousy* (*La Jalousie*, 1957), and employs at times his style of exhaustive, semi-scientific description of inanimate objects. Her next novel, *Such* (1966) concerns a psychiatrist's struggle, after his heart has briefly stopped during an operation, to reconstruct some grasp of reality out of the whirling chaos of astronomical fantasies and proliferating imaginings which have invaded his mind. What Sarraute calls 'tropisms'—scarcely formulable movements of mind on the periphery of perception or coherence—show in *Such* 'what happens to the unconscious when the body lies in a low state of life'.[34] They also contribute, in their chaos, to the sort of difficulties in 'imposing a conventional order' which interest Robbe-Grillet.

While *Such* is thus concerned in general with means of creating coherence, Brooke-Rose's *Thru* (1972) concentrates this concern much more specifically on 'the movement of the writing', and on language itself. Like Brigid Brophy's *In Transit* (1969), which it often resembles, *Thru* is a multilingual, punning, playful novel, whose inventive typographical layout creates a sort of concrete poetry, or 'concrete prose', presenting a great variety of linguistic patterns and methods of creating meaning. Many of these are discussed in the course of the novel's reflections on its own technique, or in its examinations of the operation of narrative, or even of the university teaching of literature. Such consistent reference to the nature of literature and meaning creates in *Thru* a 'prism of a language', witty but demanding to read as it is more extremely self-enclosed and much more dryly theoretical even than Beckett's trilogy. As a warning in its text suggests, readers of *Thru* find themselves 'entering the Metalinguistic Zone. All access forbidden except for Prepared Consumers'.[35] The full appeal of *Thru* may be confined to critically prepared 'consumers' such as the rather bored university teacher who figures as one of the novel's many narrators.

A strong French influence is also apparent in the work of Rayner Heppenstall. Like John Fowles, Heppenstall studied French at university, and records being 'much attracted by the French existentialists' and 'interested in the French *nouveau roman*'.[36] Heppenstall's earliest admiration, however, was for Henry Miller, whom he met with Lawrence Durrell in the thirties and whose influence appears in the extended concern with sex in his first novel, *The Blaze of Noon* (1939). This concern is unusually concentrated by the blindness of Heppenstall's narrator, whose feeling that 'from the sense of touch...there is no escape' is strongly communicated. This imparts to the novel a peculiarity and challenge to conventional expectations which perhaps accounts for the critical suggestion that *The Blaze of Noon* anticipates the development of the *nouveau roman*[37].

Heppenstall's affinities with such developments, however, do not really emerge until, encouraged by the example of Robbe-Grillet, he returned to fiction writing more than twenty years after *The Blaze of Noon*. Like some of Sarraute's fiction, his second novel, *The Connecting Door* (1962) has an unnamed narrator. Like Robbe-Grillet's, it contains some meticulously detailed description of inanimate objects, including the exercise book in which, like Beckett's Molloy, he writes his narrative. Despite such oddities, *The Connecting Door* seems for many pages a fairly straightforward account of a journalist's visit after the war to a town in Eastern France, itself something of a connecting door with the still-alien territory of Germany. The eye of the journalist makes meticulous observation, and even the vivid use of the present tense, seem plausible and natural. Later, however, as Heppenstall explains elsewhere, there appears in the novel 'a new, implicit time-dimension...an extra grammatical tense'.[38] It becomes increasingly apparent that certain characters simultaneously inhabit several different eras or planes of time, and that in some cases they are merely projections of the narrator's consciousness, or earlier versions of him. As he eventually explains to one of them 'In the past seventeen years, you've lived in occasional flickers, when I had you in mind'.[39] Some resolution of this mysterious mixture of imagination and reality is promised if the narrator can determine whether he has met again in the present a girl who has been at the centre of some earlier episodes. The novel ends, however, at the moment when he is about to investigate this possibility by opening a connecting door into the train compartment where she sleeps. In the manner of Robbe-Grillet, Heppenstall's novel thus remains a puzzle, raising and frustrating the possibility of creating a plausible pattern for its events, and eventually offering only a series of 'connecting doors' into irreconcilable planes of time or reality.

Like P.H. Newby (see Chapter Three), Heppenstall sustains his sense of mystery in a fluent, lucid prose which adds to the enjoyment of the technical ingenuity of *The Connecting Door*. Like Newby, however, Heppenstall's writing offers an example rarely taken up by later authors, although the influence of the *nouveau roman* itself is still traceable in the seventies in the work of Giles Gordon, who describes Robbe-Grillet as 'to me...probably the most influential and intriguing twentieth century fiction writer'.[40] Like Robbe-Grillet's *The Erasers*, Gordon's *Girl with red hair* (1974) is loosely a detective story, showing some of Robbe-Grillet's concentration on inanimate objects. It also strongly resembles Michel Butor's *La Modification* (1957), sharing the unusual feature of being written entirely in the second person. Some of the strangest features of *Girl with red hair*, however, such as its reference index of characters, seem to be entirely Gordon's own invention, part of a range of self-conscious experimental techniques in his fiction which has sometimes led him to be considered a natural successor to B.S. Johnson.

Free Narrative: Andrew Sinclair, Julian Mitchell, David Caute, John Berger, Alasdair Gray

Some French influence on the English fiction of the seventies continues to be apparent in the work of David Caute, who records a liking for Christine Brooke-Rose and mentions Sartre as a figure whom he admires 'above all others'.[41] Caute, however, also belongs to a small group of English novelists, including Andrew Sinclair, Julian Mitchell (whom he knew while a student at Oxford), and Thomas Hinde, all of whose work illustrates another influence on the English idiom, originating in recent American fiction. The rootlessness and alienation of many characters in modern American novels is strongly recalled, for example, by the hero of Andrew Sinclair's *Gog* (1967). His epic journey through Britain is provoked by an urge to escape from a corrupt society and remain 'alone on a road, affecting no one and nothing, merely moving from place to place, with all the useless private purpose of the truly irresponsible and the truly free'.[42] Disturbed by the violence of the war, and of his own half-mystic struggle to resist the modern machine world, Gog's mind 'does not sort the false from the true, the fantasy from the fact, but retains both with...dreadful impartiality' (p.405). Sinclair's novel likewise moves 'impartially' between realistic and fantastic, often bawdy, sections in a manner comparable to the techniques of American authors such as Joseph Heller, John Barth, Kurt Vonnegut, and Thomas Pynchon. Like these writers, Sinclair also alternates apparently arbitrarily between different and unusual textual forms: parts of *Gog* are narrated as film script, comic strip, or academic essay, for example, and even the more straightforward sections employ an unusual, highly rhetorical language.

Like Sinclair and Caute, Julian Mitchell spent time in the U.S.A. on an academic scholarship in the late fifties, and seems to have been similarly impressed by American fiction, perhaps particularly its 'impartial' alternation of fantasy and realism. Such effects are only occasionally apparent in his earlier novels (see Chapter Four). *The Undiscovered Country* (1968), however, is entirely divided into a realistic, pseudo-autobiographical first section, and a fantastic second part (supposedly the work of another author) which is set in a hotel whose surreal nature seems an image of the weird psyches of its inhabitants. *The Undiscovered Country* also displays a strong element of self-consciousness about its own devices, and about the nature of fiction generally. Much of the early part is taken up with reflection about the habits of the narrator of the second, which contains an extended, parodic commentary on its own methods and meaning.

A comparable mixture of fantasy, realistic narrative, and self-consciousness, also showing some American influence, appears in David Caute's fiction. The wild humour of *The Occupation* (1971), for example, may result from his acknowledged admiration for Philip Roth's *Portnoy's Complaint* (1969), though Caute's martyred intellectual narrator Stephen Bright also resembles the hero in another Jewish-American novel, Saul Bellow's *Herzog* (1964). Generally confused by his society, Bright takes refuge, like Herzog, increasingly within the frontiers of his own uneasy mind. The 'occupation' of the novel's title refers not only to the sixties student revolts Bright encounters, but to the multiplying fantasies which invade his thoughts, thoroughly eroding his grasp of reality. Like Thomas Hinde's *High* (1968), which *The Occupation* strongly resembles, Bright's story is correspondingly 'occupied' by competing narrative strategies—fantastic and realistic, objective and subjective —and even by competing narrators. Some of these subsidiary narrators also occasionally make the curious discovery of copies of Bright's typescript narrative, entitled 'The Occupation,' which forces them to the odd realisation that they are only characters in someone else's fiction. Elegantly and wittily assembled, such perplexities proliferate throughout *The Occupation*, undermining any secure reference to the world beyond the novel. This 'autonomy' of the fiction is confirmed, and its self-referential complexities enthusiastically compounded, by Bright's qualifications, reversals, and denials of his own narrative, sometimes extended by footnotes to the text. In the end, the reader's grasp of the fictional world is as thoroughly undermined as Bright's grasp of his own experience: as the narrator of *At Swim-Two-Birds* wishes, *The Occupation* increasingly appears 'a self-evident sham to which the reader could regulate at will the degree of his credulity'.

One of the many examinations of the nature of literature in *The Occupation* takes the form of a political and theoretical argument between Bright and a socialist critic who is committed to straightforward fictional realism. Their debate summarises some of the general interests of Caute's trilogy *The Confrontation*, of which *The Occupation* is the third part. The first, *The Demonstration* (1969) is a play in which Bright appears; the second, *The Illusion* (1970) is ostensibly his long critical essay on a subject Julian Mitchell recalls 'obsessed' all his friends at Oxford, and which contributes to Caute's admiration for Sartre—the question of politically 'committed literature'.[43] The socialist in *The Occupation* follows Georg Lukács (and other Marxist critics of the sort mentioned in Chapter Two) in severely criticising modernist and later experimental writing as irresponsible and self-indulgent. This position, however, is rejected by Bright, and further dismissed in *The Illusion*, where it is suggested 'A literature which invites its audience to question the prevailing social structure and social consciousness must constantly question and expose itself.' Caute cites *The French Lieutenant's Woman* as a 'breakthrough' and 'landmark' in making 'coherent social comment'[44] within the self-questioning, self-conscious mode he recommends. Fowles's own suggestion that *The French Lieutenant's Woman* is written in 'the age of Robbe-Grillet' and of the influential French critic Roland Barthes indicates further sources of support for Caute's opinions. Robbe-Grillet and Barthes share a suspicion of realistic fiction partly on the grounds that its conventional patterning sometimes merely conforms with and fails to challenge the 'prevailing social structure'. Their views, and those of Caute, Fowles, and others such as B.S. Johnson, are part of a general, partly political, debate about the validity and worth of modernist and later innovative writing. This debate is of especial significance for the most ostentatiously committed of recent British novelists, John Berger, for whom both 'social comment' and self-questioning are particular priorities.

Like Fowles, Berger is concerned with freedom and the possibilities for self-determination of individuals within their societies. His third novel, *Corker's Freedom* (1964), for example, concerns the difficulties of evading numbing routine and financial exigency and escaping into 'the life we would like to lead but can't...a world where we could all be ourselves. Free.'[45] Something of this world is realised in the novel's third part. Its narrative departs from relative conventionality elsewhere, following Corker's escape into the fantasies and imaginative realisations of his ideals which he formulates while watching pictures of the beautiful, distant city of Vienna. Berger himself is interested, as artist and art critic, in the sort of imaginative and visual stimuli which inspire Corker, and his best-known novel, *G.* (1972) returns in a more generally unconventional form to some of the questions *Corker's Freedom* raises about imagination and emancipation. Like John Fowles, Berger shows in *G.* a concern with political and social freedom which is amalgamated with an attempt to liberate reader and text from the constraints of conventional narrative. In particular, Berger wishes to avoid 'imposing a conventional order' whose satisfactory form or consoling sense of completeness might distract from critical alertness to the political history and social forces he depicts. He explains in the course of describing an Italian workers' revolt:

> I cannot continue this account of the eleven-year-old boy in Milan on 6 May 1898. From this point on everything I write will either converge upon a final full stop or else disperse so widely that it will become incoherent... The writer's desire to finish is fatal to the truth. The End unifies. Unity must be established in another way.[46]

Setting out, as Caute commented in a review, 'to baffle and frustrate the clients of a conventional narrative',[47] the text of *G.* resists the unity which Berger suspects, ending vaguely and made up throughout of scantily-connected paragraphs. These juxtapose statistics and historical information with critical speculation and the story of a hero who seems, rather as Berger suggests, to 'disperse...widely'. He is known only 'for the sake of convenience' (p.142) as G., and is freely conflated with Garibaldi; the pioneer aviator Geo Chavez; and Don Giovanni. Throughout the novel, like Fowles and others, Berger frequently intrudes to discuss his difficulties in describing events and his refusal to define or control his characters through a pretence of omniscience about their actions. Such authorial intrusions install the relation of art and narrative to reality and life as a central question of *G.* Its fragmentary, apparently unfinished form extends this interest. It also imposes on readers a certain responsibility for establishing for themselves a literary and historical order which the novel itself does not completely provide. As Iris Murdoch suggests (see Chapter Four) 'our sense of form, which is an aspect of our desire for consolation, can be a danger to our sense of reality.'[48] Berger's apparently disorderly combination of fiction and documentary avoids any such consoling distraction from historical reality, demonstrating instead that 'Unity must be achieved in another way', by political rather than artistic means. Though in some ways a genuinely baffling and frustrating novel, *G.* thus realises at least some of the potential for political vision which Caute and others see as a particular strength of experimental fiction.

Although very different from *G.*, Alasdair Gray's *Lanark* (1981) also employs an unusual, inventive structure partly in order to articulate a critical—even satirical or political—view of contemporary life. Though it is suggested in the novel that Glasgow is 'the sort of industrial city where most people live nowadays but nobody imagines living',[49] *Lanark* itself partly redresses this poverty of imagination through the diversity and inventiveness of its means of envisaging the city. Different parts of the novel are very differently imagined: the first and last sections show Gray's hero Lanark in Unthank, a surreal, machine-ridden, Wellsian underworld; whereas two central parts present, generally naturalistically, the life of Duncan Thaw, a sort of portrait of the artist as a young Glaswegian. These sections of fantasy and of realism are significantly interconnected. As Lanark learns from an Oracle in Unthank, Thaw may be his former self during life on earth. While Lanark is thus a sort of infernal translation of Thaw, Unthank itself is likewise a fantastic projection of the drab, mechanical life of the real city of Glasgow. Gray magnifies and dramatically clarifies in Unthank the numbing processes at work in Thaw's decaying city. Its poverty; the determining forces which shape its life; and the people whom they subjugate, are all expanded in fantasy; made actually as well as metaphorically monstrous. By this ingenious use of fantastic and realistic phases of narrative to illumine and comment on one another, Gray creates in *Lanark* an unusually complex, powerful social vision, one which Anthony Burgess calls 'a shattering work of fiction in the modern idiom'.[50]

Some of the novel's imaginative power is perhaps slightly diminished by Gray's eagerness to stress the modernity of his idiom and to flaunt the illustrious pedigree of devices he derives from modernist and other writers. He includes in *Lanark* a critical commentary on his own work, largely in the form of an index of plagiarisms which claims indebtedness to Conrad, Kafka, Sartre, Joyce, Wyndham Lewis, Joyce Cary, and Flann O'Brien, among many others. As this index seems ingenuously to admit, *Lanark* is a deeply derivative work. Duncan Thaw's doomed, obsessive life as an artist strongly recalls Gulley Jimson in Cary's *The Horse's Mouth* (1944), for example, while Lanark's encounters and interviews with his own author repeat tactics employed by Fowles, B.S. Johnson, Flann O'Brien, and others. Many more such borrowings appear and are acknowledged: Gray seems at times to act upon the suggestion in *At Swim-Two-Birds* that 'the entire corpus of existing literature should be regarded as a limbo from which discerning authors could draw' (p.25). His index even seems to follow the view of Flann O'Brien's narrator that 'the modern novel should be largely a work of reference' (p.25). *Lanark* contains not only self-conscious reference to its own methods, but introduces a more general critical consciousness about the whole context of literature in which it is written.

Conclusion

The obviousness of Alasdair Gray's borrowings, and his critical discussion of them, make *Lanark* an unusually clear demonstration of the extent of recent experimental writing's indebtedness to the modernists' developments in form and technique earlier in the twentieth century. This is not only a matter of the novel's explicit self-consciousness and direct acknowledgement of its debts. For example, the odd arrangement of *Lanark*, in which Book Three precedes Books One, Two, and Four, also illustrates the continuation in later fiction of the modernist amendment of chronological order discussed in Chapter One as a feature of the work of Conrad, Ford, Joyce, Woolf, and others. *The French Lieutenant's Woman, The Unfortunates,* and *The Alexandria Quartet* all employ like *Lanark* strategies which extend the modernists' attempt to escape what Durrell calls 'the serial form of the conventional novel: the time-saturated novel'. Other recent writers are equally sceptical of conventional fictional chronology. Berger in *G.* declares and acts upon an incomprehension for 'calendars and clocks' (p.165); Heppenstall attempts in *The Connecting Door* to present different epochs simultaneously; and Brooke-Rose in *Such* shows temporal order as one of the sources of stability which initially entirely fails her hero.

Later experimental novelists have also developed further the sort of stream of consciousness and interior monologue techniques discussed in Chapter One as a feature of modernist writing. Samuel Beckett, for example, moves beyond stream of consciousness, and at times beyond the dream-language of *Finnegans Wake*, or almost beyond language itself, into areas lost (as one of his dramatic characters remarks) in 'who knows what profounds of mind'.[51] This deepening of the novel's transcription of consciousness (also more modestly a feature of Brooke-Rose's *Such*) has often been accompanied in recent experimental fiction by a broadening multiplication of the number of figures through whose minds or narratives the material of the novel is presented. In *Ulysses*, Leopold Bloom's interest in 'parallax'—comparison of different points of view—is reciprocated in Joyce's use of the vision of Stephen, Molly, and Bloom himself. Later novelists, however, have often extended far beyond three the number of their observers or narrators. B.S. Johnson's *House Mother Normal* (1971), for example, uses nine different points of view, while as discussed already, almost all the characters in *At Swim-Two-Birds, The Occupation,* or *The Alexandria Quartet* are potential storytellers, offering alternative perspectives on the action. Like Durrell's novel, recent fiction has often engaged in 'a game of mirrors'. The 'cracked lookingglass'[52] to which Stephen Dedalus compares traditional art has subsequently shown further

219

signs of fracture, leaving the pieces and 'prisms' through which later writers reflect their complex, fragmented visions.

Expanding flexibility in point of view and chronology shows later experimental writing's extension of one set of modernist initiatives. Its most distinctive and widely-practised development, however, and the one principally discussed in this chapter, has been towards an explicit self-consciousness about art and its methods, of a sort incipiently present in the work of Joyce and some of his contemporaries. Almost all the novels mentioned above concern themselves more or less directly with 'art, the great subject of modern artists'. Reflection on 'literary activities' is a favourite occupation not only for Flann O'Brien's narrator, but for many subsequent novelists, whose commentaries on their own methods make literary criticism and creation closely connected, almost simultaneous. As Robbe-Grillet suggests,

> After *Les Faux Monnayeurs*, after Joyce, after *La Nausée*, it seems that we are more and more moving towards an age of fiction in which the problems of writing will be lucidly envisaged by the novelist, and in which his concern with critical matters, far from sterilising his creative faculties, will on the contrary supply him with motive power... Invention and imagination may finally become the subject of the book.[53]

The 'age of fiction' which Robbe-Grillet discusses is usually identified as 'post-modernist', a term which appropriately indicates the development of several of its distinctive features either directly 'after Joyce', or as an extension of the work of other intermediary authors themselves strongly influenced by Joyce and his modernist contemporaries. As Robbe-Grillet suggests in discussing his own indebtedness to Joyce, Beckett and others,

> ... the evolution has continued... we certainly don't attempt to blot out this past. In fact, it is in admiration of our predecessors that we are most united; our ambition is only to move on from there... to follow in their trail, in our own way, in our own time.[54]

This 'following in the trail' of modernist predecessors by writers of the sort discussed in this chapter has sometimes seemed less welcome in the British context than in the French literature to which Robbe-Grillet principally refers. Perhaps especially in England, post-modernism has failed to gain consistent public or critical approval. Like Stephen Bright in *The Occupation*, or Flann O'Brien's narrator in *At Swim-Two-Birds*, experimental novelists are often upbraided for retiring into the privacy of their reflections on their own methods, and for irresponsibly avoiding the artist's traditional task of representing and shaping the real world. An author in Brooke-Rose's *Thru* is accused of trying to 'run away into language... merely amusing yourself... playing with words' (p.62), and similar charges of frivolity, self-indulgence, escapism, even narcissism, are often levelled at the self-conscious idiom of post-modernism. Such charges may occasionally be justified: there may be, for example, an element of narcissism or self-aggrandisement in the apparent eagerness with which John Fowles, Alasdair Gray, or John Berger thrust themselves and their reflections into the course of their fictions.

The suggestion, however, that post-modernist art irresponsibly evades 'the real world' perhaps ignores too easily the increasingly problematic status of reality itself in twentieth-century thought. As B.S. Johnson remarks,

> Present-day reality is markedly different from say nineteenth-century reality. Then it was possible to believe in pattern and eternity, but today what characterises our reality is the probability that chaos is the most likely explanation.[55]

The continuing turbulence of twentieth century history, scarcely diminished since the modernist age, its general fragmentation and absence of 'pattern', perhaps continues to discourage direct reflection of reality in art, for some of the reasons Chapter One suggested. A further obstacle to representational, realistic art is indicated by Pursewarden's suggestion in *The Alexandria Quartet* that 'the Relativity proposition was directly responsible for abstract painting, atonal music, and formless (or at any rate cyclic forms in) literature' (p.306). The general development of twentieth century thought, scientific and philosophic, has diminished faith in the existence of a definite, objective, easily-accessible 'outer reality': in other arts as well as literature, as Pursewarden suggests, a concomitant urge has appeared to abandon conventional forms and realistic, representational styles. Instead, literature and other arts have often favoured fantasy — pure creation of the imagination — or examination of the reliability of the processes, artistic representation included, whereby reality may be known or assimilated, if indeed it exists meaningfully at all. Much twentieth-century art and literature has thus moved on into a self-conscious, 'cyclic', post-modernist idiom, developing still further than the modernists away from what Eugene Jolas called 'the epoch when the writer photographed the life about him with the mechanics of words redolent of the daguerrotype'. This movement has perhaps been further encouraged by the pace of technological development, advancing far beyond daguerrotype and photograph to motion pictures and television. Heppenstall, Julian Mitchell, Giles Gordon and B.S. Johnson have all indicated their belief that the novel was forced to develop away from realism by film and television, which are in some ways so much more adept than fiction at representing the surface of real experience. As B.S. Johnson suggests, 'the twentieth century has seen large areas of the old territory of the novelist increasingly taken over by other media', enforcing the novel's concentration on 'things it can still do best: the precise use of language, the exploitation of the technological fact of the book, the explication of thought'.[56]

In the remarks quoted earlier, however, Johnson shows his conviction that in spite of the logic of his position, 'the vast majority of British novelists' have dropped or ignored 'the baton of innovation'. Johnson's opinion of the paucity of British post-modernism is widely shared: Malcolm Bradbury, for example, remarks

> ...though there is *Finnegans Wake*, and Durrell, and Beckett...we often presume, in modern criticism, that in the English line the experimental tradition did shift or lapse, a lapse usually identified with the thirties, when realism and politics came back.[57]

Though the assessments of Bradbury and Johnson are accurate enough, a slightly more optimistic view of the innovative phase of English fiction is also possible. As this chapter has suggested, in the work of Caute, Sinclair, Fowles, Johnson and several others, experimental writing itself 'came back' in the sixties. The expansive mood of the time (especially towards the end of the decade, and in the early seventies) particularly encouraged innovation, even in the work of authors previously largely conventional in style and technique. For that matter, experiment had already 'come back' at the end of the thirties, in *Finnegans Wake* and several other novels which mark a transition from modernism to a more thoroughly self-conscious, 'experimental tradition' in later years. Some of the energies of modernism also reappear later in various recombinations with more conventional forms, in ways examined in Chapters Three and Four. The innovative nature of such combinations, and their extension of the range and technique of fiction, suggest that Malcolm Lowry, Joyce Cary, and many of the novelists discussed in Chapter Four might at least in some aspects be considered alongside the selection of experimental writers included in this chapter. Of recent novelists, Doris Lessing in *The Golden Notebook* (1962), for example, and Muriel Spark, intermittently throughout her fiction, are as radically experimental, and in some of the same ways, as many of the writers discussed above. Spark, in particular, is one of the earliest of British writers to be influenced by the *nouveau roman*.

Lessing's later development as a science fiction novelist also indicates a further area of occasional literary experiment. Some of the work of such authors as Brian Aldiss and J.G. Ballard is of an innovative quality significant beyond the genre of science fiction in which they usually write. Aldiss's *Report on Probability A* (1968), for example, is a sort of *nouveau roman* influenced by Robbe-Grillet and Michel Butor, while his 'Fantasia' *Barefoot in the Head* (1969) shows a sustained linguistic inventiveness which at times resembles *Finnegans Wake*. Several of Ballard's novels—in particular his surreal *The*

Unlimited Dream Company (1979)—likewise participate in the development of a new generation of experimental British writers, whose appearance is suggested, for example, by Giles Gordon's anthology *Beyond the Words* (1975). It contains material by Anthony Burgess, Alan Burns, Elspeth Davie, Eva Figes, Robert Nye, Gabriel Josipovici, David Plante and Maggie Ross, as well as B.S. Johnson and Giles Gordon himself.

An 'experimental tradition' is thus recognisable in twentieth-century British fiction; continues to appear in the work of several contemporary authors; and is perhaps more varied and extensive than is sometimes supposed. Nevertheless, as B.S. Johnson, Bradbury, and many others have suggested, post-modernism is not at its strongest in England, where modernist initiatives seem more often accommodated within traditional forms rather than genuinely extended. As Bradbury records, this has contributed to the way in which 'on the whole English postwar fiction has tended to come out with the reputation of one of the less exciting of contemporary fictions',[58] its 'experimental tradition' comparing unfavourably with developments abroad. Of all the authors discussed in this chapter, probably only Beckett and perhaps Durrell can be compared in terms of accomplishment and public recognition with South American writers such as Jorge Luis Borges, or Gabriel García Márquez; Americans such as Thomas Pynchon; or the continental authors of the *nouveau roman* and of other innovative novels written since. It is also significant that both Fowles and Durrell are very much more popular in the U.S.A. than in their own country, and that outside influences from Ireland, France and America have so frequently and forcefully contributed to the 'experimental tradition' within England itself. Many writers in this tradition share the view that the English context and its critics are somehow hostile to innovations and to post-modernist writing in general. B.S. Johnson remarks 'only when one has some contact with a continental European tradition of the *avant garde* does one realise just how stultifyingly philistine is the general book culture of this country.' Julian Mitchell likewise finds in English life and literature 'an enervating imaginative timidity...distinctly and depressingly parochial', and Heppenstall complains that 'in this country there is too little technical expertise. We have endless conventional novels.' David Caute similarly comments on 'a certain insularity...in the national bloodstream', and regrets that 'our collective cultural reaction to foreign aesthetic theories...continues to resemble that of a Folkestone customs officer examining a suitcase brimming with Danish pornography.'[59]

Enervated by inflexible English literary customs, many post-modernist authors seem—like the French Lieutenant's woman, Sarah Woodruff—to look forlornly across the channel for support

223

and affection they cannot find amid the conventionality which prevails within their own shores. Perhaps partly in consequence, Beckett, Durrell, Fowles, Berger and Brooke-Rose have all become more or less permanent exiles, usually in France. Neither such experimental writers' preference for exile nor the strength of foreign influence on English innovation are new phenomena, however, but an important feature of English fiction in its modernist as well as its post-modernist phase. The next, concluding, pages discuss some of the implications and significance of this feature in the development of the English novel during the twentieth century.

Postscript: 'English' Fiction
in the Twentieth Century.

'Thought you were English?'
'Certainly I am. Typical Englishman, you might say. Mother Irish.'
'And your father?'
'Russian. White Russian, of course.'[1]

International connections of the sort Yakimov outlines in Olivia
Manning's *The Balkan Trilogy* (1960-65) figure significantly in the
lives of several twentieth-century 'English' writers, and in some ways
in the development of the novel itself. Manning, for example, shares
Anglo-Irish parentage with Joyce Cary, Elizabeth Bowen, Lawrence
Durrell and Iris Murdoch, among others. George Orwell, Wyndham
Lewis, Mervyn Peake, William Gerhardie and Jean Rhys were all
born outside the British Isles and spent at least part of their
childhoods as expatriates. Many other writers were temporary exiles
at some later stage of their lives: as Chapter Four suggested,
experience of empire interested authors as otherwise diverse as
Graham Greene, Joyce Cary, E.M. Forster and Somerset Maugham,
as well as members of a younger generation such as Paul Scott. Less
distant exile in Europe has also contributed material to the work of
Christopher Isherwood and Olivia Manning, and more recently to
Frank Tuohy in *The Ice Saints* (1964). Such elements of international
background or experience are perhaps a particular stimulus to
novel-writing, establishing a critical distance from British society
which provides both an incentive and a specific perspective for its
observation. Another occasional exile, Anthony Burgess, suggests the
need for some such separate perspective when he remarks 'if you
want to write about your own people, you've got to get away from
them'. Graham Greene likewise comments of writing about London
from the vantage point of Sierra Leone that 'it is often easier to
describe something from a long way off'.[2]

Distant perspectives and foreign experience have been widely
available to British writers in a period of the final flowering of
empire and, more recently, of increasingly frequent international
travel. Though figuring fairly generally in the British novel in the
twentieth century, a degree of separateness from English society is of
particular significance for modernist authors, an unusual number of

whom were exiles, as critics have often remarked. In some cases status as an outsider may have functioned for the modernists rather as it did for some of the writers mentioned above, helping create, for example, the sort of distant vision Stephen Dedalus seeks when in *A Portrait of the Artist as a Young Man* (1916) he claims that he leaves his country in order 'to forge in the smithy of my soul the uncreated conscience of my race'.[3] Foreign experience, however, may have particularly contributed to modernists' concern with form, at least at the level of language and style. Rayner Heppenstall remarks that 'only through constant rubbing against a foreign language can a writer achieve mastery of his own'[4]: exile and other cultural circumstances often created for the modernists strong impulses towards this dominance of language. James Joyce, for example, was in some ways permanently exposed to the linguistic friction Heppenstall mentions. Its origin in his earliest days, as part of his Irish background, is suggested in *A Portrait of the Artist as a Young Man* by Stephen Dedalus's encounter with an English priest and his reflection that

> His language, so familiar and so foreign, will always be for me an acquired speech. I have not made or accepted its words. My voice holds them at bay. My soul frets in the shadow of his language. (p.189)

Stephen's 'fretting' or 'rubbing against' the English language underlies his self-conscious fascination for words, discussed in Chapter Five. Joyce's own linguistic interests were probably deepened by the shadow of other languages encountered during long periods in France and Italy; increasing his awareness of the arbitrary connection of word and world; furthering a critical distance from the English language which appears in the verbal inventiveness and concentration on words and speech in *Ulysses* (1922) and *Finnegans Wake* (1939).

Such periods of exile may also have encouraged re-assessments of the 'language' of the novel in the areas of technique and structure. Encounters with foreign culture and its alternative systems of envisaging the world may have heightened modernists' critical awareness of the conventions of their own art, adding to their readiness to reshape or abandon these conventions in favour of new techniques. As Chapter Five suggested, authors who have followed from the modernists have continued to be influenced in this way by foreign experience, ideas or models. The interest in language and the operation of narrative shown by Samuel Beckett, for example, is like Joyce's likely to have been stimulated partly by cultural and linguistic tensions encountered by an Irishman permanently resident in Paris. Comparable tensions experienced by Malcolm Lowry in Mexico perhaps contributed to the development of modernist techniques in *Under the Volcano* (1947): a particular linguistic friction, for example, is suggested by the fragments of Spanish which 'rub against' the English language throughout the novel. Exile may in more general ways have helped Beckett and Lowry sustain enthusiasm for modernist methods: each left Britain more or less permanently in the mid-thirties, thus avoiding the mood of antipathy to Joycean and other innovations which as Chapter Two suggested often appeared on the domestic scene at the time.

Not all the modernists, of course, were either foreigners or exiles. Several, however, developed in other ways a certain separateness from English society. Though Virginia Woolf's literary circle, based in Bloomsbury, apparently placed her closest of all the modernists to the centre of metropolitan culture, she nevertheless records in *A Room of One's Own* (1929):

> If one is a woman one is often surprised by a sudden splitting off of consciousness, say in walking down Whitehall, when from being the natural inheritor of that civilisation, she becomes, on the contrary, outside of it, alien and critical.[5]

As in modernist and post-modernist fiction generally, in Woolf and later women's writing a sense of being 'outside...alien and critical' encourages departure from convention and development of the novel form. As discussed in Chapter Four, the 'splitting off of consciousness' Woolf mentions requires specific techniques for the representation of women's minds and experience: the continuing evolution, for example, of the 'feminine prose' first mentioned by Dorothy Richardson. Such developments, or other extensions of modernist initiatives, are apparent in women's fiction even in the often-conservative nineteen thirties, in the novels of Stevie Smith *(Novel on Yellow Paper* (1936), for example) as well as those of Jean Rhys and Rosamond Lehmann. As Chapter Four suggested, women's writing has continued, especially since the sixties, as one of the more innovative phases of British fiction.

One of its contemporary practitioners, Emma Tennant, indicates another area of recent progress in the novel form when she suggests that 'most of the developments in fiction in the last decade that have been written in the English language are likely to have come out of Africa, or the West Indies, or India'.[6] Though the British empire has largely ceased to offer British novelists the sort of material or perspective discussed earlier, it has helped to establish a situation in which by far the majority of English speakers, and English writers, are resident outwith the United Kingdom, and there are already many signs that this legacy of empire will have more influence on English fiction than any novelist's imperial experience when British power was at its height. As Anthony Burgess suggests in *The Novel Now* (1971), 'British colonialism has exported the English language, and a new kind of British novel has been the eventual flower of this transplanting.'[7] Burgess cites Chinua Achebe, V.S. Naipaul, Wilson Harris and R.K. Narayan among many successful novelists from former colonies: others who have emerged during the past decade, such as Anita Desai, Salman Rushdie and Ruth Prawer Jhabvala might be added to his list. Many such writers inevitably experience the English language in terms suggested by Stephen Dedalus, as 'so familiar and so foreign... an acquired speech'. This 'rubbing against' the language and the need to adapt the conventions of the English novel to suit the particular interests of their own cultures have encouraged an innovative aspect in their writing. Though partly comparable to the methods of Angela Carter and Emma Tennant (see Chapter Four), Salman Rushdie's combination of fantasy and realism, for example, is most unusual in English fiction. His *Midnight's Children* (1981), in particular, imports into the novel in English some of the imaginative developments in magic narrative made in recent years by South American novelists such as Gabriel García Márqez.

The cultural and linguistic factors outlined above all suggest various ways in which 'alien and critical' distance contributes to the evolution of innovative fiction. The separateness of this sort of writing has perhaps also been a consequence of the conservatism sometimes apparent in English literature and society, a particular irritant to some of the novelists discussed in Chapter Five. In analysing 'The Ideology of Being English' in *The Situation of the Novel* (1970), Bernard Bergonzi suggests:

> ... the most important fact about contemporary English life — and one says 'English' advisedly, for Wales and Scotland have different traditions — is that it did not undergo the radical transformations that took place in countries which underwent the traumatic experiences of totalitarianism and defeat in war. Ancient traditions and continuities remained undisturbed... In cultural matters we find an unrepentant insularity and an involvement with native elements and traditions, as against the cosmopolitan innovations of the Modern Movement.[8]

Several contemporary novelists — Eva Figes and Doris Lessing, among others — share Bergonzi's view of English society as relatively untransformed by historical process, and less disposed toward a transforming, innovative fiction as a result.[9] Whereas the dark experience of the Second World War contributed, for example, to a new philosophical, existential depth in French fiction in the years which followed, many English novelists at the time continued to work within some largely-undisturbed 'traditions and continuities', often resuming interests of the Victorian and Edwardian novel such as class. C.P. Snow describes England in *The Masters* (1951) as 'the country with the subtlest social divisions'[10]: as Snow's own fiction shows, the subtlety of English social sense and class division have continued to provide promising material for the novelist, precisely differentiating characters and providing a firm framework for their interaction with each other and with their communities. Continuing concern with class, however, 'the British language' as one of William Golding's characters calls it,[11] largely removes the need for amendment of the language or technique of fiction itself. The conventions of the Victorian or Edwardian novel remain adequate for more recent examinations of social divisions and behaviour: continuing use of these realist forms adds to what David Lodge describes in *The Novelist at the Crossroads* (1971) as 'a good deal of evidence that the English literary mind is peculiarly committed to realism, and resistant to non-realistic modes'.[12] This commitment is clearly demonstrated by some of the fiction of the nineteen thirties, as well as that of C.P. Snow and his contemporaries in the fifties. Many writers in both periods concentrate on social questions; reject modernism in favour of Edwardian forms; and show at times—in some of Evelyn Waugh's novels, or in Kingsley Amis's *I Like it Here* (1958), for example—a concomitant suspicion of foreign styles and influences.

Commitment to conventional realist methods, however, is by no means uniformly apparent in the period as a whole, but only one phase of the 'perpetual action and reaction', as Cyril Connolly calls it, of traditional and innovative styles throughout the development of twentieth-century fiction.[13] 'Resistance to non-realistic modes' has been much less evident in recent decades, for example. As Chapter Four suggests, views of the English novel as predominantly conventional may be part of what Malcolm Bradbury calls 'a depressing and outdated folklore' which grew up along with prognostications about 'the death of the novel' often made in the fifties or shortly thereafter.[14] As Lodge himself suggests in *The Novelist at the Crossroads*, it would also be an oversimplification to envisage 'an incorrigibly insular England defending an obsolete realism against... life-giving invasions' (p.9). Though many impulses toward change and innovation have originated abroad, significant developments have also been made by authors largely untouched by external influences—Henry Green, for example, or D.H. Lawrence, at least in the early part of his career. Some of the charges of parochialism made by the experimental novelists quoted at the end of Chapter Five are also less than wholly justified. It is true that the thoroughgoing acceptance and extension of modernist and other cosmopolitan influences which some of them seek has rarely been forthcoming in the English novel in the later twentieth century. But it is also true, as previous chapters have suggested, that the overall tendency of the past fifty years has certainly not been to reject modernism unreservedly. Instead, there is some evidence not of parochialism but of a particular openness of outlook in the British context; of modernist addition to 'the international store of literary

229

technique'[15] existing alongside conventional realist methods which Lodge and Bergonzi see as most characteristic of English writing.

The continuing existence of this diversity of influences, modernist and traditional, is summarised in Lodge's image of the contemporary novelist 'standing at a crossroads' (p.18). He defines 'the road on which he stands' as 'the realistic novel...coming down through the Victorians and Edwardians'—very much the same 'main road of English fiction' as that on which Gerald Bullett envisaged Hugh Walpole plodding along, 'an undaunted pedestrian', in his study *Modern English Fiction* in 1926.[16] This road has remained well-trodden throughout the century: since the modernist period, however, and in the light of some of the developments which have followed, it has been less easy, and less usual, to remain 'an undaunted pedestrian'. As Lodge remarks, there are 'formidable discouragements to continuing serenely along the road of fictional realism' (p.22). Instead, particularly since the fifties, both the main road and modernist or post-modernist alternatives have seemed appealing, often simultaneously. As Chapter Four indicated, many authors have as a result struck out not altogether on either road, but on paths which mediate between the directions suggested by each. Though it would be optimistic to think such paths invariably lead to fresh woods and pastures new, their appearance and the continuing freedom of choice between several directions, old and new, suggest that the novel is in a more promising position than is sometimes supposed. Just as the richness of the English language partly derives from its absorption of foreign vocabulary alongside native elements, British novelists may continue to benefit from the opportunity of integrating or choosing between a range of native traditions, 'cosmopolitan innovations of the Modern Movement', and foreign influences likely to multiply and diversify as part of the legacy of empire.

Such diversity and the fading of the conservatism of the fifties make obituaries for the novel seem increasingly inappropriate: instead, several contemporary critics express renewed optimism about the future. Malcolm Bradbury, for example, talks of 'a vigour and talent among younger British writers which points less to the end of the British novel than to a new period of expansion and possibility'. Anthony Burgess promises that 'the contemporary novel is not doing badly. Soon, when we least expect it, it will do not merely better but magnificently'.[17] 'Rash hopes' of this sort have been expressed at several stages in past decades—by Virginia Woolf in 1924, for example, and by Cyril Connolly in 1938—without as yet being wholly fulfilled. It is nevertheless a testimony to the continuing achievement of twentieth-century fiction that such hopes are still so confidently entertained, and that the novel still holds out such promise of vision and imaginative order in a century whose difficult progress has made such qualities more precarious and yet more than ever urgently required.

References

Preface (pages 7 to 9)

1 Malcolm Bradbury, Foreword to Jay L. Halio, ed., *Dictionary of Literary Biography*, vol. 14, *British Novelists Since 1960* (Detroit: Bruccoli Clark, 1983), pp.xi, xii.
2 E.M. Forster, *The Development of English Prose between 1918 and 1939* (Glasgow: Jackson, Son and Company, 1945), p.22. Several of the commentators quoted at the start of Chapters Two and Three make particularly strong connections between the development of fiction and the history of the times.
3 Alain Robbe-Grillet, *Snapshots and Towards a New Novel*, trans. Barbara Wright (London: Calder and Boyars, 1965), p.152.

Chapter 1 (pages 11 to 29)

1 Hugh Walpole, *A Letter to a Modern Novelist* (London: Hogarth Press, 1932), pp.25, 6, 11.
2 Stephen Spender, *The Struggle of the Modern* (London: Hamish Hamilton, 1963), p.x.
3 Virginia Woolf, 'Mr. Bennett and Mrs. Brown' (1924), rpt. in *Collected Essays* (London: Hogarth Press, 1966), I, pp.326, 332, 330; and 'Modern Fiction' (1919), rpt. in *Collected Essays*, II, pp.106, 104.
4 D.H. Lawrence, 'John Galsworthy' (1928), rpt. in Anthony Beal, ed., *Selected Literary Criticism* (London: Heinemann, 1967), pp.119, 121, 120.
5 H.G. Wells, *Kipps* (1905; rpt. London: Fontana, 1973), p.241; letter to Henry James, 8 July 1915, rpt. in Leon Edel and Gordon N. Ray, eds., *Henry James and H.G.*

Wells (London: Rupert Hart Davis, 1958), p.264.
6 Henry James, 'The Younger Generation', *Times Literary Supplement*, 19 March and 2 April 1914; rpt. in Edel and Ray, *Henry James and H.G. Wells*, pp.187-8. Other quotations are taken from pp.195, 196, 200.
7 Henry James, author's preface (c. 1906) to *The Princess Casamassima* (1886; rpt. Harmondsworth: Penguin, 1977), p.16.
8 See Edel and Ray, *Henry James and H.G. Wells*, especially pp.234-68.
9 Woolf, *Collected Essays*, II, p.106.
10 Dorothy Richardson, foreword (1938) to *Pilgrimage* (1915-38; rpt. London: Virago, 1979), I, pp.9, 12; 'H.C.H.', review of *The Trap*, *The Calendar of Modern Letters*, June 1925, pp.328-9.
11 D.H. Lawrence, *The Rainbow* (1915; rpt. Harmondsworth: Penguin, 1971), p.287.
12 Alan Friedman, 'The Novel', in C.B. Cox and A.E. Dyson, eds., *The Twentieth Century Mind* (London: Oxford University Press, 1972), I, p.442.
13 Woolf, *Collected Essays*, II, p.107.
14 E.M. Forster, *Aspects of the Novel* (1927; rpt. Harmondsworth: Penguin, 1971), p.35; Bennett's description is taken from the epigraph to his novel.
15 In his 'Author's Note' to the novel.
16 Ford Madox Ford, *Joseph Conrad: A Personal Remembrance* (London: Duckworth, 1924), pp.129-30.
17 For further discussions of the wider European context of Modernism, and of its origins in the nineteenth and early twentieth centuries, see

Malcolm Bradbury and James McFarlane, eds, *Modernism 1890-1930* (Harmondsworth: Penguin, 1976).

18 J.B. Priestley, *Literature and Western Man* (London: Heinemann, 1960), p.322.

19 Ford Madox Ford, *Parade's End* (1924-28; rpt. Harmondsworth; Penguin, 1982), p.510; Virginia Woolf, 'The Leaning Tower' (1940), rpt. in *Collected Essays*, II, p.167; D.H. Lawrence, *Lady Chatterley's Lover* (1928; rpt. Harmondsworth: Penguin, 1982), p.5.

20 Woolf, 'Mr. Bennett and Mrs. Brown', *Collected Essays*, I, p.320.

21 Priestley, *Literature and Western Man*, p.327.

22 David Daiches, *The Novel and the Modern World* (London: Cambridge University Press, 1960), p.6.

23 Roland Barthes, *S/Z*, trans. Richard Miller (New York: Hill and Wang, 1974), p.4. See also Barthes's 'From Work to Text' (1971), in *Image-Music-Text*, trans. Stephen Heath.

24 Ezra Pound, 'Paris Letter', *The Dial*, June 1922, p.625.

25 John Galsworthy, preface to *The Man of Property* (1906; rpt. London: Heinemann, 1953), p.vi; see, for example, Henry James's letter to H.G. Wells, 14 October 1909; rpt. in Edel and Ray, *Henry James and H.G. Wells*, pp.121-3.

26 Gerald Bullett, *Modern English Fiction* (London: Herbert Jenkins, 1926), p.121.

27 Woolf, *Collected Essays*, I, p.337.

Chapter 2 (pages 30 to 67)

1 Virginia Woolf, 'The Leaning Tower' (1940), rpt. in *Collected Essays* (London: Hogarth Press, 1966), II, p.172.

2 George Orwell, 'Inside the Whale' (1940), rpt. in Sonia Orwell and Ian Angus, eds, *The Collected Essays, Journalism and Letters of George Orwell* (1968; rpt. Harmondsworth: Penguin, 1970), I, pp.549, 560, 561.

3 Virginia Woolf, *Between the Acts* (1941; rpt. St Albans: Panther, 1980), pp.43, 86.

4 Stephen Spender, *World Within World*

(London: Hamish Hamilton, 1951), p.137; and Spender, 'W.H. Auden and his Poetry' (1953), rpt. in Monroe K. Spears, ed., *Auden: A Collection of Critical Essays* (New Jersey: Prentice-Hall, 1964), pp.32-3.

5 See Bernard Bergonzi, *Reading the Thirties: Texts and Contexts* (London: Macmillan, 1978), p.11.

6 See Christopher Isherwood, *Lions and Shadows* (1938; rpt. London: Methuen, 1982), pp.9, 46, etc.; Cyril Connolly, *Enemies of Promise* (1938; rpt. Harmondsworth: Penguin, 1979) p.210. Auden's remark is quoted in Bergonzi, *Reading the Thirties*, p.32.

7 W.W. Robson, *Modern English Literature* (Oxford: Oxford University Press, 1970), p.127.

8 A description used by Virginia Woolf, Ford Madox Ford and D.H. Lawrence: see Chapter One, note 19.

9 Orwell and Angus, eds, *The Collected Essays, Journalism and Letters of George Orwell*, I, p.288; Philip Henderson, *The Novel Today: A Study in Contemporary Attitudes* (London: John Lane, 1936), pp.52, 14, 28.

10 Ralph Fox, *The Novel and the People* (London: Lawrence and Wishart, 1937), pp.105, 106.

11 Georg Lukács, 'The Ideology of Modernism' (1955), rpt. in David Lodge, ed., *Twentieth Century Literary Criticism: A Reader* (London: Longman, 1972), pp.474, 479.

12 J.B. Priestley, *Literature and Western Man* (London: Heinemann, 1960), pp. 425-6.

13 Henderson, *The Novel Today*, p.27.

14 Connolly, *Enemies of Promise*, p.85.

15 See Chapter One, note 24.

16 Isherwood, *Lions and Shadows*, p.49; and Christopher Isherwood, Foreword to *All the Conspirators* (1928; rpt. London: Methuen, 1984), p.7.

17 Isherwood, Foreword, p.8.

18 ibid.

19 Isherwood, *Lions and Shadows*, p.182.

20 Christopher Isherwood, *The Memorial* (1932; rpt. St Albans: Panther, 1978), pp.45-6.

21 Ford's views are quoted fully in Chapter One, see note 16; Isherwood, *Lions and Shadows*, p.182.

22 Christopher Isherwood, *Mr Norris Changes Trains* (1935; rpt. St Albans: Panther, 1977), p.7.

23 Christopher Isherwood, *Goodbye to Berlin* (1939; rpt. London: Granada, 1983), p.11, introductory note.

24 G.S. Fraser, 'The English Novel' in C.B. Cox and A.E. Dyson, eds., *The Twentieth Century Mind* (London: Oxford University Press, 1972), II, p.375.

25 Connolly, *Enemies of Promise*, p.82.

26 Bernard Crick, *George Orwell: A Life* (1980; rpt. Harmondsworth: Penguin, 1982), p.352.

27 George Orwell, 'Why I Write' (1946), rpt. in Orwell and Angus, eds, *The Collected Essays, Journalism and Letters of George Orwell*, I, p.26.

28 George Orwell, *A Clergyman's Daughter* (1935; rpt. Harmondsworth: Penguin, 1982), p.175; Orwell, 'Why I Write', pp.24, 28.

29 Paul Beard in the *New English Weekly*, 25 June 1936; quoted in Crick, *George Orwell*, p.301.

30 Robson, *Modern English Literature*, p.150.

31 George Orwell, *Coming up for Air* (1939; rpt. Harmondsworth: Penguin, 1962), p.7.

32 George Orwell, 'Shooting an Elephant' (1936), rpt. in Orwell and Angus, eds, *The Collected Essays, Journalism and Letters of George Orwell*, I, p.269.

33 Orwell, 'Why I Write', p.28.

34 Orwell, 'Inside the Whale', p.576.

35 Connolly, *Enemies of Promise*, p.93.

36 Letter to T.R. Fyvel, rpt. in Orwell and Angus, eds, *The Collected Essays, Journalism and Letters of George Orwell*, IV, p.558.

37 Graham Greene, *Ways of Escape*, (London: The Bodley Head, 1980), p.74.

38 See particularly Chapter Three of Bergonzi, *Reading the Thirties*.

39 Graham Greene, *It's a Battlefield* (1934; rpt. Harmondsworth: Penguin, 1978), p.127.

40 Greene, *Ways of Escape*, p.88.

41 Graham Greene, *The Confidential Agent* (1939; rpt. Harmondsworth: Penguin, 1967), pp.64-5.

42 Brian Finney, *Christopher Isherwood: A Critical Biography* (London: Faber, 1979), p.81; and Crick, *George Orwell*, p.256.

43 Connolly, *Enemies of Promise*, p.113.

44 Rex Warner, Author's Note to *The Aerodrome* (1941; rpt. Oxford: Oxford University Press, 1982).

45 Rex Warner, *The Wild Goose Chase* (London: Boriswood, 1937), p.111.

46 Warner, *The Aerodrome*, pp.136, 261.

47 Rex Warner, 'The Uses of Allegory', *Penguin New Writing*, 17, 1946, p.148.

48 Edward Upward, *Journey to the Border* (London: Hogarth Press, 1938), p.202.

49 Quoted in Bergonzi, *Reading the Thirties*, p.1.

50 Walter Greenwood, *Love on the Dole* (1933; rpt. Harmondsworth: Penguin, 1983), p.13.

51 Lewis Grassic Gibbon, *A Scots Quair* (1932, 1933, 1934; rpt. London: Pan, 1982), *Grey Granite*, p.48.

52 *Cloud Howe*, p.126; *Grey Granite*, pp.48, 141, 161, 167.

53 *Cloud Howe*, p.166, *Sunset Song*, p.252.

54 Wyndham Lewis, *The Art of Being Ruled* (London: Chatto and Windus, 1926), p.370.

55 Wyndham Lewis, *The Revenge for Love* (1937; rpt. London: Secker and Warburg, 1982), p.145.

56 Evelyn Waugh, *Scoop* (1938; rpt. Harmondsworth: Penguin, 1982), p.32.

57 Evelyn Waugh, *Decline and Fall* (1928; rpt. Harmondsworth: Penguin, 1982), p.100.

58 Evelyn Waugh, *Vile Bodies* (1930; rpt. Harmondsworth: Penguin, 1982), p.29.

59 Malcolm Bradbury, *Evelyn Waugh* (London: Oliver and Boyd, 1964), pp.1, 14.

60 Sonia Trumpington in Evelyn Waugh, *Black Mischief* (1932; rpt. Harmondsworth, Penguin, 1981), p.231.

61 Waugh, *Decline and Fall*, p.124; Evelyn Waugh, Preface to *Brideshead*

Revisited (1945; rpt. Harmondsworth: Penguin, 1972), p.7; *Scoop*, p.24; *Vile Bodies*, p.132.

62 L.H. Myers, *The Near and the Far* (1929 1931, 1935, 1940; rpt. London: Jonathan Cape, 1940), *The Pool of Vishnu*, p.409.

63 Robson, *Modern English Literature*, pp. 135, 136-7.

64 Quoted in P.H. Newby, *The Novel 1945-1950* (London: Longmans, Green, and Co., 1951), p.30.

65 Ivy Compton-Burnett, *Pastors and Masters* (1925; rpt. London: Gollancz, 1965), p.101.

66 John Melmoth, 'Suckfist Obsessions', *Times Literary Supplement*, 14 June 1985, p.677.

67 Angus Wilson, '"Mythology" in John Cowper Powys's Novels', *Review of English Literature*, January 1963, p.9. This special Powys number also contains approving essays by Henry Miller and J.B. Priestley.

68 T.F. Powys, *Mr Weston's Good Wine* (1927; rpt. London: Hogarth Press, 1984), p.28.

69 George Orwell, Letter to Brenda Salkeld, September? 1934, rpt. in Orwell and Angus, eds, *The Collected Essays, Journalism and Letters of George Orwell*, I, p.163. See also pp.150-154.

70 Malcolm Lowry, *Ultramarine* (1933; rpt. Harmondsworth: Penguin, 1980), p.51.

71 Rosamond Lehmann, *The Weather in the Streets* (1936; rpt. London: Virago, 1981), p.211.

72 William Gerhardie, *Of Mortal Love* (1936; rpt. Harmondsworth: Penguin, 1982), p.153.

73 Julian Symons, *The Thirties: A Dream Revolved* (London: Cresset Press, 1960), p.173, etc.

74 Charles Madge and Tom Harrisson, quoted in Samuel Hynes, *The Auden Generation: Literature and Politics in England in the 1930s* (London: Bodley Head, 1976), p.279.

75 Quoted in Finney, *Christopher Isherwood*, p.130.

76 Woolf, 'The Leaning Tower', *Collected Essays*, II, p.177.

77 Hynes, *The Auden Generation*, p.393.

78 Some reassessment of the sort suggested appears in Frank Gloversmith, ed., *Class, Culture and Social Change: A New View of the 1930s* (Brighton: Harvester, 1980) which reconsiders, among other issues, the extent and nature of political commitment among thirties authors.

79 Cyril Connolly, *The Rock Pool* (1936; rpt. Oxford: Oxford University Press, 1981), p.131.

80 Cyril Connolly, *The Modern Movement* (London: Andre Deutsch and Hamish Hamilton, 1965), p.67.

Chapter 3 (pages 68 to 122)

1 George Orwell, 'Inside the Whale' (1940), rpt. in Sonia Orwell and Ian Angus, eds, *The Collected Essays, Journalism and Letters of George Orwell* (1968; rpt. Harmondsworth: Penguin), 1970, I, p.578; Rosamond Lehmann, 'The Future of the Novel?' *Britain Today*, June 1946, pp.6-7.

2 P.H. Newby, *The Novel 1945-1950* (London: Longmans, Green and Co., 1951), p.13.

3 Robert Liddell, *Some Principles of Fiction* (London: Cape, 1953), p.13.

4 Cyril Connolly, *The Modern Movement* (London: Deutsch, 1965), p.85.

5 W.W. Robson, *Modern English Literature* (Oxford: Oxford University Press, 1970), p.146; Robert Hewison, *Under Siege* (London: Quartet Books, 1979), p.185.

6 See Elizabeth Bowen's remarks in V.S. Pritchett, ed., *Why do I Write?* (London: Percival Marshall, 1948), p.54.

7 C.S. Forester, *The Ship* (1943; rpt. Harmondsworth: Penguin, 1949), p.97.

8 Brian Howard, *New Statesman*, 7 September 1940; quoted in Hewison, *Under Siege*, p.27.

9 Evelyn Waugh, *Sword of Honour* (1952-61; rpt. Harmondsworth: Penguin, 1984), p.416.

10 Lehmann, 'The Future of the Novel?', p.5.

11 Tom Harrisson, 'War Books', December 1941, pp.417, 418, 436.

12 Samuel Hynes, *The Auden Generation* (London: The Bodley Head, 1976), p.382.

13 George Orwell, *The Lion and the Unicorn* (London: Secker and Warburg, 1941), pp.32, 95.

14 Walter Allen, 'Books and the War, VIII', *Penguin New Writing*, 1941, no.9, p.121.

15 Negley Farson, *Bomber's Moon* (London, Gollancz, 1941), p.38. Henry Green, 'Mr. Jonas', *Penguin New Writing*, 1942, no.14, p.15. Keith Douglas, *Alamein to Zem Zem* (1946; rpt. Harmondsworth: Penguin, 1966), pp.6, 20.

16 Quoted from Sansom's journal in Hewison, *Under Siege*, p.87.

17 Angus Calder, *The People's War* (London: Panther, 1971), p.590. I am also indebted to Angus Calder's unpublished lecture to the Scottish Universities' International Summer School, 'Britain in the Second World War', August 1981.

18 Graham Greene, *Ways of Escape* (London: The Bodley Head, 1980), pp.101-113; and see *Penguin New Writing*, 1941, no.4, and 1942, no.14.

19 'A Reader's Notebook, V', *Penguin New Writing*, 1943. no.17, pp.158-9.

20 J.B. Priestley, *Daylight on Saturday* (London: The Reprint Society, 1944), pp.214, 302. The other parts of the trilogy are *Black-out in Gretley: a Story of—and for—Wartime* (1942), and *Three Men in New Suits* (1945).

21 Newby, *The Novel 1945-1950*, p.14.

22 ibid., p.13.

23 Robson, *Modern English Literature*, p.143.

24 Tom Harrisson, 'War Books', *Horizon*, December 1941, p.432.

25 Anthony Burgess, *Ninety-nine Novels: the Best in English since 1939* (London: Allison and Busby, 1984) p.109.

26 Newby, *The Novel 1945-1950*, p.14.

27 James Hanley, *No Directions* (1943; rpt. London: Nicholson and Watson, 1946) p.v.

28 Walter Allen, *Tradition and Dream* (London: Dent, 1964), p.217;

Evelyn Waugh, *Put out More Flags* (1942; rpt. Harmondsworth: Penguin, 1943) p.5.

29 Henry Green, *Caught* (1943; rpt. London: Hogarth Press, 1978), p.43.

30 Lehmann, 'The Future of the Novel?' pp.6-7.

31 Allen, *Tradition and Dream*, p.214.

32 Henry Green, *Living* (1929; rpt. with *Loving* and *Party Going*, London: Picador, 1979), p.207.

33 G.S. Fraser, 'The English Novel', in C.B. Cox and A.E. Dyson, eds, *The Twentieth Century Mind* (London: Oxford University Press, 1972), II, pp.413-14.

34 Frederick R. Karl, *A Reader's Guide to the Contemporary English Novel* (London: Thames and Hudson, 1972), p.192; Henry Green, 'A Novelist to his Readers— Communication without Speech', *The Listener*, 9 November 1950, p.506.

35 See Nathalie Sarraute, *Tropisms and The Age of Suspicion*, (1939), trans. Maria Jolas, (1956; rpt. London: John Calder, 1963), p.102, etc.

36 Fraser, 'The English Novel', p.375.

37 *Penguin New Writing*, 1941, no.11, p.8; Lehmann, 'The Future of the Novel?' p.7; Newby, *The Novel 1945-1950*, p.8.

38 Lehmann, 'The Future of the Novel?' p.10.

39 Anna Kavan, 'Selected Notices', *Horizon*, February 1945, p.145.

40 Rosamond Lehmann, *The Ballad and the Source* (1944; rpt. London: Virago, 1982), p.82.

41 Elizabeth Bowen, *The House in Paris* (1935; rpt. Harmondsworth: Penguin, 1983), p.77; Elizabeth Bowen, *English Novelists* (London: Collins, 1942), p.48.

42 Elizabeth Bowen, *The Death of the Heart* (1938; rpt. Harmondsworth: Penguin, 1981), p.171.

43 Elizabeth Bowen, 'Truth and Fiction', in *Afterthought: Pieces About Writing* (London: Longmans, 1962), p.124.

44 Burgess, *Ninety-nine Novels*, p.45.

45 Elizabeth Bowen, *The Heat of the Day* (1949; rpt. Harmondsworth: Penguin, 1983), pp.90-92, 100.

46 Newby, *The Novel 1945-1950*, p.20.

47 L.P. Hartley, *Eustace and Hilda* (1944-47; rpt. London: Faber, 1979), p.180.

48 See Chapter One, note 6.

49 L.P. Hartley, *The Go-Between* (1953; rpt. Harmondsworth: Penguin, 1983), pp.7, 264.

50 Henry Reed, *The Novel since 1939* (London: Longmans, Green, and Co., 1946), p.15.

51 Forrest Reid, *Young Tom* (London: Faber, 1944), p.164.

52 John Cousins, *The Desolate Market* (London: Cape, 1948), p.23.

53 Henry Green, *Pack My Bag*, (London: Hogarth Press, 1940), p.5.

54 Newby, *The Novel 1945-1950*, p.24.

55 P.H. Newby, *A Step to Silence* (London: Cape, 1952), p.184.

56 P.H. Newby, *The Retreat* (London: Cape, 1953), p.100.

57 Stephen Spender, 'Books and the War, V' and 'Books and the War, VII', *Penguin New Writing*, 1941, nos. 6 and 8, pp.129, 130; Cyril Connolly, editorial in *Horizon*, 1941, p.6.

58 Graham Greene, *A Sort of Life* (Harmondsworth: Penguin, 1972), p.85.

59 As Greene mentions in *Ways of Escape*, p.86.

60 Graham Greene, *The Power and the Glory* (1940; rpt. Harmondsworth: Penguin, 1978), p.25.

61 Graham Greene, *The End of the Affair* (1951; rpt. Harmondsworth: Penguin, 1976), p.27.

62 Graham Greene, *Brighton Rock* (1938; rpt. Harmondsworth: Penguin, 1976) p.127.

63 'Life on the Border', (1939), in Philip Stratford, ed., *The Portable Graham Greene* (Harmondsworth: Penguin, 1981), p.7.

64 Greene, *Ways of Escape*, p.136.

65 ibid, pp.136-8.

66 W.Somerset Maugham, *The Razor's Edge* (1944; rpt. London: Pan, 1981), pp.71, 252.

67 Graham Greene, 'Some Notes on Somerset Maugham', (1935-38), rpt. in *Collected Essays* (Harmondsworth: Penguin, 1970), p.154.

68 In *The Novel Now* (London: Faber, 1971), Burgess calls *Cakes and Ale* 'one of the best novels of the twentieth century', (p.208), though he goes on to express some reservations.

69 'Prefatory Essay' to Joyce Cary, *Herself Surprised* (1941; rpt. London: Michael Joseph, 1958), p.7.

70 Joyce Cary, *Herself Surprised*, rpt. with *To be a Pilgrim* and *The Horse's Mouth* as *Triptych* (Harmondsworth: Penguin, 1985), p.80. Subsequent references to the novels are to this edition.

71 Joyce Cary, *Art and Reality* (Cambridge: Cambridge University Press, 1958), pp.149, 158.

72 Gilbert Phelps, 'The Novel Today', in Boris Ford, ed., *The Pelican Guide to English Literature: the Modern Age* (Harmondsworth: Penguin, 1973), pp.506, 509.

73 'Prefatory Essay' to *Herself Surprised*, (note 69) p.7.

74 Reed, *The Novel since 1939*, p.27.

75 Joyce Cary, 'Prefatory Essay' to *To be a Pilgrim* (1942; rpt. London: Michael Joseph, 1953), pp.7, 8.

76 Reed, *The Novel since 1939*, p.23.

77 Philip Toynbee, *The Garden to the Sea* (London: MacGibbon and Kee, 1953), title page.

78 C.S. Lewis, *Voyage to Venus (Perelandra)* (1943; rpt. London: Pan, 1953), p.8.

79 John Lehmann, Foreword to *Penguin New Writing*, 1941, no. 7, p.7. Newby's and Rosamond Lehmann's remarks are quoted earlier in this chapter; see note 37.

80 Mervyn Peake, *The Titus Books* (1946-59; rpt. Harmondsworth: Penguin, 1983), pp.228, 374, 396.

81 Burgess, *Ninety-nine Novels*, p.36.

82 See Colin Manlove's interesting study of Peake in his *Modern Fantasy* (Cambridge: Cambridge Univesity Press, 1975), p.215; and, for example, Cyril Connolly's editorials in *Horizon*, 1945-6.

83 Mervyn Peake, *Mr. Pye* (London: Heinemann, 1953), p.188.

84 Wyndham Lewis, *Malign Fiesta* (1955; rpt. London: John Calder, 1965), p.62.

85 Wyndham Lewis, *Monstre Gai* (1955;

rpt. London: John Calder, 1965),
p.19.

86 Wyndham Lewis, *Self Condemned*
(1954; rpt. Manchester: Carcanet,
1983), pp.28, 93.

87 Walter Allen, *The Novel Today*,
(London: Longmans, Green and Co.
1955), p.32.

88 Allen, *Tradition and Dream*, pp.263,
265.

89 See Malcolm Lowry, *Dark as the
Grave wherein my Friend is Laid*
(1969; rpt. Harmondsworth:
Penguin, 1975), p.77.

90 Malcolm Lowry, *Under the Volcano*
(1947; rpt. Harmondsworth:
Penguin, 1983), p.33.

91 Malcolm Lowry, letter to Jonathan
Cape, 2 January 1946, rpt. in
Harvey Breit and Margerie Bonner
Lowry, *Selected Letters of Malcolm
Lowry* (1967; rpt. Harmondsworth:
Penguin, 1985), p.66.

92 Stephen Spender, 'Books and the
War, III', *Penguin New Writing*,
1941, no.4, p.145.

93 *Selected Letters*, p.66.
94 ibid., p.73.
95 ibid., p.66.
96 ibid., p.67.
97 ibid., p.88.
98 Burgess, *Ninety-nine Novels*, p.38.
99 Lowry, *Dark as the Grave wherein my
Friend is Laid*, pp.58, 255.
100 Lowry, *Selected Letters*, p.67.
101 William Sansom, *Fireman Flower*
(1944; rpt. London: Hogarth Press,
1966), pp.233-4, 132.
102 William Sansom, *The Body* (London:
Hogarth Press, 1949), pp.20, 200.
103 Graham Greene, *The Heart of the
Matter* (1948; rpt. Harmondsworth:
Penguin, 1974), pp.260, etc.
104 Connolly's remarks are quoted
earlier, see note 4. Walter Allen,
'Books and the War, VIII', *Penguin
New Writing*, 1941, no.9, p.121;
Reed, *The Novel since 1939*, p.21;
Newby, *The Novel 1945-1950*, pp.14,
24; Liddell, *Some Principles of Fiction*,
pp.13, 14.
105 G.S. Fraser, 'The English Novel'
(note 33), p.410.
106 William Plomer, *Museum Pieces*
(1952; rpt. Harmondsworth:
Penguin, 1961), p.92.

107 Allen, *The Novel Today*, p.29.
108 Burgess, *The Novel Now*, p.49.
109 Allen, *Tradition and Dream*, p.262.
110 Newby, *The Novel 1945-1950*, p.21.
111 See remarks on Philip Henderson,
Ralph Fox, and Georg Lukács in
Chapter Two. Lukács's remark
about 'the denial of history' is in
'The Ideology of Modernism'
(1955), rpt. in David Lodge, ed.,
*Twentieth Century Literary Criticism:
A Reader* (London: Longman, 1972),
p.486.

Chapter 4 (pages 123 to 193)

1 John Wain, Introduction to *Hurry on
Down* (1953; rpt. Harmondsworth:
Penguin, 1979), pp.1-2.
2 Doris Lessing, 'The Small Personal
Voice', in Tom Maschler, ed.,
Declaration (London: MacGibbon
and Kee, 1957), pp.27, 23.
3 John Osborne, *Look Back in Anger*
(1957; rpt. London: Faber, 1978),
p.84.
4 Kenneth Allsop, *The Angry Decade: A
Survey of the Cultural Revolt of the
Nineteen-Fifties* (London: Peter
Owen, 1958), p.10.
5 William Cooper, *Scenes from
Provincial Life* (1959; rpt. London:
Methuen, 1983), p.21.
6 Quoted by Malcolm Bradbury in his
introduction to *Scenes from Provincial
Life*, p.1.
7 Walter Allen, *Tradition and Dream*
(London: Dent, 1964), p.280.
8 Wain, *Hurry on Down*, p.250.
9 John Braine, *Room at the Top* (1957;
rpt. Harmondsworth: Penguin,
1983), pp.28, 47.
10 'The State of Fiction: A Symposium',
The New Review, Summer 1978,
p.23.
11 Alan Sillitoe, *Saturday Night and
Sunday Morning* (1958; rpt. London:
Star, 1983), p.220.
12 Allan Sillitoe, *The Loneliness of the
Long Distance Runner* (1959; rpt.
London: Star, 1983), pp.9-10, 7.
13 Alan Sillitoe, *A Tree on Fire* (1967;
rpt. London: Star, 1979), p.274.
14 Lionel Stevenson, *The History of the
English Novel*, vol.11, *Yesterday and
After* (New York: Barnes and Noble,
1967), p.404.

15 Bernard Bergonzi, *The Situation of the Novel* (London: Macmillan, 1970), p.165.

16 Kingsley Amis, *Take a Girl Like You* (1960; rpt. Harmondsworth: Penguin, 1980), p.62.

17 Anthony Burgess, *Ninety-Nine Novels* (London: Allison and Busby, 1984), p.64; Bergonzi, *The Situation of the Novel*, p.166.

18 In Boris Ford, ed., *The Pelican Guide to English Literature*, vol.7, *The Modern Age* (Harmondsworth: Penguin, 1978), pp.511-13.

19 *The New Review* Symposium (note 10), p.49.

20 William Cooper, 'Reflections on Some Aspects of the Experimental Novel', in John Wain, ed., *International Literary Annual*, no.2; Kingsley Amis in the *Spectator*, 2 May 1958; both quoted in Rubin Rabinovitz, *The Reaction Against Experiment in the English Novel, 1950-1960* (New York: Columbia University Press, 1967), pp.6-7, 40.

21 C.P. Snow, 'Challenge to the Intellect', and Angus Wilson, 'Diversity and Depth', *Times Literary Supplement*, 15 August 1958, pp.iii, viii.

22 Angus Wilson, 'Arnold Bennett's Novels', *London Magazine*, October 1954, p.60.

23 David Storey, *This Sporting Life* (1960; rpt. Harmondsworth: Penguin, 1979), pp.229, 171.

24 David Storey, *Radcliffe* (1963; rpt. Harmondsworth: Penguin, 1979), p.341.

25 David Storey, *Pasmore* (1972; rpt. Harmondsworth: Penguin, 1976), pp.27, 171.

26 Angus Wilson, 'Mood of the Month—III', *London Magazine*, April 1958, p.44.

27 Angus Wilson, *Anglo-Saxon Attitudes* (1956; rpt. Harmondsworth: Penguin, 1976), p.108; Malcolm Cowley, ed., *Writers at Work: The 'Paris Review' Interviews*, first series (London: Secker and Warburg, 1958), p.231.

28 Angus Wilson, *Late Call* (1964; rpt. London: Granada, 1982), p.63.

29 Angus Wilson, *The Old Men at the Zoo* (1961; rpt. Harmondsworth: Penguin, 1976), pp.180, 229.

30 Angus Wilson in James Vinson, ed., *Contemporary Novelists* (London: St James's Press, 1976), 2nd edition, p.1516; and Wilson, 'Diversity and Depth', *Times Literary Supplement*, 15 August 1958, p.viii.

31 Angus Wilson, *No Laughing Matter* (1967; rpt. St Albans: Panther, 1979), pp.355, 478.

32 Wilson, *Late Call*, p.49.

33 Malcolm Bradbury, *Possibilities: Essays on the State of the Novel* (London: Oxford University Press, 1973), p.211.

34 These are: *Strangers and Brothers* (*George Passant* (1940)); *The Light and the Dark* (1947); *Time of Hope* (1949); *The Masters* (1951); *The New Men* (1954); *Homecomings* (1956); *The Conscience of the Rich* (1958); *The Affair* (1960); *Corridors of Power* (1964); *The Sleep of Reason* (1968); *Last Things* (1970).

35 C.P. Snow, *The New Men* (1954; rpt. Harmondsworth: Penguin, 1982), p.212.

36 C.P. Snow, *The Masters* (1951; rpt. Harmondsworth: Penguin, 1983), p.153.

37 Snow, *The New Men*, p.97.

38 Bergonzi, *The Situation of the Novel*, p.138.

39 These are: *A Question of Upbringing* (1951); *A Buyer's Market* (1952); *The Acceptance World* (1955); *At Lady Molly's* (1957); *Casanova's Chinese Restaurant* (1960); *The Kindly Ones* (1962); *The Valley of Bones* (1964); *The Soldier's Art* (1966); *The Military Philosophers* (1968); *Books do Furnish a Room* (1971); *Temporary Kings* (1973); *Hearing Secret Harmonies* (1975).

40 Anthony Powell, *The Acceptance World* (1955; rpt. London: Fontana, 1983), p.186; *A Buyer's Market* (1952; rpt. London: Fontana, 1980), p.274. *A Question of Upbringing* (1951; rpt. London: Fontana, 1980), p.202.

41 *The Acceptance World*, p.128.

42 ibid., p.173.

43 Anthony Burgess, *The Novel Now* (London: Faber, 1971), p.84.

44 Bergonzi, *The Situation of the Novel*, p.122.

45 C.P. Snow 'Challenge to the Intellect', *Times Literary Supplement*, 15 August 1958, p.iii.

46 Anthony Powell, *Books do Furnish a Room* (1971; rpt. London: Fontana, 1972), p.9.

47 These are: *The Dark Lantern* (1951); *Donkey Boy* (1952); *Young Phillip Maddison* (1953); *How Dear is Life* (1954); *A Fox under my Cloak* (1955); *The Golden Virgin* (1957); *Love and the Loveless* (1958); *A Test to Destruction* (1960); *The Innocent Moon* (1961); *It was the Nightingale* (1962); *The Power of the Dead* (1963); *The Phoenix Generation* (1965); *A Solitary War* (1966); *Lucifer Before Sunrise* (1967); *The Gale of the World* (1969).

48 Henry Williamson, *The Dark Lantern* (1951; rpt. London: Zenith, 1984), pp.172, 307.

49 Burgess, *The Novel Now*, p.19.

50 Farrell's remark is quoted in the note to Penguin editions of his novels.

51 Kingsley Amis, *The James Bond Dossier* (London: Cape, 1965), pp.88, 92, 147.

52 ibid., p.9. Amis used the name 'Robert Markham'.

53 Paul Scott, *Staying On* (1977; rpt. London: Granada, 1983), p.8.

54 J.G. Farrell, *The Siege of Krishnapur* (1973; rpt. Harmondsworth: Penguin, 1983), p.53.

55 Julian Mitchell, *The White Father* (London: Constable, 1964), p.164.

56 The phrase is taken from Margaret Drabble, *The Ice Age* (1977; rpt. Harmondsworth: Penguin, 1983), p.55.

57 Jean Rhys, *Good Morning, Midnight* (1939; rpt. Harmondsworth: Penguin, 1983), pp.37, 87.

58 Introduction to Jean Rhys, *Wide Sargasso Sea* (1966; rpt. Harmondsworth: Penguin, 1977), p.9.

59 ibid., p.62.

60 *The New Review* Symposium (note 10), p.39.

61 Eva Figes, *Waking* (London: Hamish Hamilton, 1981), p.28.

62 Anita Brookner, *Providence* (1982; rpt. London: Granada, 1983), pp.83-4.

68 Edna O'Brien, *Casualties of Peace* (1966; rpt. Harmondsworth: Penguin, 1979), p.31.

69 Margaret Drabble, *The Millstone* (1965; rpt. Harmondsworth: Penguin, 1981), p.102.

70 Drabble in Vinson, ed., *Contemporary Novelists*, p.373.

71 Drabble, *The Ice Age*, p.253.

72 *The Millstone*, p.18.

73 See note 18; pp.517-18.

74 'The Small Personal Voice', (note 2), pp.22, 14.

75 Doris Lessing, *The Golden Notebook* (1962; rpt. St Albans: Granada, 1972), p.7.

76 Title page of Doris Lessing, *Briefing for a Descent into Hell* (1971; rpt. London: Granada, 1982).

77 Doris Lessing, *The Summer Before the Dark* (1973; rpt. Harmondsworth: Penguin, 1976), pp.77-8.

78 Emma Tennant, *The Bad Sister* (1978; London: Picador, 1979), pp.63, 28, 101, 137.

79 Angela Carter, *The Infernal Desire Machines of Doctor Hoffman* (1972; rpt. Harmondsworth: Penguin, 1982), pp.207, 14, 19.

80 *The New Review* Symposium (note 10), p.65.

81 Fay Weldon, *Down among the Women* (1971; rpt. Harmondsworth: Penguin, 1983), pp.83, 40-41.

82 *The New Review* Symposium (note 10), pp.65, 51.

83 Susan Hill, *Strange Meeting*, (1971; rpt. Harmondsworth: Penguin, 1982), p.105.

84 Olivia Manning, *The Balkan Trilogy* (1960, 1962, 1965; rpt. Harmondsworth: Penguin, 1982), pp.692, 30.

85 Richard Hughes, *A High Wind in Jamaica* (1929; rpt. St Albans: Panther, 1976), p.166.

86 In his Note to *The Fox in the Attic* (1961; rpt. St Albans: Panther, 1979).

87 ibid., pp.34, 98.

88 Note to *The Fox in the Attic*.

89 Gabriel Fielding, *The Birthday King* (London: Hutchinson, 1962), p.18.

90 'Author's Note' to D.M. Thomas, *The White Hotel* (Harmondsworth: Penguin, 1981).

91 Burgess, *The Novel Now*, p.184.

92 William Golding, *Darkness Visible* (1979; rpt. London: Faber, 1980), p.20.

93 Allen, *Tradition and Dream*, p.291.

94 William Golding, *Lord of the Flies* (1954; rpt. London: Faber, 1967), p.223.

95 William Golding, *The Inheritors* (1955; rpt. London: Faber, 1979), pp.163, 194, 195.

96 William Golding, *Pincher Martin* (1956; rpt. London: Faber, 1979), p.180.

97 Interview with Frank Kermode, 'The House of Fiction', in Malcolm Bradbury, ed., *The Novel Today* (London: Fontana, 1977), p.130.

98 This charge probably originates in James Gindin's *Postwar British Fiction: New Accents and Attitudes* (Berkeley: University of California Press, 1962).

99 William Golding, *Rites of Passage* (1980; rpt. London: Faber, 1982), pp.191, 278.

100 Iris Murdoch, 'Against Dryness' (1961), rpt. in Bradbury, ed., *The Novel Today*, pp.23, 30.

101 Iris Murdoch, *A Fairly Honourable Defeat* (1970; rpt. Harmondsworth: Penguin, 1984), p.430.

102 Iris Murdoch, *Under the Net* (1954; rpt. London: Granada, 1983), p.252.

103 J.P. Donleavy, *The Ginger Man* (1955; rpt. Harmondsworth: Penguin, 1982), p.240.

104 Murdoch, 'Against Dryness' (note 100), p.30.

105 Iris Murdoch, *A Severed Head* (1961; rpt. London: Granada, 1980), p.65.

106 Interview with Frank Kermode, 'The House of Fiction' (note 97), p.115.

107 Iris Murdoch, *The Sea, The Sea* (1978; rpt. London: Granada, 1981), pp.35, 29, 163.

108 Murdoch, 'Against Dryness' (note 100), pp.30-31.

109 Anthony Burgess, *Earthly Powers* (1980; rpt. Harmondsworth: Penguin, 1981), p.634.

110 George Plimpton, ed., *Writers at Work: the 'Paris Review' Interviews*, 4th series, (1977; rpt. Harmondsworth: Penguin, 1982), pp.347, 348, 354.

111 ibid., p.349.

112 Anthony Burgess, *A Clockwork Orange* (1962; rpt. Harmondsworth: Penguin, 1976), p.34.

113 *The 'Paris Review' Interviews* (note 110), p.342.

114 Murdoch, 'Against Dryness' (note 100), p.27.

115 ibid., p.27.

116 Burgess, *The Novel Now*, p.192.

117 Muriel Spark, *The Comforters* (1957; rpt. Harmondsworth: Penguin, 1978), pp.63, 104.

118 Muriel Spark, *The Prime of Miss Jean Brodie* (1961; rpt. Harmondsworth: Penguin, 1982), p.42.

119 Ian McEwan, *The Cement Garden* (1978; rpt. London: Picador, 1980), p.81.

120 'Points of Departure', Interview with Ian Hamilton, *The New Review*, Autumn 1978, p.21.

121 Ian McEwan, *The Comfort of Strangers* (1981; rpt. London: Picador, 1982), pp.79, 125.

122 William Trevor, *The Children of Dynmouth* (1976; rpt. Harmondsworth: Penguin, 1982), p.126.

123 Malcolm Bradbury, *Rates of Exchange* (1983; rpt. London: Arena, 1984), pp.20-22.

124 Evelyn Waugh, *The Loved One* (1948; rpt. Harmondsworth: Penguin, 1983), p.33; Beryl Bainbridge, 'Purposeful Children', *Times Literary Supplement*, 17 May 1985, p.554.

125 Beryl Bainbridge, *A Quiet Life* (1976; rpt. London: Fontana, 1983), pp.56-7, 121.

126 'Amis and Connolly: the Best-Seller Boys', *Cosmopolitan*, August 1978, pp.71-2.

127 Made in his play *Huis Clos* (*In Camera*, 1945).

128 Martin Amis, *Other People: A Mystery Story* (1981; rpt. Harmondsworth: Penguin, 1982), p.205.

129 *The New Review* Symposium (note 10), p.18.

130 Angus Wilson, 'Diversity and Depth' (note 30), p.viii.

131 *The New Review* Symposium (note 10), p.49.

132 In his Afterword to *The British Museum is Falling Down* (1965; rpt. Harmondsworth: Penguin, 1983), p.170.
133 ibid., p.168.
134 Lodge in Vinson, ed., *Contemporary Novelists* (note 30), p.833.
135 ibid., p.833.
136 Malcolm Bradbury, *The History Man* (1975; rpt. London: Arrow, 1978), pp.3, 7.
137 Malcolm Bradbury, *Possibilities: Essays on the State of the Novel* (London: Oxford University Press, 1973), p.229; Foreword to Jay L. Halio, ed., *Dictionary of Literary Biography*, vol.14, *British Novelists since 1960* (Detroit: Bruccoli Clark, 1983), p.xvi; Bradbury, *The Novel Today* (note 97), p.20; *The New Review Symposium* (note 10), p.25.
138 Frederick R. Karl, *A Reader's Guide to the Contemporary English Novel* (London: Thames and Hudson, 1972), p.328.

Chapter 5 (pages 194 to 224)
1 James Joyce, *A Portrait of the Artist as a Young Man* (1916; rpt. Harmondsworth: Penguin, 1973), pp.166-7.
2 Viriginia Woolf, *To the Lighthouse* (1927; rpt. Harmondsworth: Penguin, 1972), p.202.
3 See, for example, some of the stories in *In Our Time* (1925); and *Men without Women* (1928); and *A Farewell to Arms* (1929), especially Chapter III of 'Caporetto'.
4 Eugene Jolas, 'The Revolution of Language and James Joyce', in Samuel Beckett and others, *Our Exagmination Round his Factification for Incamination of Work in Progress* (1929; rpt. London: Faber, 1972), pp.91, 79.
5 James Joyce, *Finnegans Wake* (1939; rpt. London: Faber, 1975), p.152.
6 Samuel Beckett, 'Dante...Bruno. Vico..Joyce' in *Our Exagmination Round his Factification for Incamination of Work in Progress*, p.14.
7 Samuel Beckett, *Murphy* (1938; rpt. London: Picador, 1973), pp.101, 6.
8 Samuel Beckett, *Molloy* (1950); rpt. with *Malone Dies* and *The Unnamable* as *The Beckett Trilogy* (1959; rpt. London: Picador, 1979), pp.9, 17, 97, 26, 59, 152, 121, 63, 72.
9 Samuel Beckett, *That Time* (1976), rpt. in *Collected Shorter Plays* (London: Faber, 1984), p.230.
10 Flann O'Brien, *At Swim-Two-Birds* (1939; rpt. Harmondsworth: Penguin, 1975), p.9.
11 B.S. Johnson, *Travelling People* (London: Constable, 1963), pp.11-12.
12 B.S. Johnson, 'Fat Man on a Beach', in Giles Gordon, ed., *Beyond the Words: Eleven Writers in Search of a New Fiction* (London: Hutchinson, 1975), p.155.
13 B.S. Johnson, *Christie Malry's Own Double-Entry* (1973; rpt. Harmondsworth: Penguin, 1984), p.166.
14 B.S. Johnson, *Aren't You Rather Young to be Writing your Memoirs?* (London: Hutchinson, 1973), p.22.
15 B.S. Johnson, *Albert Angelo* (London: Constable, 1964), p.167; Johnson, *Aren't You Rather Young...*, p.14.
16 Johnson, *Aren't You Rather Young...* p.25; pages of *The Unfortunates* are not numbered.
17 Johnson, *Albert Angelo*, p.176; *Aren't You Rather Young...* pp.19-20.
18 Virginia Woolf, 'Mr. Bennett and Mrs. Brown', rpt. in *Collected Essays* (London: Hogarth, 1966), I, p.334.
19 Beckett's remark is quoted on the back cover of B.S. Johnson, *House Mother Normal* (1971; rpt. Newcastle: Bloodaxe, 1984).
20 Johnson, *Aren't you rather Young...*, pp.15, 30.
21 In his 1959 preface to *The Black Book* (1938; rpt. London: Faber, 1977), p.9.
22 My translation of 'Mon côté baroque est toujours là', a remark quoted by Jean Montalbetti in 'Entretien: Lawrence Durrell en Dix Mouvements', *Magazine Littéraire*, Septembre 1984, p.82.
23 A suggestion Durrell accepts in his interview in Malcolm Cowley, ed., *Writers at Work: The 'Paris Review' Interviews* (London: Secker and Warburg, 1963), Second series, p.231.

24 Lawrence Durrell, *Justine* (1957), rpt. in *The Alexandria Quartet* (London: Faber, 1974), p.28.

25 'Un jeu de miroirs' is the description of *The Alexandria Quartet* offered by the interviewer in the *Magazine Littéraire* (see note 22). Durrell replies 'Votre choix de métaphores est très correct'. p.84.

26 Durrell in *The 'Paris Review' Interviews*, p.231.

27 ibid. p.234; and Durrell's Prefatory Note to *The Alexandria Quartet*, p.14.

28 Durrell in *The 'Paris Review' Interviews*, p.233.

29 John Fowles, *The French Lieutenant's Woman* (1969; rpt. St Albans: Panther, 1977), p.315.

30 Nigel Dennis, *Cards of Identity* (1955; rpt. Harmondsworth: Penguin, 1983), p.80.

31 Alain Robbe-Grillet, 'A Future for the Novel' (1956), trans. Richard Howard, rpt. in David Lodge, ed., *Twentieth Century Literary Criticism* (London: Longman, 1972), pp.469, 471-2.

32 Alain Robbe-Grillet, 'The Case for the New Novel', *New Statesman*, 17 February 1961, p.261.

33 Alain Robbe-Grillet, *Snapshots and Towards a New Novel* trans. Barbara Wright (London: Calder and Boyars, 1965), p.64.

34 Christine Brooke-Rose, *Such* (London: Michael Joseph, 1966), p.145.

35 Christine Brooke-Rose, *Thru* (London: Hamish Hamilton, 1975), p.51.

36 Rayner Heppenstall, *The Intellectual Part* (London: Barrie and Rockliff, 1963), pp.62, 198.

37 Rayner Heppenstall, *The Blaze of Noon* (1939; rpt. London: Barrie and Rockliff, 1962), p.198. Heppenstall notes critical comparison of his work with the *nouveau roman* in *The Intellectual Part*, p.212.

38 Heppenstall, *The Intellectual Part*, p.214.

39 Rayner Heppenstall, *The Connecting Door* (London: Barrie and Rockliff, 1962), p.121.

40 Giles Gordon, 'The Definite Article: The Novels of Robbe-Grillet', *New Edinburgh Review*, February 1981, p.26.

41 David Caute, *The Illusion* (1971; rpt. London: Panther, 1972), p.16.

42 Andrew Sinclair, *Gog* (1967; rpt. Harmondsworth: Penguin, 1970), p.278.

43 Julian Mitchell, *The Undiscovered Country* (1968; rpt. St Albans: Panther, 1970), p.83.

44 Caute, *The Illusion*, pp.22, 252-3.

45 John Berger, *Corker's Freedom* (1964; rpt. London: Writers and Readers, 1981), pp.188-91.

46 John Berger, *G.* (1972; rpt. Harmondsworth: Penguin, 1973), p.88.

47 David Caute, 'What We Might Be and What We Are: the Art of John Berger', rpt. in *Collisions: Essays and Reviews* (London: Quartet, 1974), p.136.

48 Iris Murdoch, 'Against Dryness' (1961), rpt. in Malcolm Bradbury, ed. *The Novel Today* (London: Fontana, 1977), p.31.

49 Alasdair Gray, *Lanark* (1981; rpt. London: Panther, 1982), p.105.

50 Anthony Burgess, *Ninety-nine Novels* (London: Allison and Busby, 1984), p.126.

51 Samuel Beckett, *Ohio Impromptu* (1982), rpt. in *Collected Shorter Plays*, p.288.

52 James Joyce, *Ulysses* (1922; rpt. Harmondsworth: Penguin, 1974), p.13.

53 Robbe-Grillet, *Snapshots and Towards a New Novel*, pp.46-7, 63.

54 Robbe-Grillet, 'The Case for the New Novel', p.261.

55 Johnson, *Aren't You Rather Young...* p.17.

56 ibid., p.12.

57 Malcolm Bradbury, *Possibilities: Essays on the State of the Novel* (London: Oxford University Press, 1973), p.86.

58 Malcolm Bradbury, 'The Novel', in C.B. Cox and A.E. Dyson, eds, *The Twentieth Century Mind*, (London: Oxford University Press, 1972), III, p.330.

59 Johnson, *Aren't You Rather Young to be Writing your Memoirs?* p.29; Mitchell, *The Undiscovered Country*, p.91;

Rayner Heppenstall, *The Fourfold Tradition* (London: Barrie and Rockliff, 1961), p.270; Caute, *The Illusion*, pp.13-14.

Postscript (pages 225 to 230)

1 Olivia Manning, *The Balkan Trilogy* (1960, 1962, 1965; rpt. Harmondsworth: Penguin, 1982), p.718.

2 Anthony Burgess in conversation with Edna O'Brien and Clive James in 'The Late Clive James', Channel Four Television, 11 May 1985; and Graham Greene, *Ways of Escape* (London: The Bodley Head, 1980), p.95.

3 James Joyce, *A Portrait of the Artist as a Young Man* (1916; rpt. Harmondsworth: Penguin, 1973), p.253.

4 Rayner Heppenstall, *The Intellectual Part* (London: Barrie and Rockliff, 1963), p.120.

5 Virginia Woolf, *A Room of One's Own* (1929; rpt. St Albans: Panther, 1977), p.93.

6 'The State of Fiction: A Symposium', *The New Review*, Summer 1978, p.65.

7 Anthony Burgess, *The Novel Now* (London: Faber, 1971), p.165.

8 Bernard Bergonzi, *The Situation of the Novel* (London: Macmillan, 1970), pp.58-9.

9 See Eva Figes's comments in the *New Review* Symposium (note 6 above),

pp.38-9; Doris Lessing, Preface to *The Golden Notebook* (1962; rpt. St Albans: Panther, 1972), p.14, etc.; and the comments of novelists quoted at the end of Chapter Five.

10 C.P. Snow, *The Masters* (1951; rpt. Harmondsworth: Penguin, 1983), p.312.

11 William Golding, *Rites of Passage* (1980; rpt. London: Faber, 1982), p.125.

12 David Lodge, *The Novelist at the Crossroads and Other Essays on Fiction and Criticism* (London: Routledge and Kegan Paul, 1971), p.7.

13 Connolly's view of the matter, considered more fully in Chapter Two, is taken from his *Enemies of Promise* (1938; rpt. Harmondsworth: Penguin, 1979), p.85.

14 Bradbury in the *New Review* Symposium (note 6 above), p.25. Bergonzi offers a useful conspectus of opinions about the death of the novel at the start of Chapter I of *The Situation of the Novel*.

15 See Chapter One, note 24.

16 Lodge, *The Novelist at the Crossroads*, p.18; and Gerald Bullett, *Modern English Fiction* (London: Herbert Jenkins, 1926), p.121. See also Chapter One.

17 Malcolm Bradbury, Foreword to Jay L. Halio, ed., *Dictionary of Literary Biography*, vol.14, *British Novelists Since 1960* (Detroit: Bruccoli Clark, 1983), p.xviii; Burgess, *The Novel Now*, p.217.

Select Bibliography

There follows a list of assessments and surveys useful for the study of British fiction in the twentieth century. Section I contains works of general scope, Section II studies of particular periods.

I

ALLEN, WALTER, *Tradition and Dream: The English and American Novel from the Twenties to Our Time*. London: Dent, 1964. Full judgements of the major figures and developments up to the nineteen sixties.

BERGONZI, BERNARD (ed.), *Sphere History of Literature in the English Language*, vol.7, *The Twentieth Century*. London: Sphere, 1970. A collection of essays on individual figures and general developments, including Stephen Wall's survey 'Aspects of the Novel 1930-1960'.

BRADBURY, MALCOLM, *Possibilities: Essays on the State of the Novel*. London: Oxford University Press, 1973. Bradbury's essays on phases in the development of fiction in the twentieth century, as well as on several individual authors.

BURGESS, ANTHONY, *Ninety-nine Novels: The Best in English since 1939*. London: Allison and Busby, 1984. Brief introductions to each of Burgess's personal choices of outstanding British, American and Commonwealth fiction.

BURGESS, ANTHONY, *The Novel Now: A Student's Guide to Contemporary Fiction*. London: Faber, 1971. A very wide-ranging guide and introduction to the ᵣentieth-century novel, principally British and American but with sections ᵣn European, Asian and African developments.

COX, C.B., and A.E. DYSON (eds.), *The Twentieth Century Mind*. 3 vols. London: Oxford University Press, 1972. A collection of essays on many aspects of twentieth-century intellectual history, covering the period 1900-1918 in vol.1; 1918-1945 in vol.2; 1945-1965 in vol.3. Each volume contains an assessment of the development of the novel.

CROSSLAND, MARGARET, *Beyond the Lighthouse: English Women Novelists in the Twentieth Century*. London: Constable, 1981. A general survey with an extensiᵣe bibliography.

FORD, BORIS (ed.), *The Pelican Guide to English Literature*, vol.7, *The Modern Age*. Harmondsworth: Penguin, 1964. Includes Gilbert Phelps's assessment of 'The Novel Today' and many essays on the general background of twentieth-century literature and on individual figures. Revised and reissued as the two items listed below.

FORD, BORIS (ed.), *The New Pelican Guide to English Literature*, vol.7, *From James to Eliot*. Harmondsworth: Penguin, 1983.

FORD, BORIS (ed.), *The New Pelican Guide to English Literature*, vol.8, *The Present*. Harmondsworth: Penguin, 1983. Includes an updated version of Phelps's essay.

HALIO, JAY L. (ed.), *Dictionary of Literary Biography*, vol.14, *British Novelists since 1960*. 2 vols. Detroit: Bruccoli Clark, 1983. Critical essays surveying the careers of over a hundred recent and contemporary authors. .

KARL, FREDERICK R., *A Reader's Guide to the Contemporary English Novel*. London: Thames and Hudson, 1962. Karl's essays on major figures writing since the thirties. There is also a second edition (1972) which adds a 'Postscript: 1960-1970'.

OLDSEY, BERNARD (ed.), *Dictionary of Literary Biography*, vol.15, *British Novelists 1930-1959*. Detroit: Bruccoli Clark, 1983. Uniform with Halio, ed., above.

ROBSON, W.W., *Modern English Literature*. London: Oxford University Press, 1970. A concise introduction to English literature in the twentieth century, with brief sections on most of the major novelists.

STEVENSON, LIONEL, *The History of the English Novel*, vol.11, *Yesterday and After*. New York: Barnes and Noble, 1967. A thorough descriptive survey, with brief outlines of novels by major authors.

SWINDEN, PATRICK, *The English Novel of History and Society, 1940-1980*. London: Macmillan, 1984. Chapters on Richard Hughes, Henry Green, Anthony Powell, Angus Wilson, Kingsley Amis, V.S. Naipaul.

VINSON, JAMES (ed.), *Contemporary Novelists*. London: St. James Press, 1972. A very thorough directory of English-language fiction since the fifties. Each entry includes a brief biography, a full bibliography, often a statement by the author, and a brief critical essay. A fourth edition is in preparation.

II

Items marked with an asterisk belong to a series of British Council pamphlets which provide near-contemporary assessments of the periods they discuss and include a list of the major figures writing at the time.

*ALLEN, WALTER, *The Novel Today*. London: Longmans, Green and Co., 1955. Covers the period 1950-55.

BERGONZI, BERNARD, *Reading the Thirties*. London: Macmillan, 1978. A study of the 'thirties generation' and their work in fiction and poetry.

BERGONZI, BERNARD, *The Situation of the Novel*. London: Macmillan, 1970. Opens with Bergonzi's general reflections on the current state of fiction. Later chapters are devoted to assessments of individual authors, British and American. These are updated in a second edition (1979).

BRADBURY, MALCOLM (ed.), *The Novel Today: Contemporary Writers on Modern Fiction*. Glasgow: Fontana, 1977. A collection of essays by critics and novelists on the current nature and practice of novel-writing.

BRADBURY, MALCOLM, and DAVID PALMER (eds.), *The Contemporary English Novel*. London: Arnold, 1979. A collection of essays on several aspects of the recent development of the novel.

*BURGESS, ANTHONY, *The Novel Today*. London: Longmans, Green and Co., 1963. Concentrates on the fifties and early sixties.

GINDIN, JAMES, *Postwar British Fiction: New Accents and Attitudes*. Berkeley: University of California Press, 1962. A near-contemporary assessment of the angry young men and others in the fifties.

GORDON, GILES, *Beyond the Words: Eleven Writers in Search of a New Fiction*, London: Hutchinson, 1975. Brief statements and samples of work by recent British experimental novelists.

*HAYMAN, RONALD, *The Novel Today: 1967-1975*. London: Longman, 1976.

HYNES, SAMUEL, *The Auden Generation: Literature and Politics in England in the 1930s*. London: The Bodley Head, 1976. A year-by-year analysis of the decade.

JOHNSTONE, RICHARD, *The Will to Believe: Novelists of the Nineteen-thirties*. Oxford: Oxford University Press, 1982. An introduction to aspects of nineteen-thirties fiction with chapters on six of the major authors.

LODGE, DAVID, *The Novelist at the Crossroads and other Essays on Fiction and Criticism*. London: Routledge and Kegan Paul, 1971.

McEWAN, NEIL, *The Survival of the Novel: British Fiction in the Later Twentieth Century*. London: Macmillan, 1981. McEwan's essays on the current state of fiction and on seven recent and contemporary novelists.

*NEWBY, P.H., *The Novel 1945-1950*. London: Longmans, Green and Co., 1951.

*RATCLIFFE, MICHAEL, *The Novel Today*. London: Longmans, Green and Co., 1968. Covers the period 1962-67.

*REED, HENRY, *The Novel since 1939*. London: Longmans, Green and Co., 1946.

RABINOVITZ, RUBIN, *The Reaction against Experiment in the English Novel, 1950-1960*. New York: Columbia University Press, 1967. An assessment of the angry young men and their rejection of modernism, especially useful for its survey of their comments in newspapers and journals.

Index

Farson, Negley,
  Bomber's Moon (1941), 72
Faulkner, William, 97
  The Sound and the Fury (1929), 35
'feminine prose', 16, 62, 149, 227
  see also women's writing
Fielding, Gabriel, 104, 166-7, 169
  The Birthday King (1961), 166-7,
  168
Figes, Eva, 150-51, 223, 228
  Patriarchal Attitudes (1970), 150
  Waking (1981), 150-51, 158, 159
film, *see* cinema and the novel
Finney, Brian, 44
Firbank, Ronald, 27, 53, 58, 59, 139
  *Concerning the Eccentricities of
  Cardinal Pirelli* (1926), 27
  Prancing Nigger (1924), 27
  Valmouth (1919), 27
First World War, the, 83, 89, 99,
  103, 111, 135, 137, 166
  effects on fiction: 21-3, 27, 31-2,
  35, 164-5, 195
  as subject of novels: 17, 21-3, 35,
  40, 48, 49, 50, 75, 141, 142,
  162-3
Fleming, Ian, 144-5
  Casino Royale (1953), 144
Ford, Ford Madox, 12, 16, 17,
  20-21, 35-6, 100, 121, 178, 219
  Parade's End (1924-8), 17, 21, 22,
  35, 75, 76
  The Good Soldier (1915), 20-21, 97
Forester, C.S., 73, 74
  The Ship (1943), 69, 73, 74
Forster, E.M., 7, 26-7, 34, 143, 145,
  225
  A Passage to India (1924), 27, 145,
  146
  A Room with a View (1908), 27
  Aspects of the Novel (1927), 19
  Howards End (1910), 27, 34
  The Longest Journey (1907), 27
  Where Angels Fear to Tread (1905),
  27
Fowles, John, 207-10, 213, 216, 217,
  218, 221, 222, 223, 224
  The Aristos (1965), 210
  The Collector (1963), 207
  The French Lieutenant's Woman
  (1969), 148, 207-10, 216, 219,
  223
  The Magus (1966), 207
Fox, Ralph,
  The Novel and the People (1937), 33
Franco, General, 31, 53, 70

Fraser, G.S., 80, 81, 116, 117, 122,
  quoted 37
Free Indirect Discourse, 18, 19, 80
French fiction and its influence, 21,
  81, 141, 203, 209-14, 223-4
Freud, Sigmund, 23, 165, 166, 167-8
Galsworthy, John, 12-13, 15, 19, 28,
  33, 130
  The Forsyte Saga (1906-28), 13, 26,
  135, 142
Gandhi (1982; film), 146
Genette, Gérard,
  Narrative Discourse (1980), 8
Gerhardie, William, 62-3, 225
  Of Mortal Love (1936), 62-3
Gibbon, Lewis Grassic, 47, 48-51,
  65-6, 170
  A Scot's Quair (*Sunset Song*
  (1932), *Cloud Howe* (1933),
  Grey Granite (1934)), 48-51, 66
Gide, André,
  The Counterfeiters (*Les Faux
  Monnayeurs*, 1926), 209, 220
Golding, William, 92, 169-73, 176,
  181, 182, 188, 190, 193, 229
  Darkness Visible (1979), 169,
  171-2, 173, 174, 179, 180
  Lord of the Flies (1954), 169-70,
  171
  Pincher Martin (1956), 170-71,
  173, 181
  Rites of Passage (1980), 172-3, 177,
  182
  The Inheritors (1955), 170, 171,
  172, 173
  The Spire (1964), 171
Gordon, Giles, 214, 221, 223
  Beyond the Words (1975), 223
  Girl with red hair (1974), 214
'Gothic' fiction, 106, 132, 159,
  184-189
GPO film unit, the, 64
  Night Mail (1934), 64
Gray, Alasdair, 217-9, 221
  Lanark (1981), 217-9
Green, Henry, 31, 72, 77, 78-82, 92,
  114, 119, 121, 122, 174, 229
  Back (1946), 81, 91
  Blindness (1926), 121
  Caught (1943), 78-9, 80, 81, 82,
  88, 103, 119
  Concluding (1948), 80, 81
  Doting (1952), 117
  Living (1929), 79-80, 127
  Loving (1945), 80
  Nothing (1950), 117